Media & Values

Intimate Transgressions in a Changing Moral and Cultural Landscape

For Sarah Shrive-Morrison

Media & Values

Intimate Transgressions in a Changing Moral and Cultural Landscape

David E. Morrison, Matthew Kieran,
Michael Svennevig, Sarah Ventress

intellect Bristol, UK / Chicago, USA

First Published in the UK in 2007 by
Intellect Books, PO Box 862, Bristol BS99 1DE, UK

First published in the USA in 2008 by
Intellect Books, The University of Chicago Press, 1427 E. 60th
Street, Chicago, IL 60637, USA

A catalogue record for this book is available from the British Library

Cover Design: Gabriel Solomons
Copy Editor: Holly Spradling
Typesetting: Mac Style, Nafferton, E. Yorkshire

ISBN 978-1-84150-183-3

Printed and bound by The Gutenburg Press, Malta

Contents

Acknowledgements

The recent death of James Dermot Halloran ought not to go unremarked when giving acknowledgment to those who have contributed to this book. His contribution was not direct, but nevertheless powerful. It is to James that British mass communications owes an enormous debt. He more than anyone, through the establishment and development of the renowned Centre for Mass Communications Research, at the University of Leicester, was responsible for the institutionalisation of the field in Britain. He gave due respect to theory, but also valued the benefits to be had, both intellectually and socially, to the pursuit of applied social research. In that this book offers theoretical development, and at the same time addresses applied questions, then hopefully the book will stand as a tribute to him.

At a very direct level we would wish to acknowledge the support given by the BBC, the Independent Committee for the Supervision of Standards of Telephone Information Services, the Independent Television Commission, the Institute for Public Policy Research, the Radio Authority, and most especially, the Broadcasting Standards Commission. Indeed, the BSC, in the personages of Andrea Millwood Hargrave and Colin Shaw CBE, have over the years been more than commissioners of research, they have helped to guide empirical communications research in Britain. Others beyond the Institute of Communications Studies at the University of Leeds have had reason to be glad of their presence, but we at Leeds would like to offer public thanks for their support, both intellectually and personally. It was the sheer value and appreciation for the pursuit of rigorously conducted empirical research that was so obvious in all our associations with them. Above all one could draw inspiration and belief in the value of communications research. They so clearly valued broadcasting as a force for enlightenment, and held to the conviction that neither broadcasting, nor research on broadcasting, should ever be trivialised.

In terms of helping to see the book come to public light we would like to thank Professor David Cooper, Dean of the Faculty, for his encouragement, and Dr Graham Roberts, the current Director of the Institute of Communications Studies, for his total commitment not just to the work, but for his energy and drive in making the Institute an appropriate base within which to commit to and produce such a book. In the same light we would like to thank Professor Stephen Coleman for his enthusiasm for ideas, and unflagging optimism when engaging in often difficult research areas – in short we would like to thank Stephen for being Stephen.

This is a large book, and thus we would wish to say thanks and offer respect to the Chairman of Intellect, Masoud Yazdani, for demonstrating in practice his company's stated commitment to serving the academic community by publishing original works. Manuel Alvarado, as the editor, has demonstrated not just superb professional knowledge and skill in producing the book, but has acted, not only with this work, but others written by members of the Institute, as a figure of considerable encouragement and guidance. He stands out, furthermore, as a remarkable figure showing intellectual integrity and commitment to the idea of book publishing as a cultural activity whose central purpose is to advance the world of learning – would there be more Alvarados.

We gratefully acknowledge the time given so generously by those who agreed to be interviewed in the media industry.

Biographies

David E. Morrison is currently Professor of Communications Research at the Institute of Communications Studies, University of Leeds. He gained his PhD in Mass Communications from the Centre for Mass Communications Research, University of Leicester, and has held several university research appointments. He has also worked in market research holding the position of Director at Research International where he was Head of Media. He is the author of twelve books and numerous learned papers.

Matthew Kieran is Senior Lecturer in Philosophy at the University of Leeds. His main research interests lie at the inter-sections of art, ethics and moral psychology and he is the author of various articles and books including *Revealing Art* (Routledge, 2005) and *Media Ethics: A Philosophical Approach* (Praeger, 1997).

Michael Svennevig is Senior Research Fellow at the Institute of Communications Studies, University of Leeds. He has a wide range of experience in the media and research industries, having worked in the Research Departments of both the BBC and the IBA, and has held directorships at Research International UK and Counter Point Research. He has published a range of articles and books on various aspects of media use.

Sarah Ventress is currently Research Officer at the Institute of Communications Studies, University of Leeds. She has a degree in English and an MA in Communications Studies from the University of Leeds. She has worked as a researcher on several audience research studies.

Prologue

Each new medium has been accompanied by research into its performance. The 1920s saw research undertaken on cinema,[1] the 1930s and 1940s saw interest shift to the study of radio, and the 1950s, with the introduction of television, moved the centre of research interests to the new medium. Interest in television continues, but from the late 1990s, with the spread of the Internet, an increasing number of researchers have turned their attention in that direction. Nevertheless, the primary focus for communications research is still that of television. We have omitted newsprint from the above list of research areas, although, in fact, it has always been a subject of enquiry. That enquiry, however, has tended to be a rather narrow one, generally examined for its political content. Indeed, given the political partisanship associated with newspapers, such a focus is not surprising. Yet, the research that forms the basis of this book shows that in one area, and not political reporting, newspapers (according to our respondents) occupy centre stage of concern; namely, the intrusion of privacy. Concern rested not so much on the influence that newspapers might have on the structuring of political discourse, but on the ethics of performance, of what right they had to expose aspects of individual's lives which individuals themselves wished to keep secret or private. It was also clear from the research that in the modern, or information, age, as it is sometimes referred, the individual could not expect freedom from surveillance.

Modernity is configured on communications. What we refer to as modernity (and often contemporary life as late or heightened modernity) is in large measure the story of developments that have taken place in the technology of communications. Yet, whilst the technology of communications may have underpinned and even structured contemporary social, political and economic association, and given rise to questions concerning the effects of communications, the moral framework within which such changes have taken place requires examination. Or, rather, since nothing operates in isolated spheres – social change influences moral frameworks and vice versa – we need to ask how people morally judge the communicative world.

In its turn, each new medium has given rise to new research efforts, most usually based around the concerns raised by the new medium. The basic concern has been the social roles that the new medium might play in the development of attitudes and behaviour. Not surprisingly, therefore, the dominant tradition within mass communications research has been the study of effects, most notably on anti-social behaviour, violence in particular. The association between moving images of violence and real-life violence has been strong in public accounts of causation. For example, the reporting of outrages, such as the running amok of Michael Ryan in a shooting spree, in the country town of Hungerford in the South of England in the 1980s, saw him referred to by the press as the cinematic 'Rambo' despite the fact that there was no evidence linking exposure to violent films and his behaviour. Nor in the 1990s case of the killing of the young James Bulger by two young boys was any authoritative connection made between exposure to violent video films and his death, but the press persistently attempted to make such a link.

It may be functional, in the sense of providing an explanation for behaviour that is not easily explainable, to round on violent media displays for unwanted social behaviour. Certainly it absolves the necessity of engaging in deep enquiry into the structure and moral composition of society that might prove uncomfortable, in that the answers to social ills might suggest solutions that are politically and ideologically at variance with the basic structure of society as constituted. Yet, whilst not engaging in deep critical reflection on that which might be responsible for, or assist in, the rise of behaviours found to be unacceptable, people in our study did not hold the media responsible in any strong sense. In offering understanding of behaviour they reflected on the self, which was then refracted as understanding of others. Not aware that they themselves were affected by exposure to mediated material, they had difficulty in seeing how it was that others were, or at least in areas such as violence that are strongly socially proscribed.

This is not to say that people were unconcerned or had no worries at all over the performance of the media. Rather, they did not consider there to be the type of *strong* influence on anti-social behaviour so commonly presented by newspaper reports of crime. What they did was situate, and here we are mainly talking about television, communication processes within social performance in general. They had little inclination to accept a mechanistic view of behaviour and instead saw performance as moral performance shaped by a whole range of factors, not least of which was the moral instruction engaged by the family, the school, law authorities and other arbiters of behaviour. Indeed, as we shall see later, for some of our respondents such 'arbiters' stretched to sports personalities who, by their position, were held to have responsibility for the projection of approved values.

The research reported here set out to examine how people viewed media performance across a variety of dimensions, most notably with respect to the intrusion of privacy. From the outset, however, we were keen to see how people located the media, in principle television, within the framework of not simply a changing media world but a changing social world. For example, there was general agreement in the focus groups that there had been a coarsening of everyday life, best captured perhaps by the public prevalence of swearing. It showed a lack of respect for those outside 'swearing communities' and caused offence. Unsure in any full sense of how such language had come to form acceptable forms of expression, they nevertheless held television partly responsible for giving it legitimation though exposure, especially in drama. They went further, however, and blamed television, again in part, for undermining sets of values held to be important for civilized living.

Central here were programmes, especially those aimed at young audiences, that showed a disrespect for authority, often translated as 'bad manners'.

Indeed, it was in the area of unsociable behaviour – the transgression of manners – where television was seen to be the most influential. Central to the concerns about television and society in general was the portrayal and the enactment of values that were considered antagonistic to dignified living. Or, expressed another way, those that devalued that which was valued; namely, a society characterized by the right of people not to have their sensibilities unnecessarily assaulted.

It was taken as given that people had the right not to fear physical assault or fear for their property, although, as we will see, life in contemporary society offers little by way of guarantee of this. What is intriguing, however, is that what people really objected to in contemporary life was that which can be categorized as the coarsening of experience, of which swearing was just one manifestation. Social progress or benefit had been bought at the expense of values that had once ensured a mannered social exchange that protected communally agreed ways of conduct. No one held to some notion of a glorious past – indeed, the economic prosperity of the present compared to the past ensured that, on the whole, life was considered more pleasant than previously – but elements of the past were held as preferable to those now witnessed. This can be briefly summed up as saying that people considered that there had been a deterioration in the conduct of social exchange and that individual right to self-expression had taken precedence over wider socially established forms of expression. For this, television was not blameless in the manner that it gave voice to a variety of ways of living and behaving, in drama, in factual programmes, in talk shows and so on. There seemed to be no agreed authority anymore.

Interestingly, however, what might be termed the individualizing of authority – the right of the individual not to live by common agreement over social performance – was held in part, or could be attributed to, changes in living that our respondents had themselves sought. This, they recognized themselves. For example, they regretted the passing of authority of the schoolteacher and the policeman, indeed the 'adult' as the generalized other, over children to ensure obedience and conformity to ascribed behaviour. Yet they admitted that in the confines of their own home they were not very strict with their children, or at least nowhere near as strict as their parents had been with them (when they were children). The description given was of households that were much more democratic in terms of governance than in the past. Whilst recognizing that this had led to loosening of authority and lessening of conformity to the expectations of adults, it was accepted as an improvement in family living in that it made for a greater closeness between parents and children than had been the case when they were young. Closeness was not simply approved of, but appeared to have become a family value. Indeed, the closeness of the family had led to a restriction being placed on the powers they were prepared to accede to external authorities in the sanctioning of behaviour, the very opposite of that which they lamented.

At a general level, the description of family life delivered was one of retreat of authority. That is, sanctions of behaviour were not to be undertaken by virtue of position – the teacher, the policeman, the adult other – but by kinship, and even that authority drew its legitimation from an assumed affection for the child, rather than clearly demarcated roles of power.

It would be wrong, however, to see the parents in our sample as viewing the family as a self-contained unit with little regard for the outside world's social expectations of performance. Quite the opposite. They strove to instil values and rules governing conduct that would make them 'acceptable citizens', but such training was not to be so readily given as in the past to those outside the home. It was not altogether clear here, but it seemed that distrust existed about the quality or type of training that might be received from figures in the outside world which had been coarsened by a lack of appreciation for 'correct' behaviour, or populated by individuals who now functioned in purely technical administrative roles rather than motivated by a duty of care associated with pastoral responsibility. This view of contemporary life having been coarsened by a lack of regard for values to sustain equitable exchange between people, a disregard for the feelings and sensibilities of other, not surprisingly put television as an important point of discussion in terms of the values that it carried.

Thus, whilst television was not a major concern, although it was still a cause for anxiety in portrayals of violence in the sense of producing anti-social behaviour, it was of concern in terms of the promotion of values that were seen to threaten the values held as important by parents. What we see in discussion of media performance, and of television in particular, is a conversation that is framed by the values that people hold and by the values that they wish to be seen to govern social exchange in the wider world. The retreat of authority, wherein the home operates as its absolute resting place, has great significance when we come to the discussion of the intrusion of privacy by the media.

The very fact of television's existence represents an intrusion of privacy. Such a statement is difficult to sustain in one sense, since the presence of television is permitted 'intrusion', even, for the most part, a very welcome 'intrusion', but in another sense it is intrusive in that not all programmes, and the values that they carry, are welcome. If this were not the case then there would hardly be controversy, complaint and so on, about the performance of television. As we will see, for moral campaign movements such as Mediawatch – formerly the National Viewers' and Listeners' Association founded by the late Mrs Mary Whitehouse – the values that enter the home via television confront a private world of meaning that has been sustained in the face of a world that constantly denies those meanings. Without for a moment meaning this in any derogatory manner, the Christian world inhabited by such moral campaigners does not find resonance in the symbolic universe of the world outside their homes. This is discussed at length when examining the secularization of culture, in particular the broadcasting culture of the 1960s under the then director-general of the BBC, Sir Hugh Greene, which acted as a catalyst for the establishment of the original protest by Mrs Whitehouse. The point to stress is that for the Christian moralists, such as Mrs Whitehouse, television was, and remains, an assault on values that should find protection within the home.

Whilst the above is not, in the ordinary understanding of the term, an intrusion of privacy, it can be argued, and is given support in the focus groups of the studies, that various television programmes carry values that are seen as an intrusion into the protected space of the home. Indeed, the whole idea of territory, of what space is deserving of protection, is central to how people talk about the issue of privacy. For example, whilst those in our sample talked about rights to privacy in terms of behaviour that others had no reasonable right to know about, in the way that a jurist might, by and large the question of privacy was framed by expectations to privacy organized around spatial/social location. In Part Two of this book three types of space as it relates to privacy are identified – open public space, restricted public space and closed public space. The expectation, and in effect right to privacy, is inverse to the openness of space.

The 'communications age', as drawn from our findings, is one in which people do not expect to be free from virtually constant surveillance, either in terms of commercial transactions through the electronic transfer of money, or in terms of capture of behaviour through the presence of CCTV cameras. They do, however, expect the home, that which we later label 'closed public space', to act as sanctuary wherein observation ceases. This centring of authority on the home is part of a wider reconfiguration in the organization of living. It became very obvious to us that a demand existed for intimate exchange within the family, closeness between adults and children, greater than had existed in previous generations. That which emerged, however, was a transparency to life within the home, but with an attendant refusal to submit that life to public gaze. The 'retreat of authority' to the home appeared to have been accompanied by the construction of the private as something that was assembled around the home. Thus, when one talks about the right to privacy, it is well to hold in mind, independent of performances that it could be reasonably expected others to have a legitimate interest in, the space that is to be opened to gaze.

Following the events of 11 September 2001, in talking with people in focus groups conducted as part of the research, they extended surveillance, albeit reluctantly, to realms not previously considered legitimate; namely, to children in cases where it was considered the monitoring of suspect terrorists' offspring might give valuable information concerning the suspect. The point to drive here is that no one was seen to have an inviolate right to privacy, but, more important, that changes in the nature, or assumed nature, of society led to re-examination of what the private, and rights to privacy, was taken to mean. Privacy is a dynamic construct.

In the main body of this book, discussion is given to how the idea of the private has changed over time. This in turn is linked to changing ideas of the self. The 'transgression of intimacy' proposed in the title of this book relates to what Anthony Giddens examines in his work *The Transformation of Intimacy* (1992). Here one sees generational differences. It was quite clear in talking with older participants about their childhood that the possibility of privacy within the home, of, for example, having one's own dedicated sleeping space, let alone living space, was extremely restricted compared to the situation existing for many young people today. Not only did these older participants have, so to speak, a greater public existence, but, as already noted, emotional performance within the home lacked the intimacy characteristic of contemporary families. Matters get complicated here, but suffice to say that the willingness to display intimate aspects of the self, or intimate displays of behaviour, is not a constant. Indeed, as with privacy, what the intimate is taken to be is dynamic. The changes that have occurred in definitions of the self in terms of willingness to allow others closeness previously denied or restricted to a select few, to allow non-select individuals to know that which was once guarded, is part of a long history of social transformation rooted in structural change driven in the main by economic forces.

The mobile phone is an example where technology, in changing behaviour, has perhaps changed ideas of the private, or may be a case where technology has managed to exploit changing attitudes towards the private. More likely what one witnesses is a complex interrelationship of new ways of thinking and new ways of communication that results in an extension of the former that assists the expansion of the latter. What we need to consider, in similar mode, is whether or not broadcasting can alter ideas of the private, or whether changes in the idea of the private have led to new programme formats. Again, probably neither work truly independent of the other.

We will, in the main body of the work, give sociological account of how notions of privacy as a consequence of wider transformation in the presentation of the self have been altered, but it is worthy of consideration that television itself, the subjects and topics that it handles, and the manner in which it does, has contributed to changes in ideas about what areas of life remain governed by the private. It has, in other words, opened for view and discussion terrain that was once closed to inspection, thus leading to acceptance in everyday life of greater openness of the self to others – a redrawing of what the private ought to consist.

Reality shows such as *Big Brother* are perhaps the most obvious arena for considering how television has contributed to a realignment of the private and public spheres of life. But, our earlier point concerning the secularization of culture also relates to changes in cultural vision that have reworked the permissible of public gaze. Indeed, what Mrs Whitehouse and her followers objected to in the 1960s was the manner in which television sought to depict, particularly by the social realism of *The Wednesday Play*,[2] the intimate inner-world of social life, rather than the formal outer-world of social relationships and exchange. By secularization of culture here we mean not so much the vacating of the sacred for the profane, but that, and used in its idiomatic sense, nothing was sacred. That which had previously been considered unsuitable for dramatic treatment – abortion, the despair of the homeless and so on – became legitimate subjects, but more than that, and important in terms of redefining the private, were handled in a depicted rather than suggested manner. Sex is a case in point. One of Mrs Whitehouse's objections to the 'new television' was, for example, that the camera no longer stopped at the bedroom door by which to indicate an adulterous relationship, but followed the parties into the bedroom to show much of the actual adulterous act. Taste and decency enters the frame here, but for our purposes such movements in dramatic licence has meant that private or intimate parts of life which it was previously considered had to remain in the private realm of affairs became public, and in becoming public formed points of discussion. Such programming represents an opening up of previously closed-from-view spheres of activity to general observation. This can be seen as a winnowing away of the private which arguably then feeds into a relaxation in everyday life of what can reasonably be taken as protected 'information'. In other words, the realm of the private is no longer so rigidly drawn, and, in terms of the presentation of the self, the boundary between what is legitimate to have others know is pushed back.

The participants in the various phases of our research certainly considered that television assists in constructing views of the world. Further, as already noted, they accorded television the power to influence behaviour. It is not surprising, therefore, that the performance of television readily led to discussion of regulation. Yet, although they saw cultural performance as moral performance, they did not possess a moral language by which to express judgement. Even in the realm of the right to privacy, of which people had greater ease in handling than other areas of media performance, articulation of what was correct and incorrect to make public appeared to be heavily overlain by ideas of taste and decency rather than by philosophical judgements concerning the 'rights of man'. Of course, and as we are at pains to point out, not being philosophically trained one would not expect people to present their reason in terms of systems of thought, but, and here we go back to our idea of secularization, it did not appear that any formal system of moral principles came into play when pronouncing on cultural performance. It is as if people had been left alone in the world to decide upon the value of cultural offerings. We did discern, however, first in the focus groups and then in the surveys, two basic dispositions towards the management of culture, which relate strongly to views of the role of the state in the organizing and control of its members. These we have labelled, following philosophical precedent and outlined in Chapter 1, the neo-Aristotelian and the liberal; the former adopting a view that the state has a positive role in promoting the 'good life', which extended to television sees a place for regulatory authority, and the latter merely seeing the state facilitating conditions wherein the individual can find his or her own expression of the 'good life' by ensuring the freedom of the individual to act as he or she wishes – the state only permitted to interfere where not to do so would result in harm, which extended to television sees a very weak role indeed for regulatory authority.

The studies that form the basis of the book consisted of interviews with regulators, media personnel and others, and included focus groups along with national representative questionnaire surveys. Because of the importance of the notions of neo-Aristotelian and liberal it was decided to frame the book with an opening chapter discussing these two core philosophical positions. That, however, is preceded by an introduction involving a methodological discussion of the nature of understanding to be gained by empirical approaches to the gathering of information or data. The rest of the book is fairly self-explanatory in terms of content, but in terms of style, then whilst the philosophical chapter is written in the associated form of philosophical reasoning, the bulk of the book, drawing on the interviews with media personnel and findings from the focus groups, is narrative and interpretive in style, as are the parts dealing with social change and history. The two statistical chapters, drawn from the surveys, have been kept short and are presented in report form rather than as narrative exposition of numeric data. To do otherwise would have meant, in places, repeating earlier narrative accounts drawn from the focus groups. The numeric data, however, have not been placed within the narrative findings sections of the book since it was considered that to do so would interfere with the narrative flow of the social account of how people judged the performance of television, and the moral accounts that they gave of issues raised by television.

The book is about values, and how people position themselves in face of transgression or possible transgression of their values. The effort in structuring the book, no matter what the method used to allow people to speak, has been to allow the accounts provided by people to be as clear as possible.

Notes

1. For example, the Payne Foundation Studies (Docherty, Morrison and Tracey (1987) and Young (1935)).

2. Created at the behest of Sydney Newman, head of BBC Drama, in an attempt to save the one-off play from being axed from BBC1 due to poor ratings, *The Wednesday Play* was designed to be relevant to the lives of a mainstream popular audience, using fresh new writing talents. Determined to break new ground, the plays presented the audience with a stark documentary realism and soon acquired a reputation for controversy and outrage.

Introduction

Methodology and Approach to Understanding

In calling the book *Media Values*: *Intimate Transgressions in a Changing Moral and Cultural Landscape*, we hoped to capture the idea of media performance as moral performance. Since the moral can only apply to people we also hoped, by way of the title, to give some indication of our approach; namely, to figure the individual as the central object of study. Expansion is undoubtedly necessary here.

The book grew out of empirical work undertaken on two occasions. The first occasion – Study One – was for the former Broadcasting Standards Commission (BSC), examining changing values as they related to media issues, and the question of the intrusion of the media into people's lives. The second occasion – Study Two – furthered this question of intrusion and was commissioned by a consortium of media organizations headed by the BSC.[1] We say empirical because, in the way of most administrative research, the client, sponsor, call them what one will, placed a premium on the gathering of data that it considered would assist them in making strategic or policy decisions. The BSC was, and to its credit from our position as university-based researchers, both generous and enlightened in its consideration of that which qualified as data. For the BSC, 'mere facts' always represented meaningless findings. Nevertheless, tolerance towards 'excessive' historical or theoretical working of meanings attributed to findings could not be expected or welcomed. From a policy position, then as a regulator with a duty to act, the purpose of commissioning research is not to push forward the development of a discipline, but to have a discipline draw upon its expertise or body of knowledge to assist in pushing forward the policy-making process. It is not helpful, therefore, for such organizations to receive a theoretical or historical treatise on, say, the nature of the audience that cannot be translated into 'information' which assists the decision-making process. From within academic communications research, the advantage of such 'instruction' is that one is forced to take empirical study seriously and to pay great attention to methods by which to address the world empirically.

We will have more to say on the exact nature of the methods adopted, but it is sufficient to note here that, over both studies, 27 face-to-face interviews with media personnel, regulators and members of interest groups were conducted, as well as 22 focus groups. In addition, three national representative questionnaire surveys were undertaken, with the findings from one of the surveys in Study One returned in novel manner to focus groups for discussion. To have members of the public give comment and have them interpret the findings of survey research not only operates as superb focus for discussion, but can also illuminate areas for exploration not originally considered. Thus, having returned the findings from the first survey of Study One, a further survey stage was constructed based on what we had learned from the groups, not only to refine the survey instrument but also to examine new avenues prompted by comments made in the focus groups.

This amount of fieldwork costs money. Even focus groups, if properly sampled and recruited, do not come cheap, although, and to the discredit of university-based research, they are often done on the cheap, with poor regard for sampling. (See Morrison 1998.) Indeed, focus group research, as Robert Merton, the originator of the method, lamented, is often 'misused, even abused' (Merton 1987). The simple fact is that whilst focus groups may give the range of opinions in a larger population, they cannot be used to generalize to populations as a whole in terms of the distribution of those opinions, and it is as often as not that it is the distributions one needs to know. In short, focus groups cannot be used as a surrogate for quantification, and often without quantification focus group research remains at the level of the inconsequential, even the trivial. This is not to say that focus groups are not good for theory building, but they cannot be used, or very rarely, as a stand–alone method upon which to base a research project. Other methods are required to support and validate the findings. Indeed, and something not fully appreciated by some qualitative researchers, the logic of the method is that of quantification.

Even where disclaimers are made that the findings cannot be generalized to the population as a whole, the reader is 'forced' to make such a leap, otherwise to have the views of a few people in a few groups offers little by way of giving status to the findings. But even within the confines of the group itself, the rules or logic of the method exhibits a process, although rarely recognized, of quantification at work. For example, it is common to be given some comment or statement in the course of a focus group that excites because it is unexpected, and because it seems to offer a very good insight into the matters under enquiry. One feels that one is 'on to something', only to have the excitement dissipate by finding no other person in any group approximating such thinking, and, thus, the area, or lead, is dropped. This may be referred to as the exploration of meaning, but the process of 'dropping' is quantification by another name. Indeed, the dropping of a line of enquiry because it is not reflected elsewhere, is quantification by any name.

What one is doing, following the logic of the rules governing the method, is having a finding supported by being supported by others within the sample of enquiry. Repeated confirmation gives confidence that there is something 'there' which leads inexorably to the question, 'is it elsewhere?'. But as often as not the elsewhere is never examined. Having played the quantification game, because that in fact is what the rules entail, even in the confines of the focus group exercise, the game is brought to a close by the refusal to extend the enquiry and seek confirmation of the findings, or, more accurately, to seek to confirm whether the confirmed findings of the focus group research would be found if wider groupings of people were used. (See Morrison 1998: 160.) Further, the refusal to attempt to gauge how far the findings from the focus groups are representative of wider sentiments robs the technique of political power. Why, in other words, take the findings seriously? They are little more than indicators for further research.

The above may seem a little harsh. However, as James Curran notes in his attack on the 'new revisionists' of communications research for reluctance to quantify, which he sees as a backward step in the history of the field; there is an 'over-reliance on group discussions'. (Curran 1990: 150) This 'over-reliance' on focus groups, or group discussions, as Curran and many others call them, is not merely unfortunate in terms of the production of knowledge, but shows an all too present refusal within communications studies to recognize the need, at times, to engage in survey research. There is no single, or superior, method for the social sciences and humanities. As David Morgan rightly observes in his book *Focus Groups as Qualitative Research*, 'Anything that a technique does notably well is done, at least partially, at the expense of other things that can only be done poorly'. (Morgan 1988: 20) It is regrettable then that Stuart Hall, in discussing media studies, sees fit to comment that 'Audience-based survey research, based on the large statistical sample using fixed choice questionnaires, has at last reached the terminal point it has long deserved – at least as a serious sociological enterprise'. (Hall 1980: 120)

Hall's comment is breathtaking in its arrogance and its silliness (see Morrison 1998, chapter 5, for amplification on this), but the point to stress is that, in engaging in administrative research, the internecine struggle that is so much a feature of academic life, and territorial claims to understanding, have little appeal; indeed, are often seen as immaturity on the part of academics. What is desired, as noted earlier, is the application of methods that might best lead to the appropriate intelligence for resolving policy or administrative questions. Method, or to use Paul Lazarsfeld's wonderful term 'the language of research', clearly structures the type and nature of the conversations that can be had with people. What we can say is that in undertaking the two studies which form the basis of this book, the research sponsors wished for the most full conversation possible with people. Hence, they were appreciative of an approach that combined both qualitative and quantitative conversations.

Yet, the distinction between qualitative and quantitative approaches should not be heavily drawn, or at least not to the extent that the warring factions noted above would have. Commenting on the advantage of focus group research over survey research, Stewart and Shamdasani, after noting that while focus groups 'can produce quantitative data', comment that 'focus groups almost always are conducted with the purpose of qualitative data as their primary purpose':

> That is their advantage, because focus groups produce a very rich body of data expressed in the respondents' own words and context. There is a minimum of artificiality or response, unlike survey questionnaires that ask for responses expressed on five-point rating scales or other constrained response categories. Participants can qualify their responses or identify important contingencies associated with their answers. Thus responses have a certain ecological validity not found in traditional survey research. (Stewart and Shamdasani: 1990: 12)

If by 'ecological validity' Stewart and Shamdasani wish to infer that focus groups are 'natural' in their setting, or are suggesting that they fall within ethnography, they are mistaken. There is nothing 'natural' about focus group research.

Because participants in focus groups appear to enjoy themselves and because the groups themselves are often conducted in convivial surroundings it can look as if focus groups are natural. Yet viewers do not in their everyday lives sit around and discuss programmes in the guided fashion of a focus group, nor are they asked to sit and watch a programme in the manner of some pedagogical exercise. McQuarrie, in reviewing Richard Kruegers' book, *Focus Groups: A Practical Guide for Applied Research* (Krueger 1988), takes him to task for offering focus groups as a natural method when he states: 'Participation in a focus group is just as unnatural and constrained an activity as any other social science research endeavour'. (McQuarrie 1989: 372) Indeed, falseness, as a lack of true social setting, is structured into the methodology. But then all methodology interferes, to a greater or lesser extent, with the 'natural' situation it is designed to study or understand. In the case of focus groups, they are actually less normal to most people than the completion of a questionnaire: most people are only too familiar with completing forms requesting information about themselves, be it for tax purposes or making insurance claims.

The point to stress, however, is that not only are focus groups not 'natural' but that, when added to earlier comments about the logic of the method, generalizability to large populations is usually implicit. This implicitness is not, of course, there in all qualitative research; for example, ethnography, where generalization to populations as a whole is not sought or, more importantly, desired – ethnographers are much more likely to wish to seek out what is common to cases of a particular type. But, focus groups are not ethnography, although the literature in places suggests that they are. For example, Adeline Nyamathi and Pam Shuler record:

> As a qualitative method which bears similarities to ethnography, grounded theory, phenomenology and participant observation, the major goal of data gathering is the generation of detailed narrative data as opposed to numeric data. As such, it is a systematic study of the world of everyday experience. (Nyamathi and Shuler 1990: 1282)

Whilst true that the collection of data in focus group research is narrative and not numerical, it is not the case, as Nyamathi and Shuler state, that focus group research is the 'systematic study of the world of everyday experience'. The topic under enquiry might be very distant indeed from that of everyday experience, but nevertheless one wishes to know what people think and feel about it. Such would be a project designed to understand attitudes to, say, genetic engineering, a conflict in some distant part of the world, or a European trade agreement. The subject of the focus group might be so far removed from their everyday world of experience that the participants to the group have never even thought about the topic before attending the session. Furthermore, focus groups might be conducted among very specific and specialist groups in the population: for example, investment bankers, to determine attitudes to proposed legislation affecting their area of professional operations, which is not quite the mundane 'world of everyday experience' that the phrase normally suggests in its ethnographic usage. The danger, and this is the mistake that Nyamathi and Shuler make, is in thinking that because focus group research uses the interview technique in informal settings it has a naturalism to it associated with more genuinely ethnographic approaches to social life. As already pointed out, this is wrong. The technique is not natural but a deliberately constructed exchange between the moderator and the members of the focus group, and a constructed exchange between the members of the focus group themselves, orchestrated by the moderator and often stimulated by the deliberate introduction of stimuli. There is no element of participant observation; although with the relaxed exchange of information a feeling is often generated that provokes a sense that one is observing the participants' lives. In fact, it is only their lives as recounted by them, not as actually lived.

Yet, even if one opted for a naturalistic method of observation, either overt or covert, then leaving aside the benefits of generalization, the material collected is limited by the necessity of inference. To observe is not necessarily to understand the meaning of acts but, of course, can be subject to interrogation of those observed in the acts. Even so, as social beings formed by and through interactions with the immediate world and culture and ideas cemented over time, it is not, depending of course on the level of understanding one wishes, to have individuals provide a full explanation of their actions, responses and so forth. To be raised as a Catholic, for example, and to produce in the individual a set of responses to some issue or situation different to that of a Methodist is not necessarily that the individual understands in any theological sense why his or her response should be as it is other than by the most general of appeal to Catholicism. Indeed, no matter what data are collected and by what method, the problem of understanding the *why* of responses is rarely easy and invariably involves interpretation. Nevertheless, especially if the 'language of research' is of a qualitative nature that allows respondents to explain themselves, reflect on actions and qualify thoughts, a reasoned account can be gathered that lends good assistance in explaining the *why* of actions, dispositions, beliefs and so on. Individuals are not, so to speak, 'blind to themselves', although disentangling the accounts given to provide coherence of explanation and a framework for understanding does not absolve the researcher from his or her interpretative role, despite what some feminist writers such as Reinharz (1983) and Meis (1983) might consider. There is a hierarchy to understanding. Meaning, as a way of establishing truth, must at the end of the day be imposed and cannot be left to those who are the subject of the enquiry; although, it must be pointed out, the very notion of subject would be an anathema to some feminist writers.[2]

Qualitative methods that allow the subject or participant their thinking, reasons, motivation, beliefs and so on surrounding their opinions or actions do provide a good basis for addressing the *why* aspect of understanding performance, but not the *how* in terms of the 'hiddens' of social performance. By that we mean how, for example, the beliefs and values that people hold owe themselves to currents of thought and ideas that have their roots in the past and have been carried forward to become the platforms of contemporary morality. As such, the past, reworked in the present, shapes responses to social issues or frames action. This does not mean, however, that individuals, in giving accounts of themselves, are fully appraised or have an understanding of the tradition or set of beliefs claimed to be structuring their responses. For example, for a lay member of the Catholic Church the nature of the covenant often results in weak theological understanding of the moral positions that they take. Indeed, one might operate with a set of moral precepts without any realization as to the thinking which they are owed. To think in liberal democratic terms is not necessarily to pay any tribute or recognition to John Locke, John Stuart Mill or other philosophers, nor to hold certain attitudes towards sexual behaviour is it to recognize the part that Christianity has played in the framing of sexual discourse.

It is one thing, therefore, to have, via focus group exchange or other conversations, people articulate their beliefs and provide reason for why they believe that which they do, but the question still arises of how they have come to formulate or see the world in the fashion present. The social world is, of course, human construction, otherwise it would hardly be social, but meanings are not created individually. Meaning construction is done in association with others. (See Berger and Luckmann 1966.) This includes, however, not simply others of the present, but, in a sense, others of the past. Our operating world is one made and reconstructed from past efforts at making the world, the efforts of which may be only hazily understood or recognized by most people. We can talk of formal, and informal, efforts at sense construction. The former would include the work of designated thinkers or interpreters, and the latter everyday sense construction by people in negotiation of their immediate environment. This is not to say that in making sense of the world one understands it, only that understanding is given. The individual in accounting, for example, his or her unemployment may make sense of it by reference to local conditions without locating the local within global factors impinging upon economic performance. In other words, understanding is limited and partial. If this is so with the material world then so it is in the realm of ideation. That is, expressions are made concerning the rightness or wrongness of acts, or states of affairs, but difficulty arises when attempts are made to attach statements to sets of principles that would qualify as systematic reasoning. This is to be expected given that, outside of the professional philosopher, individuals are not accustomed to such an exercise, or have need for it, relying instead on what might be termed traditions of thought. Yet what was apparent in the focus groups of Study One was the virtual absence of a moral language by which to discuss moral issues, other, that is, than with intrusion of privacy. We will account in later chapters why privacy presented few problems for moral discourse, but for the moment wish to highlight the fact that when individuals give moral accounts of the world, they do so without the benefit of a moral language by which to finalise statements. Occasionally reference would be made to Christianity to support a moral position, and reference made to the fact that, although Britain was not expressly Christian, the principles of conduct were underpinned by a Christian heritage or ethos.

As stated, the method adopted structures or facilitates the nature of the conversations with respondents, and it is not the case that methods alone, used here in the sense of technical operations, necessarily reveal what has taken place when answers to questions are given. At one level people can give good account of why they hold the opinion or belief that they do, but at another level there is restricted visibility of how it is that they have come to hold the opinions or beliefs presented. The *how* of the *why* is missing, and is missing for precisely the reasons given; namely, that the values that people hold are not formed within immediate vision. They are the product of out-of-sight activity created in the course of long history, but have, often with reworking, come into personal possession to appear as if they have been worked through rather than given: more precisely, they are deposits from the past. Mention has been made of how Christianity was at times invoked as a court of appeal for moral position, but, for example, in talking about rights within contemporary society, of the role of the individual in relation to institutions, or the function of the press, no support was given for statements by appeal to bodies of thought that might shore up, or give authority, to their articulations of why something was wrong or right.

Yet, it appeared clear to us that, although they themselves were not naming the intellectual traditions, participants to Study One's focus groups adopted stances to be characterised as neo-Aristotelian or liberal. Thus, although lacking a moral language as such by which to express moral positions, statements made could be identified as coming from distinct traditions of western thought. Once these traditions were identified, it became that much easier to understand the approaches adopted to moral questions. In other words, we could provide the *how* to their explanations of *why*. Indeed, by understanding the traditions that the participants to the groups were operating from, consistency in responses could be determined across a variety of areas, and disagreements between people be understood as a clash of philosophical traditions rather than individual moral expressions. From a regulatory point of view what this meant was that having identified the *how* of the reasoning – neo-Aristotelian or liberal – predictions could be made as to the likely public response, given that the research revealed the intellectual components of both traditions, to various moral issues posed by the media. We could say that the neo-Aristotelians in the audience would be likely to respond one way towards regulation of content, and the liberals another way. What was required, however, was to know the distribution of the two traditions within the wider population to make such findings useful at the policy level.

Our criticism of focus groups is that only very rarely should they be used as a stand-alone method. As noted, focus groups can provide the range of opinions held within the general population, but they cannot provide information on the distribution of those opinions, and it is, as often as not, the distribution of opinion that is required to give meaning, politically and socially, to a study. Without quantification insights generated from focus groups become incomplete narratives.

Accordingly, the survey was constructed to measure values associated with neo-Aristotelian and liberal positions. The key point is that getting at the values that people hold and how such values shape specific opinions, along with the determination of those attitudes, could only be achieved by the adoption of more than one 'set of words' in its language of research.

Yet, the language of research in the sense of a technical approach to collecting information or data, produced quite early on the phenomenon already noted; namely, the absence of a moral language by which to fully address moral issues. This forced consideration of factors responsible for what one might term a secularization of moral discourse. True, individuals in their orientation to cultural control represented languages of recognizable moral discourses, but what was difficult for them, although not so much the neo-Aristotelians, was to grant television a moral authority or leadership. Such questions, of course, afflict broadcasters themselves and form a deep part of discussion concerning the role and future of public service broadcasting. The absence of a moral language means the absence of a point of appeal, but it appeared that more than that was at work in the manner in which cultural issues were discussed. It appeared difficult for people to grant authority to what might be termed society itself. That is, it was difficult for people to discern a collective or common interest when it came to cultural representations. This became very obvious, for example, when examining the defence of 'in the public interest' for the justification of the intrusion of privacy. This is not to present some post-modernist reality, but merely to say that television itself in the sense of a traditional public service ideal, especially as embodied by the BBC, is a reflection of this uncertainty produced by a lack of consensus on matters of social solidarity. People found it difficult to think in terms of a totality of interests such as that implied by the idea of 'public interest'. People spoke of a variety of publics and a variety of interests. Although a community of interests would at times be mentioned, when pressed this was only to square the circle in that various communities were held to exist which, by extension, had a variety of interests, some of which were held to be in conflict.

Viewed this way it is not that the possibilities presented by technological developments allowing multiple channels have fragmented the audience, but rather that social fragmentation has opened spaces for multi-channel broadcasting. In such a situation, and in the absence of a moral language by which to reason for a moral position, it was difficult for people to come to cultural judgement. This situation we explore in Chapter 2 by an examination of the BBC and how, from the 1960s onwards, it is caught, by wider social changes, in a general secularization process; the vacating from public life in general of moral prescription with emphasis placed on technical arrangements for the satisfaction of interests – a general dismantlement of moral authority structures. The analysis here is somewhat akin to Alasdair MacIntyre's observation concerning the recession of a sacred view of the world; that it was not that man first thought differently and then behaved differently, but rather, behaved differently and then thought differently. With reference to religion he means that changes in social association and ways of living created rationalities within which there was little room for sacred explanations of the world (MacIntyre 1967). In short, religious explanations of the world no longer made sense once, to use Peter Berger's phrase, the 'plausibility structures' surrounding religious views of the world were dismantled (Berger 1973).

In using the term 'secularization' as it relates to broadcasting and cultural production, we are using it in the sense of the dismantlement of moral authority structures, and not in its strict religious sense, to indicate the deep social shifts in social associations that have occurred, limiting the possibility of overarching meaning systems so that no one voice, be that class or status group based, can expect respect due to position. Indeed, the moral protest by Mary Whitehouse and the National Viewers' and Listeners' Association of the 1970s can be seen as a tract against the times (Tracey and Morrison 1979), in that the demand was for a uniform culture that ignored the social, sexual, moral and political differences that existed, and were beginning to show themselves, even demand representation, in the cultural life of Britain. This is not to say that such differences emerged only in the 1960s and early 1970s, but that by and large such cultural fragmentation remained, at the official level, hidden from view.

In the body of the book we have attempted to place respondents within changes in the cultural and moral climate of Britain, as indeed the title of the book suggests. This is not meant in any way to be a cultural history of Britain since the ending of the Second World War, but rather offered as an exercise in understanding the *how*, to use our term, of *why* people should have responded as they did to our questions concerning media performance. We noted earlier that no matter whether qualitative or quantitative methods are adopted, there is a limit to what such conversations reveal, for, and again as already noted, individuals have a restricted vision of their place in the scheme of things and, hence, although reflective, are not well positioned to provide full accounts of their thinking in terms of factors structuring their existence or life world. For example, most people would not be in a position, when criticizing dramatic devices for attracting audiences and the pursuit of ratings, to locate such practices in the long history of the changing relationship of the 'artist' to his audience (see Lowenthal 1961), or the internal dynamics of the contemporary television industry that increase the emphasis on such practices. In other words, individuals are only partial witnesses to their own condition.

What we have tried to do, therefore, is to place that which participants and respondents told us, in terms of their experiences, observations, concerns and so on, within the dynamic of social change. The point to this is quite simple. For the most part, in questioning people about culture, and particularly when it comes to the issue of the management of culture, answers given take the form of reaction to something, which invariably leads to questions of antecedent states and events. In short, history. For example, in discussing issues of regulation, the portrayal of violence, sexual display and the use of bad language featured as points of contention. Bad language, or swearing, was seen to be on the increase on television, but then it was also felt to be more prevalent in public than in the past, especially amongst older respondents. What bothered them was how such expression, on the street, on public transport and elsewhere, was becoming normal.

Television was certainly blamed for this condition, but feelings were expressed that it was not entirely to blame and that a general loosening of 'moral restraints' had occurred which favoured such expressions. For some, this was an assault on their personal sensibilities and presents what we have called in the title of the book an 'intimate transgression', but people were at a loss to say how this had come about other than to blame a lack of corrective energy or will on the part of the agencies of social control, mainly parents and teachers. What we have tried to do, however, is to take their concerns as a focus for examining shifts in cultural authority that have favoured such expressions, in particular the rise of new social groups resting within the creative professions who have assisted, by emphatic use of previously prohibited words, to give respectability to swearing. Swearing, rather than be seen as illustration of a restrictive vocabulary, has by association of individuals, especially in the media, advertising and communications industry in general who live by the manipulation of symbols, been given respectability through creative usage to be seen as an extension of lexical ability rather than a restriction. Indeed, by featuring the rise of such groups assists in underscoring points made previously concerning the pervious nature of cultural institutions and to fragmentations that have occurred within British society; or, rather, how once dominant moral guardians representing, and one must say supposed, national agreed standards have been overthrown in the democratization of representation.

It is through such analysis that the methods employed can work to the full. The qualitative work, in particular, the manner in which people presented their concerns and expressed their views and values, offered clues as to cultural change that required reflection of a broader nature than allowed by the methods employed. Or rather, confronted the researcher with evidence of cultural consumption and response that required going beyond the data to extract the fullest meaning.

This was especially so when discussing questions of the media's intrusion of privacy. Although it first appeared that the right to privacy was inviolate, discussion revealed that it was not. It was conditional on the acts that an individual wished to keep hidden and on the social position or status of the individual. What was at work in giving reasons for those circumstances under which privacy should be respected were sets of values relating to social order and social importance. What was also present was the idea of the individual and identity in contemporary society. It was not expressed as such, but, in talking about rights to privacy, people were talking about their relationship to others and relationship to the state. The individual, that is him or herself, was presented very much as a social being, together with an awareness that the nature of the social was constantly changing. Indeed, it was vital in understanding the comments and observations that our informants made to reflect historically upon changes that have occurred in what the private is taken to be before consideration could be given to responses relating to the intrusion of privacy. In other words, methods alone could not reveal the meaning of the responses. Certainly older people offered scenes of past cramped living conditions where lack of physical opportunities restricted the possibility of being alone and hence having an enclosed unobserved space when contrasted to young people of today, but there was more in operation than physical space in making comments about the private and privacy. Generational differences existed in preparedness for openness, of exposing aspects of the self to others. This 'transformation of intimacy' (Giddens 1992) was the explanatory backdrop to how the private and privacy was framed. But it could not be expected, and by no methodology no matter how qualitative in nature, that participants could provide an account of how the *how* of the accounts they gave had come about, other than as descriptions of their own experiences. Of course, those descriptions are formed with good information for viewing transformation of intimacy, but were not of themselves explanatory accounts of the social processes producing the experiences.

What we have attempted in the main body of the book is to present our thinking in relation to how the answers given to our questions are as they were. Of course, at the most obvious of levels the answers are a product of our questions, which are invariably to some extent theory impregnated, but the answers are not simple artefacts 'caused' by the questions. This is especially so in the focus groups where participants could, and did, expand, debate and digress from the strictures of the interview guide to present their own thoughts, articulations and feelings. Respondents to the survey questions were, of course, given less opportunity for self-expression than possible in the focus groups. The answers are closely tied to the questions in survey research, leaving respondents with little room for manoeuvre. The inclusion of open-ended questions still requires the written replies to be coded in some form or other. The codes are, of course, created out of the responses, and not in any strict sense imposed, but even so the research exercise involves a greater management of responses than that witnessed in qualitative research. The creation of a restricted language suitable for questionnaire administration underscores the benefit of first conducting focus groups to assist in the development of the research instrument; to ensure that the questions are informed by the expressive language and thinking exhibited in the focus groups. However, given that we were dealing with moral issues such as the right to privacy, and when intrusion was permissible, it was decided to introduce detailed scenarios involving rights and privacy where the respondent had at least to ponder their responses in the light of information given.

By having to work through the various scenes presented and give their judgement on what would be the most appropriate or moral response, people no longer acted as respondents in the sense of responding to fixed questions, but became decision-makers within a reasonably naturalistic narrative. Thus, answers provided were far removed from being mere artefacts of questions and, we are satisfied, represented reasoned moral positions.

What we could do with the information collected from the survey questionnaire returns was to examine, among other things, for the distribution of neo-Aristotelian or liberal sentiments that had been found operating in the focus groups when discussing the regulation of mediated culture and other issues of social control. It might be assumed that what we identified as neo-Aristotelian and liberal philosophies were in fact no more than the identification and measurement of personality traits, a kind of totalitarian and liberal personality. However, leaving aside difficult questions of personality and the adoption, acceptance or attraction of particular thoughts, ideologies and so on, we can say that the discussions in the focus groups were never structured to reveal personality traits, nor did the questions in the survey include any type of scaling that might give confidence to assertions about or measurement of personality. Nevertheless, the argument could be presented that although that is not what we were doing in the sense of intention, we in fact did do exactly that but without any precision. In other words, what we call neo-Aristotelian and liberal positions are no more than to be expected from particular personality types, always providing, of course, that one accepts the existence of types as a valuable or meaningful way of categorizing individuals. Views of the world related to personality are an historical construct, although certain personality types may characterize an historical period or be more readily found in a particular historical period; all we can say is that we were neither looking for types nor, and it would have been surprising if we had, did we find them. What we found were two basic, and notably different, forms of moral language (beliefs) in circulation that discriminated responses to the moral issues that we addressed. Furthermore, and the body of the book shows this, one moral language tended to dominate over the other, the expression of a particular language was not the preserve of any particular groups or individuals. That is, neo-Aristotelian and liberal moral language was employed often by the same individual depending upon the issue under discussion. Having said that, some individuals were more likely to invoke one system of thought rather than the other, but issue dependency could not be escaped.

What we have done, therefore, in Chapter 1, is to lay out in some detail and philosophical style the components of the two systems of moral reasoning, in order to bring to the surface the principles governing various responses to moral issues. We are not saying that those responses (and here note we do not say people but responses) characterized as neo-Aristotelian or liberal should be taken to represent the philosophical positions in full as presented in Chapter 1, but that a basis of the positions has been formed from the formally worked-through positions presented. The responses witnessed in the groups and relayed in the questionnaires should be seen as the distillations of the full reasoning. Expressed another way: the responses identified as neo-Aristotelian and liberal are the product of the heritage of moral languages available for the addressing of questions of cultural control within Britain and not the application of the detailed reasoning leading to such positions. Other than the professional philosopher, and hardly likely even then, people do not go around applying philosophical systems, or, indeed, operate views of the world always from a specific rationality. A scientific rationality can coexist within the same individual as a mystical rationality. (Morrison, Svennevig and Firmstone 1999) And, as stated, people did move between applying a neo-Aristotelian thought to applying a liberal thinking to issues. The purpose of the philosophical chapter therefore is at one level presented as evidence of how it was necessary for us to understand the elements of a system of thought so that we could then understand the language in circulation that was used in judging issues, and at another level to show what it meant for someone to frame issues in a neo-Aristotelian mode and not a liberal mode. This could only be done by exposing the formal reasoning making up the two positions. Without this elementary work it would make little sense to call some statements neo-Aristotelian and other statements liberal – it was necessary to know what we were talking about.

This book is more than simply the findings of two studies dealing with changing values, cultural regulation and privacy, or, as we have titled it, media performance 'in a changing moral and cultural landscape', but offers itself also as an attempt to empirically explore moral questions rather than have them remain at a theoretical level. The veneration of theory within media studies at the expense of hard systematic empirical work is to be regretted. Social research requires theory just as it requires methods. The conducting of empirical work, as reported here, is not glamorous: it has touches of excitement but, on the whole, is tedious. It is also, especially if undertaken for a client, required to be completed within the time specified, usually to a tight deadline. The scale of the empirical work upon which the book is based required planning to ensure that slippage in reporting did not occur. Administrative research of the type reported here invariably involves teamwork and the careful management of production. Not only has the research to be executed, analysed and written up, and presentations prepared, but there is also the buying of fieldwork, both qualitative and quantitative, together with continuous liaison with the selected fieldwork supplier, especially in the case of survey research; a constant process accompanied most usually by periodic reports on progress to the client. Problems that do arise, and they are to be expected but not predicted, must be resolved quickly and smoothly without hopefully threatening the budget or timetable. It is not, as Stuart Hall was earlier quoted as saying, that survey research has 'at last reached the terminal point that it has long deserved', but hopefully a more realistic case whereby university media departments might reach the point where conducting research for the media industry is deserved.

It is hard to convert the unbeliever, and, no doubt, the efforts here at understanding audiences in the survey part of the book will not alter the views of those who agree with Hall about the place of survey research, but we would hope that the effort to orchestrate various research languages to common purpose has appeal. Empirical work using methods of quantification does not have to be 'mindless empiricism', to use C. Wright Mills' (1959) damning and damaging legacy. (See also Stein 1964, in Vidich 1964.) Nor does engaging in administrative research mean that somehow the researcher abandons critical and reflective thought, the hallmark of university-based social science research. It does mean, however, that researchers need to be sensitive to the clients' needs, to provide material that will be of use to them. Of course, if one is working within the tradition of, say, the Frankfurt School the whole idea of 'use' that is embedded within administrative research would represent a denial of the scholar's role.[3]

Which model of the scholar's role one favours is not entirely related to the methods adopted for social enquiry, but it is not entirely unrelated either. Administrative research has tended, to a certain extent, to value quantification, although qualitative work in the form of focus group research has had a strong place. Nonetheless, quantification has a special authority within contemporary rationality and certainly administrative rationality. Whether 'spurious' knowledge or not, statistics have a 'certainty' missing in more interpretive approaches to understanding. In short, they give confidence to those making policy: statistics are readily accepted as evidence upon which to make decisions. Indeed, leaving aside epistemological reasons for objecting to survey methodology as a way of providing 'correct' understanding, what cannot be escaped is that there is a correct way of doing such research, and it is the delineation of the procedures that allow judgement to be made about the correctness of the results in a way that is not open to most qualitative work.

In undertaking the work for the BSC it was obvious that our approach to the research questions would need to take a form that would provide the type and form of information considered useful. This did not mean that in providing such information work of a theoretical nature, indeed philosophical nature, did not take place. The studies were conducted, although to a shorter time spell, in the manner that one might approach research supported by a research council. In fact, the questions asked by the BSC were in the nature of questions that one might have approached the Economic and Social Research Council for funds. The difference between receiving a grant from the ESRC and accepting the research commission from the BSC rests in how material is presented and not in the manner of the research. As stated earlier, organizations that commission administrative research do not welcome theoretical writing, or placement of the research within the historical tradition related to the area of research. What they want, at the end of the day, or rather report, are succinct findings to guide decision-making. How one gets to these findings is left, once the methodology and feasibility of the study is accepted, to the researchers themselves.

From the comments made so far, it is quite clear that despite the freedom awarded to academic researchers in executing administrative research, the frame of reference of any study is very much constructed around the interests of the client. In many ways this is a challenge. What it means is that university-based researchers in accepting such research are frequently forced to address issues and questions that stand outside their own cultivated and specialized interests. It thus provides opportunities for expanding ones range of work, and in doing so presents challenges to the imagination. Rather than continue in the comfortable manner of researching the familiar one must break, so to speak, with the known and address the new. Often this involves searching for new approaches to the language of research. In the work presented here the development of scenarios is a case in point. We had never addressed the issue of media intrusion of privacy before, but it became clear to us in the course of the study that the fixed response questions that we normally worked with in gathering numeric data on attitudes would not capture in a meaningful way people's thinking on when the intrusion of privacy was legitimate and when it was not, or at least would not capture the working through of people's thinking in making moral judgements. Hence, we developed scenarios and had respondents wrestle with the moral dilemmas presented. In short, to be presented with a research question that has not been self-generated can lead to new approaches and new ways of thinking.

In attempting to address the central question of changing values as they affected perceptions of the media, and the role of the media in intruding into privacy, it meant that we had to go well beyond, in our own search for understanding, the limits of the brief as given by the BSC. However, much of the work presented in this volume was not delivered to the BSC. The reason being that the work presented here represents our intellectual attempt to place the questions as given in a broad framework beyond that desired by the BSC. Indeed, the broadening of the scope of inquiry saw us attempt to give philosophical treatment to issues in an effort to capture how it was that people thought as they did; namely, the nature of the rationality, or historical traditions of moral thought, that people accessed, or brought into play, in discussing moral issues. As stated, this type of writing is of little use, and, hence, interest, to administrators faced with concrete policy questions. Such writing is never submitted by way of report. Yet we would claim that the broadening of research in such a manner – that is, engaging in questioning and reasoning extra to specification, played a fundamental part in the clarification of the essential findings that were eventually delivered. It was such work, and which we present in this volume in expanded form, that we would claim gave a power to the delivered reports that no market research company could possibly have delivered.

We have mentioned market research, since most usually it is to market research organizations that media companies, regulators and even government turn to for their research needs. This is regrettable and a telling tale of the marginalization of universities in public life. The gathering and provision of intelligence on a whole range of social issues by market research companies is one of the most remarkable phenomena in knowledge production of the twentieth century. Nor does the influence of market research companies on policy decision-making through the supply of research show any sign of diminishing in the twenty-first century. Our position here is that they should not have the field to themselves. This does not mean that universities should produce the same type of knowledge as that of market research companies – it would be pointless to do so and an abrogation if they did of their special status and privileged position within the world of learning. The academy cannot, however, lead a self-serving existence of a self-referential community, or at least not totally. Power rests outside the university, not within it. It is to the powerful, or perhaps influential might be a more palatable word, that at least some of a university's work ought to reach; namely, policy makers whose job it is to forge change and hopefully make beneficial changes to the public at large. Without wishing to be naïve when it comes to power, and the role that reason might play when that reasoning conflicts with the interests of the powerful, one might at least consider that rigorous and deep research, which one has a right to expect of a university by virtue of its political, social and structural position, can at least give expression to the audience. It might also be expected that by carefully considered and executed research, hopefully also the mark of university-based research, that the public's voice is more fully represented than would otherwise be the case if undertaken by organizations existing outside the precincts of a university. The work presented here, which in truncated form was delivered to regulators, hopefully does just that, whilst at the same time hopefully adding in some substantive way to the basic stock of knowledge to social and communications studies.

Notes

1. British Broadcasting Corporation (BBC), Broadcasting Standards Commission (BSC), Independent Committee for the Supervision of Standards of Telephone Information Services (ICSTIS), Independent Television Commission (ITC), Institute for Public Policy Research (IPPR) and The Radio Authority. We will refer to both studies by the name of the lead sponsor, the BSC. Ofcom has now assumed the duties previously undertaken by the BSC.
2. See Hammersley (1992) for a good account of this debate and, also, Klaus Krippendorf's (1980) discussion of emic and etic data – the former having a more 'natural' or indigenous form, with the latter representing more the researchers' imposed view of the situation, although neither occur in pure form.
3. See Adorno (1969) for his experience whilst engaged with Lazarsfeld on administrative research and Morrison (1978) discussing their relationship. See also Lazarsfeld (1941) on Critical and Administrative research.

The Philosophical Underpinnings

1 The Need for a Moral Language

This chapter sets the scene for later discussion of how people in our study talked about moral issues and the requirement of regulation. Although it is argued later that there is an absence of a moral language by which to judge cultural issues, following the focus group stage of the research two traditions of thought were identified that appeared to position how issues were framed. These two traditions were neo-Aristotelian and liberal.

Briefly, liberals, going back to the Enlightenment, tend to place primary emphasis on autonomy. The function of legislation and regulation is to enable us to lead our lives as we choose. Importantly this includes the freedom to make our own mistakes. Two basic constraints follow. Firstly, our freedom of choice should be enshrined and promoted to the greatest extent possible consistent with not infringing the basic rights of others. Thus, for a liberal, regulation is likely to concern issues such as harm or privacy intrusion but, importantly, matters of offence are as such considered irrelevant. Secondly, legislative and regulatory steps may be required in order to ensure meaningful choice. The communitarian critique of liberalism claims that it fails to recognize the role traditions and social practices play in constituting our lives as meaningful. The liberal attempt to maintain neutrality over different conceptions of the good life, it is argued, is impossible. Liberals either remain blind to the importance of identity and tradition or they must effectively privilege their own in favouring autonomy above all else. This critique lends itself to the neo-Aristotelian conception of our relation to the state. The ancient Greek philosopher Aristotle held that the good of the individual is intimately bound up with the good of the state and society as a whole. The point of legislation and regulation on this view is the cultivation of our well-being. Its aim is to promote the moral and social character of us all. Hence, in principle at least, nothing is an essentially private matter nor outside the remit of state regulation. We need governance to help us develop the virtues required for fulfilment and happiness. Neo-Aristotelians will tend to be more deferential with respect to 'moral authority', be more worried about issues of offence and consider regulation more easily justifiable and wide-ranging. Liberals, by contrast, are unconcerned with these things – except in so far as they intrude on our capacity to choose freely how to go about our lives.

What we will be considering in this section is exactly what the nature of these differences comes to, their underlying rationale and how they are likely to impact on attitudes to broadcasting regulation.

Introduction

There is a generally shared agreement that the mass media can and do have the potential, at least, to have impact and influence at the social and individual levels. On this basis, regulatory structures have been created to control media content, especially broadcasting content. To produce and enact such legislation and set up necessary authorities, there has to be an underlying value-based structure and an associated set of beliefs about media content's potential impact and, equally important, media audiences' potential to be influenced in one or other ways. It is crucial, therefore, that we think about the values implicit in broadcasting regulation and the ends towards which it is directed. (See Philo 1990; McQuail 2000; Scannell 1989; and Seymore-Ure 1991.) Different assumptions about the underlying rationale of broadcasting clearly will entail substantive differences over the nature and scope of regulation. This is further underwritten by different presumptions concerning the purposes of broadcasting. It might be presumed that the primary function of the broadcasting media is to service people's proclaimed needs, providing news and information required to make decisions *qua* political citizen, and actual preferences, providing programmes that people desire to watch. Such a view is underwritten by the liberal presumption that the function of the state is to protect people's autonomy so they are free to pursue both their private and public lives as they choose provided no significant harm to others is involved. Conversely, the concept developed by John Reith, the first director of the BBC, held that the function of broadcasting should be to shape, influence and guide the culture of a society and the individuals constitutive of it in terms of cultivating the appropriate moral and social attitudes. For, the kind of public culture into which individuals are inducted, in part constituted and shaped by broadcasting, determines the kind of public and private commitments that are meaningful rather than nominal options for individuals within society. Thus, it is crucial to clarify what our actual evaluative commitments regarding broadcasting are, what they ought to be and what such considerations entail in terms of broadcasting practice and policy. Only in the light of some critical understanding of which values in broadcasting we should respect, or seek to cultivate, can we properly assess how good broadcasting in Britain really is and how it ought to be regulated.

Liberal Regulation

Standardly, liberals hold that the only point of the state is to honour and protect the autonomy of its citizens by ensuring certain basic freedoms, such as freedom from harm, and thus maintaining the minimum conditions of stability and tolerance required for people to be free to lead their lives as they choose. Laws and state regulation should be such that they are justifiable to all citizens who are subject to them. Society is conceived of as an association of self-determining individuals who contract together in order to enable each citizen to pursue autonomously their own particular ends or goals. (See Hobbes 1996 and Locke 1988.) In being treated as autonomous and rational creatures, individuals become citizens since they are the final arbiters of whether there is good reason to adhere to the State, its forms of regulation and the kind of justice it respects. (See Kant 1970.) Equally, this position carries within it the implicit contractual requirement laid upon the individual citizen to act in a 'civic' or citizen-like manner.

Hence, any of our particular substantive moral and social values should be distinguished from and not inform state governance and regulation. A state's laws and social policy should only be judged in terms of how well or badly they respect the autonomous interests and purposes of individuals. Thus, where a state attempts to prescribe how individuals ought to choose or behave it is acting illegitimately because it is attempting to circumscribe the freedom of its citizens rather than protect it.[1] As John Rawls articulates it:

> …the guiding idea is that the principles of justice for the basic structure of society are the object of the original agreement. They are the principles that free and rational persons concerned to further their own interests would accept in an initial position of equality as defining the fundamental terms of their association. These principles are to regulate all further agreements; they specify the kinds of social co-operation that can be entered into and the forms of government that can be established. This way of regarding the principles of justice I shall call justice as fairness. (Rawls 1972: 60)

Rawls argues that the first and most important principle of justice those in such an original position would arrive at is the principle that 'each person is to have an equal right to the most extensive basic liberty compatible with a similar liberty for others'. (Rawls 1972: 60) The reason individual liberty, according to the liberal, ought to be given such priority has its roots in Kant and springs from recognizing the putatively universal value of individual liberty for human beings. What is of supreme importance, and what distinguishes us from mere animals, is our autonomy. Because we are self-conscious and can reflect upon what we do and why, our capacity for self-determination in choosing how we think and act is paramount. This is so, the liberal claims, no matter how diverse our conceptions of the good life might be.

This recognition of the voluntaristic element required to pursue a meaningful human life, the liberal claims, entails that the state is never justified in interfering with, supporting or suppressing any conceptions of the good life that people choose to pursue. So, far from cultivating and promoting a particular conception of the good, the liberal state should remain impartial about distinct conceptions of the good. The state should only seek to enshrine the basic rights and conditions required for people to be able to pursue their lives as they choose; anything else would be to abrogate the very value which underwrites the justification of the state in the first place.[2]

It is important to note that the liberal is not claiming that self-determination is valuable merely because it happens to make us happy. Although many people would resent being deprived of their autonomy, some people might, superficially at least, be happier if they could just be told what to do and how to live. Rather, the liberal holds that exercising our autonomy is valuable for its own sake and only through the exercise of it do we realize our condition as rational beings:

> The will is therefore not merely subject to the law, but is so subject that it must be considered as also *making the law* for itself and precisely on this account as first of all subject to the law (of which it can regard itself as the author). (Kant 1948: 93)

Hence, liberals prize our right to self-determination and the freedom to choose how we should live above and beyond anything else. It is also important to note that liberals are not, and need not be, moral sceptics as is often presumed:

> It is not, as critics often maintain, that liberals elevate choice to the only absolute good: no liberal would applaud a life of crime merely because the criminal had chosen it. It is, however, true that most liberals have thought that the kind of autonomous individual they have admired can only become a fully autonomous being by exercising his or her powers of choice. Some people may strike lucky and find what suits them without very much exploration of alternatives; others may need to search much longer. But a person incapable of making a choice and sticking to it will have little chance of leading a happy life. (Ryan 1993: 304–5)[3]

Hence, tolerance is one of the cardinal liberal virtues. Each individual should recognize that other people have a right to say or do what that individual might judge to be deeply mistaken. True tolerance should not be mistaken for indifference or, indeed, moral subjectivism. Tolerance involves judging that someone else has done wrong and putting up with it. One person may say or do what another judges to be deeply offensive or immoral. Nonetheless, we should recognize that, as autonomous beings, they have a right to do it.

Of course, liberals recognize that we all have not just political but social and moral interests. Amongst other things, that we have families and friends we care about and who care about us, that we have careers and can support ourselves financially, that we may value a religious life and so on. But it is not the job of the state to regulate for us in determining how we should protect and promote our interests. Rather, as autonomous individuals, we have a right to choose for ourselves how we think our interests may best be pursued. Thus, what we do is ultimately our responsibility, whether what we do is right or wrong.

The function of the state is not to promote the well-being of its citizens, but merely to maintain the conditions of stability, tolerance and free choice required for us to lead our lives as we choose. Hence, moral and social values, strictly speaking, have no business informing law, education or broadcasting regulation. The only justifiable state regulation is that required to maintain and protect the personal autonomy of its individual citizens.[4] On such criteria any broadcasting or content regulation based on purely moral or social considerations would be precluded.

Recently there has been a new development in liberal thought, principally led by John Rawls, which is less ambitious. The more modest nature of political liberalism is that it does not presuppose a metaphysical conception of the nature and value of human beings as autonomous and rational agents. Rather it is motivated by the merely pragmatic, political problem that people living in the same society, but who possess different conceptions of the good, need to get along together to pursue their own lives and conceptions of the good. Thus, according to political liberalism:

Political power ... should be exercised, when constitutional essentials and basic questions of justice are at stake, only in ways that all citizens can reasonably be expected to endorse in the light of their common human reason. (Rawls 1993: 139–140)

Political liberalism, thus construed, is demanding. The basic rationale is outlined in terms of what all reasonable individuals would assent to, precisely because this kind of liberalism wants to allow for pluralism concerning the moral and social values people assent to. Yet, it is far from clear that all reasonable individuals will be able to agree, meaningfully, concerning their basic, core political values in this way.[5]

Nonetheless, both the metaphysically ambitious and more modest political variants of liberalism hold that the mere immorality of a particular act or programme is clearly insufficient to warrant any legal or regulatory proscription against it. It is not the legitimate business of the state to regulate how we should lead our lives and thus what kinds of films and programmes we should watch.[6] The state has no business interfering over the nature and content of what is broadcast as long as the programmes are legitimately provided and production of them does not involve harming people without their freely given, informed consent. If one chooses to spend much of their life on a diet of soap operas, anti-religious programming and hard-core sex films they may well be making a big mistake, but this is no one else's business but theirs. Someone may object to explicitly pornographic or violent films on the grounds that they are degrading and thereby deeply offensive or immoral. But, as long as people who would not choose to watch such programmes can avoid them, there can be no legitimate objection to such programmes being broadcast for those who do. (See Waldron 1993: 134–142.) Moreover, even if there are good reasons to believe that, for example, pornography and violent programmes may, indirectly, lead to harm to others, the liberal would not necessarily think there were sufficient grounds for prohibiting such programmes. After all, allowing pubs and bars to open on Friday nights, or allowing cars on the road, clearly leads, indirectly, to serious harm to others. But, such things are not prohibited precisely because that would constitute an abrogation of people's freedom to choose how to lead their lives and, as such, would constitute a deeply serious attack on their autonomy.

Nonetheless, despite the emphasis upon freedom, a liberal could and would accept a limited kind of broadcasting regulation. But the kind of regulation acceptable to the liberal is very limited in scope. For the liberal the state has no business guiding how we should lead our lives, and thus regulation is only justified where it maximizes autonomy. Hence, liberals are strongly against censorship because they are necessarily deeply antipathetic to regulation concerning the inherent content of programming. However, liberals would be keen to enforce regulation which ensured the fair operation of the media marketplace. For example, to avoid broadcasting monopolies from forming which might unfairly restrict viewers' choice. The point of such regulation is to protect and maximize viewer autonomy. Yet, a liberal might also accept that some positive broadcasting regulation concerning the content of programming may be required. However, this is not due to a concern with the content of programming as such, but only to protect and promote conditions of free choice. The purpose of such positive broadcasting regulation is to ensure that minority interests which are not served by the free operation of the marketplace, for example, small ethnic or cultural groups, are catered for. From this position, broadcasting regulation should not be concerned with what we ought to watch, rather it should be concerned to provide what it is that we want to watch. For the underlying rationale and justification of the state, on the liberal model, concerns our self-determination. Thus broadcasting regulation should only be concerned to protect and promote conditions of choice. What is chosen is each individual's own affair, as long as the same fundamental rights of others are respected.

Public Traditions and Meaningful Private Lives

Political liberalism's triumph over the ideological conception of politics arose from its attempt to give an account of the role of the state and the nature of distributive justice that everyone could be expected to endorse.[7] Yet, in the last decade or so, liberalism's virtue, its aspiration to provide universal, rationally grounded principles of justice which are thus neutral amongst competing conceptions of the good life, has been condemned by some as a vice. (See, for example, MacIntyre 1985; Taylor 1989; and Sandel 1982.) The fundamental problem identified is that it removes from political consideration and deliberation the assessment of many aspects, values, activities and traditions of people's lives. But this is identified as a problem for different reasons. On the one hand, Habermas has argued that such a conception precludes such aspects of people's lives from the political deliberation which is required to subject established practices to critical scrutiny. Thus, liberal neutrality, perniciously, threatens to favour established practices and reinforce false needs, desires and consciousness (Habermas 1979). On the other hand, conservative and communitarian critics, such as Roger Scruton and Alasdair MacIntyre, hold that political deliberation should be extended to the consideration of the individual good in order to promote and sustain the role of tradition. (See MacIntyre 1985 and Scruton 1978.)

Habermas' basic thought is that liberal neutrality effectively serves to mask many fundamental political and moral issues from fundamental deliberation. Thus, many important matters concerning how we lead our lives, which ought to be a matter for political debate, are treated as, and considered to be, merely managerial, value-neutral issues. So, for example, liberal neutrality reduces politics to questions concerning how we can best organize our resources and economy to serve our basic 'needs' and 'desires' without fundamentally questioning whether what is involved really does constitute needs or that which we ought to desire. Habermas goes on to argue that the evaluative presuppositions of communication, implicit in every form of society, afford a basis by which we can examine and critically evaluate, rather than remain neutral about, such fundamental assumptions. He identifies four implicit validity claims which any form of discourse or act of communication in principle presupposes and, thus, necessarily aims towards: comprehensibility, accordance with existing norms of rightness, truth or correspondence to what is the case and sincerity. Any utterance or discourse is open to challenge to the extent it fails to conform to the four validity claims. Thus, traditions and ingrained assumptions can, and should, be open to challenge and contrasted in this manner.

Yet, as articulated, this looks an unpromising critique of liberal neutrality *per se* (as distinct from claims concerning particular socio-political forms of organization aspiring to liberal neutrality). Firstly, with respect to matters considered to be the domain of the state in protecting and promoting the autonomy of its citizens, liberals are committed to honouring the very same values. Secondly, given the importance of autonomy, the liberal will reject Habermas' assumption that the critical assessment of *all* aspects of people's lives should be subject to political, and, thus, state, consideration. Many individual and communal goods are surely more appropriately subject to critical consideration in the forum of civil society constituted by the myriad groups, associations and sub-cultures within which they are pursued. Indeed, the liberal will emphasize, state neutrality protects and underwrites civil society in order for individuals not merely to pursue but to be in a position to critically deliberate about the activities, ends and goals open to them. Habermas himself has, more recently, limited the scope of his claims to the validation of universalistic or categorical claims of morality as distinct from the diverse forms of ethical life that may be manifested in various traditions and forms of civil society (Habermas 1985 and 1990). But then it remains unclear how or why the upshot of his position is not something very much like the liberal emphasis on state neutrality.

The core communitarian thought, by contrast, is that what is right cannot be understood as prior to, or independent of, our good and, moreover, that moral virtues, duties and social obligations can only be understood within their socio-historical context. Hence, the tradition that an individual is a part of, the beliefs he or she assents to and the practices participated within, significantly shapes what constitutes the good life for that person. But, so the diagnosis goes, liberalism is necessarily scornful of tradition: viewing traditions as received practices which should be subjected to the critical light of a historical reason. If something like this argument is accepted, it has crucial consequences for broadcasting regulation. For liberalism's apparent neutrality would turn out to be nothing more than a sham. Under the pretence of being neutral amongst the competing traditions, practices and kinds of lives available to individual members of society it, in effect, favours those values which place a primacy on autonomy and precludes those kinds of lives, such as traditional Christianity or Islam, which do not. The essential claim is that the public life as regulated by the state cannot, as a matter of principle, be so sharply separated off from the private in the way liberalism presumes.

A tradition is constituted by a cluster of essential beliefs and evolved socio-cultural practices which embody some conception of the good life.[8] It is important to note that traditions are not mere instantiations of general principles or tokens of a type. Both Roman Catholicism and Protestantism, for example, adhere to the same fundamental belief; that Christ is the Son of God. But the rituals of confession, the Mass and deference to clerical authority distinguish Catholicism from Protestantism. Remove the distinctive practices and the constitutive differences in the traditions are bleached away. Now the significance of tradition is not reducible to claims concerning incommensurability. We normally consider that the particular conventions, rituals and practices which help make up a distinct tradition reveal to us something about the appropriate way to understand the objects of our social concern and activities. Take something as seemingly trivial as manners. We are inducted into certain appropriate ways of behaving towards our colleagues, teachers and elders in various contexts. We are not first told that we ought always to show respect for teachers and then told how to behave. Rather we are inducted into a certain way of behaving which is itself supposed to *show* us the appropriate attitude toward teachers and what true respect amounts to. The actions involved are themselves taken to express, and cultivate within us, a certain attitude or background understanding.

Yet it seems that what we learn through participating in the social practices that constitute a tradition is distinctive in kind from that which is afforded by the rational adjudication of political principles, propositions, counter-examples and the reasoned analysis of socio-political trends. For not all social and moral understanding is reducible to matters of general principle. We can underwrite the significance of tradition, in a distinctive way, if we attend to a crucial distinction between two distinct forms of understanding that our moral and social thinking presupposes. On the one hand, there is abstract or thin understanding constituted by the kind of reflection which, for example, is typically involved in analytic philosophy. That is, a concern to formulate abstract principles which are consistent, coherent and match up to our deepest beliefs and intuitions. (See Rawls 1968 and 1971: 48–51 & 432.) Such critical reflection and explicit belief formation concerns our knowledge about human practices. By contrast, imaginative understanding (constitutively) involves grasping appropriate ways of looking upon the world as revealed to us through our actual or imaginative experience. Typically this concerns the sympathetic imagination: striving for the appropriate way to respond to, regard and feel for others. In the case of direct experience we are inducted into received ways of carrying on which reveal to us, in our experience of them, certain norms of behaviour: that we should hug our children, shake hands when introduced to a stranger, or even just that we may express love through certain gestures. From our direct experience we can also imaginatively construct what alternative norms or ways of carrying on might be like and thus entertain possibilities other than those we are familiar with (Kieran 1996).

Our experience, actual and imaginative, affords us with knowledge by acquaintance of the nature of certain conventions, practices and the traditions that underlie them. In striving to understand the practices directly encountered, we imaginatively apprehend how others think and feel. That is, we imagine under what description or self-understanding the activities concerned are rendered intelligible and significant. Imaginative understanding thus concerns our knowledge of a tradition, through our actual and imaginative acquaintance with the practices and participants involved. Abstract understanding involves the attempt to formulate and assess the beliefs implicit therein and thus concerns our knowledge about a tradition.

The point is that through experience of, and participation within, social practices which partly constitute a tradition, our social understanding is enhanced and developed in a distinctive way. (See Schiller 1910: 209–303.) Social understanding, then, depends upon the imaginative understanding of our experiences as embodied in the conventions, customs and social practices which make up the traditions we move within. To put the point differently, we participate first in the practices and, in so doing, acquire an imaginative understanding of the underlying presumptions, intuitions, norms, values and implicit beliefs involved.[9] To conceive of social conventions, rituals and practices as reducible to the adherence to certain principles is to remain blind to the nature of human social practices and traditions and is to regard them, falsely, as significant only to the extent they fall under the application of some principle of justice.[10]

To see a tradition as falling under the application of a given principle is to have learnt something. Take the current argument concerning justice and animal rights. Fox-hunting and rat poisoning may both be justified on the grounds that certain numbers must be killed in order to keep animals under control and thus protect human property from harm. But, if this is all one understands then one obviously lacks a full and proper appreciation of fox-hunting. For the practice of fox-hunting is not just a function of a given central belief, that a fox suffers less and is better controlled through hunting than culling, but constitutively includes the activities which embody a certain self-understanding. Crudely, and historically for the sake of illustration, fox-hunters gather at the lord's manor, there are fairly rigid dress codes according to differentiated social status, there are certain rituals beforehand, the hunters follow the pack in stratified layers from the aristocracy leading the way down to the farm workers straggling at the back and the hunt ranges over the country fields owned by different farmers. Remove the formal structure and rituals, say, by merely setting traps for foxes, to achieve the same putative end of getting rid of pests and not only is the hunt gone but the understanding of country life it embodies and confirms is eroded out of existence. Fox-hunting embodies and expresses, in a way rat control obviously does not, a particular conception of British life which the principle at issue does not capture. Its significance and value, both for those who take part and those who protest, inheres in its embodiment and cultivation of a particular imaginative understanding of country life.

That this is so explains why fox-hunting is so vociferously objected to, or defended, in a way that apparently similar practices such as fishing are not. For a large part of what is objected to does not merely concern the principle involved: the pain inflicted or animal life taken to protect property. Rather, implicit in the way fox-hunting is practised and understood is the presumption that country life properly involves the dominion of man over other animals and, furthermore, ought to be hierarchically structured with regard to class and privilege. For fox-hunting, in a way fishing is not, is constitutive and symbolic of a distinct conception of British country life, mediating and contributing to the imaginative understanding of those who take part in or identify themselves with it.[11]

Consider even the concepts of everyday social discourse such as courage, kindness and generosity. In order to correctly specify the relevant criteria of application we must first imaginatively understand something about (the nature of) what the relevant concept is being applied to. We gain our sense of what they mean through their embodiment in actual practices and through our imaginative acquaintance with how they might be understood in different contexts. Consider humility. We might all abstractly understand the independently specifiable nature of humility: for example, the recognition of one's true insignificance. But one cannot really appreciate what is involved unless one has some kind of imaginative understanding of the Christian tradition in which humility has a central place, and the rituals and practices which gave a distinctive shape and significance to this particular virtue. Without this kind of imaginative understanding, the virtue of humility is likely to be dismissed merely as the display of false modesty, with which it is often confused, or the risible manifestation of peculiarly low self-esteem or morbidity.[12] Our understanding of a particular social and moral virtue depends upon grasping its nature as embodied in, and expressed through, the social practices by those within the tradition in which it finds a central place. This is not to deny that abstract understanding and reasoning about principles proper play a significant role in political justification, deliberation or the evolution of traditions. But, abstract deliberation itself presupposes an imaginative understanding of what we should be aspiring to and how given social practices are and should seek to evolve.

It is important to stress that recognizing the significance of social practices and institutions which embody a tradition does not entail unreflective conservatism. True, in order to judge the justice or otherwise of practices we must appreciate the imaginative understanding of the participants involved and, thus, why the practice concerned is seen as significant. In order to understand why people believed they were witches and deserved to be burnt at the stake, or why mediaeval prosecutors believed they had a duty to seek out heresy, we have to appreciate the imaginative understanding which gave sense to their actions. Yet, such self-understandings and the historical account of a practice's evolution are themselves contestable. Understanding does not entail approval. After we have made sense of a practice it is open to us to disapprove, as in the case of witchcraft or trial by ordeal, because the presumed imaginative understanding is in some way flawed.

Established practices come up for questioning in the light of some challenge to the imaginative understanding which gives sense to them. Our critical assessment takes place in relation to a cluster of principles, beliefs and normative commitments within the relevant tradition. Nonetheless, once the rationale or claims implicit in the imaginative understanding are articulated they are then open to assessment. This may concern any one of a cluster of things from empirical claims, such as diagnosis and prediction in the case of witchcraft, to the sense of true country life embodied in fox-hunting. Such questioning may in turn lead to a revaluation of the established practice and renewed assent, modification or outright rejection. It is through the mediation of living practices and their underlying traditions that we come to learn, reaffirm, modify, extend and sometimes repudiate imaginative understandings of our human and social world. Indeed, once there is a challenge to and shift in the imaginative understanding of a given practice this may itself entail a shift in the possible horizon of beliefs open and closed to us. (See Williams 1981: 132–143.)

Consider again the case of fox-hunting, where a social practice is threatened or questioned because of a change in other cultural attitudes, beliefs or trends. We attend to the imaginative understanding presumed by the practice. In so doing we may find that those who respond to an assumed practice have a different cluster of beliefs, values and norms which perhaps glorify, or denigrate, what those within the tradition or society had previously tacitly assumed. Hence, fox-hunting may now be taken to assert what it had, at least until the not too distant past, just been assumed to reflect about the class structure of country life. Thus, it may be affirmed or rejected by virtue of what it is now taken to express. Somewhat more subtly, established practices examined in such a critical light may be extended in some way according to an appropriately modified imaginative understanding. Thus, whereas courteous men once made a point of opening doors for women, polite people may now open doors for anyone behind them irrespective of gender.

Subjecting practices to critical reflection does not require us to step outside tradition. Once the presumed understanding which made sense of trial by ordeal came up for questioning, it was rejected in the light of a more developed understanding of Christian theology. (See Bartlett 1988.) Similarly, the call for women to have the vote was affirmed because of the rejection of both an empirical claim, that women were not rational, and through appeal to an already presumed principle – that rational citizens should have a vote. An appropriate emphasis upon the significance of traditional practices and prohibitions need not entail, communitarians claim, an unthinking conformism.

It is over-simplistic to presume that traditions, and the social practices of which they make sense, are posterior to and effectively contribute nothing towards human understanding and experience: as if traditions only colonize or pervert attitudes, presumptions, thoughts and beliefs already held. Obviously, if this were so, the dissolution of traditions in a liberal society would deprive human social life of nothing but backward-looking fetters. But this is to assume, falsely, that the significance of traditions lies wholly in the rights and principles that may be extracted from them, as if the way in which they underpinned the co-mingling of human experience with social practices were of no import at all. It is the social rituals, conventions and practices that constitute our public and private lives which are the prime mediators of our deep, imaginative understanding of the world, ourselves and others. The sense and significance of these practices and rituals is given by the tradition within which they are understood.

The imaginative understanding and expression of how we might achieve our good and what our good consists in are embodied in our social practices. But the tradition which enables us to both make sense of the practices and ourselves contains implicit claims about the human world. The claims themselves may be true or false. But whether the understanding we arrive at and the goods we aim for are the appropriate ones is a matter we may only be able to see if we are inculcated into a tradition which enables us to see these things appropriately. The objects of the world, its properties and ultimately what is just and good, is a matter which is significantly mind independent. But our mind has to be directed toward the right thing in the right way to see things as they are. Hence, what our human good consists in is not just discovered through tradition but the tradition had better be the right one.

From the very first glimmerings of self-consciousness we are implicated as participants within certain forms of life. Our imaginative understanding emerges from our experience and participation in the conventions, rituals and activities of life in a particular tradition. The point of rational deliberation is to inform, critically, our understanding and participation in the practices which afford our lives a certain meaning. The point of political institutions, procedures and governing principles of justice arises from the activities, practices and institutions of civil life. The norms and values that social roles, conventions and practices embody depend upon an appropriate imaginative understanding of them. Only in the light of relatively stable, rich and informative traditions can we make sense of different possibilities open to us and question how we ought to lead our lives or what our good consists in. The problem with liberalism, communitarians claim, is its intrinsic lack of concern for certain social practices and traditions which enable people to lead meaningful lives. For example, religious practices and traditions in Britain clearly cannot expect to command universal assent. Thus, they are considered to be outside the remit of the state. If religious practice withers on the vine in the face of secular society, says the liberal, so much the worse for religion. The liberal state cannot and should not be expected to support practices and traditions rejected by many and required only by a few to lead meaningful lives. Yet the point of having a just state arises from the broader concern with pursuing the projects, activities and goods of human life which are mediated by and expressed through traditions. Thus liberalism, in defining political legitimacy in terms of what would universally be assented to, remains corrosively indifferent to distinctive traditions which enable certain people to lead meaningful lives.

Neo-Aristotelianism and Regulation

The recognition of the importance of tradition in this way is broadly Aristotelian in nature and ties in with the claim that the good of the individual is intimately bound up with the good of the State and society as a whole. For Aristotle, the purpose of the State, and thus socio-political regulation, is to cultivate land and promote the well-being of each and every citizen. Human beings are necessarily political animals, in that the fulfilment of their rational capacities and ends can only be properly fulfilled within a community. The happiness and, thus, good of the individual necessarily involves the good of fellow members of a community. (Aristotle 1976: I. 1097b7–11, p74) It is crucial that the form of the State is that of an educated democracy, which is preferable to enlightened despotism because it is inherently more stable. Better decisions are more likely to emerge from a consensus amongst a larger educated number than the dictate of an individual or small group and, as a co-operative activity, democracy involves the exercise and cultivation of essential social virtues. True happiness is not to be identified merely with a life of honour, hedonistic pleasure or the satisfaction of preferences we happen to have. (Aristotle 1976: I. 1095b14–1096a3, pp. 75–76.) For Aristotle, true honour or pleasure are more properly the mark of something worthwhile actually having been achieved rather than constituting something's value. Moreover, many pleasures or actual preferences are, in the long run, superficial or self-defeating. Excessively pursuing an appetite for drink or pornography, for example, might be self-defeating because it might undercut our ability to function in other crucial ways, from the sphere of the workplace to personal relationships. Moreover, even if such pleasures are not self-defeating they may be superficial in the sense that they do not fully realize our human nature. A lifetime devoted to pornography, for example, would be an impoverished one, since our sexual appetites would not be properly directed toward fulfilling human sexual relationships.

Happiness is not a mental state but consists in pursuing activities which exercise and enable us to fulfil our rational, human nature and capacities. A life which is not guided by reason may be good for another sort of creature, but not for a human being. It is in the exercise of our rational nature that, for Aristotle, our happiness lies:

> If we assume that the function of man is a kind of life, viz., an activity or series of actions of the soul, implying a rational principle; and if the function of a good man is to perform these well and rightly; and if every function is performed well when performed in accordance with its proper excellence; if all this is so, the conclusion is that the good for man is an activity of the soul in accordance with virtue. (Aristotle 1976: I. 1097b22–1098a20, p. 68)

This is not to downgrade the importance of pleasure in our lives. For Aristotle, as articulated in the doctrine of the mean, nothing is good or bad in itself. But rather we should be moderate in the pursuit of our appetites and desires and recognize that clearly some desires are, for the kind of rational creatures we are, more important than others (Aristotle 1976: 1106a14–1107a27, pp. 99–102).

Since Aristotle recognized that we are essentially social animals, the pursuit of happiness includes realizing to a high degree both the intellectual and the moral or social virtues. Not only should our critical faculties be developed, in order to facilitate our arriving at truth and knowledge, but we need social goods such as friendship and, thus, we require social virtues such as justice, generosity and courage, in order to achieve well-being. We need to be able to understand both our human nature and our own particular gifts so that we can rationally order our ends to achieve true happiness. State governance and regulation is required, because in order to develop the required virtues for human fulfilment and happiness we must be habituated into the right kinds of practices and ways of understanding. Without the right kind of education our natural human desires can become perverted, by being directed at the wrong kinds of ends or activities, or we may lack the self-control required to pursue and attain the ends and activities we recognize that we should pursue. Education is thus broadly construed and it is the job of the State to educate its citizenry into, and reinforce through regulation, the intellectual, social and moral virtues in whose exercise our good lies (Aristotle 1981: I. 1331b24–1332a38, pp. 427–430). Hence, in a significant sense, nothing is strictly private nor, as a matter of principle, outside the remit of State regulation. For Aristotle it is the function of the State to regulate society so that it is conducive for the development of these virtues in all its citizens and, thus, their ability to realize themselves *qua* human beings:

> The state has priority over the household and over any individual among us. For the whole must be prior to the part. Separate hand or foot from the whole body, and they will no longer be hand or foot except in name, as one might speak of a 'hand' or 'foot' sculpted in stone. That will be the condition of the spoilt ['destroyed' or 'ruined'] hand, which no longer has the capacity and the function which define it ... the state is both natural and prior to the individual. (Aristotle 1981: I. 1253a18–29, pp. 60–61)

Aristotle's conception of the human good and the inter-relationship between the private and the public in society is an essentially organic one.[13] The realization of an individual's well-being requires essentially social activities, ends and goods which are constituted both by the individual's inter-relationships to other individuals in society *and* to social institutions themselves. Political governance, law and regulation is required in order to maintain the healthy functioning of these social institutions and activities in order to enable individuals to fulfil themselves fully, through the exercise of human virtues, and thus attain a state of true well-being or happiness. The State's fundamental purpose is to shape social institutions and activities so that they cultivate the well-being of individuals within it. The aim of State regulation is thus teleological – its aim is to promote the moral and social character of its citizens. Hence, the State should seek to habituate its citizens, using a modern example, through broadcasting control and regulation, into the right dispositions so that we are naturally led towards being virtuous in our own lives.

This suggests that a neo-Aristotelian would typically be in favour of fairly heavy broadcasting regulation. For, assuming that the media affects the way we conceive of ourselves, others and society, its potential influence ought to be constrained toward promoting the virtuous life and proscribing the life of vice. An important point to note here is that neo-Aristotelians need not deny that people should have choices regarding what they watch. Having the possibility of realizing one's preferences is clearly valuable. But what matters is that the kinds of choices open to us are meaningful ones. The choices open to us should either be pleasurably innocent or good for us.

For example, certain kinds of game shows, soaps, dramas and films are pleasurably innocent in the sense that they are funny, diverting and entertaining. However, crucially, they do not concern or involve denigrating social and moral values that are assumed to be essential to our well-being. Conversely, news programmes, documentaries, natural world programmes, cultural programmes and certain kinds of dramas or films are good for us in the sense that they inform us about the world and, more significantly, deepen our understanding of human motivations, dilemmas, characters, societies and values. Ideally, such programming should be both good for us and pleasurable. But pleasure here is a mark of such programmes' true value and not where their value lies. Their real value lies in cultivating a deepened understanding of ourselves, others and the world. (See Kieran 1996.)

The point here is that neo-Aristotelians would hold that regulation should ensure that both our innocent pleasures and educative, rational and imaginative needs are realized. Hence, a public broadcasting channel which only put out mere entertainment would be open to censure for failing to meet our rational and imaginative needs. Conversely, if broadcasting consisted only of dull but worthy and informative programming something would clearly be wrong; our need for innocent, diverting pleasures would not be catered to. More negatively, neo-Aristotelians are likely to hold that pornographic films, art house films such as Pasolini's *Salò,* which explicitly depicts the orgiastic descent of small-town Italian burghers into ritualized and vicious sado-masochism, or even explicit sex game shows are objectionable and should not be allowed to be broadcast. For, far from cultivating the right kind of dispositions in us, they glorify and cultivate dispositions such as sexual excess, which lead away from virtue toward vice. As Roger Scruton puts it:

> Whatever persons are, they have a reason to avoid both the fulfilment, and also (if possible) the possession, of corrupt desires. (Scruton 1983: 27–136)

Moreover, on a neo-Aristotelian view, the State has legitimate warrant for proscribing programme content which speaks to such desires. Indeed, many non-explicit programmes depicting various forms of sexuality or relationships, for example, homosexuality, may be objected to. The problem is not so much with the sexual content as such, though that certainly figures, but more fundamentally concerns the celebration of the kinds of motivations and desires that it is held we ought, morally speaking, to suppress, sublimate or turn away from altogether.

This thought has two distinct aspects. The first is essentially a social consideration and links to familiar contemporary arguments concerning whether watching certain kinds of programs causes us to behave in certain ways. Namely, if such programmes cause anti-social and immoral behaviour, or the acceptance of it, then they ought not to be broadcast. Of course, Aristotle famously held that, far from inducing imitative behaviour, such representations performed a cathartic function (Aristotle 1965). Tragedy, according to Aristotle, serves only to express, and thus give form to, the emotions and feelings of the audience in their response to what is represented. Yet many neo-Aristotelians might hold otherwise, since the arousal and expression of such emotions might cultivate our disposition to seek their satisfaction out. There is some reason to take such a view seriously. For many programmes and films are valued not merely because of the pleasure they afford us but because they engage and prescribe us to imagine, in peculiarly powerful ways, characters, dilemmas and possible worlds.[14] Moreover, one of the primary mechanisms by which we do so is through character identification. Where we imaginatively simulate what another thinks, feels and perceives their situation to be (Whiten 1991), through programmes directing our imaginings towards certain kinds of characters and states of affairs, programmes and films may cultivate the kind of pleasure we derive from the infliction of, for example, violence upon others. Thus, our base non-rational appetites may not only be indulged and satiated but enlarged (Plato 1989: I. 491e–492c, pp. 64–65). The empirical research here is inconclusive, partly because a far too simplistic conception of the relationship between imaginative engagement, understanding and action is presumed.[15]

The second aspect of the worry does not concern the relation to action but rather concerns one's individual character, independently of questions of causal influence. The thought is that the kind of pleasure or delight certain material speaks to may itself be morally dubious in some significant sense. Underlying this presumption is the general Kantian thought articulated in one version of the categorical imperative, that one should always 'act in such a way that you always treat humanity ... never simply as a means, but always at the same time as an end' (Kant 1948: 91).

If a programme on serial killers dwells salaciously on the minute details of the killings then it is prescribing us to savour the violent nature of the act. Similarly, in pornography our attention is directed toward the sexual acts and parts of the performers displayed rather than any characters depicted. In essence, they prescribe us to look at individuals as fantastical objects subject to the whim or violence of our sexual desires. They both degrade those depicted and the viewer. If a programme is obscene in this way, and we are right to condemn it as immoral, the neo-Aristotelian is likely to hold that it should not be broadcast. For the neo-Aristotelian, unless the content and kind of programming we allow in society is heavily regulated, we may be undercutting our ability to flourish, morally and socially, as rational human beings in a decent society.

Liberalism and the Corrosion of Tradition

The typical liberal response is to point out that the State is required precisely because social practices, activities and the values they embody may come into conflict. Given that the significance of social practices emerges in the light of given traditions, liberals need not presume that traditional commitments should be cast into the abyss in favour of an abstract set of neutral procedural principles of regulation. Rather, given a plurality of different, competing traditions, it is not the job of the State to favour or protect one tradition over and above others. For people should be free to assent to or reject particular broadcasting practices and programming as they choose and, thus, the State should be impartial regarding their relative worth. The State's laws should be justifiable to everyone subject to them, whatever tradition they belong to.

Liberalism's greatest virtue would, it is claimed, be its insistence upon the need to maintain a critical distance from the practices we are inducted into. Thus, liberalism enables us to focus upon considerations, norms and principles which transcend traditional concerns. It is limited to the rules and sphere of government whilst remaining unconcerned with the broader traditions which makes sense of our lives. The whole point about any appeal to justice and regulation is that it involves an appeal to considerations which are supposed to transcend whatever established social practice or the precedence of tradition is.

The point of protecting our rights and liberties is to enable us to live, free from the threat of harm, as we would choose. The crucial point here is that we should be free to choose to assent to, modify or reject the activities, values and goals proffered to us as constituents of the good life. We aim to realize our good through the pursuit of certain activities or goals. Of course, our assessment of their significance and meaning for us depends upon various beliefs we have about what and why something is valuable. But as autonomous individuals we may critically reflect upon the purpose or value of many of our activities and the underlying beliefs. The point of such reflection lies in recognizing the true nature of an activity in order to judge whether it is worthwhile. For we should always be free to ask whether the beliefs we are acting upon are, in fact, true or warranted. We should be free not just to practice our religion but to question it without fear of threat, harm or coercion. After all, coerced worship is hardly true worship at all. The liberal State should protect and sustain the freedoms required for people to take decisions autonomously. As long as the State is able to maintain the conditions required to ensure such freedoms it has no business in seeking to sustain or promote any tradition.

Of course, in one sense, liberalism does threaten the viability of traditions in civil society: it opens them up to critical questioning. Yet it is precisely as a challenge to unreflective conservatism that liberalism possesses its greatest appeal. As Mill himself might put it, only in the free marketplace of ideas might we expect to come to recognize for ourselves what is truly valuable and good (Mill 1974: 141–162).[16]

Whether we should judge something as just or not is thus, the liberal will retort, a matter significantly independent of tradition. Hence, though perhaps not ideal, better to have a state openly sceptical about what the good life might be than one which seeks to impose a particular tradition, social practices and, thus, a conception of the good life upon all of its citizens.

However, the typical liberal response is just a little too quick. According to Rawls, fundamental questions of justice can be settled 'only in ways that *all* citizens can reasonably be expected to endorse in the light of their common human reason' (Rawls 1993: 139–140). There is a question to be asked here about just what constitutes reasonableness, which can be put in the form of a dilemma. Either, following most liberals and Rawls' earlier work, reasonableness is construed in terms of what we have good reason to believe. In which case, many apparently valuable traditions and, thus, social practices are precluded. Or, following the most recent work of Rawls and Richard Rorty, reasonableness is what everyone, as a contingent matter, is prepared to agree to. (See, for example, Rorty 1985.) In which case it is not clear the principles of justice arrived at are rationally grounded.

Most liberals, including the earlier work of Rawls, argue that only reasons amenable to rational assessment, independently of tradition, should count. (See Dworkin 1985: 191; Montefiore 1975; and Audi 1989: 278.) According to liberalism, individuals may contingently have an interest in belonging to a particular tradition that is no concern of a State whose sole aim is to protect the freedoms and rights of basic citizenship.[17] Hence, liberals are typically unwilling to countenance privileging particular traditions unless the aim is to expand liberty for all or promote the liberty of those with the least freedoms.[18] But then liberalism, far from being neutral amongst competing traditions, becomes much narrower and exclusive in favouring certain traditions over others. Of course, liberalism remains impartial between traditions which may be reasonably disputed in the sense that they are amenable to philosophical reason. But it can only remain indifferent to, or positively hostile towards, numerous substantive traditions such as Christianity, for example, which are less obviously so. For liberalism is concerned with what, rationally speaking, it is reasonable to assent to and is therefore wholly unconcerned as to whether this bears any relation to what is found valuable in religious or conservative traditions. Liberalism is indifferent, or positively hostile, toward such traditions. For if their value is not straightforwardly amenable to rational justification, liberalism must hold that they are not truly valuable and not to be protected, perhaps even rooted out from society. This rationalist construal of liberalism thus involves a substantive conception of what is valuable and claims that traditions not open to rational justification are necessarily wrong. Rationalist liberalism cannot both respect its own commitment to impartiality and respect the importance of certain traditions. It is bound to discount certain kinds of reasons, religious and conservative ones, for example, and thus be positively disdainful of social practices, traditions and programming provision for them.

Consider the case of Christianity. Many influential liberals believe there is no compelling reason to hold Christianity to be true and, thus, the liberal State should not consider religious reasons or, indeed, support it where it threatens to disappear.[19] For, we can explain and understand the human world without adverting to a divine, omnipotent creator. Thus, given Christianity is not clearly rationally justifiable, it is not a tradition that should be protected by the liberal State. People should be free to be Christians as long as their social practices, such as Sunday worship, are harmless. But no support should be given to Christianity. Public broadcasting, therefore, should not be required to provide programming of Christian worship as distinct from programming about religion. Moreover, where the Christian tradition seeks to make claims or legislate regarding the actions of others, the State should discount it, if not actively seek to preclude its provision. The liberal State, on the rationalist's interpretation of reasonableness, should not protect distinctively Christian religious programming.[20]

Yet, it might be thought, the rationalist liberal's disdain for certain traditions which are not straightforwardly amenable to rational justification, and, thus, the social practices that are constitutive of them, lends itself to the dissolution or destruction of valuable prohibitions and commitments which help to underpin civil society. Without the traditions which underpin some social practices but not obviously susceptible of rational justification it is not clear what kind of civil society we might have left. For the rationalist liberal's presumption is that once one has arrived at a rational set of first-order principles one can begin the task of appropriately reconstructing human society. Or the thought is that, released from the fetters of traditions which are not rationally justified, we are free to remake ourselves in any way we so choose consistent with constraints of impartiality. But such rationalism in politics is, at best, so the argument would be futile and, at worst, highly corruptive.

At best liberal rationalism is futile because the wholesale rooting out of certain traditions and reconstruction of society will never achieve its end. For if our imaginative understanding of how to conceive of ourselves, treat others and thus act in the human world is mediated by tradition then, outside tradition, the significance of particular ways of behaving is lost. The very attempt to impose justice along rationalistic lines will sweep away certain mediating traditions which give a point and purpose to our behaving in certain ways rather than others. Hence, liberalism, as commonly understood, has tended to neglect or corrode the social conventions, rituals and practices which embody religious or conservative social norms and values.

At its worst, where religious and conservative traditions are uprooted and previous forms of behaviour are no longer understood as bearing particular significance, liberal rationalism seems to render many kinds of action arbitrary. A heightened sense of the myriad of possibilities conjoined with the sense that the choice itself confers value naturally inclines society toward anarchy. For example, deprived of significance, the point of familial bonds is rendered motivationally inert and either chaos is likely to reign for understandable psychological reasons or our lives impoverished.[21] But there are far more insidious and subtle manifestations.

Consider the kind of rationalistic town planning thought to be a natural extension of a rational society ordered by principles of justice. Architects, glorifying in the self-appointed term 'brutalists', designed Tower Hamlets in London to break up what was regarded as the traditional conservative and, thus, reactionary social order: familial ties were regarded as holding back the progressive drive toward impartiality. For, apart from peculiar religious or conservative reasons, would anyone think that insular, familial communities were either fair or just? As Bryan Appleyard argues, through fracturing families and alienating communities, the brutalists achieved their aim by altering the established social institutions and practices. The result was chaos, deprivation and the oppression of many isolated individuals by those who grew up in circumstances where there were no families or communities left to be held accountable to. (See Appleyard 1989: 119–125.)

But the erosion of certain valuable traditions does not merely result from the attempt to break up and sweep them clean away. Rather the liberal State's mere indifference to traditions deemed not to be rationally justified threatens to bleach them out of civil society altogether. Given that religious reasons are considered outside the sphere of rational assessability, then obviously the State itself cannot but fail to take seriously religious reasons for certain practices, rituals and activities. In a State where religion is deemed to be irrationalist it may become much harder for religious traditions to flourish. Obviously the state will not prevent people from pursuing religious lives, except where religious beliefs impinge upon others, but it obviously makes it far harder do so. Consider a family who want to bring their child up to be a Christian. At home they try to show and teach him or her certain beliefs, rituals and practices. Yet, as soon as the child goes to school and encounters children from backgrounds where religion is considered merely a bizarre superstition, as manifested in the consideration and treatment meted out to it by the State, because it is not amenable to rational assessment, it becomes much harder for the parents to bring their child up as they would wish. We will see this in operation later in discussing Mary Whitehouse and her moral protest movement, The National Viewers' and Listeners' Association and the attack on television for not supporting a Christian view of the world. Indeed, as a psychological matter it is far harder for religious practices to flourish in a society which is, at best, dismissive of their significance. Hence, for example, the kind of bewilderment, arising from indifference to such matters, that faced the Moslem community when they protested about the publication of Salman Rushdie's *Satanic Verses*.[22]

Lastly, there is a significant causal relation between the indifference to and corrosion of certain kinds of valuable traditions by liberalism and the erosion of civil society *per se*. As noted, the liberal State's concern is only to protect the rights and freedoms of the individual so we are all free to choose how to live our own lives. Thus, we can only legitimately be concerned with the actions of others if they are members of groups we have voluntarily contracted into. If one individual bears no relation to another in this way then their actions are no legitimate concern of the other. If such an individual behaves in ways the other disapproves of, it is none of the other person's business. If the way in which they behave results in harm, this is, properly speaking, the State's affair and certainly not for the other individual to deal with. The backcloth of religious and conservative traditions, through which people's imaginative understanding of themselves is interwoven with natural sympathy and duties to others, tends to dissolve away in the face of liberal indifference.

But the upshot of such indifference upon civil society may be disastrous. Consider violence in everyday life. For example, one might reasonably consider a time in the past where an act of vicious, random violence is perpetrated in public, which if a person intervened they could count on others coming to their aid, but which now would not happen on the grounds that people, though, morally speaking, consider that perhaps they ought to help, it is not, properly speaking, any of their business. It is the State's business to intervene in order to prevent harm. Hence, we can no longer trust that intervention on behalf of others will meet with any form of social support.

The corrosion of this form of social understanding, once initiated, is prone to become viciously self-fulfilling. The argument would be that without role models who intervene and thus embody social responsibility, as prescribed by, say, Christianity and conservatism, people are inclined, fatalistically, to presume that no one will intervene. From this it is reasonable to assume no one will help even if they tried to intervene and, given that under such circumstances, they alone probably could not stop the violence, absolve themselves of any responsibility. By extension of this argument, the young derive the understanding that such acts really are no one's business except the State's and those unfortunate enough to be picked on. If this is the case, then the dissolution of religious and conservative conventions, customs and social practices embodying particular conceptions of the public good not only erodes the possibility of certain public goods but also threatens to allow certain fundamental private goods to be taken from particular individuals through coercion, manipulation or malicious intent.

Society itself, and, thus, the ability to pursue certain private and public goods, is just not possible where social traditions are not supported above a certain threshold. The liberal State's failure to protect certain valuable traditions which help to underpin civil society, in the name of rational justification, thus threatens to destroy the very conditions which make our rights, freedoms and rationality worth protecting. Liberalism's acidic indifference to particular traditions thus threatens to be self-defeating.

A different tack, following the recent work of Rorty, amongst others, is to embrace multifarious political, moral and religious reasons. But then liberalism is set a very strenuous task indeed. It must justify the basic liberties protected and the resultant socio-economic distribution to a huge range of often divergent traditions which need meet only a very minimal threshold in order to be considered reasonable. Such a weak threshold means that liberals can only really expect the assent of all to be met in relatively homogeneous societies. But the force of liberalism derives mainly from aspiring to arrive at a set of rationally justifiable principles of justice despite conditions of a diverse plurality of traditions. Moreover, if reasonableness is only what everyone may assent to, there seem to be hardly any grounds for assessing whether certain kinds of reasons ought to count as being any good. After all, even if everyone in a given society believed that poor people deserved to be so and, thus, social welfare is a matter of charity rather than justice it does not automatically follow that we (rationally) should assent to the consensus belief as constitutive of justice.

More plausibly, Rawls has recently claimed that all citizens ought not to, *qua* citizen, appeal to their substantive traditions. The thought is that we can maintain liberal legitimacy if we recognize that political values override non-political ones – even where liberalism conflicts with valuable traditions we still have reason to allow the political value to override the tradition and this is reasonable.[23] Since political values make fair conditions of social co-operation possible and minimize the potential for fundamental conflicts between traditions, they must be respected first.

This, however, has faced serious challenge. It may be that political values should typically override others. But the grounds for liberal legitimacy require that political values must always override non-political ones even when they conflict with valuable traditions. This is deeply counter-intuitive. The point of political protests, from anti-abortionists, peace marchers and animal rights campaigners to anti-road demonstrators, is derived from the moral and religious beliefs the protesters regard as fundamental.[24] It is reasonable to hold that the protection of innocent lives is far more important than respecting political values. So political values cannot always override values deriving from substantial religious, conservative and other valuable traditions which are not clearly rationally justified. Political values may be great but they are insufficient to override the values the protesters are striving to honour and protect. Moreover, that respecting liberal political values tends to minimize the potential for conflict still gives no reason to believe that, as and when there is conflict, political values should always override. The liberal can only do this by appeal to a substantive tradition, which we must expect ought to be assented to, instead of invoking what everyone may reasonably assent to. But then the conception of justice involved is no longer merely political.

Liberalism appears to be in a bind. As a political conception it remains blind to and corrosive of certain significant traditions, emphasizing only what we may all contingently, or politically, assent to, or itself requires rational justifiability and, thus, commitment to a substantive, comprehensive and, thus, exclusionary liberal tradition. Hence, it is far from obvious that broadcasting regulation, which is just and fair to all the traditions within our increasingly pluralistic society, is a realizable goal.

Privacy

Consider the substantial disagreement liberals and neo-Aristotelians have over the notion of the public interest. Of course, both recognize that there is, in principle, a distinction to be made between the public interest and what the public are merely interested in. But the nature and scope of the public interest is construed very differently. One area in which we can see how this is so concerns the hotly contested issue of privacy and the media. However, in order to examine the ways in which liberals and neo-Aristotelians will differ concerning invasions of privacy, we need to reflect upon how they conceive of privacy and why it is held to be so important.

A standard liberal conception of privacy holds that it concerns personal information which is not disclosed by a person or remains outside the public arena. Thus, privacy is sometimes thought to be:

> …the condition of not having undocumented personal knowledge about one possessed by others. A person's privacy is diminished exactly to the degree that others possess this kind of information about him. (Parent 1992: 92)

Facts about oneself that one chooses not to disclose concerning one's sexual life or proclivities, financial status or even age are clearly private under this conception. Of course, some people are happy to disclose certain kinds of information, others wish to remain essentially private. But, at least typically, many people think of our sexual, financial or familial affairs as private in this way. Such a conception clearly underwrites many of our intuitions about the value of privacy. We naturally recognize that such self-revelations are within our gift. Thus, friendship is partly constituted by what we are prepared to reveal about ourselves to another as distinct from what we are happy for everyone to know. Privacy, on this view, is tied up with the kind of information we allow others access to about ourselves. Hence, many naturally think it one of the marks of a totalitarian or unjust State that it does not recognize the individual citizen's right to privacy at all and, thus, nothing personal is, in principle, considered to be outside its jurisdiction. The right to privacy, on this view, is important because it prevents the State from acquiring illegitimate power over our lives; it prevents the State from coercing or manipulating us. Furthermore, it protects individuals from the vicissitudes of public opinion. Thus, for example, our sexual behaviour and peccadilloes can, if we so choose, remain outside of the public gaze so that we are shielded from the social pressures of prurience and disapprobation. Hence, we are freer to pursue our lives and desires in this respect as we so choose.

However, though plausible, such a conception of privacy cannot really be adequate. For the liberal really wants to claim that privacy concerns the areas of our lives that we choose not to be subjected to the public gaze rather than mere information about ourselves. For clearly a person's privacy can be intruded into without anyone gaining any personal information about that individual. A journalist may break into their house, gain illegitimate access to their files, overhear a confidential conversation in a public place or pursue enquiries concerning their sex life without actually being able to glean any new or undisclosed information about that person. It is not just particular bits of information about the personal life that people wish to remain undisclosed that constitute their privacy but, rather, the spheres of their lives which such information concerns. Personal information, relationships and activities are not, properly speaking, the business of others unless we choose to share them with others. Secrets, friendships, sexual liaisons, familial bonds and disputes, amongst other things, are typically the sole business of those implicated in them. Certain kinds of concerns, activities, interests and relationships people rightly consider not to be the legitimate concern of others, except those we choose to share such aspects of our lives with, and it is these spheres of our lives which the right to privacy protects.

For the liberal then the right to privacy concerns certain spheres of personal life and it is underwritten by recognizing the value of autonomy. For, liberals hold that we should be free to pursue our lives as we choose without being subject to the judgement and coercion of others into behaving differently. Its value in this respect is twofold. Firstly, privacy allows us to entertain, try out or cultivate concerns, beliefs and practices which we would not wish to do in public. So privacy allows us, autonomously, to cultivate or modify our personal character and identity. Secondly, it provides a sphere within which we are free to develop certain kinds of intimate relationships: from familial ones to friendships and loves. So the right to privacy, for the liberal, protects an area in which we can freely test or pursue certain goals, interests and relationships without being exposed to public scrutiny:

> If we cannot control who has access to us, sometimes including and sometimes excluding various people, then we cannot control the patterns of behaviour we need to adopt or the kinds of relations with other people that we will have. (Rachels 1984: 296)

A liberal will only be inclined to accept media intrusions into someone's privacy where a journalist has good reason to suppose that an individual has been acting illegitimately or corruptly and, moreover, the relevant authorities such as the police cannot or will not act. For example, where politicians, businessmen, doctors, teachers and those in positions of power and influence over the public are suspected of corruption, then the liberal will hold that the media are justified in intruding into their privacy. For the public need to know that their representatives are acting in their interests and not abusing their position for their own illegitimate ends. We need to know if our investments are being defrauded, children being abused, or our political representatives being corrupted. As the Fourth Estate, the liberal holds, the media have a duty to intrude into an individual's privacy, where they have good reason to believe that such abuses of power are taking place. Thus, on the liberal account, the *prima facie* right to privacy can be overridden where what is being kept private essentially concerns a matter of public injustice, corruption or deception. A slightly different way of putting the same point is articulated by Andrew Belsey thus:

> …the right to privacy is no more than a presumption (though an important one), and… where some information about an individual that he or she would prefer to keep private should be in the public domain, then putting it there is not overriding that individual's right to privacy because no such right ever existed concerning this aspect of the person's life. There is…no such thing as .a justifiable invasion of privacy because justification is in fact a demonstration that no privacy could properly be claimed in the first place. (Belsey 1992: 77)

A category of persons distinct from those who occupy positions of power and influence or perform roles on the public's behalf concerns those such as public celebrities whose careers have been made out of living in the public eye. Stories concerning the love life of the actress Pamela Anderson, for example, clearly concern matters which are normally private. But such people have, tacitly, entered into something akin to a Faustian pact. For their life and career is supported by the public interest that they have cultivated in areas of their private lives. Thus, such figures cannot legitimately complain about the media attention devoted to their love lives once they have invited the media, and thereby the public, in and effectively declared these aspects of their lives to be public property. Of course, there are differences of degree here but figures who publicly reveal aspects of their private lives and seek to use them for their own advantage cannot justifiably complain about continued media interest in these aspects of their lives in ways an ordinary, private individual legitimately could.

By contrast the ordinary citizen's *prima facie* right to privacy is, for the liberal, very strong indeed. Thus, their rights to consultation regarding any programme being made about them are very strong and their consent is required. Moreover, the liberal will hold that where an individual's right to privacy has unjustifiably been abrogated, they should be able to expect a public apology, a chance to set the record straight and possibly be awarded some form of compensation. The case of the politician, for example, is rather different because he has been entrusted by the public to perform a certain role on their behalf. Where the media has reason to believe he is abusing his position, they will have every right to intrude into his privacy where necessary. Nonetheless, he should be consulted and given a chance to rebut the charges a programme makes against him.

In direct contrast to liberals, however, neo-Aristotelians will reject the very idea that we have a right to privacy as such. For, as we saw above, society as a whole is considered to be prior to the individual and its function is to provide the conditions under which individuals are able to develop and flourish. Thus, for the neo-Aristotelian, in a significant sense, strictly speaking nothing is clearly private in the way the liberal maintains. Of course, the neo-Aristotelian may agree with the liberal that privacy in one sense is required to foster intimacy and the pursuit of certain personal activities, relationships and goods. But, even if true, this in no way entails a right to privacy. For individuals should be subject to, rather than protected from, the influence and assessment of the community at large. Moreover, it is far from clear that privacy is required, in the strong sense the liberal supposes, to pursue meaningful sexual, familial and intimate relationships. Indeed, there is something to the thought that such relationships and activities may be better without the liberal emphasis on the need for and right to privacy. Hypocrisy, deceit, immorality and imprudence are more likely to flourish in a culture where privacy is considered sacrosanct. As Richard Wasserstrom articulates it, under such conditions:

> Individuals see themselves as leading dual lives – public ones and private ones. They present one view of themselves to the public – to casual friends, acquaintances, and strangers – and a different view of themselves to themselves and a few intimate associates. This way of living is hypocritical because it is, in essence, a life devoted to camouflaging the real, private self from public scrutiny. It is a dualistic, unintegrated life that renders the individuals who live it needlessly vulnerable, shame ridden, and lacking in a clear sense of self. It is to be contrasted with the more open, less guarded life of the person who has so little to fear from disclosures of self because he or she has nothing that requires hiding. (Wasserstrom 1984: 331)

The reason such an individual should have nothing to fear, for neo-Aristotelians, is precisely because it is society's function to shape and guide the dispositions and values of individuals towards the common good and this is just as true concerning even the most 'private' of familial and intimate relationships and activities as the more obviously public ones concerning justice:

> As for man and wife, children and father, and the virtue that appertains to each and their intercourse with one another, what is right in that connection and what is not, and the proper pursuit of the good therein and the avoidance of the bad – all such matters it will be necessary to discuss in relation to the constitutions. For these relationships are part of the household, and every household is part of a state; and the virtue of the part ought to be examined in relation to the virtue of the whole. (Aristotle 1981: I. 1260a36–1260b26, p. 97)

Given that an individual's normative dispositions, attitudes and behaviour should be directed by society toward the appropriate goals, the community or public has an important role to play in reinforcing them, including clearly expressing disapproval or prohibition of the wrong ones and approval of behaviour, activities and relationships which manifest good normative dispositions. If there is no right to privacy as such then clearly our right to privacy cannot be abrogated. Of course, our privacy can be still be intruded in the sense that the community or State may concern itself with activities of ours we wish it would not. Nonetheless, there is no fundamental right to privacy and, for a neo-Aristotelian, such intrusions are clearly justified not only where information about injustice or corruption is at stake but, much more widely, where activities which go against the right social and moral norms are being pursued. As David Archard has pointed out this kind of exposure of private lives is akin to a kind of gossip. (See Archard 1998.) Clearly gossip can be morally dubious because of the motives involved and because of the effects or harm on those gossiped about. But these considerations, as such, do not speak against the socially valuable role of gossip the neo-Aristotelian is inclined to presume. Firstly, gossip helps a community to define itself and create or maintain its unity. But, more importantly, it concerns the propagation and cultivation of the shared values of the community or society:

> Gossip bears on conduct which is evaluable by these values and it bears on such conduct because it is evaluable. Gossip is a way of testing or rehearsing those values by exposing conduct which they would seem to proscribe. In gossip these values, and thereby also the identity and unity of the group which professes them, may be re-affirmed. Finally, gossip exposes the wrongdoer to public shame or ridicule and consequently functions as a deterrent to such wrongdoing. (Archard 1998)

The point is that neo-Aristotelians are more likely to think that the immoral and anti-social behaviour of public figures, even where it in no way affects their performance of their public role, and of private individuals ought to be exposed precisely because it reinforces and cultivates the moral and social norms required in society for individuals to be able to develop as they should and thus flourish as good human beings. The neo-Aristotelian conception of the public interest is thus much broader and stronger than the liberal's, and the neo-Aristotelian will thus accept many intrusions into privacy by the media as legitimate which the liberal would condemn as appalling abrogations of the individual's right to privacy.

Offence, Harm and Censorship

Essentially, liberals tend to be strongly anti-censorship for a cluster of reasons motivated by the primacy they give to autonomy. Even where there is *prima facie* reason to entertain the possibility of censorship, nonetheless, except in very extreme cases, liberals will think that the costs of censorship are too great a price to pay. For, the justification of the State, according to the liberal, is to provide the conditions under which people are free to lead their lives as they choose. Censorship prevents people from doing just that; hence, it constitutes a fundamental attack on their autonomy and, thus, their very status as citizens. This is to undercut the very rationale that justifies the State's authority over its citizens in the first place. The aim of censorship measures is to prevent opinions or programmes from being heard or seen and, as such, is deeply objectionable to any liberal. This holds true irrespective of the truth, falsity or tastelessness of the opinions proffered or programmes broadcast (Scanlon 1972: 204–225). They constitute an attack upon our right to freedom of expression and the freedom to listen to or view what we choose.

Clearly the liberal holds that these rights are worth protecting precisely because, as autonomous citizens, we have a deep interest in being able to communicate with, or listen to, those we wish to address or entertain seriously. Indeed, in political matters, this is clearly crucial if our participation in the democratic process can truly be said to be both free and, potentially at least, well informed. Moreover, as John Stuart Mill pointed out, we clearly have an interest in entertaining those views we disagree with (Mill 1982: 96–108). If we only entertained those we already presume, we are not likely to understand why what we hold is, putatively, true. We would not have to think about the evidential or evaluative basis and rationale for the views we hold.

Furthermore, many presumptions we hold to be commonsensically true, in common with other people, often turn out to be false. If views were not allowed to be expressed, merely on the grounds of their falsehood, then not only would our knowledge about the world not increase but also many devious, pernicious institutions and states of affairs, from slavery to the abuse of political power, would remain unchallenged. So if programmes were regulated according to their supposed 'correctness' we would never be able to find out which of our presently held views and values turn out to be misplaced. After all, many beliefs and immoral practices were only changed because people dared to challenge accepted dogmas. Hence, regulation might sacrifice the possibility of getting at a more complete understanding of what is the case, what should be the case and why. In a culture where the freedom of expression is shackled by State censorship and regulation, corruption, elitism and the reinforcement of false prejudices are far more likely to survive. Moreover, there is clearly a benefit to allowing everyone to express their views freely, no matter how unpopular, rather than pursuing censorship and content regulation, because those who otherwise consider themselves to be marginalized from society will, nonetheless, recognize that at least they have the right and opportunity to be heard (Mill 1982: 115).

The liberal will also suggest that there are plausible reasons to believe that censorship is self-defeating. By preventing certain views from being aired, false credence may be lent to them. If the public are not left to make up their own minds about a particular view, as the liberal thinks they should, then a natural assumption for the public to make is that this is because the government does not want them to entertain it. If the view really is false and without credence, one might think, clearly, they would not mind. Thus, curtailing the rights of freedom of expression regarding some views may tend to encourage interest in it and acceptance of its beliefs rather than quell it, which is presumably the intended aim (Mill 1982: 91–94, 150). For example, prohibiting IRA terrorists, or racists, from appearing on television clearly protects them from being accountable to the public. It also serves to reinforce their own presumption that there is a conspiracy to hide their 'truth' from the general public. Better to have such views out in the open where they can be autonomously assessed on their own merits by the public at large, rather than excluded and thus lent a false air of credibility.

Lastly, even if regulation or censorship is justified in a very particular case, allowing regulation and censorship may lead to censorship in other illegitimate areas, which would constitute a far greater harm. Allowing racist programmes on air may, indirectly, lead to harm, which is certainly regrettable. But, it would be far worse to allow regulation in the name of the public good since the abuse such regulation would be open to is obvious. As Thomas Scanlon articulates it, the liberal holds that the power to restrict freedom of expression or the content of programmes is illegitimate even where it may lead to harms of certain kinds, namely:

(a) harms to certain individuals which consist in their coming to have false beliefs as a result of those acts of expression; (b) harmful consequences of acts performed as a result of those acts of expression, where the connection between the acts of expression and the subsequent harmful acts consists merely in the fact that the act of expression led the agents to believe (or increased their tendency to believe) these acts to be worth performing. (Scanlon 1972: 213)

The mere fact that something causes harm to others is not sufficient reason to prohibit it. After all, we accept that having cars on the road indirectly harms hundreds of individuals who are killed or maimed each year. Nonetheless, it is considered to be a cost worth accepting. The argument is that people should be presumed to be responsible for themselves, as drivers, and should have the freedom to choose how they travel. Similarly, racist programming may be harmful even if only a few people are encouraged to adopt that viewpoint. But, people are assumed to be responsible enough to make up their own minds and should be free to do so. Ultimately, the liberal's attitude toward content regulation is deeply antipathetic. For the liberal's basic question is this: 'Why should I, as an autonomous human being, have my choice or freedom of expression restricted, and thus suffer in a very deep way, merely because other people are irresponsible about what they choose to say, watch or believe?'

For the liberal, that a programme is deeply offensive does not constitute any ground at all for modifying or prohibiting it. This is because finding a programme to be offensive is essentially the expression of a moral judgement; it goes against some moral view, value or principle which the viewer thinks ought to be upheld. But, as noted earlier, the liberal holds that the state has absolutely no business in interfering with or guiding what, morally speaking, we choose to do or watch. Hence, if there is a demand by viewers for racist, anti-religious or pornographic programmes, and those offended by them can choose not to watch them, they should not be censored or regulated. Generally we should be free to choose what to do and watch, as long as the rights and freedoms of others are respected. Hence, though offensive to many, a person should be free to watch pornography. If someone is prepared to pay money to watch something then they should be allowed to do so, as long as there is no serious harm involved to others in the programme's production, whether doing so is morally dubious or not.

In contrast to liberals, neo-Aristotelians are likely to take very seriously the question as to whether a programme is offensive or immoral. For a programme to be offensive in a minimal sense is merely to annoy someone. People may be annoyed by all sorts of things, ranging from the irksome to the distasteful, and that is merely a reflection of what they do not like or approve of. Someone may find youth programming offensive because of the way presenters speak or look. We can be offended for all sorts of reasons which may reflect peculiarities about ourselves rather than anything suspect about the nature of the programme being broadcast. Clearly, there is little reason to take this kind of offence seriously. However, neo-Aristotelians are likely to hold that there is a significant kind of offence which is deeply important and this concerns moral outrage or repugnance. Indeed, this kind of offence may well, as The Williams Report suggests, be construed as a kind of harm:

Laws against public sex would generally be thought to be consistent with the harm condition, in the sense that if members of the public are upset, distressed, disgusted, outraged or put out by witnessing some class of acts, then that constitutes a respect in which the public performance of those acts harms their interests. (Williams 1979: 99)[25]

But, although we may be traumatized or upset by a programme, this cannot really constitute a harm in a significant sense. Firstly, it is far from clear that such traumatization is harmful. After all, someone may be traumatized in just this way because their fundamentally false beliefs, racist ones, for example, have been challenged. Yet we would clearly consider this to be a good thing. So it is not clear that we should be, or indeed need to be, protected from this kind of reaction as such. Secondly, and more importantly, this reaction only arises precisely because the programme goes against or abuses moral, religious or fundamental beliefs and values we hold dear. Such feelings cannot constitute a harm, as such, if they depend upon or arise from the expression of a moral view. (See Ellis 1984: 3–23.)

However, to judge a programme to be deeply offensive is not reducible to the traumatization or deeply unpleasant phenomenology involved when we are subjected to it. Rather, to judge a programme to be offensive in a deep sense is to claim that it presents or condones that which is held to be morally or socially repugnant and this is precisely what a neo-Aristotelian, as distinct from a liberal, considers as warranting its prohibition or modification. Consider pornography or highly explicit violent films. The thought is that such programmes are obscene because they are directed toward our lascivious interests, non-rational sexual appetites or base delight in violence. The morally dubious nature of these programmes does not lie in the fact that they may contingently excite such interests. After all, perfectly acceptable programmes may excite such interests in odd or perverse people. Rather, the obscenity inheres in the fact that these programmes are made in order to pander to these aspects of our selves.

The very point of pornography, for example, is not to cultivate an interest in the nominally fictional characters and situations depicted. Rather, the programme focuses on the spectacle of the actual people and their sexual features displayed in the film. Hence, such programmes typically focus upon the sexual parts and actions of the performers concerned. Anyone who does not see this has clearly misunderstood the kind of programme being watched. Of course, we may have some reason to believe, as articulated above, that such films may, in complex ways, be causally implicated in encouraging people to behave in morally dubious ways, for instance, abusing women or committing violent acts. (See, for example, Marshall 1989: 185–214.) After all, we know that social pressure, opinions and conceived norms can distort what people are prepared to believe and deem to be acceptable. (See, for example, Asch 1955: 31–35.) However, this is clearly not just where the real objection lies. The objection inheres in the kind of interest pandered to, independently of whether anyone is then likely to act on what they have seen. For this kind of interest, directed towards satisfying our fantastical desires, cannot fulfil us as human beings in terms of our well-being or fundamental interests. Neo-Aristotelians are concerned with our realization as a rational human being, which constitutively includes our moral and social interests, and the absence of such realization as manifested in a devotion to pornography, for example, marks a decline in, or corruption in, one's self as a person.[26] For not only is the kind of interest pandered to itself dubious, but it cultivates a sense of unreality or removal from the norms and desires that society quite rightly encourages us to pursue for our own benefit. As Roger Scruton articulates it:

> The fantasy-ridden soul will tend to have a diminished sense of the objectivity of his world, and a diminished sense of his own agency within it. The habit of pursuing the 'realized unreal' seems to conflict with the habit, which we all, I believe, have reason to acquire, of pursuing what is real. There is no expenditure of effort involved in the gratification of fantasy, and hence the fantasist is engaged in no transformation of the world. On the contrary his desires invade and permeate his world, which ceases to have any independent meaning. The nature of the fantasy object is dictated by the passion which seeks to realize it; and the world therefore has no power either to control or to resist the passion. Normal passions are founded on the sense of the independent reality of their object. They do not invade, but on the contrary, are disciplined by the world. They change as understanding changes, and come, in time, to bear the imprint both of the subject's agency and of the world's reality. (Scruton 1983: 131)

It is not the mere explicitness of sex or violence that the neo-Aristotelian objects to, though that is symptomatic of a programme's being offensive. Rather, what is being objected to is the kind of interest a programme panders to through its plot, dialogue and images. It is the nature of the programme in directing our interest, approval and delight, immorally, toward certain kinds of things which speak to our non-rational, baser appetites. And these appetites are not the kind of things, morally speaking, that we ought to wallow in or cultivate. Thus, a neo-Aristotelian may not object to a programme containing sexual content *per se*. Indeed, he or she may well approve of an adaptation of *Lady Chatterley's Lover* whose sexual content is fairly high. Rather, the problem concerns what the sexual content is doing and the kind of interest it is directed towards.

In a 'good' adaptation of Lawrence's *Lady Chatterley's Lover* the point of the sexual content is to inform and develop our understanding of the character, motivations, desires and tensions felt by the central characters. But we can imagine a bad adaptation of the same novel that may well be obscene. For the story would be used merely as a pretext to display and wallow in the details of sexual congress. This, for a neo-Aristotelian, would be deeply offensive. For the interest here would not be the characters and, thus, an attempt to understand the story, but the details and sexual parts of the actors, pandering to an interest that is itself morally dubious.

Neo-Aristotelians are also likely to object to programmes, on the grounds that they are offensive, which approvingly represent attitudes, values or ways of life held to be immoral or anti-social. This enables us to make sense of just why a neo-Aristotelian is likely to find certain kinds of programmes deeply offensive, even though there may be no explicit violence or sexual content at all. A neo-Aristotelian may object to the depiction of homosexuals in the soap opera *EastEnders*, the detailing of the sexual lives of *Hollywood Girls*, or even the depiction of Christ in Scorcese's *Last Temptation of Christ* precisely because they prescribe the viewer to approve of what are taken to be morally flawed relationships, attitudes and beliefs. The neo-Aristotelian then is likely to favour heavy content regulation and the possible censorship of programmes and films which are taken to appeal to the wrong kinds of interests in us or which approvingly represent those beliefs, attitudes and activities which should be disapproved of.

The fundamental dispute between liberals and neo-Aristotelians over broadcasting regulation concerns whether the State and society should, legitimately, seek to shape, guide and protect people's moral and social values. Such a conflict may even manifest itself in the ways these distinct conceptions presume regulatory decisions should be taken in the face of disagreement. The neo-Aristotelian model will naturally favour a regulatory board made up of acknowledged experts and authority figures from the relevant moral and social groups in society. For example, figureheads of the Christian, Muslim, liberal and ethnic communities. The hope will be that, although these traditions may have disagreements about particular cases, nonetheless, they will be able to establish enough common ground regarding the appropriate treatment of issues which concern our moral and social welfare. By contrast, liberals will naturally shy away from constituting a regulatory board with figures concerned for our moral and social well-being. Liberals are, strictly speaking, not concerned with matters of offence, or our moral and social welfare, but only with protecting everyone's freedom of choice regarding programming, serving the interests of all and, where relevant, protecting sections of society from significant harm.

A Regulatory *Via Media*

The essential thrust of our research, set out in the following chapters, has been to draw out what people's fundamental values are in relation to the vexed questions articulated above; to understand where, broadly, people fall in relation to a liberal or neo-Aristotelian model and to see where the resultant tensions in people's values lie. The most obvious area of agreement concerned the kind of graded privacy rights liberals would want to enshrine in regulation as articulated above. Furthermore, despite the apparent tensions in other areas, there is some indication that a liberal *via media* might be available. After all, political liberalism cannot, nor indeed should not, be so shy of encouraging and cultivating the appropriate public conventions, activities and practices required to sustain in civil life. For if certain traditions are required to make sense of the conventions, practices and critical reflection open to us in civil life then surely we require them as a backcloth against which we are free to pursue a good life. This is not to claim what liberals would rightly shy away from: that individuals are significant only in so far as they participate within an established tradition, or that the State should seek to impose upon all its subjects a very particular, substantive conception of the good life. But, it is to recognize that, in so far as certain traditions enable and are required to mediate, guide and promote our pursuit of the good life, the liberal State should sustain, protect and, in certain cases, promote them. What must do the crucial work for liberalism cannot be reducible to what traditions happen to be valued by its citizens nor those which are rationally justified. Rather it should conjoin a commitment to liberalism's fundamental tenets with the recognition that certain traditions, which are neither clearly rationally justified nor clearly false, are valuable and legitimately require and may demand protection.[27]

Far from representing some Archimedean standpoint from which one can neutrally adjudicate amongst claims made, liberalism is a political tradition worth defending. Typically liberals do fail to recognize that the imaginative understanding which underpins the social virtues of respect, tolerance and justice are themselves historical achievements which rely upon an established civil society. Moreover, a decent civil society is sustained by institutions, practices and values which are not themselves clearly rationally justified. Far from standing back as some neutral observer the liberal State must aim to cultivate the virtues of tolerance, respect and justice and thus defend the shared public practices, conventions and communities which enable the individual freedom the State is supposed to protect. Hence, liberalism need not stand in antithesis to religious and conservative traditions, for example, but rather provides the appropriate rationale for critically examining and standing up to unjust traditions and practices which rest upon irrationalist, incoherent or false philosophical, moral, religious and empirical beliefs.

Liberalism is not, nor should it pretend to be, sceptical about what is properly speaking humanly valuable. It stands for, and seeks to protect, the rights of the individual whose life is realized in and through their ability to participate within both private and public life. Without a proper public commitment to, and defence of, certain traditions and virtues, liberalism becomes motivationally inert and corrosive of human society. A truly just State is one which cultivates the participation in and expression through public practices, rituals and conventions the norms, values and imaginative understanding of the many human goods we may choose to pursue. Thus, the State is required to sustain, protect and promote the fabric of many valuable traditions, but only those which are not falsified, fundamentally irrationalist or shown to be incoherent by clear and evident reasons. Recognizing the significance of tradition may yet reinforce rather than undermine the claims of the liberal state.

It is important to distinguish here between a weaker and a stronger claim. We have suggested that liberalism is compatible with, and ought to recognize if it is to be self-sustaining, the protection and promotion of the multiplicity of different traditions constitutive of our society in a weak sense. That is, the State should maintain the viability of valuable traditions which give sense to civil society and which we are free to reflect critically upon and thus assent to, modify or reject. The idea that the State has a duty to protect the traditions that enable us to make sense of and pursue what we consider to be a good life should not be confused with the stronger claim that the state should promote a particular tradition.[28] Freedom as the variety of valuable choices takes precedence over freedom as unrestricted choice. Thus, on this reasoning, where the Welsh language threatens to die out, the liberal State should intervene to protect the teaching of Welsh in schools and promote Welsh-language television, as the State indeed does by subsidising S4C. For without such support a central part of Welsh culture might have died out and, thus, the significance and value of what it is to be Welsh, a very important matter for some, would have become deeply emaciated.

It is vital to recognize that the liberal State may be justified in enforcing typically 'illiberal' broadcasting regulation to protect and sustain activities which form part of a valuable tradition in order to maintain them as viable options where they are rationally valued as such by members of its civil society. Hence, for example, the protection by the French of their film industry is not fundamentally illiberal but can itself be justified on liberal grounds. The State is not threatening to ban American films or prescribe what the particular character of French films should be. Far from limiting people's possible choices, it is aimed at keeping alive the very possibility of choice that the ubiquity of American films threatens to swamp. But the liberal State should not tolerate traditions which require commitments to claims, and resultant practices, which are contrary to clear and evident reasons. In other words, the mere lack of reason is insufficient for the liberal State to refrain from protecting, and supporting where required, cultural practices and traditions. Rather, powerful reasons are needed against cultural practices and traditions, such as their fundamental irrationality, for the State to refrain from supporting them where they threaten to die out.

Far from expecting a rationalistic blueprint for all societies we should expect liberal states to come in all shapes, sizes and forms. For the traditions that are live options for those in different liberal States may vary radically. What is crucial, and what any liberal State should seek to sustain, are the existence of viable, shared and valuable traditions which underpin the social practices, activities and conventions of civil life. A traditionless society is not only futile, but also dangerous, and threatens to undermine the very conditions that sustain a liberal society. The impoverishment of traditions that make sense of our social norms, practices and ways of carrying on, ultimately threatens the very imaginative understanding which underlies the liberal State. Traditions are not static: they develop, change and are sometimes threatened with extinction. But this is, for the liberal, as tradition should be. We are free to reflect upon and attempt to modify received social practices precisely because they are important to allow for and respond to the conditions of meaningful choice. On this arguing, enlightened liberal broadcasting regulation should accordingly seek to ensure broadcasting provision for the multiplicity of traditions that make up our society. Only if such provision is made can the public space of civil society be protected to ensure meaningful choice in the sphere of people's private lives.

Notes

1. Waldron (1987: 127–150) gives a useful explication of the different forms the notion of liberal legitimacy has taken.
2. Although generally liberalism is characterized in terms of the primary value it places upon freedom, in recognition of our autonomy, there are notable liberals who, as an exception, place primary emphasis upon the notion of equality. See Dworkin (1977 & 1978).
3. See also Waldron (1993: 63–87).
4. See Rawls' Dewey Lectures (1980: 515–572).
5. See Gaut (1995: 1–22) for a clear critique of Rawls' political liberalism on just this basis.
6. It should be noted here that, throughout this book, the word 'film' is used generically to describe filmic material. This includes films shown on DVD, VCR, TV and music video.
7. John Rawls offers a neo-Kantian universal justification for liberalism in *A Theory of Justice* (1972) and more recently has defended the much more qualified claim that liberalism is what we can expect people would reasonably assent to in conditions of pluralism in *Political Liberalism* (1993).
8. 'A living tradition then is an historically extended, socially embodied argument, and an argument in part about the goods which constitute that tradition...the history of a practice in our time is generally and characteristically embedded in and made intelligible in terms of the larger and longer history of the tradition through which the practice in its present form was conveyed to us.' (MacIntyre 1985: 222)

9. Hence, the need to investigate general questions of political psychology and particular self-conceptions which motivate attempts to reform or modify society in certain ways. See, for example, Elster 1993.

10. We take it that this is something like Wittgenstein's point when he talks about a society's 'form of life'. See Wittgenstein 1969, paragraph 234.

11. Note that one doesn't have to take part in or confront a practice to consider it important. We may watch others take part in fox-hunting or religious worship and value aspects of these practices, though their significance in such cases is obviously more attenuated and complex.

12. Perhaps this lack of understanding is what leads Hume to condemn the monkish virtues of celibacy, self-denial and humility. See Hume 1975: 270.

13. Alasdair MacIntyre's highly influential *After Virtue* (1981) and *Whose Justice? Which Rationality?* (1988) explicitly develop a neo-Aristotelian communitarian critique of liberalism.

14. See Walton (1990) where it is argued that games of make-believe are central to our engagement with representations of any kind. Psychological research which supports such a conception in relation to broadcasting includes Singer, J. L. and D. G. (1981).

15. See, for example, Gauntlett (1995) and Newsome (1994) for conflicting speculations based upon empirical research. See also Cumberbatch and Howitt (1989) and Freedman (1984: 227–246).

16. Even if the state imposed the appropriate conception of the good life we should be free to assent to or reject it because only then will we come to see for ourselves why our good really does lie in the activities and practices suggested.

17. Thus, Rawls at the very outset of *A Theory of Justice* (1971: 3–4) states that 'each person possesses an inviolability founded on justice that even the welfare of society as a whole cannot override... Therefore in a just society the liberties of equal citizenship are taken as settled; the rights secured by justice are not subject to political bargaining or to the calculus of social interests.'

18. See Rawls (1972: 18–19) where he states that the original position entails that 'persons' conceptions of their good do not affect the principles adopted.'

19. A paradigmatic liberal for whom this was true is obviously David Hume, *A Treatise of Human Nature* (1978: 477–501, 534–567), but contemporary liberals from Isaiah Berlin, 'Two Concepts of Liberty' in Anthony Quinton (ed.), *Political Philosophy* (1967: 150–151) and Robert Nozick, *Anarchy, State and Utopia* (1974: 26–33) to Robert Audi, "The Separation of Church and State and the Obligations of Citizenship", *Philosophy and Public Affairs* (1989: 278–279), obviously hold that religious traditions as such are not worthy, legitimately, of the liberal State's consideration or support.

20. Note this is not claiming that Christianity or conservatism are required to underwrite the value of altruism or the prohibitions of conventional morality. Rather, they underwrite these values, as other traditions might, in a valuable way which, for some at least, gives point and purpose both to the values themselves and their own lives.

21. The French revolution was perhaps one of the most extreme results of such political rationalism. See Edmund Burke, *Reflections on the Revolution in France* (1960).

22. This refers to the case where some British Muslims unsuccessfully called for author Salman Rushdie to be tried under the law of blasphemy after the publication of his controversial novel, *The Satanic Verses*. However, the law only recognizes blasphemy against the Church of England.

23. See Rawls, *Political Liberalism* (1993), pp. xlv-l, 29–35, 77–81, 140–144 and 213–254.

24. Gaut (1995: 13–14) makes this point.

25. For a similar line of thought see also Feinberg (1973: 36–54).
26. See Aristotle (1976: 1. 1097b22–1098a2, pp75–75) for the distinction relied on here between the mere satisfaction of desires and desires which satisfy our well-being.
27. Hence, the strategy pursued by Bruce Ackerman (1980) is deeply flawed. The liberal cannot remain neutral about the justification of liberal impartiality over what the good life consists in.
28. Though which tradition the claim is made on behalf of predictably varies from the extremes of progressive feminism to ethnic nationalism or Moslem theocratic states.

PART ONE

The Historical Context: The Moral Void

2 The Question of Regulation: The Absence of a Moral Language

This chapter traces the secularization of society in both a religious and value sense. It looks at how the social construction of the world in religious terms gives way to a secular construction. The exercise here is to show the development of a moral void and examines such institutions as marriage as a contractual rather than religious state, but in particular shows how the dismantlement of religious authority is mirrored in the dismantlement of moral authority within broadcasting. The chapter also looks at social fragmentation, which undermined a consensus over values and shows how the lack of any overarching appeal to an agreed set of norms has led to the absence of a moral language by which to discuss moral issues as they relate to cultural performance.

Introduction

The mechanization of production that began in the eighteenth century, and that accelerated in the nineteenth century, captured by the term 'the Industrial Revolution', ushered in not simply changes in economic organization, but changes in human relationships to the means of production, and, hence, political change. In the western world at least, then, standing at the vantage point of the early twenty-first century, the dominant political system of organization to have emerged is that of liberal democracy, and with it sets of values, beliefs and ideals that denote the acceptance of the liberal democratic model of political economy.

There is nothing 'given' about this acceptance of the liberal democratic model. The contest about how social, economic and political life shall be organized, if bitter in the nineteenth century, was brutal in the twentieth century. The emergence of Communism, Fascism and National Socialism all represented extremes of human effort to determine how man shall live and what his or her relationship to the social world should be; indeed, what the social world was to be. These were 'export struggles', carried to countries removed from the original site of battle. Although Britain was no idle onlooker to the clash of forces of continental Europe, the wash of change cut a different, and less dramatic, political path than in countries beyond, but close to, its shores. Nevertheless, the economic changes of the nineteenth and early to middle twentieth centuries produced reflection and action on the structure of social, political and economic organization.

C. Wright Mills (1959), reflecting on his discipline, commented that it was all about understanding how biography cuts history. Focus groups are not historical method, but what is most apparent, particularly in this study, is that culture as the sediments of experiences of generations of people are given living expression in the present by the manner in which respondents address the contemporary world and contemporary problems. Wright Mills also made the methodological, or rather epistemological, point that the purpose of facts was to act as a discipline on the imagination. Survey research is even less of an historical method than focus group research; that is, the structured nature of the conversation between researcher and respondent allows little possibility for the introduction by the respondent of generational experiences: the methodology, or the language of research, does not represent naturally occurring conversation in the manner of focus group research. Where survey research comes into its own is in the collection of facts and, as an instrument of conversation, allowing, through sampling and the computerization of data, the possibility of talking with large numbers of people. Whereas focus groups, as stated, are good for establishing the *range* of opinions likely to be found in the population as a whole, they cannot establish the *distribution* of those opinions among the population as a whole. For that, one requires survey research.

Survey research has often been attacked as 'abstracted empiricism' or 'mindless' fact-gathering, and, indeed, Wright Mills, as already noted, was a foremost critic of an overdependence of social research on such a method. However, what we see in our surveys, particularly the second survey, is the operation in practice of the working through, by the respondent, of moral dilemmas. The treatment of opinion on issues as one that involves the provision of answers through moral reasoning gives pointers to the historical stock of thought that the respondent is drawing upon in their effort to answer the questions posed. The research draws upon the contours of beliefs that form the currency for moral reasoning in Britain, or at least, since they have empirical existence, form the basic set of orientation to moral questions in terms of social responsibility construed in terms of the control or management of culture. These two basic moral positions, described in detail in Chapter 1, have been categorized as neo-Aristotelian and liberal.

Although the survey results show that the dominant philosophical precepts which underpin moral thinking in relation to cultural control are those of the neo-Aristotelian, it is also clear from the survey, and from the findings of the focus groups, that the placement of people into the neo-Aristotelian or liberal frames of thinking is empirically possible. However, it is also the case that considerable movement takes place within the same individual between these two categories of thought.

No individual ever, or very rarely, steadfastly occupies a consistent philosophical position in relationship to cultural control. In some ways this can be accounted for by the lack of intellectual training. After all, unlike some European educational systems, English education has not favoured the addressing of abstract thought, instead preferring concrete problem solving as an approach to learning and definition of knowledge. Having said that, hardly anyone, and probably not even the professional philosopher, conducts their daily life by reference to philosophical position. To do so would lead to inaction at best, and mental breakdown at worst. The squeeze of space and time, especially in contemporary life, requires decisions unencumbered by lengthy reflection on the moral consistency of action taken through reference to some struggled-for philosophical consistency. In acting morally in everyday life the individual has no need to examine the basic structure of their ethics. Actions are taken which simply appear right. And they appear right because they have the force of the time-honoured practice of cultural performance, set within demarcated moral communities. Not to behave in a certain way feels wrong, because that is how people in a particular moral community behave, and to do otherwise is to risk social sanction, and even legal sanction. In other words, our moral performances are values cemented over time in social practice, but both are informed by the other. Whether some act makes social sense depends on whether it is seen as appropriate to the situation the individual inhabits as a recurring experience, but nevertheless it will at some point require collective legitimation by a body of theory of how to behave; in short, be given the force of moral principle.

Moral communities are empirical entities, but appeal to what people do in certain communities cannot provide an absolute basis for moral position. One of the dangers of using empirical research for policy-making – the application of values to practice – is that no matter how many people believe something to be right, or behave in a certain way, does not make what they believe, or how they act, right. Good and evil are not enshrined as foundational truths in the statistics of practices. Yet, most people, and it is fortunate that this is the case since for it to be otherwise would leave the individual in a state of permanent psychological tension and crisis, do not have to confront fundamental moral questions.

For the most part we operate with a digested moral code that barely requires examination in dealing with the mundanities of the world around us, and, hence, we are not used, in any strong intellectual sense, to having to justify our actions by appeal to formal workings of how to behave. Thus, when we subject acts to moral scrutiny, unpack our taken-for-granted thinking on a particular issue, it is often difficult to give expression to the moral base of our reasoning. Unless asked to do so, it is usually not called for. The difficulty faced by our research, therefore, was that we were asking people to search for explanations, or apply moral reason, as to why they thought as they did about moral issues raised by broadcasting practice.

Broadcasting is part of the mundane world of everyday life, although the issues that are broadcast are not. Thus, while people may have an opinion that a particular programme was wrong because it invaded someone's privacy, to ask them why such an invasion was wrong involved the much more fundamental philosophical question of rights, and hence demanded of the respondent a considerable amount of intellectual effort. Not used to working with abstract concepts, or at least not used to having to interrogate their thoughts for consistencies that might then provide a coherent set of principles by which to address moral dilemmas, it was decided that the survey instrument should allow the respondent to work through sets of possible responses to moral questions, but to do so from a personal position that would allow the respondent to identify with the dilemmas. In other words, given that many of the areas we wished to address involved abstract notions, such as rights, justice, and public and private interests, it was considered that what was required was the transferring of abstract ideas to the realm of individual relevance. Respondents were on the solid terrain of the familiar and, not surprisingly, could reason with confidence through the grounded nature of the questioning about the moral dilemmas which the research set. So, although the concepts that required address were abstract, as indeed all concepts are, the language of the research itself, the methodological procedure, was not.

In reference to Wright Mills, whilst it is true that survey research forms no part of the historical method, and that to varying degrees, even with latent structure analysis, responses do remain somewhat abstracted from the situated experience of the respondent, nevertheless, the answers that respondents give do not come *ex nihilo*. In asking about matters such as the management or control of culture, the responses given are the worked-through experiences of a lived culture, both present and past. Although the survey responses do not give direct access to history (that collection of experiences that are reworked over time to provide thought in and about the present), they nevertheless allow historical consideration of how the responses are as they are. What we see, in fact, from both the survey and the focus groups, is a lack of any single moral community. This finding alone must give trouble to any broadcasting system that wishes to speak to the nation, or if it wishes to explore human experience in any creative or imaginative manner. This lack of a single moral community is the source of many of the problems that current broadcasting faces at the level of practice. However, even with the fragmentation of the audience (moral commonalties or taste communities) to be catered for by having an increased variety of broadcasting outlets, this does not obviate basic moral problems concerning the regulation of culture.

It would certainly be wrong to view the past in Britain as having held some point where a moral community could be identified, that there was some Elysian field of national moral agreement. But it is not wrong to consider that a moral/social fracturing has taken place wherein it is increasingly difficult to identify distinct moral communities that have a clearly bounded geographic or social cohesion, or at least one of any scale.

The idea of moral community, perhaps most popularly or commonly associated with Richard Rorty (1989 & 1999) (see also MacIntyre 1981), may have leverage in philosophy, and is no doubt useful analytically for the problems philosophy sets itself, but the idea of a moral community – that in judging something to be right or wrong ought to include reference to community standards – must in practice mean that such communities exist empirically. There is little point, for example, in discussing the right to hunt foxes by horse and hound by appeal to the values of the moral community of rural England if no such community exists. However, even if such a community did exist, it would still not be right, necessarily, to hunt the fox, simply that certain conditions existed for a particular defence of a moral reason. The conditions for such a defence certainly falls away if rural England is found to be heavily populated by escapees from the cities who through economic prosperity and availability of transport can commute between work and cottage. If this is the case then new meaning and existence is given to bucolic life that might preclude the empirical realities of the assumed moral community that gives support to fox-hunting. Or it may be that the 'escapees from the city' actually did ride to hound, but did so only because of some idea of the idyll of rural life that they wished to belong, but nevertheless considered fox-hunting to be morally wrong. Where, in other words, is the moral community of rural life that someone such as Roger Scruton would invoke by which to appeal for a moral defence of fox-hunting? In short, some defence other than appeal to moral community must be mounted to defend fox-hunting – as indeed, in fairness to Scruton he does invoke by drawing basic distinctions between the rights of humans and those of animals (Scruton 1996 & 1998).

Whatever the value in utilizing the idea of moral community for problems in moral philosophy, it has a certain purchase for a sociological discussion of social change and moral agreement. It matters nothing, for our purpose, whether the notion of moral community is useful for deciding how one determines moral value, but it is useful for deciding the existence of moral agreement and the problems that broadcasting might face in the absence of moral communities.

A mediaevalist might well point to moral communities as empirical fact. The relatively unchanging nature of mediaeval society certainly allows the identification of geographic areas and social strata locked into time-honoured ways of behaving and thought. Although a whole history of social change could be written here, the social transformations witnessed in the late eighteenth and nineteenth centuries, particularly advanced in Britain as a consequence of the early transformation of the production base of economic life, gave rise to new problems of social solidarity; indeed, social solidarity is seen to become a problem. Whole new classes and groups came into being and with them new expressions of political claims. The transformation of a pastoral agricultural life to an urban industrial life, in terms of common conditions and life experiences, drew lines of conflict over the distribution of resources to produce, at one and the same time, a sense of solidarity within groups and a sense of difference to other groups.

However, it is not necessary to document the historical detail of social change to make the point that political communities tend also to be moral communities: that similarities of life experiences tend to give rise to common interpretations of the world and what is, or is not, correct behaviour. It is in the establishment of what is correct in a moral sense that cultural production almost invariably involves political struggle.

Moral judgements need to be applied to the world in a way that makes sense, at an effective level, to the material world that they are to be applied to. It makes little sense, for example, at the level of the collective, to hold to a morality about the non-exploitation of nature – a green ideology – when the collective itself is faced by wretched material deprivation that might be overcome by the exploitation of nature. The enjoyment of clean air that might come from silent factories is nothing like the pleasure to be gained from the material comforts to be had from being in employment. In other words, to hold to a certain view of the world is to exist in a world where the plausibility structures supporting that view make sense.

This making sense of the world, and part of making sense of the world is to make moral sense of it, is not an individual act. It is done in association with others. Nor is this making sense of the world, or reality building, begun afresh by each generation, although it is a never-ending project of renewal and change. Entry to the world, on birth, is entry to an existing world. In short, it is entry to a particular cultural world that the individual must make his or her own; the subjective internalizing of the objective world, the basic tool for which is language, and language itself, the actual lexicon, is the product of a social activity.

It is the accomplishment of this reality construction that then allows the individual to participate in the surrounding world through the inhabitation of shared meaning, and that includes moral meaning. But, as stated, this exercise of construction is a never-ending project and in a dynamically changing world the structure is likely to be fragile as new information and change has to be made sense of.

If we now return to the observations concerning solidarity and the transformation brought about through rapid urbanization and industrialization, we are faced with the position of a separation of experiences from what has gone before, a distinct break, and separation of experiences between groups that are proximate to each other in socio-economic status. Clearly, the congregation of the labouring classes in the towns during the nineteenth century provided sufficient communality of experience to allow these experiences to be given resonance, and collective voice, in new political parties. Even so, the conditions are set, with the failure of revolutionary European labour movements to seize power and transform capital along collective lines to create a common enterprise, for a collective language of morality to become increasingly problematic and unlikely.

We are not arguing here that there ever was a universal language of morality, but rather that what might once have appeared a possibility has historically been dashed against the rocks of fragmented experience. The early labour movement spoke not simply against iniquities in the distribution of wealth, but with the voice of values and ideals beyond economic management. It was not technocratic rationality that drove the movement, but moral vision. What we see in effect is that the burgeoning conditions of the nineteenth century, which made for collective experience of large sections of the population, and, hence, the possibility of an all-encompassing moral appeal, do not last out the twentieth century. In the organizing of experience the appeal is no longer to grand schemes of moral certitude, nor is it possible anymore, post-industrialization, to have the world made sense of by the sheer act of existence through cementation in time-honoured and time-set patterns of relationships. In the long history of social change the rhythm of existence of pastoral society that gave it the appearance of a natural order, indeed an ordained order, was ruptured by industrialization and urbanization, not to be replaced, although great efforts were made, by a politically engineered universal moral order.

The dismantlement of grand moral systems and the erosion of community-set patterns of moral performance, present themselves in our work as a confusion on the respondents' part to know where to turn for authoritative appeal to support the values that they hold. There is no collective that they can reach out to, either in social, or ideational, association, in which to anchor their moral judgement about acts.

The very social forces which are to be found in the unfolding changes of the nineteenth century that gave rise to mass political movements were responsible at the same time for undermining religious views of the world. It was not that religion as an organizing point of reality was defeated by intellectual argument, but that it suffered erosion in the face of technocratic and scientific rationality released by the industrializing process. It was not, as Alasdair MacIntyre states: 'that men first stopped believing in God and in the authority of the Church, and then subsequently started behaving differently. It seems clear that men first of all lost any overall social agreement on the right ways to live together, and so ceased to be able to make sense of any claims to moral authority' (MacIntyre 1967: 54). This lack of moral authority, of an overarching court of common moral appeal, rests at the heart of much of the confusion exhibited by people in our study in deciding what is or is not moral: the decline of religious belief has meant that people have been left on their own in the world to make sense of it as they will. Consequently, people have difficulty in supporting their moral judgements by institutionally shored sets of beliefs, or, in the absence of formally organized moral knowledge – politics – by reason. This requires exploration in order to ground the difficulties respondents faced in deciding moral issues we put to them and, also, in accounting for the lack of uniformity of judgement among respondents.

It was mentioned earlier, and by no means intended pejoratively, that people in our study had difficulty in handling abstract concepts. One of the advantages of a 'given' belief system is that its acceptance armours the individual against uncertainty and that they can then apply moral principles safe in the understanding that a wider authority than themselves would agree with their decisions. To know which principle to apply might be difficult, but at least the individual has a body of theory by which to guide him or her, and the satisfaction of knowing that they have not simply acted empirically: that their acts make sense other than by reference to themselves. In other words, the individual is imposing a structure of meaning on the world, rather than merely responding to it as benefits the individual at the moment, or in some manner which, if repeated and built upon, will benefit him or her in accord with some long-term plan of operations where the self is the central logic of action. The imposed meaning, however, to make sense, must also be imposed by others, otherwise it becomes impossible, and maybe even dangerous, to conduct life on lines of a personalized view.

What we witnessed at times in our research was reference by participants to the focus groups to having their moral beliefs drawn from Christian teaching, indeed, as a moral system, it was the only one referred to. But to have some idea of what it was to act as a Christian appeared to afford poor protection in the modern world in making moral judgements when confronted by secular institutions and practices that denied religious meaning. Christian litany, for example, may surround church weddings, but the legal scaffolding of marriage is decidedly secular. And, indeed, as we shall see later from the findings of the focus groups relating to the role of State authority in regulating the dissolution of marriage, consciousness was secular, not religious. Marriage was seen as a private contract between two individuals sanctioned by the State. People regretted the impermanence of many marriages and, as we shall see, some people considered that the State had a right of interference in personal arrangements, but what requires consideration at the moment is the role that law plays in the arrangement of social attitudes. Undoubtedly the law can effect changes in consciousness, and at other times changes in the law simply enshrine the empirical realities of states of existence. This is something that requires consideration in terms of regulating changes in broadcasting when set against social attitudes towards broadcasting and patterns of existing behaviour. In short, can regulation oversee that which is actually happening – can a moral position be held to in light of actual practice? The moral framework surrounding the dissolution of marriage is worth examining as a good working example of both the law interfering in moral life and attempting relevance to actual practice.

By mediaeval times, marriage as a holy bond that could not be broken whilst the partners to it were alive was firmly established in most of Western Europe. In England, the exclusive jurisdiction of the Church over marriage was cemented by the twelfth century, and remained pretty much in place until the close of the seventeenth century when marriage could be dissolved by private parliamentary act. Before that marriages could be declared invalid where rules governing who could marry were broken, but still under the jurisdiction of the Church. The introduction of annulment by Parliament in the seventeenth century, although only open to the rich and influential, nevertheless sees the encroachment of the secular on the spiritual. It was not until the passing of the Matrimonial Causes Act of 1857 that valid marriages could be dissolved other than by Private Act of Parliament. The significance of this is 'that it transferred jurisdiction over marriage to the civil courts and allowed judicial divorce' (Elliot 1986: 136). However, as Elliot continues: '...it did not go very far towards making marriage a voluntary terminable contract'. Such divorces were expensive, and thus remained the preserve of the aristocracy and upper middle class. More importantly, 'the 1857 Act retained the notion that church and/or state have an interest in the continuation of marriage which takes priority over the wishes of the parties involved' (Elliot 1986: 136). Central to divorce under this legislation was the doctrine of 'matrimonial offence'. 'Divorce was thus defined as arising out of the contravention of basic moral principles' and even though the Church may have been replaced by secular authority, the principles of the 1857 Act 'was structured by religious ideals ... and contained no trace of the individualistic, privatised, person-focused ideals which were to lead to pressures for divorce by consent in the 1960s.' Indeed, the law 'which sought to maintain the overall stability of marriage by making access to divorce difficult was out of step with the increasingly individualistic, person-focused and privatised ideals of the mid-twentieth century.' (Elliot 1986: 137).

The Established Church, in recognition of the public pressure for reform and private practice of separation, withdrew, quite suddenly, its opposition to the 1969 Divorce Reform Act which became operative from 1971. For the first time the irretrievable breakdown of marriage became the sole basis for divorce in England and Wales, with Scotland following seven years later. What the 1971 act did was to 'formally redefine marriage as a secular and terminable arrangement between a man and a woman' (Elliot 1986: 138). The idea that divorce should be available on proof that marriage had broken down irretrievably, and that a matrimonial offence or a period of separation should be treated as evidence of that breakdown, shows a vital shift in the fading of theology as a relevant framework for judgement; the transgression of a moral code having been reduced to the level of evidence. As Davies noted, 'the issue of innocence or guilt is no longer the crucial one and the law, instead of asking the question who is to blame asks rather what is the best course of action to take in this situation' (Davies 1975: 18).

The precise interplay of ideas, beliefs and values on social practices need not detain us, sufficient to say, however, that alteration in divorce laws is not just a matter of religious retreat, but changes in the nature of the family itself over time. As Elliot notes:

...the ideology of the conjugal family is said to entail the legitimation of divorce: it is argued that a family ideology which emphasises individual rights and achievement of personal happiness through sexual and emotional fulfilment presumes that marriages which do not provide these satisfactions are without a *raison d'être* and should be dissolved. (Elliot 1986: 135)

Such views of the family have their tracks in wide-reaching changes in social and economic organization, and not simply a loosening grip of the sacred over the profane, although such a loosening itself has at base, as hinted at earlier by MacIntyre, social factors and not simply ideational struggle. This requires examination in some detail since, as hinted, moral reformation is not just ideational, but material, and has significant bearing on the question of the moral authority underpinning the regulation of culture.

An interesting fact about modern western societies is that they no longer produce anti-Christian zealots bent on attacking and undermining religion. The Bertrand Russells of the world are now an anachronism, read only for their historical interest or for their other intellectual contributions. This fact alone points to the present everyday status of religion. It is innocuous. It is not that some great anti-theological work has collapsed the relevance of religion, or shown it to be false, or that it has even fallen victim and been replaced by some other similar total conception of reality. No battle has been fought; the simple fact of the matter is that in the process of secularization the plausibility structures upon which religion stood have been dismantled. Indeed, the loss of belief, the declining importance of religion as a meaningful way of organizing reality, was contingent, upon alterations in the structures which gave religion meaning and content. (See Berger 1973.)

The key explanatory factor in accounting for secularization is that of industrialization, although one ought to accept that Christianity is a particular secular religion, especially its Calvinist branch, and had within it the seeds of its own destruction. That is, that Christianity is a peculiarly secular religion,[1] which allowed man to stand in a non-mystical relationship with 'nature', and thereby fostered the development of science.[2]

Secularization is the 'defatalisation' of history; the 'discovery by man that he has been left with the world on his hands, that he can no longer blame fortune or the furies for what he does with it' (Cox 1965: 2). Or, to use a phrase from the theologian Dietrich Bonhoeffer, it is 'Man's coming of age' in which man is alone within his own man-made world. But, as we shall shortly see, and of importance in understanding the absence of a moral authority in contemporary Britain, be it religious or secular, it is not man in a man-made world that is so troublesome, but many men standing in different relationships to each other that forbids common appeal to a central moral authority by which to give coherence to views about issues that broadcasting raise, either in approach or topics covered.

The forces making for secularization, whilst agreeing with David Martin (1969: 16,17), that they are not unitary, are nevertheless not mysterious. Traditional religion, its symbolism, its ritual, its institutions and its social importance have been eroded under the twin process of industrialization and urbanization. As Berger notes, 'for the individual, existing in a particular religious world implies existing in the particular social context within which that world can retain its plausibility' (Berger 1973: 58). The plausibility structures supporting religion were dismantled at an unprecedented rate in the course of industrialization and the consequent urbanization. Indeed, as Berger further notes, the original 'locale' of secularization 'was in the economic area, specifically, in those sectors of the economy being formed by the capitalistic and industrial processes.' The erosion of belief was, therefore, differential. Industrial society produced 'a centrally "located" sector that is something like a "liberated territory" with respect to religion. Secularisation has moved "outwards" from this sector into other areas of society' (Berger 1973: 133).

Secularization has a subjective as well as an objective side. It is more than social-structural process in that it involves culture and symbols, to be observed in the 'decline of religious contents in the arts, in philosophy, in literature and, most important of all, in the rise of science as an autonomous, thoroughly secular perspective on the world' (Berger 1973: 113). Secularization involves not just the removal of the sacred from society and culture, but the secularization of consciousness. The process by which this secularity has been carried is, then, the spread of industrialization, but, at the same time, the change in man's consciousness is due in part to the rationality demanded by industrialization. Industry has to be organized along rationally functional lines; it has its own logic. Thus, modern industrial production has demanded and created a whole battery of scientific and technological personnel whose 'training and ongoing social organisation presupposes a high degree of rationalisation, not only on the level of infrastructure but also on that of consciousness' (Berger 1973: 136).

The functioning of the industrial world, the structural cementing of it, depends upon rationalization and not tradition. Indeed, the modern industrial complex had its own relentless logic, which broke and shattered not only traditional ways of acting, but traditional ways of viewing the world. Authority itself was seen to shift from the traditional to the rational-legal. The conclusion, in so far as Berger is concerned, is that the configuration of meanings which constitute the symbolic realities of traditional church religion appears to be unrelated to the culture of modern industrial society, and that the internalization of the symbolic reality is neither enforced nor, in the typical case, favoured by the social structure of contemporary society (Berger 1973).

Although we are talking about 'long history', and not moments of history, it was the urbanization consequent upon the industrial revolution that finally destroyed the features of the old social structure to which religion gave symbolic expression. The repetitive cycle and stability of 'community' associated with pre-industrial rural life informed social order and gave it, despite differences in social rank, an apparancy of harmony with 'nature'. It was this harmony which according to MacIntyre (1967) found universal expression in religious symbolism and which was broken down with the development of industrial society.

In considering changes in literature, MacIntyre notes that the key difference between the seventeenth and the eighteenth centuries is the 'consciousness of the emerging autonomy of secular life'. If this split or separation was there in literature, new social divisions were seen to emerge as a consequence of social change that not only robbed the Church of its authority by being able to appeal *en masse* to people, but thrust apace secular thought. In discussing the new kinds of class divisions that emerged in the course of industrialization, MacIntyre reflects on the consequences for this of any recourse to common moral appeal. Throughout the class conflicts there were attempts by the Church 'to continue the appeal to common norms and to revive the older social and moral values, but the changing structure of society make it only too obvious to all parties that the alleged authoritative norms to which the appeal is made are, in fact, man-made, and that they are not the norms of the whole community to which in their own way men of every rank are equally subject'. Indeed, this fragmentation meant that the norms which did govern the new 'economic, political and social relations between classes' when given religious significance meant that religion was 'invoked to justify the norms which one class wishes and is able to use against the other' (MacIntyre 1967: 13, 14). This was not a matter of the Established Church invoking religion in defence of the landed or middle classes, but dissenting religious groups invoking religion for the political defence and support of the aspirations of lower classes.

What MacIntyre captures is the increasing fragmentation of the social world into classes and groups which came to stand in recognized opposition to each other. Furthermore, not only did 'community' fracture and split, but individuals' lives became compartmentalized so that interaction with others was not seen as a totality, but increasingly in terms of a specialization of roles. In this context any appeal to a common universe of meanings became difficult to support. As the process of secularization continued, traditional religious forms and practices were driven out of more and more areas of life. As Berger has suggested, the locus of this process was in those areas closest to the new modes of industrial production. The tensions of social relationships, the autonomy of production from the rest of experience, and its own needs meant that as industrial production developed it created classes, cultures and groups which could no longer be bridged by symbols drawn and developed from previous historical forms.

This is not to argue that all mystical symbols or elements of religiosity were removed from consciousness, or that individuals do not hold views that could be considered magical. Clearly, ritual is also still a feature of the English social scene, however, as a means of totally organizing experience, traditional Christianity has lost its power of persuasion and, in doing so, can no longer offer moral guidance in anything like a general manner. The implications here for regulating culture are obvious.

The decline of religion in the western industrial world as an organizing point of reality does not mean that the erosion has been equally smooth; ground away by the cadence of waves on Matthew Arnold's 'Dover Beach'. It was not some general doubt, a humanist intellectual attack that left the waves that washed Dover Beach incompatible with the waves that lapped the shores of Galilee, but social condition that robbed the narrative of its meaning for those existing in an all too obviously man-made world.

Farming communities and even communities based on extraction, either on land or sea, were less affected by the secularizing process than those employed in production. Pockets of religiosity remained in Britain throughout the period under description, and the general movement away from the Church, although an historical occurrence through the nineteenth and twentieth centuries, should not be overplayed in terms of the working class, since with geographical exceptions, as David Martin (1969) wishes to stress in countering the secularization thesis, the working class were never especially churched. The Irish labourer in England was a different matter. As émigrés, then to be Catholic was a source of identity with the 'old country'.

The cultural function of religion, as opposed to its inner universe of meaning, is important in determining its impact on the structuring of moral universes. The Pole, the Lithuanian, the Italian, who formed the 'huddled masses' of nineteenth- and early-twentieth-century American society, and made up the ghetto populations of the great

American cities, in bringing their religion with them brought more than a faith, they brought the world they had left behind: the constructed meanings of a past life and past situation. Religious belief thus acted as a bridge between worlds and often at more than a symbolic level with the Church forming a haven, often linguistically, in an alien world – the priest negotiating between cultures.

In England, the establishing by Catholics of 'fortresses' of religion – Catholic schools, Catholic social clubs and so on – helped hold at bay, through self-enclosure, contamination of secular thinking. Through deliberate social arrangement this meant the establishment of sub-cultures that have managed to be, in relative terms, resistant to external factors. Even so, Catholicism could not resist the forces ranged against a religious definition of reality, and although of a slower rate of decline than Anglicanism, the general curve of decline is similar to the Established Church.

Each culture must be examined separately for the meaning that religion holds and for the meanings of institutional attachment, a point Bryan Wilson (1966: 114,115) makes in discussing the marked differences in church affiliation between the United States of America and England. His argument is that levels of American religious affiliation ought not to be taken as autonomous since they are derived from the wider values of American life. To be 'American', for a majority, is to have an affiliation to a church, as any US president is aware: indeed, America can be considered to have a 'civic religion'. Furthermore, church attendance cannot necessarily be equated with religiosity, especially where religious emphasis may be on attitudes of faith and trust rather than outward moral observance, and many of the current evangelical movements would be difficult to plot in terms of observance rates.

'Invisible Religion', to use Thomas Luckmann's term (Luckmann 1967), although an undoubted presence, can be shunted to the sidings in terms of impact at a national level on culture and moral thought. What we are interested in is not sects, or small groupings of religious thought, but the general process by which a religious definition of the world is no longer to be found in popular consciousness, and the vacating from the national scene of any all-encompassing moral framework by which people can, in common with each other, address moral issues. There is an absence of a moral language, and those who wish to use a moral language have difficulty in making themselves understood to broad audiences – this is the consequence of social fragmentation, and a problem that broadcasting, as opposed to narrowcasting, faces, or, the regulation of narrowcasting faces if the general governance of broadcasting, with its assumed communality of audience, is applied. However, we can return to this question later and do so through the voices of those in our focus groups.

The removal of ecclesiastical authority from the area of marriage was used as an illustration of the evacuation by the Church of an area previously under its control and was seen as a part of the general secularization of civic life. Nevertheless marriages are still sanctified by the Church for the very reason that secular society has not been good at producing solemn rituals with which to signify key moments in human affairs, such as birth, marriage and death. However, although the Church may well be called upon when needed, the secularizing process has nevertheless altered the meaning of its liturgy for most people. Indeed, the Church itself, its internal universe of meaning, has not escaped the erosive and corrosive force of secularization. As an administration, it must address its congregation and in doing so has exposed itself to forces that have threatened it as a medium for expressing foundational truths of ageless applicability.

This is not to suggest that the necessity of keeping falling congregations has, in the way of a television company faced by falling ratings, engaged in audience-building devices, although there is an element of that, but rather that it has faced a genuine difficulty, theologically, of not being able to successfully segment its market. If the churches, as Luckmann points out, wish to 'maintain their institutional claims to represent and mediate the traditional religious universe of meaning, they survive primarily by association with social groups and social strata which continue to be orientated towards values of a past social order'. To accommodate, however, to the 'dominant culture of modern industrial society they necessarily take on the function of legitimating' it. To engage in this latter exercise has meant that 'the universe of meaning traditionally represented by the Church becomes increasingly irrelevant'. In summing up the snare within which the Church has been caught, Luckmann comments, 'the so-called process of secularisation has decisively altered either the social location of church religion or its inner universe of meaning' (Luckmann 1967: 37).

In agreement with David Martin (1969: 16) that because there has been 'no unitary process of secularisation one cannot talk in a unitary way about the causes of secularisation', and that the process may not be irreversible. Yet it is quite clear from where the engine of change was driven, and in the foreseeable future it is hard to envisage how the forces released that were responsible for secularization could shift to have the body placed back in the cave of the Garden in Gethsemane. This is not to say that the mystical has been removed from modern life, or that vigorous efforts will not be made to restore religious meaning to the world, but it is to say that religion as a central organizing point of reality, sufficient once more to infuse art, philosophy, music, drama, literature, the legal system and master institutions of society, or to be taken as knowledge about the world, has been banished from public performance.

An interpretation of the world that has a totalizing meaning structure, such as a religious view of reality, faces a difficulty of performance, over time, if located at the margins of society. It is constantly in threat of being overwhelmed by the infidel. Retreatism is one response to ensure the intactness of the social context within which a religious view of the world can retain its plausibility, or some conquistador revivalism to reclaim the world in the face of oppositional definitions of reality might be mounted by which to 'force' a favourable climate for the continuation of beliefs. The former is a possible option, but the interlocked nature of modern society makes escape difficult from those realities that stand in opposition to religious truths, the latter, not possible as anymore than a skirmish with the enemy.

The above discussion of the fate of religion has been engaged to help lay out – but only in one direction, many other roads could have been laid and followed – transformations in culture brought about by transformations in economic and social organization. What we have attempted to do is to take a body of ideas, Christianity in this case, and show that alterations in the way man began to live altered man's beliefs about the world. Christianity appeared to be a particularly good cultural case to focus upon in light of the research task at hand in that not only does Christianity, like most religions, involve views of how the world is ordered, but also views about how it *ought* to be ordered; that is, it has a prescriptive or moral loading about self-conduct. It is, if nothing, judgmental, but what we witness in our research is that people have difficulty in being judgemental in any ordered moral sense when it comes to assessing cultural products. True, firm expression is offered on programmes or scenes that they do not like or approve of, but little moral arguing is engaged by way of support for their responses. The absence of this, although perhaps not too surprising, goes hand in hand with not being able to formulate a clear position on how culture ought to be regulated.

The Politics of a Moral Language

The description of the Church of England as the 'Tory Party at prayer', while lacking absolute veracity, nevertheless captures a process of religious socio–political fusion. This association, furthermore, has allowed the permeation of Christianity into general culture, so that even classes and groups that formally were removed from clerical Christianity could not escape its influence on the mind. The Church of England, as the Established Church, and closely interlocked with 'Establishment' Britain, has had 'permission' to address audiences, most notably in the nation's schools, where it would not have been invited otherwise. Thus, although secularization and the differential erosion of beliefs meant that Christianity was never a 'lived religion' for the labouring classes of Britain, it has had a cultural and moral presence that has been difficult to escape. The taking of oath in the courts as a legal necessity for the creation of perjury, but done so by swearing on the Bible, illustrates the intertwining of Christianity with established authority. No matter that many habitués of the courts would be more familiar with the rules of arrest than the strictures of the Bible, Christianity in Britain, once its organic days were spent, has had a 'forced' presence. It has permeated the master institutions and those areas of culture falling under their influence which would not have been possible without entry as a practising faith by those classes making up the British establishment. Christianity had, and still has, a voice, in other words, far in excess of its numeric support. It can be invoked on occasion of national appeal to provide through moral sanctification of acts, or to solemnize moments of national significance.

As a framework for moral performance, the Church has hugged the nation in its embrace. At times it has involved itself in distinct practical moral reform or sharp effort at moral improvement, particularly in the nineteenth and early twentieth century when, on firmer social foundation, interference was possible. As a mechanism of social control through the installation of Christian values by Sunday Schools, the attachment of the Boy Scouts to churches, or the preaching of a sober life through the Temperance Movement and valuation of Christian family life by organizations such as the Mothers Union, the effectiveness of Christianity as a regulatory force is open to question. The facts of life for much of the industrial working classes was not one that left much space for 'spiritual development', even if the hope was that Christian cultivation might dampen brute passion, both politically and morally. The point to underscore, however, is that, although actual places of worship may have had restricted entry, the placement of Christianity within cultural practice and thought has been wide. But it is to Luckmann's point concerning the process of secularization, thinking here in terms of long history, that has decisively altered the social location of church religion (or its inner universe of meaning) that we must return in terms of broadcasting and the language of moral judgement. Both broadcasting and the language of moral judgement must both be situated in terms of wider social change.

Tom Burns, writing in the early 1960s, commented that 'If the social function of broadcasting is properly construed as the provision of political, social and cultural navigation charts, the job Reith chose for the BBC to carry out was that of maintaining a kind of pilot service'. Although Burns' description of Reith is a good one, it is not so easy to imagine a current commentator, nearly half a century on, holding so solidly to the social function of broadcasting in such a manner. It may still be held by some as an ideal, but not necessarily as a descriptive state. Burns further likened the early days of Reith's BBC to the diplomatic service:

> ...the BBC developed as a kind of internal diplomatic service, representing the British – best of the British – to the British. 'BBC culture' like the BBC's standard English vocabulary and pronunciation, was not peculiar to itself but an intellectual audience composed of the values, standards and beliefs of the professional middle classes. (Burns 1964: 20)

Although Reith's particular 'muscular Christianity' may not have been shared by the British upper and upper middle classes to which the output of the BBC was addressed – the rest of the population having to learn to enjoy that which was authoritatively offered – nevertheless, Christianity had a common enough drawing-room presence among such groups to provide a sense of refracted common culture; although in effect, a sectionalized culture which operated as 'official' culture. This culture was enthused with a moral language and purpose drawn from Christian sentiment. The application of moral purpose to broadcasting was, of course, made all the more possible by the absence of any alternative channels to carry a variety of voices, but this should not obscure the rather lengthy holding of a Christian ethos within national culture consequent on the mass communicative nature of broadcasting.

In examining the history of broadcasting in Britain, one can, in fact, detect a shift in the expressed intellectual location of senior policy-makers within broadcasting away from a distinctly Christian informed rule. Thus, one can compare statements of principle by Reith (in Stuart 1975), Haley (1948), Greene (1965) and Curran (1971); and detect quite readily a shift from the clear exposition of broadcasting's commitment to lead in the evocation of solid Christian principles to Greene's commitment to what he described as 'basic moral values' (i.e. non-Christian)[3] and Curran's argument during his reign that since we now live in a post-Christian era the responsibility of broadcasting is to give full voice to all the various ideas current within society.

Social change can be cast in many ways. But from the point of view of examining viewers' ideas concerning the regulation of culture, then what one sees in relation to television in the 1960s, particularly under Hugh Greene's stewardship, is social change operating as a focal point of tensions emerging from general cultural changes that began to redefine authority relationships, both at the individual and societal level, but which also entailed a retreat of the religious in the face of the secular. One might even argue that there was an epistemological rupture within broadcasting during the 1950s and 1960s, especially with the advent of ITV, in the sense of having to rethink broadcasting – its purpose and place within national culture.

Charles Curran's argument when director-general (in Stuart 1975) that, because of now living in a post-Christian society, broadcasting had to give full voice to a range of ideas existing in society, found support from no less an institution than the Independent Television Authority[4] in its submission to the Longford Committee in early 1970. The ITA, in discussing the organizational directives on production in the form of codes of practice, argued that 'One of the main difficulties underlying [the codes of practice] has come as a result of the philosophical shift over the last few years. The black and white value system accepted in the 50s emerged into the grey area of the 60s and led to the rejection of absolute standards in the thinking of many in today's society' (Longford 1972: 247). It is interesting that around the same time the Church of England's Broadcasting Commission (1973), in asking within what moral context decisions about programme content will be made, noted: 'It would...be useless for the broadcasting authorities to seek for such principles from the practice of modern society. The trouble is that the present pluralist society not only lacks any universally, or even generally, accepted moral norms, but instead simultaneously pursues the widest variety of independent aims.' In short, like the ITA (only from a theological perspective), they were saying that the 'problem' with broadcasting is that it had become netted within the prevailing orthodoxy of the 'new morality', which is 'often sheer social expediency, its ethics are situational and its ultimate goals seldom bear any relationship to Christian hope'.

If one can see the fault lines of stress appearing within broadcasting in the 1960s, with it losing its claim to speak for an identifiable set of values drawn from established cultural assumptions about Britain as a Christian nation, then broadcasting was no different from the Church itself in having to find itself in the 'dark night of the soul'. The fact that broadcasting speaks from the studio and not the pulpit means that it is not required to engage in higher order intellectual reasoning to understand, or justify, its performance. The recognition that its audience is a plurality that can be spoken to in many ways undoubtedly frees it to the pursuit of standards without reference to a totalizing belief system, or values drawn from such a belief system: the artist has been freed from ecclesiastic control and, as often the case with artists, has pushed form and symbol to the point where no control exists other than the limits of the artist's own imagination. The fact that for the artist to live requires an audience, and for the artist living within and off broadcasting an audience of considerable size, popularity of appeal becomes a constraining force on the imagination as practice. The attempt to hold a congregation or the attempt to hold an audience by reference to the existence of taste is, at a fundamental level, a sign of a loosened moral purpose in the first instance, and a sign of a loosened cultural purpose in the second instance.

It would be foolish not to consider, however, that to prosper even the most assured of cultural or moral missions must take note of its communicative appeal and reception. Furthermore, although the idea within communication research of the 'active audience' engaging with the message may be recent, as an empirical fact its existence is longer than the idea. One can presume, for example, that the good burghers of Geneva favoured those

Calvinist pastors that reflected in their sermons the ethic of industry as insurance against not being among the elected, rather than those who espoused a more quietistic response to the uncertainty of grace. While quietism is a perfectly logical response to the message delivered by Calvin, it is not one likely to be taken up by an 'active audience' made up of people engaged in commerce.

The position identified by Tom Burns concerning the early days of the BBC acting as a kind of 'internal diplomatic service' representing the British people based on a narrow drawing of the cultural map of Britain, the trigonometry point for which was the professional middle classes, could not be sustained when faced by the necessity of having to appeal to a broader audience. The BBC had to reposition itself, as indeed it is currently having to do, in light of changes in the topography of the broadcasting landscape and in doing so released its purchase on an all-embracing cultural purpose. It could no longer, especially in the 1960s, operate without challenge by those who it hoped to claim as an audience. It no longer had any moral authority to have an all-embracing cultural purpose. The consequent change in practice was something which dismayed Lord Reith, as evidenced by his letter bitterly attacking what he saw as the BBC's desertion of its cultural duty: 'The BBC has lost dignity and repute; in the upper reaches of intellectual and ethical and social leadership it has abdicated its responsibility and its privilege. Its influence is disruptive and subversive, it is no longer "on the Lord's side"' (Letter to Sir Arthur Fforde, 18 May 1964 – in Stuart (1975)).

The move from the theologically informed culture of Reith to the secular informed culture of Greene's 'basic moral values' represents a recognition of some basic sociological facts of modern industrial life. Roy Wallis, writing on the moral campaign of Mary Whitehouse to 'clean up TV' makes the pertinent observation that

> In modern industrial society, occupational and social differentiation give rise to a wider range of sub-cultures embodying more or less distinctive life styles, consumption and behaviour patterns. While these continually threaten to impinge upon each other and hence provide the grounds for conflict, there is nevertheless a degree of segregation and insulation of competing sub-cultures. (Wallis 1976: 25)

At the sub-cultural level then, there has been a fragmentation of beliefs such that 'no man can expect his norms and values to hold exclusive sway' (Wallis 1976: 27–28).

Mary Whitehouse and her followers in the National Viewers' and Listeners' Association expected their norms and values to 'hold exclusive sway'. Whitehouse and her followers are deeply Christian, and the overhaul of British Broadcasting that she demanded during the heyday of her movement in the 1960s and 1970s was, if nothing, an attempt at Christian revival.[5] The protest of the NVALA may have been focused on television, but it was a symbolic protest in that its real goal was the re-invigoration of Britain as a Christian society.[6] Whitehouse was correct in her fundamental judgement of British television, that it was 'ungodly', or rather, that a Christian country would not have the broadcasting culture that emerged in Britain in the 1960s and continues to this day; namely, one devoid of moral certitudes.

The structural fact about Whitehouse and NVALA was that they were cut off from mainstream shifts in British culture. It was television in the 1960s, particularly with its exploration through drama of the private worlds of the inhabitants of inner-city life, and the treatment of social and sexual issues, that proved to be the educational tool by which Whitehouse and members of NVALA learnt how ungodly British society had become. To live, as previously noted, 'in a particular religious world implies existing in a particular social context within which that world can retain its plausibility' (Berger 1967: 58), and it was television, coming into the sanctuary and sanctity of members homes, that posed a direct threat to the plausibility structures supporting their beliefs. Television offered a different definition of reality to that constructed by the members. The protest by NVALA had, therefore, twin drives: alerted to the ungodly nature of British society, members had a Christian duty to recapture the world for God and at the same time possessed a fear that if they did not do so they would be overwhelmed by the unchristian culture beamed at them. In short, although television was the focus of their protests, and a genuine affront to members' sensibilities and values, it was a symbol of deeper ills in British society which required a moral crusade to correct.

The social nature of moral consciousness that occupied classical sociology, most notably Durkheim, is as problematic as ever, but Durkheim's 'conscious collective' gives the impression of a uniform, knowable entity such that abnormal behaviour is recognized precisely because the orthodoxy of normative behaviour and belief is so pervasive. This is no place to rehearse critiques of Durkheim, but to simply note that with the complexity and ideological pluralism of industrial society it becomes questionable as to what extent one can talk of commonly held and recognized social norms. Further, and in terms of addressing social cohesion, since one can no longer discern the unanimity of shared norms, and since one is confronted with a whole range of norms, tolerance rather than approbation of differing value systems would appear to be the most functionally necessary response. The central point to stress is that cultural fragmentation within modern society means that there no longer exists a vocabulary, a common framework of discourse, within which moral questions applicable to the whole of society can be discussed.

The changes to broadcasting, the manner in which it unshackled itself, especially the BBC under the director-generalship of Sir Hugh Greene, from an ethical framework of performance underpinned by notions of Christian stewardship has been part of a general transformation of defined morality within British life in the post-1945 world. One needs only to look at parliamentary legislation in the 1950s to support this assertion. How far parliamentary legislation was both a cause and effect of changing mores is hard to say, but legislation reached a peak in a series of acts that seemed to herald the new 'permissive age' by articulating and defining a transformation from the morality of a Christian ethic to the ethical propositions of a secular society; in particular the Obscene Publications Act 1959; the Murder (Abolition of the Death Penalty) Act 1965; the Abortion Act 1967; the Sexual Offences Act 1967; the Theatres Act 1968; and the already discussed Divorce Act of 1969.[7]

Why Whitehouse and NVALA could still talk about broadcasting in terms of moral purpose, when broadcasting could not, is that there was no recognition by them of social realities: theirs was a moral world in which the scripture of performance was of equal applicability and value to everyone. Judgement was not to be modified by any recognition of the social circumstances within which acts occurred. Thus instruction on how to behave was to be the same for the young of some inner-city slum, as it was for the young of some leafy grove in a middle-class suburb. The fact that the message had no possibility of any bridging relevance, a communality of meaning, emptied the message of content. The long process of cultural fragmentation that forbid the existence of a framework of discourse within which moral questions applicable to the whole society could be discussed was lost to her and her members, but not lost to broadcasters. As far as Mary Whitehouse was concerned, Sir Hugh Greene became not simply wrong to recognize the plurality of values of contemporary Britain during his office at the BBC, but was a figure of evil.

The accommodation of broadcasting to the empirical fact of the values of the empirical audience, necessitated in part by competition, that not to do so might mean it had no audience at all, although enmeshing broadcasting at times in controversy as it explored the cultural boundaries of the existences of values/taste, was something entirely within its power. Yet, if broadcasting has lost the right of cultural imposition by no longer being able to appeal to absolute moral standards, as indicated in the submission by the ITA to the Longford Committee, and supported by the Church of England's Broadcasting Commission, the question remains: with what moral authority does broadcasting act? One response is not to see itself as having any moral purpose, and stake its defence of content by appeal to professional values internal to the programme itself framed by the legal edicts that govern performance. This is not a response that would satisfy most moralists, but therein lies the problem – what language to adopt in judging performance, and from what universe should that language be drawn?

Throughout our discussion of moral universes and the language adopted in display of those universes, we have really being talking about the changing relationship of broadcasting to its audience, and the changing nature of the audience itself in terms of its construction of meanings, as part of a long historical process that has left the world, more or less, viewed as humanly constructed. In the present, although the mystical or magical still breaks though the idea of the humanness of the world as a totalizing system of belief, the 'otherness' of the world is no longer an organizing principle of reality. Man faces the world as his own product, and as such has a right of say in its performance.

The stripping of the sacred or mystical from culture provides cultural products with a transparency hitherto unknown. The individual can see representations of themselves in secular form rather than appearing as part of some wider tapestry of fundamental meaning. Figures appearing can have actual biographies rather than as representational entries of other states – Faith, Hope, Charity and Christian can give way to real names.

Democratization

In the development of popular culture consequent on catering to the entertainment needs of the growing urban populations of the late nineteenth century and developments in the mechanical reproduction of cultural artefacts, and, later, the electronic mass delivery of culture, it becomes a small step for people to demand a direct representation of themselves. At the furthest extreme this is a demand for the inclusion of groups to which they belong: for example, homosexuals.

The existence of sub-groups in industrial society always offers the possibility of conflict. But, for the reasons given by Roy Wallis (1976), conflict is reduced by the very complexities of industrial society in that, hidden from each other, each individual can, to a certain extent, go their own discrete way. However, the demand for representation by sub-groups means that the insularity they were once afforded, and which provided them with an invisibility, is no longer the case. Homosexuals, for example, have become visible through the portrayal of their lifestyle, which has produced conflict at an ideational level. Indeed, this was something that became very apparent by comments made in the course of the focus groups. Although claiming tolerance towards homosexuals because of a sense of the self as decent, where to be decent was defined within an ideology of tolerance, the legitimization of homosexuality in *EastEnders,* by the presentation of the homosexual characters as 'normal' people, caused deep offence and concern. Homosexuality as a lifestyle was not to be normatively sanctioned, although homosexuals themselves were to be tolerated.

The changed relationship of the audience to broadcasting that has foregrounded the existence of the viewer, symbolized by the BARB audience measurement service, has given a democratic play to broadcasting that makes it increasingly difficult to make moral pronouncements on the management of culture drawn from a distinct set of values.

Popular art is not a modern phenomenon, but the intellectual and moral controversy that surrounds it is. The controversy has its roots in social change as much as the changed nature of popular art. Social change has resulted in a visibility of all groups to each other (their leisure, behaviour and culture) and has meant an increased critical inspection of cultural denominators.

Historically, because there was no cultural contact between the elite and the masses, nor a bridging middle class, the existing discrete cultural worlds went their own way without alarm or concern. It is difficult, as Leo Lowenthal stresses, to determine the exact point when the gap closed and controversy ensued. He considers that, in England, the controversy began in the eighteenth century and, by the mid-eighteenth century, the problems of modern commercial culture were apparent. According to Lowenthal, 'the artist, traditionally dependent for his subsistence on the direct consumers of his art, no longer had to please only one rich or powerful patron; he had now to worry about the demands of an increasingly broader, more 'popular' audience' (Lowenthal 1961: xvii).

This process took place in the great European nations with varying speeds, but by the middle of the eighteenth century there had arisen in each of them a group of writers and playwrights who specialized in caring for the needs of these broad audiences. Lowenthal states that it was about then that the controversy over the threat of popular art to civilization began. The challenge to popular art was no mere question of aesthetic taste; rather, it asked whether the individual ought to engage in leisure pursuits that did nothing to contribute to the salvation of the soul. At the philosophical level, the task of thinkers was to reconcile the individual's religious responsibilities and moral heritage to the requirements of an emerging national and capitalist economy. As Lowenthal argued: for the first time in modern history, discussion posed the problem of the value of serious against relatively frivolous leisure-time pursuits (Lowenthal 1961: xviii).

Production began to depend on the ability to attract a broad audience, and, thus, a form of production emerged featuring audience-building devices and fed a transformation in the definition of cultural merit that rested on the popularity of the product. The ultimate triumph of this process can be seen in the broadcasting industry, symbolized by the establishment of research departments to measure and quantify the popularity of programs.

The industrialization of western societies, although uneven in its pace and place of development, gathered momentum in the nineteenth century and saw its grip firmly embrace cultural production in the twentieth century. The industrialization of culture, the mechanical reproduction of 'art', was both a consequence of technological developments and the social change wrought by industrialization itself. Transport developments and the growth of populations in discrete areas all presented new and definable markets, which were accompanied by a cultural loosening of the distinctiveness of populations under the new shared conditions of concentrated capital. In Britain, organic art, or folk art, expressive of local conditions and experiences, that was characterized by little separation of experience between the performer and audience, lived on only in isolated pockets, giving way to the professional performer and the marketing of performance. Secondary industries such as market research developed and grew rich on the efforts to limit artistic failure. Furthermore, in branches of electronically delivered 'art' the separation of the artist from his or her product as it moves down the production line of delivery has been such that it is often difficult to distinguish any author at all. This development of a manufacturing base of artistic production lends strength to the oft-quoted argument that television is no different from any other industry. If this is so, then it should be treated accordingly and allowed to let markets and market forces decide what is, and what is not, worthy of production.

But we would argue that television *is* different from other areas of consumption; culture is political and represents a struggle to define how we wish to represent the world to ourselves. It is because of this that one has the type of intellectual and moral controversy referred to by Lowenthal, and the political debate concerning how cultural expression is to be managed.

As stressed, however, there is no longer an all-encompassing or shared moral language by which to articulate and give meaning to moral discussion. The crucial difficulty, however, in making appeal to performance through moral precepts, or to the congealed tastes of a dominant cultural group or class, is that the fragmentation of populations within advanced industrial societies has also been accompanied by technological advances offering a multitude of channels that threaten to undermine the possibility of genuine national broadcasting. If viewing is to no longer be a public act in the sense of accessing a nationally common offering, but a private act of consumption reflecting individual preferences, which at the same time does not interfere with the preferences or values of others, it becomes difficult to mount a defence of the management of culture by appeal to a commonweal of values or taste, or by appeal to the protection of a specific culture. It may be that the possibility of viewers being able to desert the offerings of a particular culture undermines the power of its presence, but it does not mean that it cannot be represented – it must find its 'true' place within the expressive preferences of the population.

The explosion of channels, and the arrival of new delivery systems and direct payment for programmes, along with smart cards to protect exposure to non-intended viewers such as children, requires a particular language of reasoning for the management of culture. The notion of 'harm' is one, or if a programme is likely to 'deprave' or 'corrupt' is another, but basically these are behavioural tests and have nothing to do with moral ideas concerning how a society should represent itself to itself: what, through culture, is the picture we wish to paint as marking the values by which we wish to live? And that is what, at base, the question of taste is really about.

It might be argued that individuals have a right not to be offended by what they watch. However, the changed relationship of the viewer to broadcasting means that material which might offend quite a lot of people, if they viewed it, does not give offence because those viewing it have deliberately exposed themselves to it and done so by the democratic method of the market. That is, they have paid for it as a specialized contract between themselves and the supplier. What we witness, therefore, is a new arrangement in the consumption of culture, and with this new arrangement a shift in social responsibilities for the management of that culture. What people appear to be saying, and we will see evidence of this later, is that if someone directly pays for a service or programme then the onus is more likely to be put upon the individual to decide the value of content. And this decision ought not to involve the interests of others. What this means, in effect, is that the existence of desires for cultural products is to be the determining factor in deciding cultural expression. It is as if the manner in which something is consumed, the absolute arrangement of consumption, forgoes the necessity of considering the ethics of aesthetics. To adopt such a position, and many in our focus groups did, is to leave unexamined the whole question of the purpose of culture, and to see culture as having no moral implications in terms of how we see the world and how we represent social order to ourselves. It is to put the individual at the epicentre of social life without reference to any collective.

It might be expected that most people would not give an account of culture as involving moral stories, but at a pre-theoretical level they did see that certain stories ought not to be told, and that it was thus necessary to have some management of the storytellers. Why management was considered not so necessary as a result of a private contract between the individual and the storyteller was not easy to determine. But clearly it had something to do with the acceptance that private payment gave personal rights. Indeed, that personal ambitions could and ought to be satisfied at the site of the individual without reference to wider ambitions involving community. In other words many people did not have a moral language that encompassed the collective, and as such had difficulty in addressing cultural issues other than through reference to the self as an economic being.

The central role of payment as the arbiter of consumption is the language of economics, not the language of morals. One might erect from political philosophy a moral system which argued that non-interference in the market fostered collective political freedoms, some general good, but it is difficult to see how the interference by a regulatory agency was held to be fine in one set of circumstances, but not in another. That is, if the point was to protect the individual against exposure to certain cultural display which was held to be bad, it was difficult to see how such display became good through a different contractual arrangement for its consumption – the nature of the contract did not alter the nature of the content.

We will later examine the various reasons respondents put forward in arguing for less management of television if viewers pay directly for programmes. What cannot be overlooked is that, while culture was seen to involve moral questions, an unshackling of the individual from a discourse that allowed the expression of wider truths than individual interest does, nevertheless, appear to have taken place. This unshackling of language from the language of universal truths – religion – that has stunted the ability to address moral issues, has its consequential counterpart in the unshackling of political language from moral ambition.

Politics and Moral Ambition

The establishment of the BBC in 1922 as a limited company and then it becoming a public corporation in 1927, funded by a licence fee charged on all wireless owners, was undertaken within a political atmosphere that favoured public boards. Water and Electricity, as Barnett and Curry point out in their account of changes in the ethos of the BBC, were already, at the time of the BBC's founding, 'administered as public corporations'. The First World War, furthermore, 'had produced a number of civil servants well versed in both the philosophy and the practice of centralised control' (Barnett and Curry 1994: 6). The times that favoured the establishment of public boards to reform social life through collective provision of service is a far cry from present-day zeal to privatize institutions and services that once stood as civic statements of collective aspirations.

At the time of the Peacock Committee (1986), enquiry into the future of broadcasting, set up under that privatizer of all privatizers, the then Prime Minister Margaret Thatcher, several opinion polls were conducted by market research companies to test attitudes towards the financing of the BBC. Indeed, the Peacock Committee itself commissioned NOP to conduct such a survey. The surveys and polls were in agreement that a majority of the general public would favour the BBC accepting advertising if, by doing so, this meant a reduction in the licence fee. This was good news for those who wished to 'sell off' what had been seen for so long as a national asset supported by pubic donation, albeit compulsory public donation. It no longer seemed that public service broadcasting was held to as an ideal by the bulk of the British people. Morrison, however, told a different story in his study, *Invisible Citizens* (1986), of the publics' attitudes towards the BBC and how it ought to be funded.

The questions put by the market research companies presented respondents with the possibility of a 'free meal'; that is, by agreeing to the BBC accepting advertising, they would not have to pay a license fee. Not surprisingly most people took the opportunity to avail themselves of such an offer. Troubled by the apparent readiness of the public to sever its historical relationship with the BBC and turn it over to the market to be funded by advertising, the BBC commissioned its own survey to test if the response of 65% wishing to commercialize the BBC was an artefact of question order – that if the questions were asked in a different sequence to that of the original surveys the response might differ. Question order can affect responses, but in this case the differences achieved were marginal: the 'problem' was in the questions themselves, not the order in which they were asked.

The survey for *Invisible Citizens* asked the same questions as those adopted by the market research companies and got roughly the same responses as they had. The questionnaire then sought, however, to ground those questions within the context of what accepting advertising by the BBC might mean in practice. By so doing it not only dignified the respondents by allowing them to judge whether or not the meal offered by the BBC accepting advertising would genuinely be free, but allowed the survey to get at values upon which opinions are based.

All decisions have consequences, some intended and others not intended; therefore, the questionnaire offered realistic scenarios of what the consequences might be if the BBC accepted advertising. Only a small percentage of those originally wishing the BBC to accept advertising held to their original decision when allowed to respond to what doing so might mean in practice. What the research gathered through this approach, especially when combined with focus group research, was that the ideal of public service broadcasting appeared to rest on, and be enmeshed with, civic values. By civic values it is meant that institutions and practices are valued as a public good and not just as a private pleasure. It matters nothing in other words that the totality of service might not be utilised by any single individual, but is supported because without collective commitment aspects of the service that an individual might wish to use would not be provided. In short, behind civic values is the idea that individual well-being can only be guaranteed through the whole community sharing in the provisions of some service. It is the opposite of the idea of the individual being left to make their own provisions for themselves. The notion of civic values also embodies the egalitarian sentiment that certain individuals might be in a privileged position to furnish themselves with a service, but the service remains just that, a privilege, the satisfaction granted being undermined through the moral consideration that others are not enjoying such benefits.

It must remain open to question as to whether, if the *Invisible Citizens* study was repeated now, nearly twenty years later, one would find such strong support for a public culture provided by a licence fee, or the presence of the type of civic values that underpinned such support. Even when the original study was undertaken, it may well have been that what it captured, although real enough, was no more than the light from a dying star of some past galaxy of beliefs. It is certainly the case that technical arrangements rather than moral meaning have come to occupy the heartland of public political discourse, and notions such as Citizen's Charter (Conservative) and Social Contract (Labour) and, more recently, Ofcom's use of the term 'citizen-consumer' do nothing to disguise this fact.

The long march of history has served to transform meanings into technical questions. It has already been noted how one of the primary definers of how life ought to be conducted, namely religion, has vacated consciousness, not to be replaced by any other totalizing belief system through which to give moral purpose. Religion may now be a private domain organising the inner world of some individuals, but not an external force imprinting itself as collective endeavour on the social, political and moral life of the country.

The twentieth century has certainly witnessed political attempts at the central organization of meaning through state domination of social life, but these efforts feature, in Britain in the early twenty-first century, only as historical lessons rather than as any living expression of organized hope. Indeed, what is remarkable about the contemporary political scene is the absence of a political language with which to address moral issues. Politics itself has, at core, an absence of the moral ambition that characterized politics even in the recent past. What one has witnessed is an increased appeal by all sections of the political spectrum to managerial ability as a rationale for support rather than moral purpose, and this is so despite Prime Minister Tony Blair's invocation to accept him as a moral man.

Admittedly, the Conservative Party has always had management as an intertwined part of its ideology. Its presentation as the natural party of government in a capitalist economy through its support base in capital allows it the privilege of appearing non-ideological while at the same time holding very strong sets of ideological positions. This was bound to be so once the basic features of the British economy became settled, and alternative definitions to capital ceased to be a living force. The difficulty now, in the absence of a moral alternative to capital, or the introduction into capital of moral beliefs based on past threats of alterations to the social order, is that of finding a vocabulary to express moral purpose. Appeal for political support has had to be based on technical competence and not righteousness.

A whole history of socio-political change is captured in the above description of the closure of party differences – the absence of moral management as a central feature of the contemporary political scene, replaced by that of technocratic management – but the social bases from which the parties were established, and drew their core support, have undergone alteration so that both must speak in a language different from the past and in doing so have come to speak with a voice similar to each other. Past social divisions, that had both an objective and a subjective reality to make possible appeal to large sections of the population in bold ideological terms, have undergone such alteration that to do so now would threaten electoral success.

The similarities in the political discourse of the parties is not simply due to changes that have gone on in the economic base of society – the move away from production to services which has led to new social formations and in doing so altered identities and symbols with which people identify – but the increased technocratization of society, particularly the electronicization of communication, leading to impersonalized contact with institutions, has meant that social life does indeed appear to be more managed. Politics is thus transformed from the moral to the technical, since the objective fact appears that the successful running of such depends on management skills and not moral vision. The expressive aspect of politics has necessarily given way to technical competence and, in doing so, has altered the very language with which political struggle is fought out. The difficulty of the Labour Party is in knowing what language to use to give purpose to its foundational spirit, when that language of its foundational spirit is no longer relevant to people's lives as they now perceive them; indeed, it has no meaning. It is an archaic language, drawn from a forgotten country. Yet, at the same time it wishes to claim moral ground over the Conservative Party, but without any grand moral purpose. Its right to govern is based on the claim of managerial competence, and not the creation of a moral order through the rearrangement of its relationship to the economy or of people to each other.

The point to register is that, in the absence of a moral language, the regulation of culture, as both a value in itself and as valuable in practice, becomes extremely problematic. The regulation of culture will undoubtedly become increasingly technically difficult with the promised explosion in sources of access to culture, but that is not the central problem. The real problem is to know by what authority regulation can take place in the absence of a language to discuss cultural moral issues. However, in the absence of a moral language by which to discuss control, another language has been found; one much more suited to technocratic rationality – science.

Given the absence of a shared moral language by which to discuss cultural value, it is not surprising that much of the demand for the control of culture has had to stand, and be defended, by appeals to science and not moral reasoning. That is, the demand for regulation is empirically grounded: moral issues have become transformed into technical questions, in that certain cultural offerings are held to have undesirable behavioural effects. Whether this is true or not matters nothing, what is significant is that moral questions have become research questions to be answered by the methods of the social sciences, which, although perhaps value-impregnated, do not start from moral premises and, furthermore, are not capable of providing moral answers.

What was heard from the focus groups was the absence of any real notion of moral authority. However, respondents would frequently, whilst claiming not to be religious, admit to being guided in their moral judgements by Christian teaching. Although, there was no evidence that such judgements were accompanied by any theological reasoning: Christianity appeared to stand as a metaphor for decency, and as such was secular. What was decent and what was not decent was to be judged by experience of that which was harmful, underpinned by the socialization into a set of norms drawn from their experiences and lessons of family life that allowed, but only in the most vague of ways, the application of a moral code. That moral code, however, was not an instructed moral code as in the form of receiving a set of codified moral principles, *vide* Christian instruction, but sets of standards their parents had applied in their negotiations with other people.

One of the difficulties, however, in applying standards which are simply ways of living, rather than operating with sets of principles, either philosophically or theologically reasoned, is that what is operationally appropriate in one generation may not be valid for other generations faced by totally different social conditions. For example, to 'love one's neighbour' and offer friendship and support to them, in that it makes good sense reciprocally in terms of applied living, does not make the same sense if one does not know one's neighbour. Indeed, it might even be foolish to trust one's neighbour. We found that people were confused about how they should live, and that they were left adrift in an indeterminate sea of uncertainty, but all the time anchored by the pragmatic principle of protecting themselves and those close to them from harm. Perhaps there is nothing new in this, but what did appear new, at least according to people's accounts of their own childhood, was that 'protection' was a more central organizing point of their lives than they cared for it to be.

This concentration on the self as at risk from harm is a mark of not trusting the world of others. Although respondents felt that they were decent and raised their children to behave in a decent manner towards others, their performance was not seen to be given support by the performance of the wider community. There was a general feeling that the family was forced back in on itself in terms of moral instruction. The existing culture outside the home, in schools and the everyday performances of others that they witnessed, such as the extension of courtesy and politeness, was antagonistic to moral directives that they wished to give their children. Of particular importance in this direction was the cultural performance of television.

While very few people held television responsible for distinct behaviour, such as acting violently, they nevertheless objected to the images that television gave of the world; that is, the moral lessons it offered. Yet, this concern about culture, taking culture here to embody reflections of the world and the moral stories told, was not accompanied by any moral language by which to debate, in any consistent fashion, where regulation of culture might start or end. The artist was certainly not to be given free rein to his or her imagination, but neither were they, as adults, to be told what they could or could not watch, especially if they had made special arrangements to view material by paying for it directly via cable or satellite delivery.

What we see in effect is an absence in contemporary culture of the intellectual equipment to make moral judgements, or, perhaps more accurately, that there has occurred a fragmentation of moral certitude so that there is no overall agreement as to what constitutes the moral, only a general feeling of what is decent. There is not a moral community, but then, without the moral, one does not have community. Perhaps that is what people were really saying, and in so doing expressing the source of much of their concern about life in contemporary Britain.

Notes

1. See Cox (1965) chapter 1 for a good succinct discussion of this.
2. See Merton (1968) chapter 20 for a discussion of Puritanism and science.
3. See Tracey (1983) for a detailed account of the development of Greene's thinking, and Tracey and Morrison (1979) for his vehement opposition to Christian moralists such as the late Mary Whitehouse and her organization, The National Viewers' and Listeners' Association (now MediaWatch).
4. The ITA was the first regulatory authority for commercial broadcasting, which became the Independent Broadcasting Authority and then the Independent Television Commission. In 2003, Ofcom became the super-authority of mass communications.
5. See Tracey and Morrison (1979) and Morrison and Tracey (1976) for a full discussion of this.
6. See Gusfield (1972), study of the American Temperance Movement; Zurcher et al. (1971), study of American anti-pornography campaigns; and Parkin's (1968), study of the Campaign for Nuclear Disarmament, for a discussion of symbolic protest.
7. See Pym 1974 for a good discussion of this parliamentary legislation and the reforming nature of the new generation of Labour MPs in Parliament, especially following the Labour victory of 1966.

Cultural Contestation

3 Culture in Practice

This chapter examines the confusion that exists at a terminological level between anti-social behaviour and unsociable behaviour and stresses that clarification is required over the meaning of the terms if discussion of the influence of television is to be meaningfully advanced. It discusses the place of lifestyle and how the media may play a role in furthering certain lifestyles that are taken to be anti-social, but in effect are better viewed as unsociable. It also considers the place of swearing in everyday life and swearing on television. The chapter identifies new social groups engaged in the 'expressive' professions that use swearing as a mark of distinction and that such groups, often through their portrayal on television, have helped legitimate a style of language once only associated with low social status groups. The chapter examines the democratization of television that has resulted in a variety of cultural sub-groups either being given voice or forming the object of portrayal, and how this process has undermined the appearance of moral authority associated with a single dominant culture.

The central argument of the previous chapter dealing with the social basis of values was that the location of the individual within contemporary society did not favour the occupation of any totalizing belief system, and that this had led to an inability, or difficulty, through the absence of a moral language, to discuss moral issues. This is not to say that what we have witnessed as the century has unfolded is the defeat of hope, but it is to say that in general people exist without the comfort of moral or political purpose. How many people in the past have stood facing the world not buoyed by such feelings is impossible to say, but one can characterize ages as being canopied by sentiments of total meaning even if not all individuals managed to find shelter.

This is not to paint a picture of the miserableness of modern life, far from it. Most people in our study considered their lives to be more pleasant than their parents' lives were, and, of those who had children, most considered that relationships between themselves and their children were closer than, and preferable to, that which had existed between themselves and their parents. There was much to be thankful for in terms of the routines of daily living and in terms of family life, even though the impermanence of marriage was often commented upon. What people in the focus groups possessed was a kind of fractured Whig view of history: that history is progressive, that tomorrow is better than yesterday, but that not all things are for the better.

A Whig view of history is often mocked, but very few people would like to change the present for the past. This is not a case of 'this is what we have got, therefore this is what we love,' but one of analytical judgement. However, although the past was definitely not pictured in pastel colours, much was seen in the present that was not viewed as an improvement on the past, and it was held that if nothing was done to correct matters the future would be worse than the present. Whig history was fractured by what J. K. Galbraith memorably referred to as 'private wealth and public squalor' (Galbraith 1958); that is, a rising living standard for the individual, but a diminished quality of life through lack of attention to public services.

Galbraith being an economist, it was perhaps not surprising that his attention should focus primarily on the economic provision of well-being. What surfaced in the focus groups was a position somewhat similar to Galbraith's dictum, but relating more to the moral provision of well-being rather than its economic provision. One had private moral wealth, but public moral squalor. It was agreed that improvement had taken place in the realm of individual well-being, but this had not been accompanied by any improvement in public well-being. They looked at their own private situation as one of improvement over the past, but could not find, on opening their door, a world that offered the same kind of pleasantness as in the past. There was a coarseness to modern life that they did not like, a coarseness, furthermore, that threatened the private gains in well-being that had been made. At the most brutal level, the outside world threatened, and more than just figuratively, to kick in the front door to their sanctuary. What one witnessed in the focus groups was a cultural dismay and a dismay at culture. People could not understand, nor give meaning to, the moral organization of contemporary society.

In discussing the absence of a moral language with which to frame cultural questions, we mentioned that shifts had taken place whereby authority now rested with the language of science and not ethics. The argument was that, in the absence of shared agreement about moral order, no agency could rule on such matters and expect to find general support among the disparate populations and groups that now make up contemporary society. Consequently, rather than appeal to sets of foundational truths, or make statements that exposed values, the settlement of cultural issues had been given over to science. This had been achieved by turning the question of culture into a behavioural question amenable to measurement. Thus, harm has become a central plank in the debate over symbolic representations of the world. However, harm is not construed in a manner that suggests the transgression of values, but as the transmission of forms of behaviour that if acted upon would break legal codes governing behaviour. Legal codes do, of course, embody values, but, as we have seen in the previous section, the law has become increasingly secular in its administration of social control. The law certainly prohibits behaviour, but does not promote it in any evocational sense of operating as a promotional moral force.

Culture has come to be debated in terms of the effect it might have in its ability to promote acts that others need protecting from, it is not debated in terms of the harm it might have on the individual as a moral being. No such debate is possible where there is no longer a valid currency by which to purchase agreement. The question of taste, however, does appear to include ideas of cultural value unrelated to the question of harm. Even so, taste has become a matter of offence; that is, who was offended, how many were offended, what programme were they offended by, what time was the programme transmitted, on what channel was the programme shown and so on. This is technical reasoning, and not moral judgement. Indeed, the 'professionalization' of regulation has meant that the 'legislators' have deliberately tried to stay clear of the imposition of values.

Codes of practice, which often form the basis of technical judgement, are of course impregnated with notions of what is right drawn from a sense of acceptable standards, and what constitutes an acceptable standard is culturally informed. It could be no other way, since it is impossible to step outside the world that one is a part of. But the point to stress is that the standards that are imposed are constituted by direct reference to the audience as an empirical reality. The reality taken of the audience is one which might be upset by various representations and, in the examination of the acceptance of images, great attention is given to demographic variables as a predictor of acceptance. Thus, taste becomes a research question; the 'scientific' exploration of how we shall live. It does not involve the imposition of standards drawn from an ordered moral position.

Causation

The transformation of moral questions into research questions, the most obvious being the attempt to discover the relationship of filmic violence on real-life violence, as if to find that if it had no effect then that would make any, and all, filmic violence right, represents the triumph of practical reason. Indeed, it is this triumph that gives a peculiar slant to the findings from the focus groups. Participants did not, with some qualification, believe that filmic violence was responsible for real-life violence. Thus, they had to make a judgement about such images without being able to shelter behind any scientific (causal) reasoning. Instead they had to make objection on cultural/moral grounds. This they found difficult to do for the reasons already advanced – they lacked the language by which to do so. Had they accepted an effects model of television then they would have been home and dry in coming to a position on the control of culture. They could have come to a judgement based on technical reasoning. What we see, however, is that any power television is held to have in terms of influencing behaviour is marginalized by consideration of more personal influences.

Personal Experience

In the second wave of focus groups it was decided to ask people if they had been a victim of crime. Our purpose in doing so was to see if exposure to crime influenced how they thought about crime. We begin by looking at the responses of 18 to 24–year-old women living in London.

The discussion was started by presenting to the participants some of the findings from our first questionnaire survey. The figures given related to the proportion of people who said they were concerned about crime in Britain. When the focus group participants were asked if they were surprised by the large percentage of people who had said that they were concerned about the level of crime in Britain, one woman immediately responded, '*it hasn't happened to me yet'*. The assumption here being that one could expect to be a victim of crime. Indeed, whether people had experienced crime or not, Britain was seen as a place where crime took place at a level so common that it was difficult to protect against. The possibility of being a victim of crime was accepted as a fact of life. The crime most likely to occur against them was seen to be that of burglary and not assault. It must be said, however, that, given that any crime is an intrusion of protected space, vulnerability to the power of others is a common consequence of theft. One of the women had clearly been frightened by an attempt to break into her car.

> *I've had someone try to break into my car while I was sitting in it. I was parked outside the bank waiting for my boyfriend when these three young men came round the corner and were larking about. One of them suddenly grabbed the door handle and tried to wrench it open. Lucky I had my doors locked. I dread to think what would have happened if it hadn't been.*

She was asked if this experience had coloured her response to other events and happenings around her. Was she nervous about going into her house in the evening when it was dark?: 'No. Not so much outside the car. But going out in the car and having to park and get out and go, say, into the bank, yes, I'm very wary now.' Although a traumatic experience her fear appeared to be kept localized. She did add, however, 'I know you shouldn't be racist, but they were black – it's made me very aware of when I am on my own, especially going to the bank. When I got home I rang the police and reported it because they were obviously out looking for trouble'.

What is interesting here is that, although she did not wish to be seen as racist, and there was no suggestion that she was, the fact that the perpetrators were black forced a response in her that she did not want; that is, to be suspicious of young black men when getting out of her car. A whole category of people has thus been caught in the web of her fear spun by one particular incident.

The point to underscore here is the power of personal experiences. And it is an understanding of the power of personal experiences that tends to lead people, but not leader writers, to downplay mediated experiences. One or two others in this group had experienced minor theft, such as a purse being stolen from a locker. One woman, however, mentioned that she had been burgled. Even though she had not been home at the time of the burglary, the effect on her was marked: *'It made me a bit worried about the way they got into the house – they got in through a very small window'*. The upshot was, as she commented, *'I don't like being in the house on my own'*.

Clearly, a direct experience is likely to have greater psychological impact than the experience of watching the comparable act on television. This is not to say that those who have been the victim of a crime might not watch a similar crime portrayed on television with greater unease than someone who had not being a victim, but the point to underscore is that people live in a world where real things happen to them and, although watching television is real enough, the events shown act as 'removed experience', not direct experience.

One of the mistakes that media research has frequently made is to regard viewers as an audience, rather than as people who happen, as part of daily-life, to watch television. In other words, people have biographies independent to that of an audience, and consequently draw upon a vast range of experiences in giving causation and meanings to the world. The above woman, for example, in a brief moment of exposure to danger in the otherwise routine of her life, completely transformed her thinking in terms of the organization of her own safety. Parking her car to go to a bank would never hold the same meaning again. Doubtless, the absolute uncertainty of what might lay in store on such a trip will recede in time, but such experiences force a reposition to the world and to what the world includes. Similarly, the woman who had been burgled was now nervous about remaining in her house alone.

These are direct and disturbing experiences which, necessarily, force a rethinking about the world, and also force reflection on the world and the circumstances of its structure. Quite clearly, the traumatic happening of three young men attempting to force entry into her car left the woman with a sense of danger. Her fear was based on a real event, but the fear transformed to provide her with an unrealistic fear of the world; that is, and virtually admitted to by herself, a fear of young black men. Thus, experiences in the world do not necessarily provide knowledge about it, or, more accurately, complete knowledge. In the same way that one 'reads' media messages, one 'reads' the signs of the non-mediated world, and different individuals can come to different readings of both. What was quite clear from the focus groups was that what took primacy in understanding the world was the act of living in it, and not the act of watching television. This requires qualification.

It was not that individuals did not learn about the world from television, or other media for that matter, they certainly did, but such information gained was digested and interpreted through existing understandings of the world. Information was tested against the givens of experience and, where no direct experience was to be had, pulled through a theoretical understanding to judge whether something was plausible or not. For example, in one focus group, discussing the question of rights to privacy, it was argued that the actor Hugh Grant, who had been arrested for lewd behaviour in a car with a prostitute, had little claim on the right to privacy, but that his girlfriend at the time, the fashion model Liz Hurley, did have such a right. She was not in any way involved in the incident that took place.

One man, however, considered that Hurley's own behaviour lessened her claims to privacy. His view was that she wanted the attention of the media. Given that this respondent had no access to Hurley's thinking, other members of the group asked him as to how he knew that Hurley desired media attention. He worked theoretically. He took known facts and placed those facts within general understanding to provide an account of happenings that could not be derived from the facts alone. On learning of Hugh Grant's sexual misbehaviour, and on Grant's return to their large country house, Hurley had insisted that Grant no longer share her bed. She had consequently contacted a local store to have a new bed delivered to the house. This respondent considered that the act of ordering this bed, given that journalists were swarming all around the property, was a deliberate attempt by Hurley to bring public attention to her displeasure over Grant's behaviour. The respondent could not accept that a house of the size that Hurley and Grant were renting did not have more than one bed: after all, he himself lived in a modest-sized house and even he had more than one bed.

We will return later to rules governing privacy, but what the above shows is that information gained from the media operates on existing understandings of the world. This is not to say that the media play no part in creating those understandings, far from it, but it is to say that people operate with accumulated knowledge that is the product of worked-through understandings created in the course of a life that consists of more than mediated knowledge of the world. As witnessed, information provided by the media is not evidence for something, but rather forms part of the material out of which knowledge is fashioned. And this is so, as the above case amply illustrates, where the viewer, listener or reader, has no direct access to events by which to test the veracity of statements, or even where past experiences would not readily equip them to test for truth. Information is interrogated against general accumulated knowledge of the likelihood of something being true, and by a theoretical construction of how the world functions. In the absence of any access to existing 'versions' of the world to apply information received, such as an event in some far-flung region of the world involving some unknown political regime, information, as likely as not, becomes knowledge. That is, it becomes the complete account of what is taking place. Even so, the information might still not be accepted as forming the basis by which to reach an understanding if the source of the information is not trusted, or if those commenting on the events have been unreliable in the past when discussing events or topics where the viewer has prior knowledge.

The interrogation of information against accumulated knowledge and theories of social life, no matter how shaky, means that the media, although occupying a powerful position in rendering meaning, have no taken-for-granted authority. If this is so, then it is also the case that social behaviour that is accounted for in terms of media performance is subject to similar scrutiny. But, given that people have close experience of media, and either direct experience of some of the behaviour that is accounted for by reference to the media, it is far from automatic that the social ills blamed on the media, television in particular, are accepted. Indeed, when it comes to matters of human behaviour in recognizable contexts, people claim for themselves privileged understanding.

The understandings that people offer for behaviour based on common sense or everyday experience do not make them superior to the understandings provided by those offered through formal enquiry, but it does mean that people stand in a peculiar position to knowledge in the social sciences when compared to knowledge in the natural sciences. Each individual, by virtue of being human, has the ability to reflect on their own experiences and, although not recognizing or even being aware of all the factors and forces that go to make up who they are, are nevertheless in considerable provision of the facts of their lives. This understanding of the self readily leads to the assumption of the understanding of others. And, indeed, people do, in a general anthropological way, have an understanding of how others are by virtue of the understanding of the self. What this means is that, through introspection, individuals come to an understanding of the salience of factors that make for particular behaviour.

Introspection alone is not a sufficient method to account for all behaviour, or for giving a completeness to the behavioural narrative. Understanding is supplemented by knowledge filtered from more formal and theoretical accounts of social behaviour, in the main, those coming down from the social sciences. Also, although not possessing a formal body of knowledge or theory to assist observation, individuals confront the behaviour of others on a daily basis and must make sense of it in order to participate effectively in social life. Some behaviour, however, is so different from anything that the individual might recognize by introspective appeal, or so normatively odd as not to be recognized through experiential contact, that no sense can be given to it and is thus bracketed off as 'mad', requiring no further explanation. The expertness of the individual – by deft of their existence in the world – at understanding social behaviour, means that the media are not the ready source for explaining social behaviour that one might assume. People, on the whole, do not foreground the media, and we are really talking about television, video and cinema films here, when seeking explanation for anti-social behaviour.

Anti-social and Unsociable Behaviour

We must make a distinction here been *anti-social* behaviour and *unsociable* behaviour, since it takes on vital importance later in discussing regulation. These terms are almost invariably used wrongly and result in a great deal of analytical confusion. The term *anti-social* refers to behaviour or acts that can be said to be against society; that is, they have a dimension that threatens social solidarity. Such acts would, for example, include practically all forms of violence and theft, since they threaten the operation of the community. Swearing, on the other hand, is not anti-social. It does not, although it might make life unpleasant, threaten the operations of the community. To swear, or to spit on the floor, in a community where such behaviour is not normative, is simply to act *unsociably* – to be uncivil, but not threatening. Of course, a line can be crossed where the unsociable or uncivil might transfer to the anti-social. For example, spitting in the soup tureen at a dinner party so that the community could no longer hold together in the enterprise of collective eating for which it had gathered. Such behaviour could be held not only as unsociable, in that it fell foul of the rules governing correct conduct and thus caused offence to the sensibilities, but anti-social in that it threatened the community.

However, one needs to consider whether unsociable behaviour is related in any way to anti-social behaviour. It is highly likely that those who engage in anti-social behaviour, such as forcing their position through violence, also act unsociably. Someone who has scant regard for someone else's physical well-being is not likely to have much regard for rules that govern manners and the protection of other people's sensibilities. Yet, while someone who acts anti-socially is also likely to act unsociably, this does not mean that those who act unsociably are likely to act anti-socially. Nevertheless, and this was seen in the groups, the fear is there that unsociable behaviour might lead to anti-social behaviour. This is a tenable proposition, but the connection between unsociable and anti-social behaviour is not capable of ready observation for the simple reason that one is looking at a process and not practice as some kind of 'leaped' performance; that is, that the engagement in sets of behaviour acts as a springboard to another set of behaviour. This can be illustrated by considering whether there is a connection between taking hard drugs and soft drugs.

It may be that taking soft drugs in some clinical physical sense leads to a progression to hard drugs. But it may also be that in taking soft drugs a set of attitudes towards soft drugs that refuses to accept the taking of them as wrong is developed, which promotes attitudes towards drugs in general and fosters a framework for the acceptance of hard drugs.

What we need to consider is whether unsociable behaviour is the demonstration of a set of attitudes that may dispose an individual to include anti-social behaviour in their repertoire of performances. But, if this is the case, what would these attitudes be? The answer, in fact, is to be found within the concerns expressed in the groups towards something such as swearing – a loosening of authority and definitions of correct behaviour that then allows the incorporation of more serious forms of behaviour; that is, anti-social acts.

In any given case one would need to know what the unsociable behaviour represented. If it was no more than adolescent exploration of the bounds of the acceptable, then the unsociable behaviour is likely to be contained at the level of what it is, a disregard for manners as normatively accepted. If, however, it represents an emerging challenge to authority and accepted ways of behaving at a fundamental level, then it is possible, but only as part of an overall development, for it to lead to anti-social behaviour. This is not to say that one has caused the other, but that the acceptance of one provides the territory for the acceptance of the other. We could imagine, for example, that a young man appropriating swearing as a means of demonstrating toughness, begins to be regarded as tough through such appropriations and enjoys the distinction such regard affords, which then results in a repositioning of the self with regard to other acts of toughness, such as violence. In short, the individual enters on a career of toughness where the world of the 'respectable' is no longer valued. A set of values gives a re-evaluation of the world around him or her that includes meanings that were previously absent.

This distinction between anti-social and unsociable behaviour is vital in understanding how people talk about the media, and in what it means for regulation. In terms of an influence on anti-social behaviour then the media falls away when compared to its influence on unsociable behaviour. That is, the media, television in particular, is held responsible for unsociable behaviour – swearing – but not for anti-social behaviour – violence.

As past surveys of the public have shown over the years,[1] both violence and bad language have consistently topped the list of concerns viewers have about the content of television. Both forms of behaviour upset viewers, but in terms of regulating for the possible undesirable (behavioural) effects of television, it is the unsociable conduct, the less serious socially of the behaviours, that requires special attention.

If the participants to the focus groups are correct, then one is faced with the possibility that unsociable behaviour shown by television could, over time, become sociable as it becomes normative.

One can measure the offence given by language and, in principle, measure the effect of mediated language on language as actual behaviour, but that does not have the same power of justification in taking regulatory action as to measure the effect of mediated violence on violence as actual behaviour. In the latter case, because advanced industrial societies are premised on the absence of violence, then 'scientific' pursuit of its eradication would universally be held as a good thing, but in the former case, since there would not be universal agreement that in all situations certain expressive forms are wrong, the 'scientific' pursuit of their eradication would not universally be held as a good thing. What one is left with, therefore, in the realm of un-sociable behaviour, the most readily imitated, is the imposition of values about what is right and wrong when, as repeatedly argued, it is, in the fractured nature of modern societies, hard to appeal to a set of values that embrace all groups. No group holds sway or has moral authority over any other group, and any appeal to standards has the transparency of their source, be this a social class, gender or age group.

Nevertheless, it is the case that 'bad language' on television is widely deplored by British viewers, and so support is given by them to its containment. For example, the Ofcom data shows at the time of the research that majorities of adult viewers in the UK thought there was too much swearing (54%) and violence (56%) on TV. Also, 63% felt that there was too much intrusion into other people's lives by television.[2] But such an empirical fact has an uneasy relationship to the audience in practice. Objection can be modified by the context of usage, either by consideration of the likely audience – for example, children before 9 o'clock – or after 9 o'clock by consideration of the genre or situation within which they are employed. In short, bad language is evaluated and not judged by a set of values that simply prohibits its usage whatever the context. Right and wrong become negotiable by reference to performance and circumstance.

It is this fact alone that makes the application of a code of practice extremely problematic and pushes legislators ever-increasingly down the frantic path laid by the liberal of searching out the empirical audience through research. To be able to make judgements then the liberal legislator, as opposed to the neo-Aristotelian legislator, is required to know the audience's desires and preferences, of what gives offence and what does not give offence. This search for truth is a constant moveable feast befitting the valueless age in which it is practised, while, at the same time, collective assumptions of what is right and wrong do exist as the congealed preferences of how to live. These preferences, however, have little bearing to any moral system that might afford certainty to performance. They offer themselves as an inheritance to be grimly held onto, the force of which is born of popular dismay at current social behaviour and cultural performances.

The adoption of unsociable behaviour is easier to trace to television than anti-social behaviour, but even then the root is not straightforward; rather a tangled mess of interplays in the establishment and presentation of the self. The use of bad language as a routine of speech may simply be a product of the lexical preferences of a particular group, and contained to that group cause offence to no one; indeed, be so natural that the words are not even registered as constituting swear words. Within such groups such words only take on offensive meaning when the deliberate intention is to be abusive. Yet, there can be no doubt, according to those interviewed, that the use of bad language has increased, particularly in the young.

Whether it has actually increased is an open question, but the fact that adults believe it to have done so must mean one of two things; that they have become more sensitive towards certain words and therefore register them more readily when they hear them than in the past, or that words previously prohibited have gained wider circulation. If the latter is the case, and one suspects that it is, then we can consider that what has happened is that swear words are either deliberately employed as a way of marking territory, or that they are assumed to be appropriate for public display. Both are possible, and television may be responsible in some measure.

To mark territory by the use of swearing is to deny the space of others. Used in this sense swearing is a technique for denying the authority of others, in that the user wilfully refuses to recognize that world where swearing is not the norm and, by doing so, through language, makes claims for his or her world having at least equal right of recognition, if not more right of recognition, than the world of others. It is, in an absolute sense, disrespectful. It is as if to say, through verbal encroachment on linguistic territory, that the other is not more important than you are.

The Use of Language

Language as practice does embody lifestyle. The fondness of academics for Latin words is not necessarily because of the lack of suitability of English words, and thus used as an aid to improve communication, but to inflict confusion on an audience who do not have access to an arcane language that is the peculiar preserve of scholars and the older professions. Such use forces recognition of a superior educational status. Karl Marx was particularly fond of doing this when confronted by clever artisans. Given the lack of mastery within Britain of any language other than English, French can easily, and now more commonly the case, be substituted for Latin to serve the purpose of 'intimidation'. French is good for this in that, unlike other European languages, it has the benefit of the distant reminder that it was once the court language. Although the use of Latin, and to a lesser extent French, may force recognition of a superior educational status, it can also make one look very silly. The establishment of status, however, is often about drawing distinctions and not in appearing sensible. If this were not the case, it is hard to imagine how some forms of dress are adopted at all. We will see later how the adoption of clothing styles by the young, of shirt tails, for example, being deliberately worn outside trousers rather than inside the trouser as intended, clearly worried some group participants. It was taken as marking a lack of respect for adult authority. The breaking of sartorial codes, particularly this latter one, was blamed on *Grange Hill*,[3] and carried with it, so far as one man was concerned, all the values that *Grange Hill* enshrined – a lack of respect for traditional authority as represented by teachers and parents.

It would appear, judging by the focus groups' discussions, that bad language has come to flourish in terrains where it was previously absent. It has, in other words, come to the attention of adults in circumstances that they find offensive. It may be that bad language is being used in the functional manner documented; that is, as a juridical device laying down the boundaries of authority to serve notice that respect and homage will no longer be paid to traditional authority. Or it may be that there is an increasing lack of awareness of the social rules governing language, or that new rules have been created by acts of performance that have pushed aside the old rules. If this is the case then it would be seen as perfectly correct to now use bad language within those circles or places where it was once prohibited. The perceived spread of bad language is objected to in real life, as it is objected to on television. The two are held to be related.

Attention has been given to how language can function to provide distinction and establish authority. Firstly, by imposing feelings of inferiority through exclusion of others to the discourse, that the linguistic performance must be learnt and can only be learnt through access to institutions which teach that language and are themselves exclusive – the conferring of social capital through language. Secondly, by causing offence through the use of language to demonstrate a refusal to accept the other as in any way superior, and by extension the cultural world that that person inhabits and represents.

It would seem unlikely in any strong sense that a deliberate confrontational game is at work in the increased visibility of bad language, but something does not have to be deliberate to be effective. The visibility of bad language does in every practical way stand to serve notice that forms of authority have changed, that those groups who convened the rules of correct language are no longer in the ascendancy, and consequently will no longer be accorded the respect associated with status as cemented in language.

To unravel this process would take us into a long tract of cultural history and the subtle shifts of power relationships between groups, but there can be little doubt that the prominence of bad language holds much to the prominence of new status groups that use such language. The use and non-use of bad language can be seen as the battleground of cultural conflict between modernists and traditionalists, which in turn rests on differences in social formations and the status position of those formations.

Although many forms of behaviour are capable of capturing the lifestyle of a group, what is essential, *vis-à-vis* status, is that the behaviour sufficiently differentiates between social groups and is recognized as doing so. For example, if one examines the history of the Temperance Movement in America, then Prohibition is not simply a story about consumption of alcohol, but what that consumption or non-consumption represented in terms of cultural politics and the fate of various social groups within American society. Very briefly, there are two discernible phases in the development of the American Temperance Movement. The first phase was based on the reaction of the old Federalist aristocracy to a loss of power. This loss of power stretched from the social and religious to the economic. Indeed, this group suffered a series of political defeats in the early part of the nineteenth century which saw its grip loosen on both cultural and political control of the country to the increasingly powerful middle classes. If the old Federalist aristocracy could no longer control the political life of the country, it was determined to control the morals of the nation and be accorded the respect owing to moral authority. The second phase of the movement, culminating in Prohibition, represented the efforts of the established urban middle classes to consolidate their respectability through the non-consumption of alcohol and, in doing so, stand in sharp distinction to the lifestyles of the new, and often immigrant, middle classes, as well as other social groups such as the labourer and farmer. (See Gusfield 1972.)

The point about alcohol as a focus of concern was that it encapsulated differing lifestyles. Drinking and non-drinking was more than just a group custom, since it also had a moral connotation associated with a certain lifestyle. The consumption of alcohol shifts prestige from one's ability to produce to one's performance as a consumer, to what Martha Wolfenstein refers to as a 'fun morality' (Wolfenstein 1958). The old middle-class culture was one firmly based on the ethic of work, self-control, planning and industriousness. Abstention was not only essential to such a way of life, but epitomized the very essence of the culture. Counterpoint to this was the impulse gratification of a new, rising middle class, whose ascendancy was characterized by consumption and pleasure, symbolized for the Temperance mind by alcohol.

The abstinence doctrine of the old American middle class was not only embedded in the ascetic character of its culture, but was institutionally preserved as well. It was a mark of note and stood in distinct contrast to the lifestyles of socially inferior groups. However, the rising economic and consequent political power of the new middle classes meant that the prestige of the old class could no longer be taken for granted and had to be demonstrated and established. There is no more profound demonstration of power, prestige and status than to have the capacity to institutionalize one's beliefs within the law of the land. The fact that the enforcement of Prohibition was very patchy mattered nothing, the fact is that the drinker had to recognize the interference in his or her life by a social group and culture, and award it, although admittedly extracted, prestige. With the repeal of the 18th Amendment in 1933 even that was no longer possible, sounding as it did the death knell of one social order and heralding the legitimacy of a new set of social relationships.

If we examine the rise of swearing in this fashion, then offence is at least amenable to some kind of structural understanding and is not seen as simply a question of tastes. Taste must be understood, especially from a position of regulation, like drinking, as representing the norms of particular groups, and the position that they occupy in society. To hear words on television that one objects to, most especially if that service is provided a common levy such as the licence fee, is to witness a rebuttal of the values that one lives by, and the triumph of the values of other groups who enshrine such language in their lifestyle. If that language is then carried by youngsters, it represents a faded power in the generational transmission of one's own culture.

It is not suggested that one can locate swearing in any precise fashion to structural groups in the manner that the consumption of alcohol could in America. Rather, it seems that what has occurred is the ascendancy within our culture of groups and lifestyles that are an anathema to other groups. In short, that there has been a re-allocation of prestige, which in part has been fostered by the media, but which in other ways the media, particularly television, offers itself as no more than a demonstration of such changes. On this last point then what one can say is that if television has not been absolutely formative in fostering change it has at least legitimated the lifestyle of certain new groups through exposure given to them and thus helped to cement their cultural position. In doing so, television has assisted in the spread of forms of expression – swearing – that characterize the manner in which these groups address the world.

Reference has already been made to the idea of a 'fun morality' in which prestige shifts from one's ability to produce to one's ability to consume, and that the former is underpinned by the ethic of work, self-control, planning and industriousness, and the latter more settled around the gratification of impulses. It has within it the idea of pleasure unrelated to any moral purpose.

The rise of consumerism has witnessed whole new industries dedicated to ephemeral spend; to the constant sweeping of the market with new products, each just slightly different from the last, but with sufficient difference to provide novelty of experience through possession. It has brought with it not just the desire of possession of the new, and dissatisfaction with the old, but occupational groups dedicated to the provision of style. What has happened is a relocation of the basis of performance from an appreciation of character to an appreciation of personality; that is, from an appreciation of qualities that are grounded in some set of moral values which the individual might embody, to an appreciation of an individual's ability to capture attention merely by the manner of their presentation. To be noticed is a key component of a consumer culture, but to be noticed not for what one embodies in terms of foundational qualities of the personality that are admired or respected (character), but for what one captures at the moment of appearance through the projection of the self (personality) and is taken as admirable.

If being noticed is vital to consumer culture, to be known by and through one's consumption, then its psychic quality is the admiration of appearances. Thus, consumer culture has brought new figures to the fore of public display that have little to do with settled ways of living, and instead represent commitment only to that which keeps them before the public gaze; that is, the ability to capture attention through outward display.

On the one hand, therefore, consumerism with its frenetic appeal to change – style – has thrown up public performances that must constantly seek to keep up with change itself, and, in doing so, has no appeal to set standards. On the other hand, it has given rise to new forms of expression that owe little to the past, or even to one particular culture. In the pursuit of style that will allow the establishment of presence, nothing is sacred. Other cultures are raided as a means of providing distinction. And this goes for all social classes. Thus, the clothing of black youth of the inner-city slums of America is transported as a style statement, and the signification of difference, by white youth in Britain. And it has been television, cinema and music that have been the carriers of these cultures.

What consumerism has done is unshackle, in part, traditional forms of establishing identity and redistributed it along lines of consumption. It has also thrust to the fore those groups that embody its rationale and the values that go with it, and has done so through the outputs of display available to their command, most principally those medium of entertainment, such as television, that live in constant search for the new. There is, therefore, a new type of individual in popular entertainment that represents nothing other than the fast moving world of consumption that he or she is a part of. To validate one's life through consumption is to live by outward appearance and, in the process, to strip away at the critical faculty of being able to judge the lasting importance of something: the world is tested by appearances without search for what the substance of the appearance might be.

This rise in consumerism represents more than the pursuit of goods, it signals a change in consciousness. It is an empirical question, however, how far and to what extent individuals give meaning to their lives by and through consumption. For our purposes, however, this question can remain at the theoretical level, apart from noting that the possession of goods and the transferring of those goods to statements about the self has gone on, and at its furthest reaches can be witnessed as life lived as style. What this means is that there has been an undermining of traditional authority structures in terms of how individuals, but particularly the young, draw support for definitions of who they are. If life becomes style, then not to be stylish is not to be valued, nor respect given to the values of those who do not live by style. This gives rise to particular problems for those, such as teachers, engaged in the transmission of values. It can also produce the sight of teachers adopting the styles of those who are valued in the attempt to engage with their charges. Dress becomes more than a sartorial question, it becomes an educational issue.

If we return to television, then what this means is that a cultural space is created loaded with more than straightforward narrative, but one which is to be raided for style – of dress, manner and speech. There is nothing new in this, especially among the young, since youth is a time of establishing identity, and one way of establishing identity is through a separateness from the parental world. Yet, the advance of consumerism has put a premium on establishing that identity through the commoditization of the personality; that is, through the collected meanings that have become attached to display. These meanings are made in the practice of daily life, but the raw material can be drawn from any world – the borrowing of the street styles of black America by young Britons.

This raiding of styles, made possible on a grand scale by the media, has meant a loosening of local authority in the governance of manners. The dismay of the old at the manners of the young is nothing new, indeed is chronicled in Chaucer, but what we witnessed in the focus groups differed in more than just degree from age-old complaints concerning the lack of respect by youth for their elders, it involved an objection to the models that the young were basing their manners on.

Swearing, to take our original discussion point, might be seen as part of the rebelliousness associated with growing up, the testing of the tolerance of the surrounding world in order to establish the parameters of the permissible, but it might also be seen as the establishment of a new code of conduct that needs no permission because it is seen as right. That is what worried parents, and they rounded on television for providing the belief that swearing was right, that it had a natural place in language. Parents, along with other moral authorities, had lost local control.

Again, there is nothing new to this. From the time of the first picture houses the young had the opportunity to adopt the styles of figures seen on the screen, and to include the performances witnessed on the screen in their own play. But what has altered is not just screen content, but the space for adoption of style opened up by the pursuit of style. The celebration of style, furthermore, that is part of consumerism, is not restricted to any one aspect of life, but, as a general movement, invests performance. Thus, what one has is a drawing into mediated culture of the portrayal of groups who themselves have deliberately created styles as marks of distinction, which are then carried forward on screen to become the material for stylistic raids. It is not art mirroring life or life mirroring art, but a disposition that has collapsed the boundaries between the authentic and the false. That is, that authentic expressions of life drawn from a particular cultural setting become the base of media portrayal, which are then borrowed and, even though now false, not only become interwoven into the cultures of their non-original setting but also reworked in authentic fashion to carry statements about the holder. This borrowing is made possible, and is in its form new, because of the move away from production as an organizing point of experience to consumption.

What this has meant in practice is that all kinds of lifestyles have been brought forward as possibly valid ways of living. There is no moral judgement. Style is its own defender and does not need validation by appeals to community authority because it works at an individual level. Although style is not an individual creation, it is individual in the sense of time and space in that the presenter offers themselves at the psychic level either to imagined communities or communities that are not necessarily local; that is, to others that wish to present themselves in similar manner. But something such as swearing as style does require local support.

The general democratizing of social life, commented upon earlier, whereby the right of representation has brought minority groups into the studio discussion programme, for example, has also made practically any group, or sub-culture, the rightful subject of dramatic attention. What this has meant is that it is not simply that groups have appeared which might provide the basis for a raid on style in the sense of dress, but equally for a raid on their manners.

The term 'manners' is here meant to denote the ways in which individuals signify themselves through their expressive acts. These ways will, of course, include dress but, also, and more important in the present context, language. It also includes attitudes and not just attitudes as expressed through language, but attitudes expressed by deportment. Indeed, for those individuals living in cultures that place high store on style as deliberate statement, then the presentation of the self is part of a carefully worked-out and practised whole, each part of expression must support the central statement. Thus, language, clothes, personal possessions, consumption of types of alcohol, manner of walk and stance and so on, all come together to draw the meanings from each other to present a collective front in the provision of identity. Worked on to this level then style of this nature becomes a political statement drawing a clear distinction of who one is and who one is not, with the implicit demand that rights be accorded to the persona presented.

The opening up of social groupings for portrayal by both television and cinema has meant the display of cultures, which includes manners that, if transferred as practice to other cultures, sit uneasily with existing forms of expression and can easily give rise to offence. Of course, the transference of any cultural expression to another culture runs the risk of being seen as odd, but does not necessarily give rise to offence. The fact is that television and cinema have imported lifestyles that include swearing as a natural part of their language, or figures from occupational cultures that, whilst swearing is not a part of occupational procedure, have an acceptance that swearing will be used on occasion for persuasive effect. In short, much of the adult world is seen to swear. But it is to cultural groups which embody swearing as part of a style statement that we must turn for confirmation of the threat to local control over manners.

To adopt a style of dress from one culture represents more than approval for the way in which such individuals dress. It also signifies approval of the meanings that that dress signifies. The street clothes of black youths in the inner-city slums of America, although no doubt possessing meanings internal to style as fashion, carry a further meaning, and that is defiance of the values and norms of the white dominant society. With that statement go other statements and manners, not all of which are racial but nevertheless relate to the circumstances of life in an inner-city slum. The central statement of these manners is one that is functional for survival; namely, toughness.

The full package of all the manners that designate toughness need not detain us. But part of the public display of toughness involves breaking the rules of politeness, the presenting of the self as uncivilized and, therefore, dangerous. An obvious way of breaking the rules of politeness is the refusal to accept the conventions of language that have been created to facilitate non-aggressive exchange. One of these conventions is not to use words that have been classified through common consensus as offensive, and these, almost universally, have come to be words that have a sexual reference or sometimes a religious reference.

If swear words have come in some cultures to form a frequent part of naturally occurring language, then their offensive nature is likely to be less than in those cultures where they are not commonly used, but they never lose their power to offend if used with precision. In other words, swearing always has the power to denote toughness because it is never fully incorporated into the rules of exchange. More important, however, is that no matter how much swear words may be accepted in specific cultural settings, they are never sanctioned by official or dominant culture. But what has happened is that the portrayal of cultures, particularly in film, that, as a matter of course, use this form of expression, means that the language has been given a visibility hitherto hidden. More than that, it has brought such language into the mainstream of cultural display.

To buy the symbols of a culture is in a sense to buy into the values of that culture. However, the acquisition of clothes that in their original setting signalled a defiance of dominant white values and norms, cannot function in the same way in a society that is not organized along ethnic lines. Nevertheless, even though the full meaning of the clothes cannot be transposed they can, through association of what they signify at a general level, a defiance of authority, be taken up to serve a somewhat similar purpose as they did in the culture from which they were grafted. Indeed, the adoption of a style of dress in the manner described here implicitly involves an admiration for the culture from which they came, or, rather, admiration for some aspects of that culture, since one might hold the culture, in general, or its occupants, in low regard. It might simply be that it is the toughness of American street culture that is admired and nothing more.

If style, in the terms of clothes, is borrowed, and the above is only introduced for illustrative purpose, then so too can language as a signifier of a style. If clothes are borrowed that signify streetwise toughness, it is hardly likely that other aspects, such as swearing that is part of the combined package of the presentation of the self as tough, will not be taken up. This is not to suggest that those who might adopt street tough clothes did not exercise a vocabulary frequented by swear words before exposure to cultures where swearing was the norm. But it is to suggest, however, that the use of swear words is given credibility and legitimization through association with groups that are taken as representative of an admired style, and also that other manners encrusted with the verbal expressions might well become incorporated as a new presentation of the self.

At no point are we suggesting that culture is created by simple mimicry. Culture is the creation of lived experience, but symbolic representations of culture feed into, and give expression to, lived culture. What the rise of consumerism has meant is that localized culture – the lived experience – now has a whole variety of forms, by which to represent its inner meaning as outward display, that owe little to the origins of their production and owe little to the localized culture. This is not to argue some post-modernist thesis here that all is appearance, and deny the importance of the material fact of social life, but to say that the expressive forms of mediated culture have allowed a reformulating of localized expression, and that some already existing facets of localized culture/experiences have been encouraged at the expense of others.

To those who exist in worlds where to talk is to swear, even to the point of using swear words to hyphenate nouns, then the portrayal by the media of individuals and groups who swear, will, apart from perhaps picking up a few novelties of expression, lead to no change. But many people use swear words on occasion, and it is these non-habitual uses of swearing that must form the focus of our attention.

The coarsening of everyday life by the unsociable act of swearing was something that bothered and upset people in the focus groups. Although not laying all the blame on television for such behaviour they nevertheless wished to place it firmly in the dock. The quantitative survey results discussed later on also show that television was perceived as an influence on children swearing. The suggestion is that parts of expression that have previously been prohibited, or kept for special occasions, have been encouraged by finding support from the media. That is, that the private realms of those groups and individuals who swear as a routine part of speech have been put on public display through the attention given to them by film and television. Such portrayals, furthermore, often have a documentary realism to them: plot gives way to the capture of situation. Such portrayals have assisted in providing approval to those words that were once 'secret', used only in trusted situations or among a particular language community, and, in doing so, offer the suggestion that they might be suitable for more general usage.

The suggestion here is not that of copying, that is, some imitative effect, but of the reinforcement of words through the legitimization provided by familiarity of usage and source of deployment. By source of deployment is meant both the medium of delivery and authority of those delivering the speech. In the first instance then to have private words become public property through television is part and parcel of the creation of a public culture. Such words are given 'official' blessing, or at least begin to lose outright opprobrium. In the second instance, and here we return to the question of style, is that such words become valuable possessions through association with their authors and come to be used to make statements about the self. This might appear that we are suggesting an imitative effect. The notion of direct imitation, however, is too crude to capture the complexities of media influence.

The individual is not passive. All behaviour is rule-governed, and that includes language, but individuals themselves are part of the rule-generating game and are, thus, deeply implicated in the construction of the influences that the media have. Indeed, to appreciate mediated forms of expression and incorporate them into one's own speech is an interpretative act of some significance. Words have to possess some relevance and be made to work in the way the individual wishes. For example, hearing a small child use a swear word can produce shock and even amusement in the adult listener for the reason that the word cannot possibly work for such a young person, in that the circumstances of a child's life is not one in which the word can be put to the purpose it was created for. The rules governing the engagement of the young child with the external world, the sets of circumstances that structure the child's existence, not least of which is the total dependency on adults, are not those which can be given expression by such language – the rules will not allow it. And here we do not mean moral rules, in the sense of sanctions on expression, but the sheer incapacity for the child's world and experiences of it to be rendered intelligible by such words.

The rules of behaviour are in permanent flux, but sufficiently set for all practical purposes at any point in time for performance in the world to take place so that the individual can, in a sense, know 'the other'. However, as indicated in the discussion of style and what style can mean in terms of the presentation of the self and the role that style has come to occupy in a consumer society, mediated lifestyles can be recreated in the lives of viewers should such lifestyles say something to them. To use our past example of the adoption by British youth of the street look of black inner-city American youth, then such adoption does not represent some fantasy claim upon their life, but the reworking of the meaning of the clothes in a manner appropriate to their own definitions of themselves and then projecting those means through the style of the other. Thus, if to be a 'hard man' can be captured by the style of a 'hard culture', then that style might well be adopted. Equally, if individuals wish to dissociate themselves from normative ideas of correctness, such styles might also be adopted. The meanings of such presentations can only be discovered by the examination of both cultures: what the nature of the portrayed culture is, what the nature of the host culture is, what meanings are given by the adopter of a style to his own culture, the meanings they ascribe to the viewed culture, and, finally, an examination of what is being bridged by the adoption of styles.

All kinds of styles can enter the life of viewers in this way and, indeed, so can styles of expression. Some can be very innocuous. New words and terms, such as 'sleepover', 'grounded', 'hang-out', decorate the vocabulary of children because they serve to express the circumstances of their lives. Although the adoption of words and terms such as these may be annoying to some adults, they do not cause offence. It is the perceived rise of swearing that gives offence, although the adoption process is somewhat the same in each case.

It has been argued that what mediated swearing has done is to assist the more common usage of words that were already in use, but which previously tended to be restricted to particular language communities. Certain previously prohibited words have been legitimated through repetitive use on screen. It is not simply, however, the fact that the unfamiliar has been given familiarity that has helped the legitimization process, but that such words, due to the public nature of television, have been given official sanction. And this is so despite the increasing fragmentation of the audience. Television for the moment acts as a single language community. There are exceptions, as, indeed, regulators recognize in their adjudications of offence; for example, certain programmes on Channel Four are held to address specific taste communities and this is taken into account in determining the taste or decency of a programme.

What needs to be considered, however, is not simply the sanctioning of language, or the 'demystifying' of certain words through repetitive use, but, as with style in general, what it is that makes these words attractive. For that one must examine the reasons for the ease with which they enter a culture that has previously resisted their incorporation as correct speech. It may signal two things: one, a loosening of traditional authority so that users no longer pay it respect, and therefore feel free to use such language, or two, that the language is used to confront traditional authority by refusing to pay it respect through conforming to its strictures.

In discussing the Temperance Movement in America it was stated that many forms of behaviour are capable of capturing the lifestyle of a group, and that the consumption and non-consumption of alcohol did just that. What was being played out during the Temperance years leading to Prohibition was status politics. It was noted that, in the second phase of the movement, Prohibition was the attempt by the old native middle classes to impose its values on the rising new commercial middle classes who threatened the former's political power. The fight to control the drinking of others was symbolic political struggle. However, in using the Temperance Movement to address the question of swearing, it was not suggested that one could locate swearing in any precise fashion to structural groups in the manner that the consumption of alcohol could be in America, but it was suggested that what has occurred is the ascendancy within our culture of groups and lifestyles that are an anathema to other groups, and that swearing has formed the battle site of the relocation of prestige. In other words, a process of cultural restructuring has occurred that has disadvantaged certain social groups in the claim to have their culture represented, made manifest by the utterances of language they themselves would not use, or, if they did, would do so only to discrete audiences.

What has happened is the opening up for inspection of a whole variety of lifestyles, at an almost documentary level, that has privileged forms of expression of groups that hitherto would not have had a public platform. We can in a sense take this back to the 1960s and the Greene years, and concur with Mary Whitehouse that a set of values was appearing in broadcasting that no longer represented a distinct cultural group, but which instead sought to portray the plurality of social life and, in doing so, did not favour a particular definition of culture. Sir Hugh Greene may have been the individual agent of change, but, as already pointed out, the changes to broadcasting were part of a general transformation in British social life. Whitehouse was correct, the removal from Broadcasting of a particular moral ethos – neo-Aristotelian – to be replaced by a recognition of a plurality of rights where none held superior claim over the other – liberal – has led to the present-day situation of the portrayal of groups whose lifestyle is characterized by swearing. It has also led to the appearance of individuals who use such language and have a reduced inhibition in employing it when broadcasting. The more innocuous use of such language finds ready appearance in popular music radio stations, often, it must be admitted, in ludic manner. Indeed, the social rise of the disk jockey, his or her prominence in popular culture, is significant of the processes being discussed. They bring with them not just music, but the culture from which that music emanates.

Popular music, which for ease of description may be placed under the rubric of rock music,[4] has always resisted incorporation into the respectable, or at least those segments of the music that represent in some way or other the non-powerful in society. It is not meant to speak for, or to, social order, either in its harmonic arrangement or its inner core of meaning. Neither are its representatives supposed to represent respectability, since to do so robs the music of the lifestyle statement it is often supposedly making. What is not understood is rarely appreciated, and lack of exposure to such music by adults can in part account for their revulsion at its sound, but there is also a social objection to that which it represents, symbolically captured by the lifestyle, language and behaviour of the representatives of the music. Nor is wealth, usually a calming influence on behaviour through the incorporation into the respectable, seen to stand in the way of the achievement of unruliness; indeed, is used to support it with extravagant indulgence. Its leading, and often extremely rich, figures often in their lifestyle demonstrating a contempt for restraint.

Popular music, or the element referred to above, will always be looked down upon by those that exist in an ordered cultural world, especially if order is the basis for its foundation, success and survival. A culture that is based on the ethic of work, self-control, planning and industriousness, is not one to enjoy or applaud the non-tidy world of the merchants of rock. That is, it is produced, in its most raw form, and especially so historically, by those at the margins of society and who have little investment, through exclusion, in its continuation. Leaving absolute structural groups aside, it is not surprising that youth, as a transitional stage, both locationally and emotionally, should be drawn to support such music. Such music is also sexual, and although accounting for its appeal among a particular age group – it expresses their own sexuality – offers, what all sex threatens, the sublimation of reason to passion. Order cannot exist without reason, and 'rock' music is disrespectful of order. It has never been brought totally under the control of the music or culture industry, try as it might. If it has escaped inclusion into the respectable because of the grounds of its practice in excluded groups, then it is useful to see swearing in a similar manner. Swearing, like music, represents more than just a preferred form of speech. It represents a preferred universe of meaning.

Swearing can present itself as a challenge to order, at least in contemporary society, by association with low-economic social groups. This is particularly so for those on the fringes of society for whom attention to language as a matter of propriety serves no practical advantage. Their condition will not be altered by gaining the approval of those in superior social position.

New Social Groups

Swearing, in contemporary society, does challenge the principle components of an ordered life. The non-use of swear words is bourgeois, in that bourgeois society was structured on regulation and conformity. The very success of bourgeois society was the creation of ordered economic order and financial exchange, which both presumed and created a moral order based on the control of expression. And these forms leached down to orders other than the bourgeois itself in the instruction of manners. Non-swearing is a heritage, but one which still has a practical life.

What has changed, however, is that although those in very low socio-economic status swore, and in doing so offered a sure sign that they stood outside the control of bourgeois or respectable societies, there are now groups that swear who are very much part and parcel of economic performance; namely, those in creative occupations where conformity is neither demanded nor functional. That is, those individuals, and the artistic community would perhaps be the best example, who cannot perform by the standardization of expression are likely to pay scant attention to the conventions of language drawn from an ordered world.

Creativity, although it might have its own rules, and cannot proceed without the organization of its own forms, is crushed by the conformities to the rules of others. This might manifest itself in normatively breaking the rules of consumption, sex or language, but it does not necessarily have to. All it means is that individuals who live by artistic creativity have a greater option to do so than those in other sectors of production. Indeed, the closer to 'pure art' then the greater the need for freedom of expression. However, to break with convention in one sector of one's life, namely production, the more likely it is to break with convention in other sectors of one's life. On such a basis, bohemian culture is born, indeed, bohemian culture as an identifiable lifestyle and historical placement took its shape only by reference to the conformity of bourgeois culture. For the 'pure artist' then the investment of the personality in production is so high that it is not useful to speak of a separation between productive life and life in general, and one might expect the breaking of conventions of correctness to be a mark of his or her life.

The 'pure artist' is not an occupational group of much presence, but there has increasingly flourished groups which, while not artists in the sense already used, nevertheless, and to a greater and lesser degree, have proximity to them in terms of creativity. That is, they work with symbolic representations of the world. Within this category would include all those who work within television itself, producers, writers, directors and even managers. Taken as a whole, the communications industry, and here one includes advertising agencies, market research companies, graphic artists, public relation firms and so on, is an essential part of a modern economy.

What has occurred is that a whole stratum of individuals has come into being that, more so than ever in the past, exists by the creation and manipulation of symbols. It was mentioned in discussing the development of industrialization that its need for rational organization gave rise to new forms of consciousness that excluded the mystical from an understanding of the world. The development of the communications industry, however, has produced individuals whose job now is to provide interpretative understanding, indeed, create the symbols by which we understand the world, and they do so on an industrial scale. Whether the world makes any sense by this effort is by the by, but what it has meant is that 'industrial' life is now distinguished by the creation of meaning as deliberate activity. It might be expected, as with the 'pure artist', that people in these occupations, who are employed for their 'artistic' creativity where the breaking of convention is rewarded, would not break, in their social lives, the conventions of language.

Swearing is common among such middle-class groups, the 'new artists', and is often used, as befitting groups who live by symbolic expression, with great skill and communicative richness. Such language is used inside the office and outside the office. Given their erstwhile glamorous life, or a life that can easily be ported as glamorous and dramatic, especially the lives of media personnel, they frequently form the subject of dramatic portrayal by the cinema and television. They could hardly, furthermore, given their sheer presence as a workforce and place in contemporary cultural life, be excluded from representation in observations on the modern world. What this has meant is that once more, but from a different direction, swearing as a natural part of language has been given a visibility it did not have. One might even argue that given the social status of such individuals they assist in legitimating swearing in a way that lower socio-economic groups, or those marginal to society, can not.

We have said that the groups that embody swearing can not, unlike the groups identified in the Temperance Movement, be given precise structural location, although clearly we have attempted to do so to some extent by the locating of them within the industrial sector of the new communication industries. Swearing is nothing new and workers in the old sectors of industrial production, the building trades and the extraction industries can certainly be associated with such language – swearing is not associated with those working within the older professions or in commerce and banking.

The fact that working-class speech was interspersed with swear words matters nothing for our central argument or the public rise of swearing. The 'vulgarity' of the speech of the traditional working class, although not universal within that class, occurred within a contained place both in work and leisure. It was a specific language community wherein such speech could flourish unhindered even by considerations of gender. The occupations were male proscribed and workingmen's clubs, as their name suggests, prohibited women or allowed entry only on designated nights or special occasions. Swearing as part of language was thus recognized and even institutionalized. Many public houses, for example, had rooms dedicated for men only, so that men could feel free to express without inhibition in similar manner to their enclosed regime of work. The 'new artists' have no such inhibitions about swearing, and theirs is not a gendered exclusive world. In both work and leisure there is a democratic meeting of the sexes, and a democratic use of swear words, although some particular words may still be ring-fenced as inappropriate for open use.

Although one might see these 'new artists' as structural groups, the new middle classes located in those sectors of the economy that demand a high level of artistic creative thought and expression, it is perhaps best to see them as cultural groups which have loose associations to each other. That is, they are more identifiable by a shared lifestyle than any precise shared position in the economy; although clearly the similarity of their lifestyle is related to them having a sufficiently related structural position to make this possible. However, financial reward among the 'new artists' is often very unevenly distributed to make material lifestyle also somewhat uneven. Yet there is a shared cultural orientation and a shared set of values that makes each, even at the material level of possessions, a reflection of the other. They are spoken to and for by the same designs. The difference being that some of the 'new artists' may buy 'the design' made-to-measure, while others buy off-the-shelf.

Such groups have given semi-respectability to swear words through their command of the 'artistic' heights of the economy. They are, furthermore, because of their creative imaginations, the shock troops of the fashion sectors of the consumer society. They are style leaders, and who, as part of style, include swear words as an adornment to language. But it is the rise of these 'cultural groups', and their population of the media itself, that has given rise to the issue of language as forming the battle lines of cultural dispute. On the one hand, as producers of dramatic representations of life, they have a high tolerance to swearing and therefore find little wrong, in terms of appeal to their own sensibilities, of including such expressions in their products – although mindful of the audience – and at another level have come to form rightful groups for dramatic portrayal. They have become key representatives of modern society.

Unlike the status politics of the Temperance Movement there is no structural clash between these groups and others (there does not exist a firm socio-political base of an easily identifiable nature), but there nevertheless exists a clash of cultures which can be identified as having its roots in economic reorganization and re-allocation of prestige that such reorganization has brought about. Traditional values drawn from a world of production have given way to modernist values based on consumption, and, in particular of late, to the ascendancy of values belonging to those groups who live by communication. Swearing in British contemporary culture, like alcohol in past American culture, can be seen as an organizing point for protest. Swearing is taken by the traditional holders of authority on manners as symbolically representing the state of the modern world; that is, a world that has become coarsened and debased. Language then is taken as a statement of moral decline, and as a statement about the decline in respect for authority. However, the idea of authority necessarily entails ideas of who the authority holders are, and in that direction, as we have endeavoured to show, it is not so much a decline in respect for authority that has been witnessed, but a decline in respect for those who traditionally have held authority, both culturally and personally.

Notes

1. For example, the annual surveys formerly run by the Broadcasting Standards Council and the Independent Television Commission and now run by Ofcom. See Svennevig (1998) for more detailed analysis of these surveys.
2. Source: Ofcom, 2004, The Communications Market 2004 – Television. Appendix: *The Public's View* Survey Results, Table 32 (p. 12).
3. *Grange Hill* is a BBC drama series designed for older children, set in a secondary school in the UK. It has run since 1978.
4. Popular music, in its general and older sense, is a very broad umbrella term and illustrates the difficulty in the definition and labelling of music categories. However, for our descriptive purpose, the term 'popular music' was created as a synonym of 'rock-n-roll' during the birth of the rock era in the 1950s in order to separate the then-new and controversial form of music from that which had come before it.

Moral Decline and the Rights of the Individual

4a What Constitutes Social and Anti-Social Behaviour? Views of Authority – Voices from Focus Groups

This chapter begins by examining the public's thinking about social causation. Do people consider causes of crime, for example, to be rooted in material factors such as unemployment and poverty or in failure in moral upbringing? Having examined this, the chapter explores the role that people consider television plays in creating anti-social and unsociable behaviour. The chapter then examines issues of authority – authority within the family, and state- sanctioned authority and the part it plays in social control. This extends to how people view the regulation of culture and the limits of regulation. The chapter ends by an examination of the right of the media to intrude into people's private lives, and who and in what circumstances might individuals expect privacy to be protected.

The distinction made in Chapter 3 between unsociable behaviour and anti-social behaviour is useful in assessing the possible social influences of the media. Unsociable behaviour was categorized as that behaviour which stood not as a threat to a community, but nevertheless broke rules governing social exchange. Swearing was held to fall into the category of unsociable behaviour rather than anti-social behaviour.

Effort was made to account for the increased public visibility afforded to swearing by reference to general cultural shifts. Although we held that these changes accounted for the acceptance by the media of swearing, the idea of direct copying of swearing by people following exposure to mediated swearing was abandoned in favour of a framework of analysis that tried to place swearing in the context of people's actual lives. At one level, we argued, swear words might be carried into everyday usage by their sheer use by the media so that they come to be seen as an acceptable part of speech. It was also argued, however, that swear words might be given legitimation through association with the individuals who employ such words. It was argued that a whole new stratum of people – the 'new artists' – has emerged where swear words are a common part of their everyday speech. However, in the case of young people, it was argued that it was much more likely that the acceptability of such speech derives support not from its use on screen by the 'new artists', but from the attachment of such language to marginal groups in society, or from individuals, such as law enforcement and associated agents, that deal with such groups. The reason for this is that the use of swear words by these groups focuses on power; that is, bad language is used to handle hostile situations. It has, therefore, a sense of assertiveness about it that is attractive to certain youths. When used by the 'new artists' bad language is merely the extension of an already rich descriptive vocabulary.

Swear words when used by marginal groups function as the organization of street culture. What this in effect means is that such language has a relatively easy passage into the language of youths who might wish to construct similar meanings to their own lives to those that have been witnessed on screen. That is, they represent proximate meaning for their own life as they did for the lives of those within the original culture from which they were drawn. Used by marginal groups, swearing often represents assertiveness through appearing tough. The striking of 'hard man' poses was something that worried some parents, as we shall see later.

There is little to be said from effects studies on this question that has not been said before. While not agreeing with the simple effects model of mediated behaviour, we would consider that behaviour can be carried across from the media to social life, but whether it is or not depends on social life itself, and the nature of the behaviour to be carried across. Violence has its base in social conditions and in personality. Although there is no convincing argument that violent behaviour is instigated by the media in the sense of copied behaviour, film violence may nevertheless assist the legitimation of existing violent behaviour. Screen violence may assist in supporting definitions of the self as tough in communities where toughness is an appreciated trait. The argument being made is that the primary influences on the development of attitudes and personality are given assistance by media portrayals of violence through non-contradiction of those violent features of the individual. For the individual already given to violent behaviour, then, the media can be seen, in the way that it might position him or her in relation to violence, to be a secondary influence.

Anti-social behaviour, as its name suggests, is behaviour against society (community), but it is also behaviour that is gained in society. The participants to our focus groups understood this, and drew a distinction between anti-social and unsociable behaviour. The two forms of behaviour involve different levels of moral grammar. The latter is more open to modification because the moral grammar governing performance is of a lower order. What is being ruled on are manners, the superficialities of behaviour. Manners, furthermore, are volatile to circumstance. That is, as ways of regulating exchange they need to change and adapt to local conditions. Anti-social behaviour, on the other hand, has a stubborn brutality to it. It is formed on the basis of deep experiences, and thus tends to be a permanent feature of the individual.

Explanations for Crime

If we now move to the statements made by the focus groups, and return to the 18 to 24-year-old women from London who were talking about their experience of violence, what we see is an appreciation of how the social world operates. In terms of violent criminal behaviour, the media are not seen as an important source of influence. These people are not alone in their view, as the national survey clearly showed – very few people considered the influence of television as a major cause of violent crime. They do this because, as previously commented, to live in this world is to think about it and offer sociological explanations of causation. This is not to say that an explanation that privileged the media would not, of itself, count as sociological. This is because, in examining daily existence, most people have a great deal of difficulty, at both a theoretical and empirical level, in visualizing how the media can be responsible for that which they witness in terms of anti-social behaviour as opposed to unsociable behaviour. They cannot imagine themselves influenced in such a way and, thus, with some exceptions, such as in the case of children and the mentally unbalanced, they cannot imagine other people being influenced in such a way. The importance of this in terms of regulation is that if people do not establish a link between the media and behaviour then this necessarily structures their positions on regulation.

The above women, after providing their own experiences of crime, were asked what they thought was responsible for the rise in crime. The main, and most immediate, response was 'drugs': 'Drugs, that's the main one I would have thought'. So immediate was this response that the group was questioned as to whether or not they had seen a documentary programme the previous night about heroin users in the City of Leeds. The programme linked drugs with a rise in theft as a consequence of the addicts' need for money to support their habit. Not all the women had seen it. Those who had viewed the programme were asked if they considered that their response to the cause of crime had been influenced by the programme. They considered that they would have offered drugs as a major reason for the rise in crime without watching the programme. 'They need the money to feed their hit – it's mainly mugging and burglary'. Another woman responded, 'Generally it's young people under 25 who perpetuate most of the crimes I would have thought'. This was picked up by another member: 'A lot of young people not having anything to fill their time. If they're not employed they need money to enable them to go to clubs. Boredom …greed'. Commenting on this last statement, someone said, 'It's the easy way, isn't it, rather than earning money'. Someone else in the group gave 'unemployment'.

These comments were made by women without children aged 18–24. Yet, the comments made by older women with children were similar. Their experience of crime was not as first-hand as that of the younger women. It was mainly other members of their family who had direct experience of crime. For example, when we asked the women living in Walsall, aged under 55, if they had had experience of crime they said they had, but when asked what the crimes were, practically all the crimes related to events occurring to their children or to their husbands. Thus, when asked had they experienced crime, the replies were: 'My son had his bike stolen'. 'My son had his car broken into'. Such comments were interwoven with statements of concern about the general dangers of modern life: 'I'm very concerned about crime, especially when you've got children. I think it's a terrible world we're bringing them up in. These days everything is matter of fact – drugs, bad language'.

It is interesting here that bad language is rolled into a discussion of crime when swearing itself is not a crime unless it is likely to lead to some breach of the peace. What this signifies, as discussed in Chapter 3, is that bad language is taken as a metaphor for social malaise. It has come to symbolically represent all that which is seen as wrong with the modern world. And there was, according to these women, much to object to and worry about. For example, one of the women volunteered; *'It's not just burglaries at home – they're taking things off them in the street. You never heard of that ten years ago'*. Ten years is not long history. Her statement shows a picture of people caught in the grip of rapid change, which they feel helpless to confront and stand against. To support the above woman's statement, another member added the information: *'My son had his trainers taken off him'*, to which someone else said, *'Children do things today that we'd never heard of when we were their age. You've got to watch them all the time – then you're accused of not letting go and not giving them their freedom'*.

We will return later to this idea of how current social life has led to an imprisonment of children in a protective cocoon. Indeed, it is a classic case of where a subjective state, fear of crime, has led to an objective state, changes in how parents raise their children. Although fear of crime may be out of all proportion to the level of actual crime and the statistical possibility of being a victim of crime, we encountered sufficient personal experience of crime to suggest that apprehension was a reasonable response to the actuality of the real world. What we did find was that what might be taken as minor events were rolled out to be taken as warnings that very serious things might happen to them. This was particularly so when parents reflected on the safety of their children. We will see evidence later of this billowing of fear, but there was little doubt in talking with these women that the significance of these events was not contained within the events themselves. The imagination spiralled the danger of any single act. As one member of this group related: *'There was a gang of kids kicking my husband's car a couple of weeks ago – one of them was only 8, she was using abusive language as well'*. When asked what did her husband do, she replied: *'Well, obviously he told them to leave the car alone, and we got in and drove home from the pub. Then he walked back to the pub and they were there doing it to everybody's car. So he went to the police and told them'*. Asked how the police responded, she replied, *'they did nothing'*, and then added, *'I even phoned 999 just in case they'd got knives'*.

What we witness here is unsociable behaviour (bad language) accompanied by anti-social behaviour (violence against property). What we also witness is a framework of perception of contemporary society that allowed a particular act, damage to a car, to be conflated with more serious acts, the carrying of knives, to then make her fear that her husband might be stabbed. This spiralling of consequences whereby specific acts are taken as signifiers that more serious possible acts might occur, shows the uncertainty with which people now confront the world. Maybe it was ever thus, but not on the evidence of oral history gained from talking with our respondents. But we will return to that shortly.

There is little point in documenting similar comments made in the other groups. The main point to extract is that whether one had experience of crime at first-hand, or vicarious experience of crime, the media was not held as primarily responsible for anti-social acts. They were held, however, to be responsible for unsociable acts.

The discussion with the young women took place, as noted, the evening following the documentary in which crime was linked with drug-taking. Several police officers interviewed for the programme made this connection, and made it convincingly. The reason why these women offered drugs as an explanation for the rise in crime may have been as a direct result of this programme, even though the woman refuted this. It is difficult to say. But the fact is, whether or not they were influenced by the programme, they did not consider that watching crime on television influenced real-life crime. In other words, it is one thing to be influenced in one's knowledge about crime, but another thing altogether to be influenced by mediated crime and then go and commit a crime.

In giving accounts of the causation of crime what these women did was draw upon their own direct experience of the world, and their theoretical understanding, which when allied together was used to judge the plausibility of reasons given for the existence of crime. In the circulation of ideas about the causes of crime, television as a source of its presence was not one that found ready favour. Or at least if it was accepted as a cause of crime, this was circumscribed by other claims of causation of more explanatory power.

Following the comment already quoted, that theft was an easy way of people obtaining money, it was put to the whole group: *'But lots of people don't have much money, do you think there is anything else behind it?'* The responses given were a far cry from the imitative effects model of television: *'The way they were brought up as well. If their parents or brothers are into it they become influenced by them'.* Here there is a recognition of the power of the 'real' world to shape who and what we are. Personal influences were seen as much stronger than mediated influences in determining behaviour.

One of the other participants in this group said: *'It amazes me how these people think they have the right to go into your house and take things. Whereas people who go out to work save and buy something, other people feel they have the right to go in and take it'.* Her indignation at people presuming they have a right to other people's property was hard to escape, but we asked her, *'do you think they think they have the right to take your property?'* to which she replied: *'They think you've got the money and you won't miss it'.* This was followed by us asking, *'Does that mean they don't feel guilty?'* She answered: *'No, I don't think they do'.* Her explanation was: *'If they do something and get away with it, then they'll do it again'.* In other words, one of the causes of crime is the lack of development of a moral consciousness within which theft is seen as wrong.

This idea of people repeating behaviour if not corrected quickly moved the discussion into child rearing and ideas of how children are taught right from wrong. We will return to this area later, since it has implications for how people see moral standards, and the part that 'regulation' plays in the management not just of individual behaviour, but the management of the moral cultural ethos of society. For the moment, however, we wish to explore further the reasons people gave for crime.

The London men, aged under 55, saw the world in similar fashion to the young London women. They saw crime as having a structural basis, for example, unemployment. Like the women also, they saw crime as having a moral basis, that is, located in the ways people are socialized into sets of values. When the figures from our national survey were put to them, showing a high level of concern over crime (90% of adults), none claimed to be surprised.[1] When asked why they were not surprised, one man in the group simply said: *'Because we're in a recession, and crime increases in a recession'.* When asked where he had got such information, he replied: *'I must have read it somewhere, but it makes sense'.* What happened here, and is illustrative of the points made earlier about how people establish facts, is that information had been received that was tested against what he knew about the world, knowledge informed both by theory and by experience, before making a judgement as to the plausibility of the claims he had read for the causes of crime. For him, unemployment was a plausible explanation for the cause of crime. Later we shall see this same procedure applied to the causation of violence.

This group was asked, like other groups, whether they had ever been a victim of crime, and what crimes concerned them. The reply from one man was: *'Certain types of crime – theft I would think would concern us most. What you've worked so hard to get you don't want somebody to come along and take it away from you'.* Asked if he had ever been burgled, he answered:

I've been burgled twice. It wasn't the robbery as such – they didn't take that much. It's the fact that you've got to get someone round to fix the back door, take time off work for the insurance assessors to come round – its all the inconvenience of it rather than the actual theft itself. If you're insured you don't worry about that so much. I just felt angry at the inconvenience.

There is a clear difference in this man's reply from the response the young woman gave, who, having been burgled, did not like to remain at home at night on her own. The possibility that burglary might be accompanied by sexual assault is a fear that men do not carry. To see burglary, however, as just an inconvenience is interesting, especially his comments relating to insurance. It is as if actuarial science has smothered moral meaning: repeat exposure to burglary normalized the act so that the wrongness of it was transformed to a question of accountancy. Another man in the group commented:

I think people have adjusted to the level of crime over the years. I know lots of people who've been burgled. I've been burgled; my car's been done. The more it happens the more you get used to it. Years ago it was a shock to hear of someone being burgled. Now it's almost commonplace.

We wondered if these men considered that the high rate of crime experienced by them owed something to living in a large capital city. They did not think so. They refused to think in terms of specific locations when discussing crime because they considered crime to have causal underpinnings which affected the whole of Britain, principally unemployment. To the question concerning the relationship between crime and living in London, one man said: *'It's a sign of the times. It's a sign of what this government's done to the country'.* Asked if he really blamed the government, he replied: *'I think some of their policies are to blame for it, yes'.* We were back onto unemployment and its relationship to crime. The discussion that followed, however, raised the question of the nature of human behaviour. On the one hand what was offered was a rather mechanistic or behaviourist position on human behaviour, where the individual responds to structural facts, and on the other hand what was offered was a more voluntaristic position where the individual controls his or her behaviour by reference to ideas of moral performance. Again the later survey showed that, nationally, people ranked lack of discipline as a cause of crime very highly indeed. What we see in effect is interplay between structural and personal factors as responsible for crime, but not television. The exchange between members of the group was as follows, prompted by our rhetorical question, *'So you see a direct link between the rise in unemployment and the rise in crime?'*

I don't see that crime is a symptom. It is the government and society that are causing it.

It could be, but I think the rise in drugs is probably linked too.

Yes, that's because of social deprivation in certain areas. In London crime is more rife in certain areas than others and that can be put down to social deprivation, unemployment.

Glasgow has one of the highest crime rates.

It's cause and effect, isn't it — people need money.

Crime is big business now isn't it. I think there's an underclass of people who make a living out of it.

If there is a recession there's bound to be more crime.

Yes, but if the recession goes the crime rate will stay up.

I think the drug culture has created a lot of it.

What we see here is an appreciation of the structure of people's lives that promotes certain behaviour. The high level of crime in London was put down, as one man said, to 'social deprivation'. Thus, if social deprivation was the cause of crime then one would expect crime to surface wherever social deprivation occurred, hence, the mentioning of Glasgow, historically associated with deprivation. This appears to be a classic use of correlation as causation: the presence of Y always appearing with X, and Y causing X. In fact, however, these respondents did not use correlation to establish causation. What they demonstrated was a rather sophisticated understanding of causation. The constant occurrence of two variables offered the starting point for examining why the two variables should always appear together, and then used theory to establish causation; in this case what unemployment meant in terms of access to the material needs of existence.

What also emerged from the conversations was that they tested hypotheses by examining for alternative cases to that which the theory stated ought to occur. Their thinking was that if social deprivation causes crime, then how was it that one has differential rates of crime once unemployment is held constant? For example, the man who pointed out that *'crime is more rife in certain areas'* which could be *'put down to social deprivation'*, was comparing areas of London with similar levels of deprivation, and then, because crime was unevenly distributed between these areas, ruled out social deprivation as the independent variable. Of course, his reasoning was never expressed in such a way, but the conclusion he reached by this intellectual process was that one had to look elsewhere for the causes of crime. Indeed, the further comment *'if the recession goes the crime rate will stay up'* takes the causation of crime away from structural factors and places the emphasis on a more voluntaristic approach. Crime, for him, must take account of the type of person who engages in crime. One of the men argued from this position when putting forward reasons why he did not turn to crime when he was unemployed: *'I've got four kids, and I've got too much to lose. I know people who've been put away and you lose too much'*.

His reason for not engaging in crime is not particularly moral. The fact that he did not turn to theft because the risk of doing so was too high demonstrates instrumental reasoning and not moral reasoning. What he is at pains to illustrate, however, is that the individual is not a prisoner of material circumstances, that the individual has free will and can choose for him or herself how to act. In short, that the individual is a moral being because he can act morally. This is not, of course, offering a very sophisticated explanation for crime. One can still hold to a free will position by claiming, as most criminologists would, that crime is made more likely by the presence of social deprivation: that only the rate of crime can be predicted, not which individuals will commit crime. To engage in the last type of enquiry one would need to know a great deal about any particular individual, including their moral beliefs and attitudes. We will see later, however, that people consider an individual's moral structure and attitudes to be very important in accounting for anti-social and unsociable acts.

The more we examined what people were saying about social conduct, the more apparent it became that major store was put on an individual's performance as learnt behaviour, but not behaviour that was learnt from television, at least not anti-social behaviour, but learnt by association with others. The term 'learnt behaviour' is used here to include not just learning how to behave by the examples set by others, but learning of a moral code that is brought into play in acting, and the learning of sets of values that structure judgement about behaviour.

The Decline in the Quality of Life

The very first focus group was with 25- to 44-year-old men in Leeds with children living at home, and who also had multichannel television. It was decided to begin the discussion by deliberately asking a very general question open to wide interpretation. We simply said, *'What power do you think the media have?'* We did not say what media, or what we meant by power. The response was: *'It's very powerful'*. We followed this by asking, *'When we said media what did you think of?'* Although one man said, *'newspapers'*, the more immediate general response was: *'TV'*. There can be no doubt about the primacy of television in people's media consciousness. Although, having said that, this is not the case when people think of specific issues related to the media.

When we asked in what way television was powerful, what was surprising, or at least to us, was that the question of privacy was raised immediately. Although we were extremely interested in the ethical question of media intrusion into peoples' lives, the responses given were totally unprompted. They flowed naturally from our initial, and very open, question concerning media power. One man, for example, mentioned that the media *'tend to lead'*, but said he was not bothered by bias in television, *'because I've got the option to turn it off if I don't like it'*, to which someone immediately responded, *'I don't think the TV is that bad – it's the papers who go over the top'*. Again, being careful not to prompt, we simply asked, *'What sort of stuff?'* Back came the reply: *'Things to do with the Royal Family and privacy – they go well over the top'*.

Women of the same age living in Redditch, also unprompted, raised privacy as an issue when asked about the power of the media: *'I sometimes think they paint a false picture'* was the first reply given, the second being, *'They can invade your privacy – they'll think nothing of jumping over your fence to get a photo'*. Asked if they thought that the media would *'go beyond the law even'*, back came the reply: *'Yes. To get a good story they would'*. We then asked, *'Who would they be?'* – *'The papers'*, was the ready response.

These are concerns about the media, but what is interesting is that they do not focus on that most traditional of concerns, violence in the media promoting real-life violence. What we see, in effect, is a much wider judgement about the media that includes, indeed focuses on, the rights of individuals, and how the media might infringe those rights. But what we also found is a concern, particularly in relation to television, over the infringement of people's values. That is, the showing of material that went against the values of people and their sense of decency. Not to respect someone's privacy was not to behave decently. It went against a central value that everyone had a right to private space. We will see later, however, that this right was not to be universally awarded. It could be withdrawn if the individual behaved in a way that lost respect.

Given that we were interested in privacy, and it had been raised so early in the proceedings, the order of the discussion guide was abandoned to allow us to follow up what had so naturally been raised. For the moment, however, we will leave any detailed discussion of privacy to one side and concentrate instead simply on the type of concerns that people voiced.

Areas of Offence

The infringement of rights as an assault on values and a focus of concern came particularly to the fore in those focus groups that were recruited on the basis that they had either complained, or wanted to complain, about something that they had seen on television. We asked the male group in Redditch, aged 35–65, what they had objected to: *'The gay scene on EastEnders. Not that I'm against gays, but with children watching I don't think it's right'*. Someone else agreed that they did not like that particular scene, but concluded: *'I think it is more the time it's shown than anything else'*.

We were not convinced that the portrayal of gays in the soap opera *EastEnders* was just a matter of timing. We did not readily accept that they would have considered the scene permissible if it had gone out later at night when children might not be watching. Indeed, the protection of children, it struck us, was often used as a cover for what was in their thoughts, but more difficult to admit to – the protection of their own values. Let us therefore follow this group's discussion of the scene in *EastEnders* where two gay men were witnessed kissing.

After one man had said: *'I turned it off. I've got 9- and 12-year-old sons and I think it's terrible'*, we responded by saying, *'What about the argument that there are gay men in our society? What would your argument be to people who say it's natural for your sons to be exposed to gays?'*

I think my argument would be that if you're an adult you know that this does go on, it's part of society, but when you're young you're trying to tell them that's the norm – I don't think it is the norm.

I'd be shocked myself if I saw gay people kissing. I've never actually seen it happen.

I know gay people – I've got some gay friends and they don't do that in public.

In this country it's not legal unless you're over 21, that's because you've got to be an adult to be able to decide.

There's a situation in [Channel 4's soap opera] Brookside as well where two children are having an incestuous affair – I have a daughter of 17 and a son of 15 and I found that embarrassing. I had no reason to find it embarrassing, but I did. I'd heard that there was going to be something about it, but I honestly didn't believe that you would see them in bed together.

I think the trouble is with that sort of situation is that if you speak up against gays you're homophobic – you're the odd one out. I'd be the one that was slated so it's very difficult to explain to kids that just because everybody else says its ok it doesn't mean its right.

We followed up this last comment by asking, *'Do you begin to feel that you're being … persecuted is the wrong word, but…'* He replied: *'Yes, that's what I'm saying. I'm not homophobic, but what I am saying is there's a lot of things that I do and don't believe in, but I don't push my beliefs in the face of other people'.* Another man supported him by adding: *'We don't want it forced on us do we?'* We returned to the argument often made by people in the face of not liking something on television: *'There is the argument that says you don't have to watch it'.* This brought the response: *'Yes, but it is something that you follow, you watch all the time and it's only a particular part of it…'* This man was saying that he was affronted by the gay kissing scene on two fronts: he did not want homosexuals portrayed on screen in an intimate way, and he objected to the contamination of a programme that he always watched by the inclusion of such a scene. His rights, therefore, were breached on two scores. He had a right not to have his values assaulted, and he had a right to enjoy a programme that he normally enjoyed. This led to a discussion of the placement of such material on minority channels. We asked, *'So if, as Channel 4 has done now and then, they had a lesbian evening and at other times they've had a gay evening – is that better?'* One response was, *'Yes, I think so'*, followed by someone else saying, *'If it's something that's not incorporated into everyday situations then it's something that stands apart because it is something that should stand apart'.*

The idea that gay sexual portrayal should 'stand apart' is interesting. What he was objecting to was having homosexuality normalized by giving it wide public display. Hence, it was perfectly all right for such scenes to be bracketed-off from mainstream culture by having it consigned to specialist performance. The theme was further taken up:

If they want to put a new channel on that's purely for gays then that's okay. If they want to have a channel for religious beliefs like they do in America, they can do that. You're not talking about everyday television where, especially soaps, they're a big influence on people's lives.

We will see this idea of specialist performance emerge later in discussing regulation. However, it seemed far from clear to us that this man and others in the same group would sanction such behaviour on minority or specialist channels. The enclosing of behaviour away from mainstream broadcasting might appear fine, but this man's view of television was of a medium that could influence people's lives. Yet, this same man, much later in the discussion, did not consider that the portrayal of violence on television was responsible for violence in society. As he prosaically put it, with reference to the veterinary drama series *All*

Creatures Great and Small, '*I used to watch* All Creatures Great and Small, *but it didn't make me want to stick my arm up a cow's arse*'.

It is difficult to say if this man had a theory of sexuality that incorporated a belief that sexual preferences can be readily acquired by mediated exposure to sexual behaviour. Perhaps. But it is much more likely that gay sexual practice worried him because it represented an alternative definition of sexuality to the one that he held. In short, such portrayals confronted and affronted his values concerning correct sexual practice and what the correct gender relationships ought to be. It might be that his worry about correct sexual practices was so strong that he did allow television to have an influence in that area of human performance, but not in other areas that he was not so worried about, or that gave him no such mental anguish. However, the interesting question is, if he did believe such sexual behaviour might be imitated, and since he objected to such behaviour, why was it permissible to have it shown at all, exclusive channel or non-exclusive channel?

One of the difficulties in examining the values people hold, and the controls they wish to place on the portrayal of values that offend them, is that values are not stable entities. It is not simply a matter of a particular individual's values competing for space with other people's values, but that, within the same individual, internal competition takes place as to what aspect of a particular value set will be given precedence in deciding how to act, or in making judgements. For example, while one particular man was affronted by a scene of a gay couple kissing, he could not bring himself to approve an outright ban on such material because, and this came out at several points in the course of the evening's discussion, he saw himself as decent, and to be decent was to be liberal.

At one point in the evening, after several times saying he was not homophobic, he wished to demonstrate how liberal he was by saying:

When we started off we talked about the gay situation. My daughter's just got a boyfriend – should I be happy that she has got a boyfriend or should I be expecting her to come home with a girlfriend? Have I got to be happy whether my son comes home with a girl or a boyfriend?

Someone in the group responded, '*Well, that's up to you*'. He replied that he wasn't homophobic and said: '*I feel that as long as he's happy I don't care*', to which the man sat next to him muttered, very quietly, '*I think you would*'. To us there was no doubt that he would be extremely unhappy. It was hard to imagine that the loving couple would be well received in his house, but the point to express is that, as a liberal, he felt he ought to be tolerant to that which he could not tolerate. In other words, the ideology of liberalism served to define what decency was: tolerance for the other person's point of view. Yet, how to be tolerant when being tolerant involved the exposure to values that ran counter to his own? But there is more than just that at play here.

If we examine his quote we notice the introduction of the word 'should' – '*should I be happy*' because his daughter has got a boyfriend, or should he only be happy if she had a girlfriend as a lover. And as he also said, '*Have I got to be happy*' if his son comes home with a boyfriend. What he is actually saying here, and he is quite right, is that cultural projections tell us not just about the world, but inform us as to how we should live our lives. That is why cultural struggle over the definitions of meanings is always a political struggle. He felt he should, or had to, accept the unacceptable. We can return to his much earlier statement for evidence of this: '*I think the trouble is … is that if you speak up against gays you're homophobic – you're the odd one out… It's very difficult to explain to kids that just because everyone else says it's okay it doesn't mean it's right*'.

This man had a very firm idea of what was sexually right and wrong. And it is doubtful that he really thought that his son, watching a gay couple kiss on *EastEnders*, would, always presuming that his son was strictly heterosexual, follow such practices in his own life. What had occurred is that the walls of his moral garden were breached by the display of gay affection on television, and if he objected to the representation of gay culture he would be held to be morally at fault – '*to be the odd one out*' – as if he was the one in the wrong, and not the programme maker. What the programme represented in terms of cultural and moral space was that his values no longer, in contemporary society, held sway. The definers of morality were no longer people like him. Moral authority had moved its location to groups that did not represent his lifestyle or beliefs. Furthermore, and again rightly so, he saw the promotion of gay culture as a political act. For example, when it was put to him: '*But presumably gays would turn round and say, "hang on", we are part of everyday life*', he replied:

They're entitled to their opinion – I don't thrust my opinion on them. It's the same with religion – I have my beliefs but I don't thrust them on everybody else. You don't see a situation on EastEnders *with a Roman Catholic who says everybody who isn't a Roman Catholic has something wrong with them.*

The liberal in him is there in the sense of agreeing that everyone is entitled to his or her opinion, but it is not there when it comes to having to confront someone else's beliefs as practice. It is hard to imagine a Roman Catholic behaving in a soap opera as he imagines. But, it is not difficult to imagine a scene with a Roman Catholic priest dispensing the Eucharist; that is what Catholic priests do. And what gay lovers do is kiss. The kiss was more than a piece of behaviour, it embodied a statement that kissing between men was right, and, as far as he was concerned – implied in his statement of the Catholic not telling others that there was something wrong with them if they were not a Catholic – that if you were not gay there was also something wrong with you. The programme, in other words, was seen not simply as promoting a set of relationships as right, but, by doing so, because they were not condemned, denying the validity of other types of relationships such as those that ought to be supported because they are right; namely, heterosexual relationships. The fact that *EastEnders* is full of heterosexual relationships does not serve to overcome the message of the single homosexual kiss for this individual. Such kissing shows a lack of respect for dominant values, even in a series where the heterosexual relationship consists, often, of illicit affairs.

The women who had been recruited on the same basis as the above men, in that they had complained, or felt like complaining, about something they had seen, lived in London and were aged between 35 and 65. They also objected to homosexual scenes: '*I think soaps that are on quite early – there's too much homosexuality*'. Asked what programmes she was thinking about, this woman replied, '*EastEnders. I know it all goes on but if you've got young children watching I don't think it is necessary*'. Immediately following this comment one woman added her objection to the teenage soap opera *Grange Hill*, to which others added further comment:

> *I turned the television on the other afternoon and* Grange Hill *came on. My daughter's 15 and she said: 'I can remember you never let us watch this'. I watched it and said 'now you can see why'. I can't beat that programme.*

> *I dislike it but the children say it's real. They behave like that.*

> *They treat adults like dirt.* Grange Hill *was the start of it, but it's the same in* EastEnders *and I think it's very bad. Children see it on TV then they do it to their parents.*

One woman was much taken up by the subject of premature ejaculation. She said: *'I'm going to be really controversial here – a few months ago on* [Australian soap opera] Neighbours *this couple were having trouble in bed – it was obviously premature ejaculation. This storyline went on for weeks and I thought why – do we need this at 5.35 in the evening?'* Asked, *'is it that you don't want it showing at all or is it just on at the wrong time?'* all agreed that 5.35pm was a bit early, and that such a subject matter ought only to be included late at night, on the grounds that *'It's up to you whether you choose to watch it, but at 5.35pm I don't think it's necessary. I don't see why we should have to censor our children at that time of night'.* Asked as to when they expected to have to censor their children, the reply was, *'after 9 o'clock'.* This prompted a flood of comments:

> *The trouble is, so many children have got televisions in their bedroom these days, so you put them to bed and they watch it anyway.*

> *We are all guilty. I used to make my son watch* EastEnders *in the bedroom so my daughter didn't see it. I don't like it. I think to make a convicted murderer into a hero is awful – I won't watch anything with that man in.*[2]

> *They have the 9 o'clock watershed and at one minute past the language floods out.*

> *It's the same language you hear on the school bus.*

> *Yes, the children will pick it up from school anyway even if they don't watch it on TV.*

> *You can't blame television for bad language really can you?*

> *No, I don't think you can. You've only got to walk down the street and hear adults speaking like that.*

> *I just think you try to bring your children up speaking nicely and they don't speak nicely now do they?*

> *There was a time when you couldn't get on TV if you had any sort of accent – even if it was a Northern one. They used to have elocution lessons to get rid of their accents.*

What we witness here is a collision of manners as much as anything; although it is interesting that the gay scene in *EastEnders* should once more appear. However, it is also noteworthy that two other soap operas were picked out for attention: *Neighbours* and *Grange Hill*. Given their early evening slots it is, to an extent, understandable that soap operas should feature so highly as being in need of close scrutiny. Yet, timing alone should not obscure another fact about soap operas. They purport to chronicle everyday life. Indeed, British soap operas have an almost documentary-like quality to them. As moral stories, therefore, they do engage the viewer in debate about contemporary culture and act as a commentary on social relationships.

The lack, furthermore, of established, and therefore well-known, actors in the roles helps transform the actor into the character played in a way which can foster the impression that the character and the real-life person acting the part are one and the same person. There is a distinct lack of breakage, so to speak, between the real and the fictional world. Thus, it is not too surprising that soap operas should be singled out for special attention in terms of the moral tales that they tell. As one of the 45–64 year old Leeds women said: '*I never let my children (grandchildren) watch* Grange Hill *because I think it is a dreadful way to behave in class. If you listen to young people talking on the bus they really believe that* EastEnders *is real*'.

Whether the young people she overheard talking on the bus really did believe *EastEnders* to be real is not the real issue. What her statement captures is a worry that such a programme, because of its dramatic closeness to real life in East London, might be taken as entirely true to life by those who view it. It is this attempt by such soap operas to ground themselves very firmly in the here and now of everyday life that adds to their authenticity. However, such authenticity means that it is difficult for them to remain aloof from social movement and change, or, more accurately, since there is nothing in principle to say that they reflect in absolute detail the supposed world of their setting, they are open to the ready adoption, as a dramatic device, of controversial social issues. Homosexuality, abortion, suicide, drug-taking, incest, underage sex, bullying at school and a host of similar issues can produce drama through moral contention.

One man, for example, in the 45- to 64-year-old London group, began his complaint against portrayals of sex on television by rounding on Channel 4. He considered that Channel 4 had an agenda designed to promote the acceptability of homosexuality: '*If you are going to ask me for specific programmes* [that he objected to] *I won't be able to identify them, but I'm getting fed up with having the gay agenda rammed down my throat. Stuff which you find on Channel 4.* He finished by saying: '*It's on BBC 1 now – EastEnders.*' Someone else supported his position: '*Yes, you're right. There is an agenda there which is being pushed. It isn't just on television either*'.

The idea of an agenda '*being pushed*' is one way of viewing the inclusion of groups and lifestyles that have previously been 'hidden'. Another is to view the inclusion of groups such as homosexuals within the framework already laid out in the previous sections: the loosening of the moral authority structure of contemporary life, where no group has automatic claim to superiority, has meant a democratization of social life. Representation of diverse lifestyles and diverse behaviours is not only possible but increasingly likely. This would especially apply to programmes claiming to capture life as it is lived in real communities. Hitherto 'hidden' groups not only become visible, but social problems also become the subject of entertainment and, it must be added, social commentary. The restructuring, furthermore, of British television and the rise of independent production houses, originally supported by Channel 4 with its remit to be 'experimental', has encouraged the pushing forward of the boundaries of the acceptable. Two soap operas that were singled out for special commentary were those made by Phil Redmond, Chairman of Mersey Television – *Brookside* and *Grange Hill*.

Redmond studied sociology, but, perhaps of more significance, he associates himself, more than is customary for most media executives, with the community and culture that forms the base for his material. When Redmond was interviewed in the course of this study he showed no defensiveness over representations his company gave of culture. He reflected that

> I am interested in writing about what people label as 'social issues' because they're only social issues because they affect people and they affect a lot of people. If it doesn't affect a lot of people it doesn't become a social issue. Another good example is what we're doing now – the incest issue. We've got regulators crawling all over our backs, but at the same time I've got newspaper cuttings on my desk which is the result of a campaign to see what people think about this issue in Brookside – 66% think we have gone too far and 73% say it's very interesting and we've handled it sensitively. [...] Our research shows that 10% to 12% of people will admit to having some sibling sexual contact – therefore, as you will know, the incidence is probably three times as high.

Leaving aside Redmond's obvious familiarity with audience-building devices, his position was that there was little point in denying the existence of incest, homosexuality, or behaviours that went with social depravation. Intellectually, as far as he was concerned, the local community was open for inspection in an almost anthropological fashion. The 'reality' of a child's life in a comprehensive school such as *Grange Hill*, and its catchment area, may have, as we have seen, offended adults, but not the audience it was made for. *Grange Hill* is not made to appeal to, or be approved by, traditional definers of moral authority – adults. It is made to appeal to the very subjects that appear in the drama – young people. The teenagers that appear figured by Redmond's approach, the behaviour and manners of their incorporation, are not drawn from the 'ought' of the acceptable, but from the 'is' of the empirical.

Whether it involves the inclusion of homosexuals, or the inclusion of disrespectful children, this supposed portrayal of real life by British soap operas, and the reactions to such programmes, which are widely enjoyed, captures much about the problems of regulation. These and other programmes, which feature everyday life, open doors on cultural tension points which in the past have been relatively closed. The point made by Wallis (1976), as noted earlier, that modern society, in creating occupational and social differentiation, has given rise to a wide range of sub-cultures and lifestyles which threaten to impinge on each other and thus provide the ground for cultural conflict, is worth raising again. Wallis's observation that conflict has been to a great extent avoided because of the 'segregation and insulation of competing subcultures' is, however, no longer quite so true. The reason for this is the visibility given to these sub-cultures through the insistence of television not to exclude them; indeed, to make varied behaviours the focus of attention.

At the structural level, Wallis' comments still hold. Members of different sub-groups rarely come into direct contact with each other, or, in some cases, do not knowingly come into contact with each other. As the man in the Redditch group said: *'I'd be shocked myself if I saw gay people kissing. I've never actually seen it happen'*. But he did see it on *EastEnders*. Thus, what has happened is that it has become increasingly difficult to avoid the existence of behaviours of which one disapproves. What one does about these behaviours, however, is a different matter. If operating with the value structure of the liberal, where tolerance is a cardinal virtue, it is not easy to proclaim against them to the extent of demanding their outlaw. Furthermore, although certain behaviours may be an assault on one's values, the fact is that such behaviours are portrayed behaviours, and not those that one necessarily comes into contact with at the personal level of living. To that extent, although swearing is a slightly different matter, they do not pose a direct threat in negotiating concrete daily living. Such worlds, so to speak, can be kept at bay. Yet, this is only true up to a point.

The offence given by media portrayals of values or behaviour, and those which run counter to those of the viewer, should never be underestimated. Having said that, it is not the case that the media threaten their immediate world except in one direction. For example, people in the focus groups did see media portrayals as a direct threat to the immediacy of their world, and the entry point of this threat was through their children. The battle on this score was an almost physical fight to ensure that their values were reproduced in their children. The battle was a daily one. Socialisation is a continuous and continual process to ensure correct performance both morally and behaviourally. As such, there is nothing removed about media portrayals if they offer the possibility of becoming enactments, no matter how modified, within a parent's own physical space through the manner in which their children present themselves.

To have children is to have responsibilities. But, it is also, by the act of being in society, to have a social responsibility to the community for ensuring that the child is brought up to see him or herself as having responsibilities to the community. We can now return to learned behaviour and how people view the influence of the media, and, in so doing, lay the groundwork for discussing attitudes towards regulation, but being able to do so through the understandings people give to such matters.

The Family, Discipline and Influence

It was clear that the focus group participants tended to feature structural facts as being strongly linked with anti-social behaviour, the most significant being unemployment or social deprivation associated with specific structural locations. The media, although not entirely absent in accounting for anti-social behaviour, were not seen as having the powerful force that is often ascribed to them. The material facts of life override mediated portrayals of life as an influence. Yet, it was apparent that the group members we talked with did not settle for some crude behaviourist model of individual performances. They saw individuals as moral beings who act on the world. An individual's behaviour was not determined by the objective material circumstances of their lives, they only made some behaviour more, and not less, likely.

The crucial intervening variable acting on objective material conditions was seen to be that of discipline. We need to give some attention to this since what discipline means is control – control in the sense of putting strictures on emotional expression and behaviour, together with the control of exposure to influences.

The Walsall men aged under 55, with older children, spoke at length about crime in their area.

I leave my car open, they don't damage it then.

Car theft is so rife the police don't seem too bothered about it.

I think we all accept it now.

A friend of mine had his stolen. The police phoned him a few days later to say they'd found it. They told him where it was and he was there within the hour. When he got there it had been stolen again.

My father-in-law had his stolen last year – they found it and rang him and he said he'd be over there to collect it in the morning – they said it might be pinched again before then.

Others in the group said that they had been victims of burglary. When asked *'what do you think is responsible for this rise in crime?'* one man replied, *'I think that children are growing up without any fear at all'*. We asked, *'fear of what?'* This opened a floodgate:

They've never been punished. When I was a lad at school if they walked in everybody stood up. At my son's school you actually hear the kids cheeking the headmaster.

The vast majority of juniors these days don't really care about responsibility.

I told a couple of 8 year olds off the other day for doing something. When I was 8 years old and was doing something wrong and an adult came along I'd be off up the road but these kids stood there as if to say 'you can't do anything so what are you shouting at me for?' Now you can't do anything about it.

It's definitely the deprived areas. I'm in the fire service; we've done surveys on where they have the worst fires and its nearly all inner city. It does tend to be the trend that parental guidance is low in these areas, education I believe is lower. Whereas my children went to school at 5 already reading and writing because we took time to teach them, they can't. I firmly believe that it comes from within the home to start with.

These were pretty damning indictments of modern life. But we asked these men whether or not such behaviour had got worse in recent years.

It's definitely got worse. There's no discipline at all is there? There is nothing for them to be frightened of. I knew tough kids when I was at school but they still grew up with discipline. They were still frightened of the police.

It used to be a minority of kids like that but it's becoming a majority now I think.

I don't think it's just to do with the parents either because I know some kids who are unruly and their parents are lovely people.

This last remark prompted us to ask: *'Are you talking about discipline in the home?'* to which he responded: *'Discipline throughout life'*. We then asked: *'How has this come about?'* The responses were more descriptive than analytical, and tended to reinforce earlier points: *'They can't punish children at school. When I was at school if you did something wrong then you knew what you were in for. Now the teachers can't do anything to them'*. *'Most of the parents blame the teachers – they never blame the kids do they?'* *'It all comes down to the parents in the end. Discipline comes from within the home'.* This general sentiment was also clearly evident from the survey data (Chapter 4b).

The women in Redditch talked about their years at school in the days when corporal punishment was allowed. The conversation was begun by one woman commenting on a news item on television of a boy who had been disruptive in school:

> *There is this case at the moment with a lad who's been expelled. His mum came on the television and said 'he's a good boy really'. Well, he obviously isn't, he's kicking teachers, he's taking dinner money off all the children but they sit there and say he's a good boy.*

Asked what their judgement was of the situation, the general response was summed up by one woman who said: *'I thought immediately it was the parents' fault'.* Somebody else added: *'Unfortunately they haven't got him out though because the law says they can't'* and then continued, *'the law has been brought by parents who've said they don't want their kids to be caned at school'.* When asked the reasons for this, the answer was: *'Because they don't like other people disciplining their own children'.* It was a position generally shared by members of this group. One person recalling her school days said: *'When we were at school we were caned',* and another added, *'If you did wrong you got the cane and that was it',* to which someone rejoined, *'some children didn't do wrong and they still got the cane'.* However, these women were not in agreement with corporal punishment in schools. For example, when asked directly whether corporal punishment was a good or bad thing, the position was, and held by all but one woman, that it was right that corporal punishment was now prohibited in schools: *'I think it is a good thing, I wouldn't want my child to be caned'.* One objection was: *'A lot of people say violence breeds violence which is why I think a lot of people have said they don't want their children caned in school – there are other ways of disciplining them'.*

What we see here, therefore, is the limitation of 'power' discussed previously. These parents had a heightened sense that their children belonged to them, and were not prepared to give their discipline over to the control of others to decide how it should be administered. Children, in other words, fell, even when outside the home, under parental jurisdiction and not other authority figures. Part of this 'belonging' was probably a product of the closer relationship that they had with their children than their parents had had with them. Children were, in a very strict sense, members of the family, and not mere residents. As one of the older participants said, in describing her childhood: *'You never thought of your parents like friends. They were, I don't know, people who were there – they looked after you when you came home, gave you food and things. It's changed now'.*

There can be no escaping the fact that the lack of discipline of children was held as crucial in accounting for the rise in crime, and that the blame for this lack of discipline was the invasion of the right of self-determination that crisscrossed social life in general. Children were held to *'know their rights'.* For example, in discussing the question of discipline and authority with the young women in London, they were asked, if they were to have children at some point in the future, would they expect the schools their children would attend to teach moral values? *'Not entirely'* was one response, *'but you would expect them to give them some morals'.* Another women agreed: *'I think it's up to them* [teachers] *to tell them what's right and what's wrong'.* She continued, however, by saying: *'But then the system lets them down because teachers have no power over pupils anymore. You're not allowed to touch them. If a child is running riot round the classroom you cannot physically haul them back into their seat. Teachers can't do that any more'.* When asked why not, the response was: *'People's rights have come into it haven't they?'*

This idea of a child's rights, and children knowing their rights, meant that adults, by virtue of being adult, could not punish them. Schools had only a limited authority of correction and even the police had to abide by strict rules governing the right of intervention in behaviour. On more than one occasion it was mentioned that even parents cannot smack their own children, and reference was made in this context to the European Court of Human Rights, symbolising for them a general feeling of powerlessness.

But we should be cautious in interpreting what these respondents are saying, or at least when examined in terms of other attitudes that they expressed. On the one hand they regretted lawlessness and held lack of discipline, or, as one person has already put it, lack of *'discipline throughout life'*, as responsible, but on the other hand they were unwilling to sanction the disciplining of their children by other adults. Part of the rise of child centeredness is that children are no longer seen as 'community property'. This is not unrelated to the decline of traditional community itself – although one ought to be careful not to overplay the idea of traditional community any more than one should see past rural life as made up of the village smithy and the spreading chestnut tree over the village green. However, if the child is no longer community property then it follows that community authority has shrunk, to be reduced, as we have seen, to little larger than the immediate family.

What we see in the above comments is a loosening of traditional State sanctioned authority – the police and teachers – and a decline in personal authority – parental. The media hardly get a mention, and when they do it is as a source for information on how to behave: *'Television is like a university for crime. They show you exactly what you can get away with and what your rights are.'* To suggest that children have rights is to suggest what the limitations of the rights of others over them are.

Authority, in other words, has become formalised, and in doing so has undermined assumptive authority: authority, in this case, is assumed to exist by virtue of status alone and not legal power. The teacher and the policeman, who once had the power of interference through being accorded respect, now only have to be respected in accordance with the law. Indeed, the man who said that he had tried to correct the behaviour of *'a couple of 8 year olds for doing something'*, found that his assumptive power based on his status as an adult had no force because it lacked legal power. As he said about his inability to successfully chastise the culprits: *'Now you can't do a thing about it'*.

The decline in assumptive power has undoubtedly circumscribed the effectiveness of social control of children. The degree of surveillance of children has declined now, since categories of behaviour can only be corrected by those who witness such behaviour and are formally charged with the authority or power to correct it. This means whole areas of behaviour go unchallenged. For example, the policeman cannot correct general 'loutish' behaviour because he no longer has the assumptive authority to do so, he can only correct that category of behaviour he has formal authority over. As one woman in the Redditch group noted: *'I honestly believe that years ago the police had more control over what they could do with people than they have today'.* And as one of the Redditch men, aged about 40, said: *'Society isn't policing itself any more. When I was 7 or 8 you only had to hear the words, 'there's a copper coming', and that was it. Everything stopped – you stopped playing football in the street, you stopped climbing people's fences, you stopped climbing the lamp post – everything stopped'.*

The teacher outside professional hours of authority has lost assumptive authority, and may even have difficulty asserting authority within ascribed hours if such behaviour is not strictly an educational disciplinary matter. If that is so for the teacher and the policeman, it is even more so for the 'generalised' adult. They have no authority whatsoever to take assumptive power by virtue of simply being an adult. It is still probably the case, however, that in some traditional tightly-knit communities the assumptive authority of the adult still operates; that is, any adult can act as the guardian of community standards in the policing of behaviour.

Practically all those in our discussion groups believed that there has been a widespread decline in discipline of the young, and believed that this lack of discipline had given rise to anti-social and unsociable behaviour. Indeed, that perceived lack of discipline was the single fact held most responsible for such behaviour. What they are really talking about, of course, is moral decline, where moral decline is defined as the privileging of the individual over the collective. The point of reference in judging one's own behaviour is the self and not others. This type of moral decline means that very limited authority is given to others to decide how one should behave. It is not the right of the schoolteacher to say what company a child ought to keep, or to comment on his or her dress, or to take action against rowdy behaviour on the bus home from school. The authority of the teacher in such a situation has been redistributed along educationally functional lines, where education itself has become defined in instrumental rather than moral terms.

There has undoubtedly been a redrawing of the boundaries of authority, and, with that, a reduction in moral figures. This whole process is of a dialectical nature. If there is a shrinkage of the boundaries of authority, then, authority holders not only see a shrinkage in their traditional area of performance, but change the nature of their own performances to become no longer figures of moral worth and respect. If one is no longer given rights of intervention in behaviour, then, equally, others have no right to comment on your behaviour in those areas from which authority has been withdrawn. The performance of the individual in such circumstances reduces itself to comment only on those areas of which he or she has been charged with formally – assumptive moral responsibility giving way to formal moral responsibility. In other words, providing the individual performs his or her professional duty satisfactorily, then how they perform in the rest of their lives is of no concern to anyone. This process means that, apart from those areas of responsibility the individual has been formally charged to execute, they are released from acting as a moral example in other areas of their life and, not surprisingly, released from such responsibility, may well change their behaviour accordingly.

In general, whatever a politician does in his or her private life, providing he or she performs their political duties correctly, offers no reason for not supporting him or her in their professional capacity as a politician. This would be so for the teacher, the local dignitary, the businessman, and so on. We will see this rationality coming into play later when discussing attitudes to privacy, but for the moment it is worth noting that personal lives, if known, cannot escape judgement. The judgement may not be to remove the person from office, but judgement will be made – it is almost an inescapable fact of life – about the individual as a person, should the behaviour be considered morally wrong. In doing so, respect for that individual declines and, if associated with any frequency with particular posts, such as the post of politician, then the position itself loses respect. The outcome of this process is an inability for anyone in that position or post, no matter who the person is, to make moral points or act as moral exemplars. Indeed, one woman mentioned that *'in our street one of the neighbours has assaulted the next door neighbour'* and then added, *'he's just got on the Labour Council'* and in disgust said *'because he hadn't been imprisoned for 3 months he could still sit as a Labour Councillor'*.[3] In other words, what we see is a social process set in motion that feeds on itself in a non-intended way.

One might argue here that this process of the lowering of moral regard opens up a space for other influences on behaviour to be drawn from other than traditional sources. One of these sources might be the media, or figures in the media that offer attractive styles and behaviour, but which at the same time are not anchored in any moral foundation. Although this might be true, it would be difficult to sustain without strong evidence. However, it has been argued earlier that 'manners' can be taken over from mediated behaviour in situations where they have meaning. One needs to account, therefore, in explaining how this could happen, by reference to the circumstances of individuals – what do media messages have to contend against?

Closeness and Lack of Discipline
What was obvious in the course of the focus groups was that adults were aware that their relationships with their children, especially in terms of discipline, were different from the relationships they had had with their own parents. The older the group, the more marked the difference that members observed between how they raised their children and how they themselves were raised. Although it does not necessarily follow that differences between generations in childrearing practices lead to differences in values between generations, it is nevertheless noteworthy that in the national survey half of those questioned considered their values to be different to those of their parents (Table 9, Chapter 4b). Clearly, values are not simply derived from parents but, as Table 11 shows, parental figures were nominated by the great majority as the most influential in the transmission of values.

For many in our groups, what had made a difference to the way they responded to their children was, undoubtedly, the difference in affluence between themselves and their parents when they the group members were themselves young. Discipline often entails denial, but as one woman in Redditch commented, and similar attitudes were found in other groups, *'I think children get too much'*. When asked why, if they thought that their children got too much, they did not do something about it, one woman said: *'You always like your kids to have what you didn't have. You want them to go away from home in the future and say 'my mum and dad did everything possible they could for me''*. Another woman in the same group explained her reason for giving in to her daughter's requests by reference to the lack of energy and time she had to give her children. In short, it was easier to say 'Yes', than argue through the 'No'.

My daughter who is coming up to 8 will just about take no but will try it on a bit, whereas my mum, if 'No' was said, 'No' was meant. I remember always feeling that with my parents – the level of respect was always there, there wasn't the questioning and testing all the time. I think our parents just stuck to a limit of how far they could be pushed. They were fair. But I think the pace of life is so fast now you're under pressure as a mother to deal with your own needs, your part-time work needs, your husband's needs, you haven't got that crucial time to pay to your kids that they always need. You do become guilty of saying 'amuse yourself, watch the telly' until you've got the time to give them. But the special time that you give them isn't always when they need it.

Quite a few of the women in this Redditch group worked either full or part-time. One other woman said:

I'm fortunate in that I do a term-time job so I work when the schools work. This is the first year that I've done that and I had six weeks' holiday in the summer. I felt that for the first time my lads had a full-time mum and the atmosphere in the house was definitely more relaxed. It was just because I hadn't got the pressures. When you come in from work you've got the tea to sort out, bags to empty, uniforms to iron etc. And that's when the kids are getting under your feet, you end up saying, 'put the telly on for 5 minutes, I want to sit down with a cup of tea'. That's the time maybe if you give them one to one you wouldn't have the battles you have sometimes.

As mentioned, all agreed that they were less strict with their children than their parents had been with them. One woman in this group said: *'I had no freedom. When I was 16 and I started work I still had to be in at 9 o'clock. I think I've given my children a little bit more freedom because I think they go behind your back'.* That might seem a pragmatic approach to freedom, but she then added: *'I want them to be honest with me'.*

Indeed, there was a desire among these women for, and an appreciation of, closeness to their children. When asked if they thought that the way they brought up their children was an improvement on their parents' day, the responses were: *'I think my children tell me more'. 'I think my daughter's closer to me than I ever was to my parents'. 'Perhaps men have changed a bit over the years, they've become more involved'.*

Regulation of Viewing
It is difficult to talk about families in general. They differ enormously in terms of the ethos between them, even within those that share similar structural location to each other. One can, however, still discern general patterns.

To say that relationships between parents and children are now more intense than in the past may be difficult to sustain, but we have seen that an ideal of family life is closeness, and closeness does suggest an intensity of sorts. Closeness comes about through the allocation of independence to others so that the emotional tie, captured by the term 'closeness', is one that is awarded in the negotiation of living. Closeness involves, among other things, liking, and to be liked cannot be the product of force, or the dictating of behaviour by fiat. The democracy that we have seen infect social life in general has also infected, with obvious degrees of difference, the family. What we have, in other words, both at the public and private level, are liberal pronouncements on the world – the tolerance of difference. Yet, one cannot, either at the public or private level, easily regulate by such a principle. Certainly at the level of the family a neo–Aristotelian position overlays much of the liberal. Parents do have a view on what is good for their children, and are not shy in imposing their views on their offspring.

Regulation of viewing can be cast as a matter of external and internal control; that is, an issue involving external agencies and an issue involving the internal agency of the family. The above point, therefore, concerning the ethos of the family being marked by the ideal of closeness, with its presumption of a liberal outlook, has implications for viewing. If closeness is fostered by negotiation of differences and the granting of rights to others, then what children watch becomes unsettled territory, or at least at the margins of what is acceptable to the parent.

The close family is one in which decisions must be accompanied by reasons for the decisions given, otherwise the participatory process by which closeness is established breaks down. Television, therefore, becomes more than just the site of entertainment, but the site of authority. It also plays a part in the establishment of relationships. Television is, after all, a central feature of domestic living. It is not too difficult to see why even the liberal, who was a parent with children, might welcome strict guidelines on viewing, at a practical, if not necessarily a philosophical, level. Strict guidelines obviate the parent from having to negotiate authority. For the liberal, as parent, such matters have been taken out of their hands by the enforcement of a broadcasting policy that, for example, classifies material or forbids certain types of material for transmission before certain hours. The point to stress is that, in the question of regulation, one needs to understand what regulation means within the family. It also means understanding what powers people attribute to the media.

We have mentioned closeness as an ideal of family life as an important factor in understanding the mechanisms of social control as it impinges on discipline, and discipline, it was mentioned, was seen as the key factor in practically all social control, both inside and outside the family. Yet, no one in the focus groups really spelt out what they meant by discipline. They simply noted that it had declined. Physical punishment clearly signified discipline, but that was most definitely ruled out as a form of discipline if inflicted by anyone other than parents, and was not that popular within the confines of the family either. Although physical punishment as a form of discipline was occasionally used in some families of those interviewed, it was not a favoured method of discipline. Indeed, it could not be a favoured method if closeness as an ideal was to be achieved. Given that no one willingly agrees to being hurt, the inflicting of physical harm can hardly be said to be a negotiated act, and thus hinders the development of closeness. For example, one man in the Redditch group reflected on the strict nature of his upbringing and compared it to how he now raised his children:

My parents were Irish Roman Catholics and very, very strict and I ended up a responsible person. Ok, you might want to rebel against the discipline but you maintain a certain amount of self-respect and self-discipline. That's what kept you. If our curtains weren't drawn at a certain time or there was a crack in them we were given a smack for it with a stick. It only happened a couple of times – the curtains were drawn properly after that. Now at 15 I got out, but one thing I don't do is smack my kids. What you have to do is teach them very early on that some things are right and some things are wrong and they've got to carry that with them. The fact is you have discipline and you see you are a responsible parent to your kids.

The emphasis here is on discipline as a matter of teaching correct behaviour rather than as an enforcement of the will through punishment. But closeness as an ideal has probably arisen, or been made possible, by the reduced necessity to control domestic space along ordered lines. That is, the removal of most individuals from the hardship of straightforward material existence, a life of long hours and drudgery, allows the opening of space for emotional fulfilment. We have already seen that the woman who went out to work and had innumerable domestic tasks when she came home, admitted to the children getting *'under her feet'*. If such pressure is a constant of domestic space then the organising of that space is essential, and must be done in a routine manner, or if not by routine then at least organised on the principle that tasks will be carried out when instructed. Order is assured by orders, and not through discussion of the rightfulness of decisions.

Affluence alone does not account for the changes in exchanges within the family, but it goes some way towards it in terms of shifting emphasis from economic performance and efficiency within the home to greater emphasis on emotional development and satisfactions. The command of 'Do it!' gives way to the reasoned 'why I would like you to do it'. The former approach has tended to categorise working-class homes, whilst the latter approach has tended to typify middle-class homes. The latter approach is more suited to the development of closeness and is, one might suggest from the evidence of the focus groups, in general ascendancy. For example, had the Redditch mother above typified her relationship with her child through command and instruction rather than reason, it is unlikely that the closeness with her child that she valued would have developed to the extent that it had.

We have seen that when under domestic pressure this woman's response was to sit her child in front of the television. By her own admittance, she felt guilty about doing this. Yet, it is quite clear, and we will see shortly, that not as much control goes on over what children watch on television within the home as parents would think proper. As with most aspects of life, one can have an opinion about what one ought to do, but whether one does it is another matter. Whatever guilt parents might have over not exercising more control over the viewing habits of their children, the simple fact is, for all the reasons given, that the modern household is not one that is easily open to command. To dictate viewing behaviour, or to dictate viewing behaviour within grey areas of the acceptable, does not sit easily with the ethos of the modern family, especially when children have a democratic voice and might appeal for support for their preferences by reference to the viewing habits of their friends.

Yet the protection parents have, based on their own reasoning, against the possible influences of television, and we will now look at this in some detail, is that they believe that the moral instruction that they have instilled in their children serves as a barrier to 'corruption'. In discussing influences on behaviour with the above group of women, it was heard how one woman did blame television as a negative influence, but in an interesting fashion. She said: *'I think I would put TV fairly highly because a lot of single parent families stick children in front of the TV so they can have time to themselves. The children then take that into school'.*

Earlier in this group, one woman, after mentioning that the primary influence on children's behaviour was that of parents, said: *'But sometimes they come under peer pressure at school and get into bad company'*.

What we have here is a model of the circulation of influences; that is, from the television to particularly exposed children, and then from those children, via personal influence, to other children. This model is in fact the 'two step flow' model of influence introduced into communications research by Paul Lazarsfeld, but without, in this woman's example, the presence of opinion leaders. When asked *'what type of things do they take into school?'* one response was: *'Things they watch on TV. My 7 year old does if he watches Power Rangers'*. Even so, when asked by another member of the group, *'but is it the telly that's to blame or is it the parents?'* back came the response: *'The parents are the ones in control of the television'*.

What is witnessed here is a discussion of quite a complicated process, and shows the difficulties in any attempt to isolate the variables of influence, let alone accord strength to the variables. For example, if a child who watches lots of programmes that are generally taken to be unsuitable for children then manifests anti-social behaviour, the true variable at work may not be television, but that of childrearing. That is, the parent who allows such unregulated viewing might well, and indeed it is highly likely, not regulate the child in other directions either. In other words, the real cause of the child's behaviour is a general lack of social control. The child has not been instructed in behaviour, but instead allowed to follow whatever he or she wishes to do. When this group was asked, *'Would anybody put television in that mix* [of influences] *in any way?'* the reply from one person was: *'It comes from the home I think'*. But clearly, on their own confession, it was not always the case that the parents were in control of the television. It did not seem to matter, however, if children watched material that was considered unsuitable, if other conditions applied: *'I still think that if they see something on the telly that's wrong you've already taught them it's wrong. Say like with EastEnders when they were selling all those drugs, the kids know that's wrong. They know right from wrong'*.

The Impact of Television

If a moral upbringing, through what might be described as 'nurtured discipline' as opposed to forced compliance to rules, is seen as affording protection against the likelihood of children engaging in anti-social behaviour, then this is not quite the case with unsociable behaviour.

Much attention was given in previous sections to the manner in which television might influence unsociable behaviour through the incorporation of style, and what style meant for people in terms of social indicators. The Redditch male group, it will be remembered, were specifically recruited because they had complained about programmes they had seen, or had objected strongly enough to what they saw to take avoiding action, either by switching the television off, changing channels or walking out of the room. The following comments are therefore particularly interesting, since they show that one of the foci for objection can be style and not necessarily something that prompts outright shock or revulsion.

The discussion in the group readily moved from addressing violence on television to other issues, such as bad language. One man started the ball rolling by discussing the content of films that are now shown on television:

> *Some of the language is awful. If you look at some of the Eddie Murphy films the language spoils what could be a regular family film. If it were just the odd bit of bad language and it fitted in with the story, okay, but when it goes all the way through it just becomes a bore.*

Boring it might be, but this man was saying more than that: he objected to it because the repetitive use of bad language made it unsuitable for family viewing. He had a teenage son, and said he had switched the television off on occasions to prevent his son being exposed to material.

The idea that he would not mind if there was *'the odd bit of bad language and it fitted in with the story'* is to miss the idea of the genre within which, to an extent, Eddie Murphy films fit. On the one hand they are often comic, but on the other they fit into the portrayal of inner-city American street culture. Close attention to the forms of expression of those who inhabit that culture, or have to deal with it in some regulatory way, are a mark of the films. Indeed, this goes back to the point made in earlier sections about the opening up by film and television, in almost documentary fashion, of sub-cultures that have remained hidden, or, if not exactly hidden in the past, dusted down to be presented in 'respectable' fashion.

This group were certainly far from what one might call genteel; that is, they had a robustness to them that suggested they were not precious in any way. Comments they made about their lives, especially past behaviour when younger, supported this. They saw current portrayals of language and behaviour as indicative of a wider social malaise. We asked them about their responses towards material that they saw on television, by saying: *'Is it simply because you don't like it or because you think it is dangerous in some way?'*

> *I don't think it's helpful if you have a society breaking down anyway – 5- and 6-year-olds kicking teachers and not respecting anything. I don't think you're helping it by portraying the rest of the world as being exactly the same. It is teaching disrespect.*

> *Television lacks discipline. We saw a documentary about glue sniffing – up until then we didn't know anything about it. I reckon the whole country started sniffing glue after that.*

Glue-sniffing would come into the category of unsociable behaviour and not anti-social, in the same way that heavy consumption of alcohol would. Both are 'crimes' without victims and, thus, cannot be said to threaten community. Behaviour, of course, might follow from the habit that is anti-social, but that does not make the original behaviour anti-social. The interesting point about the above comments, however, is not simply the reference to unsociable behaviour, and the teaching of certain attitudes by the media, leading to a disrespectfulness towards adults, but the reference to a *'society breaking down'*. This was followed by opening his comment to everyone for answer – did they think it was breaking down? Assent was not universal, or, as one man put it, *'I don't. I think it goes through cycles'*. It was not quite clear what he meant by this, but the feeling was given that societies hit low patches in their performance, and that one should not be too pessimistic about the future.

Those who did think society was breaking down, which really probably means no more than that it is in some kind of crisis of solidarity, as referenced by the performance of agreed behaviour, rather than that it is about to collapse in some fundamental way, were asked: *'What do you think is responsible for this breaking down?* One man said, *'I think America's 10 years ahead of us and I think we import a lot of beliefs from America'.*

In order to explore further what this group meant by society breaking down, we made a more direct enquiry: *'When you say society is breaking down, what do you mean by that?'*

Kids seem to want to damage things just because it doesn't belong to them. They seem to want to swear because it sets them out as being hard and they think they will gain respect from other people. This is what I mean by society breaking down – you've got a situation where kids have got no respect for anything. I consider myself to be a reasonable parent, but I still have to tell my kids not to do things because as soon as they walk out of the house there's nothing I can do. They go to school and come home with their shirt hanging out. You see that on Neighbours *– in* Neighbours *they go to school in jeans with their shirt hanging out, so our kids start doing it. It's only small things, but how far away are they from the more serious things. That's what worries me. I think there are certain things that you have to do if society is not going to break down completely.*

What is interesting in this context is that when respondents in our national sample were asked where they thought their values had come from, television was mentioned as influential, but no one said that it was the most important source. Yet, when we asked where they thought today's children got their values from, television as a source of influence dramatically rose, and some people nominated television as the most important source.

Where influences were likely to enter, even in those families where all the protective support structures were in place, was in the area of unsociable behaviour. Indeed, as we saw above, what may be innocent behaviour, the shirt worn outside the jeans, was not innocent to that particular parent. It represented to him more than just an unconventional way of dressing. It carried with it sets of attitudes that threatened the discarding of values that he had attempted to transmit to his children. He was aware of the trivial nature of the 'offence', but saw it linked to the deeper question of respect. In his view, once respect goes, and here he meant respect for traditional authority-holders, society as a functioning unit was directly challenged. Or, as pointed out earlier in discussing cultural politics, his type of authority-holder and his vision of what values society should operate on, and by, were threatened.

This idea of cultural strain was captured well in talking with the 18 to 24-year-old men in Leeds. For example, we presented them with the results of our questionnaire for comment. At one point, one of the young men asked us what the actual question in our survey had been in relation to sexual attitudes. Not remembering the precise wording of the question, we gave a rather clumsy interpretation, translated as: *'Do you as a group of young men think that our sexual standards have declined or remained the same?'* A bad question brought forth an insightful response: *'I wouldn't say they've declined, but they've changed'.* In terms of cultural politics, then, one group's idea of change becomes another group's idea of decline.

To the response that sexual standards had not declined, but simply changed, we asked, '*in what way?*' to which the answer was, '*It's more open*'. Indeed, they proceeded to discuss sexual matters with a great deal of openness, and expressed attitudes in the process that many in our other groups would have held as evidence for decline. It was quite clear that these young men were not going to live their lives or express themselves through the values and attitudes of other cultural groups. Nor did they accept that films might influence their behaviour. For example, they discussed the controversial film *Crash*, which deals with sexual excitement engendered by car accidents. One young man said: '*The reason I heard they wanted it banned was because they said it was going to influence people when they see violence*'. His dismissive response was: '*I think that's insane. If I had a car crash I wouldn't want to get out and bonk someone*'.

His position does have a certain brutal clarity to it, but what was interesting was that, later in the discussion, members in this group unhesitatingly admitted to having been influenced by the media. This came out in the course of discussing the incest scene in *Brookside*. It was mentioned to them that Phil Redmond had been interviewed in the course of the research. We relayed to them that his justification for including incest was that it was a soap opera reflecting the 'grittiness' of real life, and that incest is a fact of life. One of the young men said: '*I wasn't the slightest bit shocked by any of it. You knew what was going to happen. It didn't bother me at all*'. We then asked the group: '*But isn't that a bad thing?*'

I watched it – I thought it was dealt with very well. The best thing is that they're dealing with the consequences, it's not just finished. It went into how it tore the family apart and they dealt with it.

It was brilliant TV but I didn't entirely approve of it. It wasn't saying it was ok but it just seemed to be saying to me like 'it happens'. It wasn't soap opera material in my opinion. Incest isn't something that soap opera deals with. Soap opera is everyday life – incest is not everyday life. That's what it's implying. It made out that maybe it's a little bit more common than it actually is.

Thus, on the one hand the incest in *Brookside* was approved of because it offered a moral tale – that it can tear families apart – and on the other hand it was objected to because it was felt that the incidence of incest is not common enough to form part of everyday life and, thus, had no place in a genre based on the portrayal of everyday life. What was interesting about these young men, and evidenced by the way they handled not just the topic of incest but other sexual matters such as bestiality, was how comfortably they talked about sex. We mentioned this to them and said that we doubted we could have had such a conversation, say, twenty years ago. We then said: '*How would you account for your relaxed attitude to discussing sex?*' The reply given by one man, to the assent of others, was: '*The media*'.

Their relaxed attitude was not all put down to the media. For example, someone else, after commenting that '*Attitudes have changed a lot in the last ten years*', went on to say:

The issues of homosexuals and lesbians and the Act going through Parliament about the age of consent. Suddenly all these famous actors came out of the closet and it was perfectly ok. It became part of society. If you ask a lot of older people they can't deal with it. The younger generation have to accept it and if they don't they're left behind.

To underscore the point about their relaxed attitude towards discussing sex, another young man added: *'It's because it's more talked about and you get used to it. It would take a lot to shock most of us'*. What one has here is the interweaving of legislator influences (the legislation, although shaping attitudes, is reflective at the same time of changes in public attitudes) with public discussion to produce a relaxed approach to such issues.

If we now hold these comments against the comments made by the man in Redditch, concerning his worry about the significance of codes of dress and language, we can see that there is ground for his concern. It is at this level – how we address the world – that the media can push aside the restraining forces that have been put in place by the family to protect against the likelihood of children adopting anti-social behaviour by exposure to anti-social behaviour on television.

There is no need to rehearse the argument of the previous chapter concerning what swearing or dress codes can represent, and how meanings can be incorporated, often through alteration of the positions that they carried in their original setting. One of the 25- to 44-year-old men in the Leeds group commented on the decline in regulatory control over the years. Someone else described current regulation as 'slack'. The first man then focused on bad language: *'I think there has been a deterioration over the years. When I was 15 you hardly heard any bad language on television. Now it's just normal to hear it'*. The worry here is that the repetitive use of bad language has normalized and legitimized its presence in everyday language. His major worry, however, was that swearing exposed more than a particular selection of words that an individual has access to. Such words represented a particular attitude and approach to the world that he objected to and was worried by: it showed that the individual wanted to present themselves as, in his words, 'hard', and demonstrated a lack of respect for others. Thus, the adoption of styles, be it in clothes or language, is the adoption of manners. The exact meaning of those manners, whether it is 'surface play' or 'deep play', must always be open to empirical inspection. However, even as 'surface play' they can worry groups who do not incorporate such play into their repertoire, and especially cause worry if that play is interpreted as standing against, or offering a challenge to, their own values and, by extension, the structure of the lives out of which their values developed. One thing is for sure, unsociable behaviour, and swearing and forms of dress, if they break accepted codes of presentation, have an easier mediated passage into people's lives than mediated anti-social behaviour. Such concerns over culture usually involve calls for regulation.

Regulation, Confusion and Moral Language

A key aim of the research we undertook was to examine individuals' attitudes to the control of culture. We wanted to explore the manner in which individuals want, and perhaps even expect, external agencies to interject in cultural expression. Our intention was not so much to find out what offends, but what ought to be done when offence is given. We wished, in other words, to explore tolerance, and the basis upon which tolerance functioned. On the one hand, someone might hold that no matter how graphic or how much violence was shown on television there are no grounds for prohibiting the material, or making alterations to it, since it could not have any effect on behaviour in real life. On the other hand, they might still wish such material to be prohibited because they considered the scenes shown to be in some way immoral or in bad taste.

We wished to know what authority people were prepared to give to external agencies to control what they watched. In short, we wanted to examine respondents' own attitudes and preferred relationship to authority. In what way, and in what manner, did they consent to control of their own lives? We began by exploring, across a variety of situations, what power they were willing to give the state in controlling their behaviour. We deliberately took areas of performance where it is at least arguable that, in a liberal democracy, the state has no right of intrusion; those areas of social performance where it is not automatically obvious that anyone is at risk from their behaviour other than themselves, or areas of personal life where the individual has traditionally had great claim over its administration.

We begin with the London women, aged 18–24, in the focus groups. We asked them whether *'married couples who wish to divorce should be made to attend counselling before a divorce is granted?'* These are their responses:

Personally I'd say no. Once your feelings have gone for a person you can't make them come back so counselling isn't going to help.

I think it depends how late you leave counselling. If it's gone too far you can't make them come back

People become very irrational when marriages break down and I think counselling could help. It may be that people just don't want to talk about things and sometimes I think they should be made to talk to each other and sort things out.

We pressed this further by saying: *'So you think it is a good idea to be made to have counselling?'* The response was, *'Yes I think they should be made to.'* Someone else thought that *'It's up to the person – whether they want to or not'*, to which another young woman added: *'I think if there was any domestic violence involved then you shouldn't be made to go, but if it's just a marriage break-up I think they should be made to go'*. A dissenting opinion was offered: *'I don't think people should be made to go'*. When asked why, she replied: *'If you're made to go you don't want to go'*.

What is interesting about their responses is their practical nature. Rather than showing any regard for the issue of the moral right of the state to interfere in something so personal as marriage, they focused instead on whether counselling was a good idea as a practical solution in the correction of lost affection. The only time they considered counselling ought not to be forced on a couple was where domestic violence was involved. The reason for this was presumably on the grounds that the individual has a higher right not to be molested than the state has to try and make the marriage work. Even the person who said that she did not agree that people should be forced to attend counselling, when asked why, did not give the reason of the rights of the individual to decide action in that area of their lives. Instead, her reason was based on the practical grounds that, if a person were forced to go, it would show that they did not wish to go – the assumption being that to go under duress would render the whole exercise pointless.

These young women were not married, but the responses were surprisingly similar among women who were married. The same question about counselling was put to the women living in the Bristol area, who had children between the ages of 10 and 16. One woman said: *'I agree'*, while another said: *'It would probably help'*. Another gave a more considered response:

I think it depends on the circumstances. You just don't know everyone's circumstances, do you? It might not be an ideal situation. If it was just a tiff and they decided they might get divorced then maybe that might help them realize they made a mistake.

Again we see a concentration on the practical and not on the rights of the situation. We asked men in Walsall, aged under 55 with children at home between the ages of 10 and 16, the same question to see if there were any gender differences in responses. This time we expressed the question even more forcefully, just in case the idea of being *made* to have counselling was getting lost and that respondents were somehow responding to the question in terms of whether the idea of counselling itself was a good idea. We presented the question in its standard form and then followed it by saying: *'Should one be forced to have counselling if their marriage broke up?'*: *'I think it should be part of the system'*. This was not met by total agreement. For example, one man gave the qualified response: *'It depends on the grounds for the divorce. If it's just a gradual breakdown then maybe, but if you came home and found your wife in bed with another bloke…'* This introduction of sexual betrayal confused the discussion a little bit, from which it never really recovered. But someone else thought that counselling in such a situation was not necessarily wrong, since, as he delicately put it, *'there could be a reason for that though couldn't there'*, referring to why the other man's wife might be in bed with someone other than him. One person did say, which we took as a dissenting voice: *'It's a very personal thing – marriage – between two individuals'*.

To try and refocus the discussion we straightforwardly asked: *'Should the State interfere in how you want to run your life?'* Several responses followed, including puzzlement that it should want to: *'Why should they want to do it anyway?'* This then produced reasons why the State might wish to, the leading one presented being 'cost implications'. Even when it was put to them that to make people have counselling *'impinged on individual freedom, doesn't it'*, there was no great clamour to defend the rights of the individual over the State. One man even said: *'You have got to impinge occasionally on people to enable you to enforce law and order'*.

What we witnessed through this question was either a ready willingness for the State to regulate a very private aspect of individuals' lives, and a lack of willingness, or an inability to detect that a moral principle was involved, choosing instead to address the question from the position of whether counselling offered a practical solution to the breakdown of relationships.

We moved away from marriage as our focus in trying to establish what rights people gave the State to regulate their personal lives, by having members of the group consider alcoholism, and whether or not such drinkers should be forced to seek treatment. The pattern of responses was not that much different from those given in the case of making people seek counselling upon the break-up of marriage. These are the responses from the 18 to 24-year-old London women. The question put to the group was: *'If someone lost their job because they are an alcoholic should they be legally required to seek treatment?'*

I think they should – they're not likely to go on their own accord, and it would probably sort their lives out for them.

It's like getting people to go to drugs counselling – unless you want to go you're never going to do it. If it became law they would have to do it. Alcoholism normally leads to other things – violence, drugs.

To explore this question of rights as fully as possible, we deliberately began to argue the case for non-interference to see if that prompted a different response. We said, *'but do they have the right to pass this law though? What if a university lecturer was drinking heavily and it was affecting the way he taught the students?'* The response from one woman to this was: *'No, I don't think they do. It's freedom of choice'*. We then followed this by saying: *'So you see this as a question of freedom of choice, whereas you didn't with marriage counselling. Is there a difference between the two?'* Her reply was: *'Yes because alcoholism is self-inflicted whereas with marriage, it's a breakdown in communication a lot of the time'*. Again, although it looks as if this person is viewing the question as a moral one, in fact she has still seen it as an applied question. She thought that counselling might work because the problem has roots that talking to someone about might help to resolve, but not in the case of self-inflicted alcoholism. Someone else added: *'Then again, it's creating the same circle isn't it? If you're an alcoholic it could lead to violence, it could lead to crime. It could have been prevented if a law had been brought in to make that person go and seek help'*. Then, as an afterthought, she said, *'But you're always going to have alcoholics'*.

The question is still not being cast in moral terms, or, if it is, then it is clearly the case that the State has the right of interference. When examined though, that right of interference is not so much based on the principle of the State having the right to circumscribe the right to self-determination, as protecting against the lawlessness that might follow from alcohol abuse. Thus, we pressed further and asked: *'What if the person really enjoyed being an alcoholic – he was happy being smashed most of the time? Do you think the law ought to impinge or interfere in people's lives?'* To this, one of the women said: *'Not if they're not affecting anybody else. There shouldn't be somebody telling you what you should and shouldn't do. It's like the nanny State'*.

This was the first time, and only as a result of our pressing questioning, that the question was seen as involving a moral issue. In this case she mentioned the 'nanny State', implying that it had no right over such individual behaviour. To have stated the opposite, that the State did have a right over such individual behaviour, would have equally counted as operating a moral language.

The Walsall men adopted the same pragmatic approach to this question as they did to the questioning of marriage counselling. For example: *'Alcoholism is an illness, isn't it? Alcoholics need help and it would help everybody if they did have treatment'*. One man did say, however, *'I don't think so. I think if you want to drink a lot, it's up to you. It's got to be a voluntary thing'*.

The Walsall women's responses to the issue of alcoholism again did not differ much from their responses in relation to the question of marriage counselling, except one person did say this time: *'It's up to them, isn't it?'* Others said: *'He's got to want to stop drinking himself, hasn't he?'* *'You can't make anybody do anything, can you?'* by which they did not mean that the State had no moral right to compel the drinker to seek treatment, but that, as in the case of marriage counselling, if the person did not wish by their own volition to seek help, the counselling or treatment would not work.

These questions were also asked of respondents in our national questionnaire. The results show high proportions opting for forcible treatment (58%) and, to a lesser extent, for making people attend marriage counselling (44%). (See Table 1.) The detailed results of the survey are given in the following chapter. Allied with responses to other questions, one can use these responses to place individuals within a neo-Aristotelian or liberal set of values. However, both the groups and the surveys show that people can have difficulty in confronting moral questions. They seem to turn moral questions into those capable of technical resolution. There is no longer, as expressed in the earlier section, a moral language by which people can readily sort through moral issues.

The main reason for asking questions about how far the State could regulate individuals' lives was to provide a setting for addressing how far external agencies, the State, or another agent, were given permission to regulate cultural consumption. If the State was given a great deal of authority to interfere in personal aspects of individuals' lives, then the question was, is culture an exception? What we come across, however, is a difficulty of people to address central moral issues, not just of control, but also of handling value distinctions. Indeed, what was of central importance in the acceptance of control was the individuals' relationship not to culture as such – the real moral question – but their relationship to how culture was supplied, the nature of the contract between the receiver and the supplier. In many ways regulation itself was not the issue, but rather how culture was consumed. Regulation was fine in some circumstances but not in others, but what made regulation appropriate or not appropriate remained morally unresolved. That is, how content in one set of circumstances required regulation, but the same content in another set of circumstances did not, looked at times as if culture was non-problematic. But yet, we have seen, in the body of focus group findings, that culture was indeed problematic – it had all kinds of worries and concerns attached.

It was argued earlier that cultural struggle is political struggle. The case we took as relevant to our project was swearing. We showed how the use of bad language could act as notification that the power of the traditional holders of moral authority was in decline, or, at the very least, that their power was being challenged by groups that failed to recognize their authority, and did so by non-compliance with the cultural rules governing language.

This clash of social and cultural groups, however, represents more than a cultural struggle to have one's own values accepted as the dominant values and model for social performance. It stretches tolerance to the limit, or, perhaps more accurately, is a test of tolerance, especially in a society organized around, and living by, liberal democratic values. We need to know, therefore, how prepared people are to put the other before the self; that is, to agree that something should not be shown if others find material offensive, but which they themselves do not.

We asked the young men in Leeds whether if a programme was blasphemous, and this offended a small section of the population, it should be shown? The case we used was the controversial film *The Last Temptation of Christ*,[4] and we asked if this should be given general release at the cinema. There was general agreement that it should. When asked why: *'They don't have to watch it if they don't agree with it. There's plenty of things that I wouldn't watch'*. We then moved from the cinema to television and asked: *'Should it be shown after 10 o'clock on the main channels if it was going to "deeply offend" some people?'*

> No. They don't have to watch it. As long as it's known that it is one man's interpretation of the last hours of Christ. I don't think it's up to a regulator to decide that one man's opinion can't be shown.

It's obviously different on TV to the cinema. A lot of people turn the TV on by accident. At the cinema you know what you are going to see.

Anyone who watches the Last Temptation of Christ *knows beforehand whether they're going to get offended if they watch it.*

Even here we witness a change in attitude to cultural performance as a dependent of the contract made with the supplier; in going to the cinema the viewer deliberately exposes themselves to the message. But, we also have the idea of artistic freedom. It would also appear that knowingly exposing oneself to something makes a difference to the acceptability of the content. We pushed on by asking what their response would be to a devout Christian who would not watch a film portraying Jesus Christ as a homosexual, but did not want anyone else to watch it either: *'That's saying it should never be made, it's not saying it should be censored'*. *'I think it should be made – it's freedom of expression'*.

We followed this by saying that Muslims might find many things on television offensive and then took the extreme case by asking, *'what if it was decided to make a serialization of the* Satanic Verses?*'*

A serialization of the Satanic Verses *would be asking for trouble.*

I don't think anyone would make that, not because it would shock people but because there really is no need for that after all the trouble with the book. You're offending so many people with deep moral and religious feeling. They'd have to be very stupid to do that.

Certain things you can make an argument for and certain things you can't. I don't think you can make an argument for serialising Satanic Verses.

Even with bestiality in a way you could have an argument about it I suppose, but with something like Satanic Verses *there would be so much trouble.*

I think if Salman Rushdie said he really wanted to make a film in this country then he has every right to.

I don't say that they can stop him, I'm just saying that if he did it would be a wrong decision.

I don't think the Muslims could stop him. He's in our country and they can't be in our country and not accept the values that our country upholds. We wouldn't go to any Muslim country and walk around naked because that would offend – we don't do it. It works both ways.

These young men hardly addressed the question in any moral way. The issue of freedom of expression is not really raised, nor is the question of offence addressed in any moral fashion; that is, the right of someone not to have their beliefs assaulted by a film. The main thrust for not making such a film is not the offence it might cause, and therefore giving up one's own rights in deference to others, but the pragmatic reason that to make such a film would cause trouble. Moral issues quickly become applied politics. It is interesting, however, that perceived 'out-groups' such as Muslims lose rights because they are cultural strangers. They lose voice because the dominant culture is not Muslim. Here we see culture not as a struggle for expression, the making of meanings, but the right of one group through its position in society to have its definitions of the world culturally enforced.

What is particularly interesting in examining the responses in the focus groups to the idea of acknowledging the rights of people not to be offended, and the sacrificing of programmes to protect others from offence, is, as in the above, the idea of cultural domination. What is also interesting is the appeal to numeric presence as an arbiter of what is right. Indeed, even where one has the sense of appeal to a shared culture – domination – there lurks numeric justification; that most people are not Muslims, therefore, their voice is reduced accordingly. This came out even more forcibly in some other groups. For example, the same scenario was given to the young women in London as was given to the young men in Leeds: *'Yes, it should still be made'. 'They* [Muslims] *are the minority, aren't they? The majority want to see a film like that'. 'They have the choice, don't they? They don't have to see a film if they don't want to. Why should the majority be dictated to by the minority?'*

Rights thus become a question of measurement. But we have seen that, in so far as culture is concerned, to simply take a majority ruling solves nothing. There is no general agreement of a core set of values that one can appeal to for support of cultural material. Culture is the expressions of people, and modern society is too fragmented to even talk in terms of sets of shared experiences that will allow appeal to agreed norms. What is missing, as commented upon at length in earlier parts of this book, is a language by which to debate such issues. In the absence of such ability, one has appeal to numbers as a way of salvation. What those numbers might mean in moral terms is never discussed. No real arguments were put forward, although they could have been, for a moral defence of cultural portrayals based on the maximization of satisfactions. Numbers were used as a way of resolving a problem through accountancy, and no higher justification than that was given.

If we leave the area of religion aside and talk in terms of representing sexual lifestyles, the problem of not facing up to cultural questions as moral questions becomes clear. We asked the London men, aged under 55, about representations of groups and cultural material that might reflect those groups' interests based on their lifestyle. There was general agreement in this group that ethnic minorities ought to appear in programmes: *'There used to be programmes all the time on TV where you never saw a black person and yet you look around London and they're everywhere. Programmes like* EastEnders *and* Coronation Street *should have black people in them'.* We asked, *'but would you extend that to homosexuals?'*

> There's a moral code. Is it the ITC who does all the checking? There are things that are right and things that are wrong and I think that's all got clouded. It's making it harder for people to realise what is right and what is wrong, but instinctively we know what is right and what is wrong.

> You're wrong there because homosexuality isn't wrong if you're over 21.

> It's different having ethnic groups because they're part of our society – although homosexuals are, it doesn't make them right in my mind. It's a moral point – I'm a Christian and that's what my views are.

Subscription Channels

As he pointed out, the last person quoted above was a Christian and thought homosexuality was wrong on scriptural grounds; that it was *'against God's law'*. It would appear, therefore, that cultural portrayal here was easily resolved by appeal to an all-embracing system of moral belief. But it did not turn out that way once we moved away from the question of the relationship of people to culture and the relationship of each to the other – the homosexual and the heterosexual – and turned to the relationship of the consumer to the supplier. We asked him, *'What if somebody was paying to watch a satellite channel where there was quite graphic material?'* He thought that was permissible, so we replied: *'That's fine is it, but isn't it still against God's law?'* His reply was; *'It doesn't affect me or my family, does it?'* The point was pursued: *'But surely in a general sense, if one is a Christian, aren't you saying that nobody should watch it? Or are you saying that if you pay for it it's different?'* This was a bit hectoring but we wished to clarify an important issue; namely, did a person who had a strong set of moral beliefs, in this case a sanctified set of beliefs, consider that how one consumed culture, in this case by payment, makes the consumption of certain material permissible in a way that was not permissible if the contractual relationship was different? His reply was: *'It is a bit cloudy, isn't it? Obviously there are homosexuals in this country and they want to watch this sort of thing. If it's on a certain channel then they're not doing any harm by watching it'.*

It did not seem to us a very theologically pure position, but what we did find throughout the focus groups was that if someone paid for material then any general rule that might govern the consumption of culture did not apply, or, perhaps more accurately, had a weakened case. For example, the under-55 women in Walsall did not especially approve of the amount of sexual display on television, and when asked, *'Do you think they should tighten up regulations in relation to television?'* the response was one of general consent. They also said that regulation governing bad language should be more strictly applied, but when we asked about *'adult movies on satellite stations, is it fine for people to watch them or would you regulate those?'* the response was: *'I don't think there is anything wrong with it'.*

We were aware that in responding to questions of satellite delivery, or delivery by cable, people had in mind control through smart cards and so on, so that children could not access programmes with the ease that they might on terrestrial channels. This was allowed for in their responses. It was clear that people brought a different set of standards to the newer delivery systems than the older systems that were based on the changed nature of the contractual relationship. For example, the national survey revealed marked differences over the acceptability of such material depending on whether it is shown on a channel that is paid for directly or not. See, for example, Table 21 in Chapter 4b. The contract through the licence fee had a totally different logic attached to it than the contract with satellite or cable. For example, the above women, who had earlier talked about protecting children from access to unsuitable channels, showed that what was in operation for many people was that the direct purchase of something became an individual decision and had little or no relationship to collective interests. That is, that the State, or some external agency, or community values and interests, call it what one wants, had no right, or at least a reduced one, in limiting the freedom of the individual.

We asked the group, if someone was paying for a channel and it showed a particularly savage rape, was that acceptable? The response from one woman was: *'I think it is their choice'*. It must be said that there was one dissenting voice, *'I don't think it should be shown, full stop'*. Other responses were: *'You've got to have freedom of choice, haven't you?'* and *'You're encroaching on people's liberty'*, although this last person did worry about *'kids who have access to it'*. This latter question is a technical issue and not a matter of principle. In principle, adults were given permission to watch material if they paid for it, that they were not given if it was received for 'free'.

It would appear that the new delivery systems sit at a far point on a continuum of acceptance of what delivery systems are allowed to transmit. This was given clear voice by the 45- to 64-year-old Leeds women. After agreeing that *'there should be some regulations'* governing material on terrestrial television, they were asked if the same rules should apply to the cinema: *'I don't think it's as necessary as for television'* responded one woman, to which another added, to general agreement, *'I don't think anything goes'*. They were then asked for their comment on videos. Back came the reply: *'The same as cinema'*. A different judgement, however, was made with regard to satellite television: *'It's choice really with that one – I suppose if you want to watch dirty movies from Germany you can'*.

From the focus groups it would be difficult to say where each medium sat precisely on the continuum of regulation, but it was absolutely clear that terrestrial television was at one end of control and satellite television, whilst perhaps not being at the furthest end of the scale, was certainly grouped with cinema and video in terms of the relaxation of control. Some people even considered that there should be no control, or hardly any control, if a person paid directly for a service.

The entry of direct payment is therefore seen to change not only the public's relationship to regulators but also its attitude towards each other as viewers. It was almost as if what one did in one's own home was nobody else's business. What people are overlooking here is, of course, that whilst one might pay directly for a service, so are other people paying directly for the same service, and, thus, other homes are still culturally connected to theirs. It is as if the act of payment creates private space, which the State or some other agency ought not to enter. If this is the case, then a relaxation of the rules of cultural surveillance is interesting in light of the finding that many people gave the State permission to enter a most private area of their personal lives by agreeing that couples ought to be made to attend marriage counselling before dissolving a marriage. Perhaps, ill-equipped to make moral judgements in any systematic way, then money, and what that means for access to goods and privileges in a consumption society, becomes the criterion of what is right.

Privacy: An Easily Understood Outrage

When we opened the discussion in the focus groups by asking what power the media have, without any prompting, the question of privacy arose. It was held that the media abused their power by transgressing individuals' rights to privacy. From these initial reactions, it did seem that individuals have an inalienable right to privacy, but it became obvious at that early stage of our questioning that this was not so, for example, when the case of Hugh Grant and his relationship with a prostitute was examined. The question of a right to privacy became even more complicated when the right to privacy of his girlfriend, Liz Hurley, was examined. Indeed, what emerged was that there was no automatic right to privacy for anyone. This is shown quite clearly in the national survey where people were asked to judge the degree of privacy that various types of individuals had a right to expect. The results show that a pivotal factor in determining privacy is that of innocence. (See Table 23, Chapter 4b.) The right to privacy had to be merited. It is, therefore, how one merits privacy that requires examination.

One of the rules that emerged, governing whether material ought to be published, was whether or not the exposure of information served the public interest. The notion of 'the public interest' is not easily defined. Once more we bump up against the idea of differential groups with differential interests that caused so many problems in deciding whether there was a commonly held set of values to which one could make an appeal in deciding the merit of cultural products. The invoking of public interest is, more often than not, really the invoking of the interests of one particular group. The ideological trick, of course, is to pass off one's own group's interests as the interest of all. That is what hegemony is.

It is probably the case, however, that the neo-Aristotelian has less difficulty than the liberal in applying the notion of public interest, if for no other reason than that he or she operates with a moral direction that more readily subsumes the individual as part of a collective enterprise.

One of the oldest groups, men aged over 55 in the Bristol area, considered that, even though the public might be interested in the goings-on of people, such as famous sportsmen, they had no right to know. Their argument was not out of concern for the distress it might cause a sportsman who engaged in some miscreant behaviour, but that the public needed protecting from knowledge about their behaviour. These men considered that what young people require are heroes to look up to and model themselves on, even if what they are taking as their model is false.

> *You are influenced by the media. I was greatly influenced by certain sportsmen – footballers or cricketers. We wanted to be like them when we were young. What you read in the papers in those days certainly affected the way you lived. [...] A few years ago there was a programme on about the Middlesex twins Compton and Edridge [cricketers] who were my idols in the post-war years. They were reminiscing about their on-tour parties. Edridge said to Compton across the table 'remember the one when we had...' and Compton shut him up immediately. They [the press] could have dug up all the dirt, like they do with Botham now.*

This man was then asked, *'is it not good that people are told what they are like in private rather than admiring a clean living sportsman when in fact he is living a lie?'* Talking about the footballer George Best, he commented:

> *I think if George Best is womanizing and drinking to make that public is probably encouraging young people who are keen on George Best to think that maybe that's what you have to do to be a good footballer. As far as I am concerned that was his private life and I don't think that should be intruded on.*

It was not just the behaviour of sportsmen which it was claimed should be kept quiet, but pop stars also, or at least their views censored if what they said was not in the public interest: *'I was watching the news before I came out tonight and the lead singer of East 17 has just announced that taking the drug Ecstasy is ok. Should that have been covered? Definitely not!'* There was common agreement on this, the reason being that: *'You get kids hanging on to every word they say'.* Someone else added: *'Years ago they wouldn't have interviewed him, it wouldn't have been allowed'.*

What these men are saying is that 'hero' figures, such as sportsmen or pop stars, should not have their privacy invaded, not out of consideration for the sensibilities and rights of those involved, but out of consideration for the public interest. This is pure neo-Aristotelianism, in that only those aspects of 'heroes'' behaviour which act as a good model for the young should be portrayed and not those aspects of behaviour that set a bad example.

For most respondents, whether or not sportsmen had a right to privacy would not be decided by a consideration of public interest, but rather by focusing on the interests of the individual whose privacy was breached. As a general rule, most people held that those in the public eye had less right to privacy than someone who was not. Sportsmen would more than likely have greater protection on this principle than film stars, on the grounds that film stars court publicity to promote their films, and often engage in behaviour to attract attention to themselves.

Politicians have low rights, but they are probably higher than those of film stars. We asked about David Mellor, a married junior minister in John Major's Conservative Government, and his affair with actress Antonia de Sancha. The young men in Leeds thought he had a reduced right to privacy because, as one of them said: '*A politician has elected himself to public life*'. Asked if David Mellor's wife had a right to privacy, then all thought, in a moral sense, she did. However, they realized the practical difficulties of her not being dragged into the limelight. As one of the young men said: '*I'd like to say leave Mrs Mellor alone, but it is not as simple as that, is it?*' Another member of the group added: '*She should have privacy, but if you're married to someone who is in the spotlight and they do something wrong, then unfortunately you have to take the consequences*'. In other words, she has a very high right to privacy, certainly more than Mellor himself, but not as high as someone married to a non-public figure.

Some of the groups, in discussing Mellor's affair, extrapolated to politicians in general. For example, one of the men in the Redditch group said:

> The thing that I don't like about privacy is that if you've got an MP who wants to be elected he can't get his face on the telly enough, he's there with his wife and kids. And then a bit later when he's been elected and something comes out about his past – if that would have affected the way people voted if they had known about it then I think it should be publicised. I think if they are going to set themselves up as guardians of our morality then they should be spotless – one thing I don't like is somebody telling me what I should and shouldn't be doing when they are doing it themselves.

This last point can be referred back to the point made earlier in discussing the decline of moral authority; namely, the dialectical nature of expectation and behaviour. The general loosening of positional moral authority produces a change in the behaviour of those who occupy positions that, in the past, commanded moral authority. People in these positions now feel free to engage in behaviour which, if it becomes public, lowers respect for the position and further adds to the decline in positional moral authority.

If we now turn to people who are not in the glare of the public spotlight we see the right to privacy does become more sacrosanct. Much depends on the behaviour itself that might warrant attention and, also, on the context of the performance. A victim of a crime, or those injured in an accident, are presumed totally innocent of anything and therefore their right to privacy is sacrosanct. For example, when asked what rights victims have, one man from the Walsall group replied: *'I think it's dreadful, it's dreadful when something's happened and they get hounded by cameras and people saying "how do you feel?"'* Someone else added: *'It's other people's suffering'*. *'And another thing they do is when there has been an inquest they'll show the family coming out – I don't like that.'*

Permission

This is not to say that such scenes should not be shown, or that victims and other innocent parties should not be interviewed, but that there is no right of access to them. Their permission must be first sought before an interview is undertaken or filming takes place. As one man in this group said: *'I think they should ask the victims first, or their families'*.

If victims have total rights, then, depending on the seriousness of the crime, the guilty have no rights to privacy and neither do they need to be consulted, or their permission gained, in order to film or seek interviews with other people about them. For example, it was held by women in Leeds that the serial killer known as the Yorkshire Ripper had no rights to privacy, but his victims, as innocent parties, did. However, given that they were dead, those rights were extended as rights to their family. Permission in such a situation had to be sought and received before any interview or filming could take place.

Clearly the dead cannot give permission to have the media intrude, and it is interesting that, in such a situation, the rights given to the innocent become extended to their family. What we wished to know, however, is what rights do the living have who are not in control of their rights to privacy. In this case, and drawing for example on a documentary about Alzheimer's disease, we asked what right a camera crew had to film patients in a hospital. A young man in our Leeds group said:

> *They would need to get the family's permission because it's not going to affect the person with Alzheimer's. It makes no real difference to them, but to the families who have to go through the tragedy of watching this relative deteriorate and all the people who know the family. If a producer asks the family's permission and they give it because they think people should know about it, then its fine, but they just can't go ahead and make the film without the family's permission and they are sitting at home watching it, that wouldn't be right.*

What we witness here is more than one set of rights to be taken into account. The family have rights over whether their relative should be shown because it might upset them, but the patient also has a right, which is delegated to his or her relatives on the assumption that the family will have the interests of the patient at heart, and that they will act as a proxy voice. The presumption here is that all are acting with good intention, signified by the statement that filming can go ahead, *'if they think people should know about it'*. This introduction of intentions into the family's decision must, by extension, apply to the producer. That is, if his or her intention is not respectable, for example, they simply wish to make a sensational programme, then it would not be permissible to film and intrude into the patient's privacy. When asked what would be the case where the family refused permission, this man considered that the right to privacy should not be broken, but that perhaps, *'there would be one way of doing it, they could maybe do it on a medical video for doctors'.* Thus, the motive for breaching privacy in such a case would seem all-important.

The feelings of the family are also important, but this does appear to be reduced if the motive for making the item has a strong claim to recommend it, for instance, in the above case where it would benefit medicine itself, but also where it might benefit general understanding of the illness. In the under-55 Walsall male group, one of the discussants had watched his father die of Alzheimer's. He said:

> *My dad died of Alzheimer's so I've been through that. I saw it right from the start when he started losing his memory, to when he wasted away. I don't think I would have liked that to be shown. It might be all right watching someone else's dad. I wasn't even close to my dad, but I wouldn't like to see that.*

This moving statement opened up the conversation to rather sensitive commentary. One man said: *'Once somebody involved with you gets Alzheimer's and you start going to the hospital it's amazing how many people you see that you've known through your life. If you don't highlight some aspects of the illness then you'll never get people to understand it'.*

Here was a genuine moral dilemma, and it was being discussed in moral terms. Indeed, people could handle the question of privacy more successfully than other issues they were asked to comment on. Privacy did not need the type of ordering of thought that questions of culture required. It was not necessary to have access to a system of beliefs, as it was seen to come down to a matter of decency, and respect for other people as individuals. In relation to privacy, as in the case of understanding other people's behaviour and motive mentioned earlier, it was easy for people to put themselves in the place of the other person in coming to a judgement of what was right and what was wrong.

In summary, two main factors appear to be involved in the management of privacy: the moral status of the individual; and the public's right to know about that individual. These two factors then determine the right to privacy and the degree of consultation required before entering an individual's private space. The importance of these two factors in deciding the rights to privacy can be seen in operation by consulting the schematic overview laid out in the Appendix.

Notes
1. See Table 14 in Chapter 4b for details.
2. This refers to one of the lead actors, who, in the 1960s, was convicted of manslaughter and served eleven years in prison.
3. You cannot stand for local Council if you have served a prison sentence (including suspended sentences) of 3 months or more within 5 years prior to the election.
4. Based on Nikos Kazantzakis' novel of the same name, *The Last Temptation of Christ* met with controversy from various Christian groups protesting the way Christ was depicted (even before most of the protesters had seen the film). The outcry over the alleged blasphemous content came predominantly from Fundamentalist groups who had heard that the film contained a sex scene between Jesus and Mary Magdalene.

4b What Constitutes Social and Anti-Social Behaviour? Views of Authority – Voices from Surveys

This chapter analyses the results from two linked nationally representative survey waves conducted into public perceptions of key issues relating to privacy, the media and values. The surveys also formed the basis for an operational classification of individuals into two broad 'value types' – neo-Aristotelian and liberal – based on those outlined theoretically in Chapter 1. This categorization indicates that the majority of adults in the UK tend to hold neo-Aristotelian rather than liberal views on a range of moral and social issues, together with a minority who appear to have somewhat inconsistent views on these. Moreover, when these categories are applied to opinions about issues of who has rights over the media and those who do not, and what the consequent media 'rules of engagement' should be, strong and consistent differences are found in many cases. Equally, though, the survey evidence shows that there are key issues where there is effectively universal agreement over the relative rights of individuals and the media, regardless of overall moral orientation.

So far, in discussing values and cultural control, the reporting has been guided by the two philosophical notions of the liberal and the neo-Aristotelian, developed from comments made in the course of the initial focus groups. The focus groups were also used for theoretical development of issues relating to social and cultural control, and also for presenting information concerning how people saw and constructed the social and communicative world. As stated, however, the accounts given in focus groups, although offering rich material giving insights into thinking in terms of representativeness to wider populations, can only be used for making statements about the range of opinion; they can say nothing about the distribution of the opinions or thinking collected within the groups. It must be stressed, indeed forcefully stressed, that qualitative measures cannot alone represent how a given population think or feel. To base our argument solely upon focus group material would be to run the very real risk of profoundly misrepresenting the public point of view about the issues covered. From the outset, therefore, the study incorporated a substantial survey research element designed to complement the other elements of the study, and so give a sound statistically representative basis to our analysis.

Thus, the research design included two discrete survey stages. Both surveys were designed to be representative of adults (aged 16 or older) in the UK and were administered by a professional market research company. Survey 1 involved a sample of 1,062 adults and Survey 2, 535 adults. (See Appendix for further details of the surveys.)

Survey Goals

The dual-stage survey design was chosen in order to be able to explore a range of key issues in detail, in particular seeking evidence for the structuration of individuals' values and beliefs along a broadly liberal to neo-Aristotelian basis. The design also allowed for the first survey wave results, together with the intermediate focus groups stage, to inform the design of the second survey wave. The second set of focus groups concentrated primarily upon the findings from the first survey wave, interpreting them and refining shades of meaning, and providing further lines of questioning which the second survey followed up. This approach avoided the inevitable pitfalls which occur when a single survey attempts to be comprehensive without being able to return to issues highlighted by responses for further consideration. It also reduces the risk of respondent 'contamination', which might occur if a single, hour-long questionnaire homing in on a set of linked topics had been used. Further, for some key questions repeated on each wave, the design provides the benefit of independently repeated measures.

In a later chapter (8b), we also analyse the findings from a third survey, which addressed the meaning of the term 'the public interest' and its role in privacy in greater detail.

The questionnaires covered a range of issues in varying degrees of depth. In this chapter, three broad themes, developed from the issues discussed in the preceding chapters, are covered. While these are not necessarily entirely separate issues, they were covered in particular depth and follow a natural logic, starting with the basic 'building blocks' of values and going on to the expression of these values.

- First, the personal values which people hold to, the development of these values, and the influences upon them. These value structures appear to underlie many other reactions to questions, and influence specific opinions about media and other issues.
- Second, the joint issues of potential offence and possible harm which the media may inflict upon the public, in particular offence against people's beliefs and the perceived impact of violent television and video content. Of particular interest here is the seemingly irrational and widely held view that something which could pose harm to individuals becomes acceptable when it is paid for, as in pay-per-view or video or DVD rental.
- Third, the complex issue of the balance between legitimate public interest and the need for protection of individual privacy. The research aimed to chart the boundaries of acceptability in a variety of domains and media, while focussing on one particular form of television programming – the 'fly on the wall' documentary.

Survey 1 1062 adults	**Survey 2** 535 adults
Patterns of media use	Patterns of media use
Opinions about causation of social problems (full list)	Opinions about causation of social problems (reduced list)
Influences on personal development	Influence of experts on media effects
The right to privacy	Invasion of privacy by documentary
Violence and different media	Offending deeply held beliefs
Personal Values (full list)	Personal Values (reduced list)

Figure 1: Surveys and Topics.

The Distribution of Values

Questions asked in surveys are, by necessity, somewhat logical and formal, rather than expressive and loosely worded. However, the fact that focus groups preceded the actual survey design phase meant that a number of terms and expressions, topics and examples, which are well understood and unambiguous, could be identified and used in the questionnaires. Therefore, notwithstanding the difficulty of assessing values, the design of suitable survey questions was, from the outset, located within a corpus of authentic statements generated by the group members and not simply imposed from *a priori* assumptions.

One primary aim of the surveys was to be able to produce a value-based classification of individuals – reflecting topics raised and positions held which emerged within the focus groups – which could serve to place the often highly individualistic responses and judgements which people make about the media within an overall analytical framework. For example, a typical survey question might obtain results showing, say, 60% in favour of X and 40% opposed to X. Rarely, though, can such a result be satisfactorily 'explained', except by using a limited range of analytical concepts such as social grade, educational level or life-stage (itself a function, *inter alia* of age and sex). The present surveys, though, aimed from the outset to impose a high degree of analytical rigour and to characterize individuals on how they perceived the rules of society, rather than on their social characteristics alone.

The questions aimed to allow an operational partitioning of the samples equivalent to neo-Aristotelian and liberal – if such a dichotomy was indeed to be found. Importantly, the questions asked did not require individuals to 'self-classify' themselves into such overarching categories. On each item, people were free to agree or disagree, or to give a neutral or 'don't know' response.

The first survey included a range of attitude items designed to segregate individuals according to how they viewed the moral and social world. These items referred both to their own feelings and beliefs, and to other people's apparent values and behaviours. They also made reference to well-publicized real-life events in which questions of individual freedom and social mores featured prominently. For example, there were items about sadomasochism, the wearing of seat belts, and the possibility of there being 'conditions'

	Agree Strongly	Agree	Neither/ Don't know	Disagree	Disagree Strongly
Children can grow up to be decent citizens even if they are not taught what is right and wrong	5	16	12	34	34
It should be up to the individual to decide to protect themselves by wearing seat belts, and not for the law to insist on it	7	19	10	33	31
People who never go to a public library should not have to pay that part of the poll tax which covers libraries	6	16	21	37	20
If adults freely consent to inflict pain to each other for sexual pleasure they should be allowed to do so	6	27	33	18	16
Married couples who wish to divorce should be made to attend counselling before a divorce is granted	11	33	23	24	9
If someone has lost their job because they are an alcoholic, they should be legally required to seek treatment	19	39	21	16	4

Table 1. Questions relating to values: Survey 1.
Survey 1 (n= 1062).[1] Figures in percentages.

imposed to the granting of divorce: these serve as indicators of underlying values about individual versus public freedoms and about the role of the State.

From the distributions of replies to the different statements, it is immediately apparent that these questions are not merely eliciting a 'standard' response. The sample proportions strongly disagreeing with each one ranged from 4% through to 34%, and, for each statement, there were sizeable differences in opinions between varying proportions of the sample. This is clear evidence that there are opposing opinions at play, and that, therefore, there is not a national 'moral consensus' at work. However, it is also the case that in each item, bar one, there is a 'majority' view with the greater part of the overall sample opting to agree or disagree, and with an opposing 'minority' view. The one item where this pattern is *not* found is the one relating to sadomasochism, where opinions were split almost exactly into three camps: agreement (33%), disagreement (34%) and neutrality (33%).

These overall patterns suggest that, for each topic addressed, there are two (or more) broadly contrasting moral orientations at play within the adult population. The key question is whether or not these represent consistent individual positions, or whether they are simply artefacts arising from the particular questions and wordings used in the survey itself. As an example, Table 2 shows the cross-tabulation of two of the above items, revealing a high degree of consistency operating between people's judgements between items: 57% were consistent (in bold type, either agreeing, having no strong view either way or disagreeing with *both* items), and 20% were inconsistent (in italics, agreeing with one and disagreeing with the other), with a further 24% holding a definite opinion on one item to a neutral response on the other. Similar patterns were found among comparisons between each of the remaining the items.

Four in ten (42%) of the sample disagreed with both items, and could be termed neo-Aristotelian in the sense that these people believed that there is a civic or legal duty on individuals to undertake certain behaviours, regardless of individual predilections. In contrast, a much smaller proportion (11%) consistently agreed with the items, in effect arguing that individual rights overrode public obligations, and represents a consistently liberal orientation. Overall, 53% showed consistency in terms of their moral position on these two separate questions. Only 20% showed complete inconsistency – agreeing with one and disagreeing with the other – while a very small proportion (4%) did not have a clear opinion on either issue.

In order to establish whether or not there were consistent relationships between all the items used, a factor analysis of the six items shown in Table 1 was undertaken.[2] This

		People who never go to a public library should not have to pay that part of the poll tax which covers libraries		
		Agree Strongly/ Agree	Neither/ Don't know	Disagree Strongly/ Disagree
It should be up to the individual to decide to protect themselves by wearing seat belts, and not for the law to insist on it	**Agree Strongly/ Agree**	**11**	5	*10*
	Neither/ Don't know	2	**4**	5
	Disagree Strongly/ Disagree	*10*	12	**42**

Table 2. Patterns of Response: Survey 1. Figures in percentages.

technique allows underlying linkages between responses on a number of questions to be identified statistically. The analysis resulted in two main factors being clearly identified. Table 3 shows the factor analysis results in terms of the relative contribution of each item to each factor, with the two main question items which were most strongly linked to four of the six items shown in bold text.

The two factors relate to different levels of social behaviour: Factor 1 reflecting the 'public' – wearing seat belts and paying for libraries; and Factor 2 the 'private' – divorce and alcoholism (and, to a lesser degree, sexual license).

The four highest-scoring items on the two factors (in bold type in Table 3) were used as the basis for creating a categorization of individuals in terms of their overall orientations to the questions. This involved adding each individual's scores on the four items in three different ways, set out in Table 4. Classified on this basis into 4 discrete groups, the sample consists of a large group of people who mainly gave neo-Aristotelian answers to the questions, together with a much smaller liberal group.

	Factor 1 loading	Factor 2 loading
Factor 1		
It should be up to the individual to decide to protect themselves by wearing seat belts, and not for the law to insist on it	**0.72**	0.14
People who never go to a public library should not have to pay that part of the poll tax which covers libraries	**0.72**	0.04
Factor 2		
Married couples who wish to divorce should be made to attend counselling before a divorce is granted	–0.07	**0.71**
If someone has lost their job because they are an alcoholic, they should be legally required to seek treatment	–0.01	**0.74**
Neither		
Children can grow up to be decent citizens even if they are not taught what is right and wrong	–0.58	0.04
If adults freely consent to inflict pain to each other for sexual pleasure they should be allowed to do so	0.11	0.49

Survey 1 (n= 1062) Rotated factor components shown.

Table 3. Factor Analysis of Items: Survey 1.

Derivation of Scores	Maximum possible
'Neo-Aristotelian' Strongly agreeing (score 2) or Agreeing (score 1) with items 3 & 4 plus Strongly disagreeing (score 2) or Disagreeing (score 1) with items 3 & 4	8
'Undecided' Neither agree nor disagree or 'Don't know' (score 1) in items 1–4	4
'Liberal' Strongly disagreeing (score 2) or Disagreeing (score 1) with items 3 & 4 plus Strongly agreeing (score 2) or Agreeing (score 1) with items 3 & 4	8

Final Categorization of Individuals in Sample		% of sample
NEO-ARISTOTELIAN:	Neo-Aristotelian score greater than Liberal score	65
NEUTRAL:	Neo-Aristotelian score equal to Liberal score or Undecided score of 3 or 4	18
LIBERAL:	Liberal score greater than Neo-Aristotelian score	17

Table 4. Creation of Values Categories: Survey 1.

The four questions upon which this classification system was based were repeated in the second survey, with almost identical results (shown in Table 5), showing that these responses are robust and repeatable. While there are minor differences between the two surveys, these are most likely due to the different structure of the two questionnaires. Certainly they do not show any statistically significant differences in overall pattern between the two surveys.

The categorization of the individuals in the second sample was undertaken in the same way as described for Sample 1, with very similar results. Again, those classed as neo-Aristotelian form by far the largest grouping in the sample, with liberals a small minority.

However, this classification scheme does not mean that many people hold 'pure' neo-Aristotelian or liberal values. Rather, most show mixed responses to the questions used in the surveys, and the classification scheme reflects the *dominant pattern* found for each individual survey participant (Table 7). While the analysis rests upon a small number of question responses, it appears to be the case that many people do not hold to a fixed set of 'rules' by which to interpret events. Rather, the more likely picture that emerges is one whereby individual cases are often dealt with on the specific merits and circumstances involved. There is a marked tendency, however, for those giving neo-Aristotelian responses to be more likely to give only these responses, while among those giving liberal responses, most gave one or more neo-Aristotelian responses as well as liberal ones.

	Agree Strongly	Agreee	Neither/ Don't know	Disagree	Disagree Strongly
It should be up to the individual to decide to protect themselves by wearing seat belts, and not for the law to insist on it	7 (11)	19 (23)	10 (9)	33 (32)	31 (25)
People who never go to a public library should not have to pay that part of the poll tax which covers libraries	6 (7)	16 (14)	21 (19)	37 (36)	20 (23)
Married couples who wish to divorce should be made to attend counselling before a divorce is granted	11 (16)	33 (27)	23 (23)	24 (22)	9 (13)
If someone has lost their job because they are an alcoholic, they should be legally required to seek treatment	19 (24)	39 (38)	21 (15)	16 (17)	4 (6)

Table 5. Questions relating to values: Both surveys.
Survey 1 n = 1062, Survey 2 n = 535. Figures in percentages.

	% of sample 1	% of sample 2
Neo–Aristotelian	65.2	63.6
Undecided/Neutral	17.9	17.0
Liberal	16.9	19.4

Table 6. Distribution of values categories: Both surveys.
Survey 1 n = 1062, Survey 2 n = 535

Following the first survey, these issues were followed up in the second set of focus groups, where one particular interpretation of some of the items tended to dominate. This interpretation was based upon a general principle of extenuating circumstances: for example, whether or not an alcoholic should be compulsorily treated depended upon whether he/she was causing harm to others such as children or relatives, or whether failure to do a job effectively had wider repercussions.

	% of survey 1	% of survey 2
Giving only neo-Aristotelian responses	37	28
Giving mainly neo-Aristotelian responses	31	36
Giving mainly liberal responses	12	14
Giving only liberal responses	6	6
Giving equal liberal & neo-aristotelian responses	13	16
Giving only 'don't know' responses	1	1

Table 7. Distribution of values categories: Both surveys.
Survey 1 n = 1062, Survey 2 n = 535.

However, this does not mean that all such judgements are in any formal sense liberal; rather, the rules people are operating under include the need to establish the precise circumstances before making a final judgement. A reasonable conclusion, which can be drawn from these data, is that most people are neo-Aristotelian in their values rather than liberal. This may well mean that the public are considerably at variance with the media producers' views on these issues. Certainly, during the focus groups, people were not hesitant in describing programme-makers as holding values which were different from theirs, and as deliberately seeking to change the moral 'map' of the country or extending the bounds of the acceptable.

Survey 1 data only

Social Grade:[3]	ABC1	C2	DE
Neo-Aristotelian	52	23	25
Neutral	39	26	35
Liberal	33	29	38

Age:	16–34	35–54	55+
Neo-Aristotelian	36	36	28
Neutral	43	36	21
Liberal	49	34	16

Sex:	Male	Female
Neo-Aristotelian	45	55
Neutral	52	48
Liberal	57	43

Table 8. Demographic and value categories. Figures in percentages.

It is, of course, possible that these different sets of values are simply a reflection of some other underlying individual characteristic such as age or sex or social position. There are indeed some differences found between the sexes, as well as between different age groups and social grades (Table 8). To a degree, neo-Aristotelian values – supporting the notion of the public good and the need for individuals to follow behaviour which benefits the public good – are most likely to be found among the higher (ABC1) social grades; more affluent, longer educated, than among the lower grades (C2 and DE). Liberal values, stressing individual rather than social benefits and values, are in turn somewhat more likely to be found among C2s and DEs. These two social grades are also the most likely to demonstrate neutral and undecided opinions.

However, these demographic variations do not 'explain' the differences found in moral positions. Detailed statistical analysis of the relations between demographic variables and the values categorization showed that there are few overall consistent linkages, and that the influence of the values held by the sample has an impact beyond that of demographics alone.

Importantly then, the evidence strongly suggests that the broad distinctions found between these two types of values system are not merely a reflection of existing demographic differences, but in fact represent a real and profound division in outlooks between people in British society, going beyond the differences one might expect to arise simply from social status, gender or age. Later sections of this chapter illustrate how vital this measure is in understanding the different patterns of response to broadcasting regulation issues which people offer.

Moral Beliefs
The surveys also aimed to explore moral beliefs and moral development in some detail. A further set of questions asked about personal beliefs in the context of their own lives.[4] Not surprisingly, almost everyone said they have a firm set of standards.

Most also agreed that *'other people's points of view are as valid as mine are'*: in some ways, this should be treated with a degree of suspicion. Similar sentiments were voiced during the focus groups, but tended to reduce or even disappear as the group members relaxed into the group setting. What then emerged were much less tolerant views on other people's beliefs. This phenomenon has been researched elsewhere – the so-called 'Spiral of Silence' (see, for example, Noelle-Neumann 1991) – and there is good evidence that 'politically incorrect' opinions can be suppressed in public (and in surveys), and socially acceptable replies given in their place.

More varied results are seen where the concept of shared value systems and opinions about other people's behaviour are concerned. Across the various demographic groupings, and across the value groups, the overall balance of opinion on these items, bar two, was very uniform. Most people share a largely relativistic view of the moral world: while there are different value systems around, they personally aim to hold to their own values. However, there are also important differences between key groups on two specific items: *other people's behaviour* and *parents' values*.

Overall, one in two adults sees themselves as having different values from their parents. Within this overall picture are large-scale differences of opinion related to age. Younger

	Agree Strongly	Agree	Neither/ Don't know	Disagree	Disagree Strongly
I have a firm set of standards that I try to live by	60	30	6	3	1
Other people's points of view are as valid as mine are	58	30	6	3	2
There is no common set of values that people agree on	22	39	17	15	6
My values are different from those of my parents	17	34	11	18	20
I don't really care how other people behave as long as it doesn't affect me	11	15	10	27	37

Table 9. Moral beliefs.
Survey 1 n = 1062. Figures in percentages.

% Agreeing/strongly agreeing	16–24	25–44	45–64	65+	Total Sample
My values are different from those of my parents'	64	55	46	39	51
I don't really care how other people behave as long as it doesn't affect me	41	26	23	22	26

	Neo-Aristotelian	Neutral	Liberal
My values are different from those of my parents	41	52	58
I don't really care how other people behave as long as it doesn't affect me	12	27	40

Table 10. Distribution of values categories: Both surveys.
Survey 1 n = 1062

individuals in the sample were far more likely to agree than were older ones (Table 10). The under-45s effectively represent those who grew up from the late 1950s up to the late 1980s and encompass the post-1960s generation. These younger age groups are distinctly more likely than the older groups to see themselves as holding different values from their parents. This offers support for the earlier suggestion that the well-charted shift in social and political values, which occurred in the 1960s, has had a substantial effect on individuals.

The other item which shows widely different views concealed within the overall average result is '*I don't really care how other people behave as long as it doesn't affect me*'. Overall, one in four says they do not really care about other people's behaviour. Those holding predominantly liberal values differ greatly from those with neo-Aristotelian values: over three times as many (40% compared with 12%) agreed with the statement.

In short, from our findings, people are in favour of cultural control. This is further supported in Tables 20 and 21, where opinions about the acceptability of late-night violence and pornography on terrestrial TV are very different between the two types.

The Development of Moral Values

The first survey asked about how individuals' value systems were formed – both for the individual sample members' own childhood and upbringing and for today's children. It should be borne in mind that these are people's *perceptions* rather than actual 'hard' facts.

A comparison of the two sets of opinions (Table 11) shows some striking differences between the past and the present, together with a number of highly stable features. The immediate family – parents, grandparents, aunts, uncles and siblings – were, and remain, *the* main sources of values. However, the relative influence of some family members may be shifting; the role of the mother – while still dominant – is noticeably reduced. At the same time, other social figures are coming to take a more prominent role: friends and siblings.

These results also show a major shift towards the media as sources of perceived influence. As far as their *own* upbringing is concerned, most people did not feel that any of the main media had much influence. However, an overall majority believe that television is an influence on today's children, and further large minorities feel that the various other media are also influential. While these beliefs about media influence do differ from the past, it is also the case that the media are not seen as the most important influences on today's children; these results echo the types of comment made in the focus groups, whereby people worry about the media but simultaneously admit that the social and physical world probably has the most direct impact on how people live, think and behave.

A particularly noticeable trend shown by the results is the general decline in the more traditional sources of moral authority and education: religion and school. For about one in five of the sample, these were influences on their own upbringing. For today's children, far fewer see these as potential sources of moral influence. Importantly, opinions about these particular changes are generally shared by all individuals. While there are some differences between the social grades, age groups and values groups, the broad overall picture remains the same. Indeed, the views of parents within the overall sample are not different overall from the average, apart from a modest tendency to rate the media and traditional influences as being somewhat less potent.

While people may differ about what they perceive the role of society to be, and what its citizens' duties and responsibilities are, they do share a similar view on what influences are brought to bear on children.

Causes of Anti-social and Unsociable Behaviour

We also asked about the causation of anti-social (violent crime) and unsociable (swearing) behaviours. For each topic, a range of possible influences was used, derived largely from the

	Extremely/very influential on own sense of values	Extremely/very influential on children's sense of values	
	Total sample	Total sample	Parents only
Media:	%	%	%
Novels/ books	20	16	17
TV programmes	14	54	48
Cinema films	11	40	32
Magazines	10	34	29
Advertising	10	40	37
Radio programmes	10	17	15
Comics	9	26	21
Traditional:			
Schoolteacher	53	41	33
Scouts, Guides etc.	23	17	14
Sunday school	22	11	8
Religious leader	18	11	9
Religious books	15	8	8
People:			
Mother	86	79	84
Father	78	75	78
Grandparents	46	46	48
Friends	41	58	58
Brother	29	41	40
Sister	29	39	39
Aunt or Uncle	27	22	23
Friends of parents	27	24	27
Godparents	12	14	15
Neighbours	12	11	9
Survey 1 sample size	n = 1062		n =455

Table 11. Influence on personal values.

focus groups. As the results in Table 12 show, the main factors which people believe to be the root cause of these key forms of unwanted behaviour were essentially social and economic – lack of parental discipline, unemployment, 'weak' courts, school discipline – rather than attributable to the media. The results below come from asking the sample to rank a number of possible causes of violent behaviour.

Causes of violent crime	% saying this has the most effect on violent crime (rank of 1)	Average rank of effect on violent crime	% saying this has no effect at all on violent crime
Lack of discipline in the home	32	3.5	7
Unemployment	17	5.5	18
Lack of tough sentencing by the courts	17	5.2	13
Lack of discipline in schools	9	4.7	11
Poor housing/ poverty	7	6.1	19
Video films	5	7.0	24
TV programmes	4	7.6	28
Break-up of old communities	3	8.4	36
Lack of will power	3	8.7	33
Cinema films	2	8.3	32
The decline of religion	2	9.7	50

Table 12. Causes of violent crime.
Survey 1.

While people do have a marked tendency to draw attention to perceived media deficiencies – in focus groups, or in more vaguely worded surveys – in terms of themes and content which they might object to, they did not rank the mass media as *strong* influences to any real degree. For a very small group of people, though, the media are seen as the main factor underlying violent crime.

There were minor differences in opinion between the values groups, and between other demographic groups, but these are small-scale and do not affect the overall relative ratings of importance of the factors shown below. These beliefs about causation are shared between the great majority of the public.

A similar emphasis on the real world rather than the media world is seen in people's beliefs about the factors causing swearing amongst children. Parents and friends are believed to be the main causes of children swearing, with the media falling well behind. Among the media asked about, television is thought to be the most influential, closely followed by video films. What is particularly noticeable here is that the media – especially TV and video – were believed to have a markedly more central role in encouraging swearing than it does in promoting criminal behaviour.

Again, the same overall relative levels of importance of the factors were the same across demographic sub-groups and across the three value groups.

Causes of children swearing	% saying this has the most effect on children swearing	Average rank of effect on children swearing	% saying this has no effect at all on children swearing
Parents	32	4.3	14
Friends	30	3.6	8
Lack of respect for other people	11	5.9	15
TV programmes	8	5.7	17
Other people in the neighbourhood	6	6.0	18
Video films	5	5.8	14
Brothers and Sisters	2	5.3	16
Cinema films	2	6.9	23
Teachers	1	9.5	65
Pop and youth magazines	1	8.8	47

Table 13. Causes of children swearing.
Survey 1.

Concerns about Society

From the focus groups, it was clear that people are concerned at all levels – at home, at work, at leisure – about anti-social and unsociable behaviour in their everyday lives. The types of issues they were concerned about included <u>anti-social acts</u> – theft, violence drug-related crime – and <u>unsociable behaviour</u> – swearing and rudeness, especially from the young.

These concerns are equally prominently displayed in the survey results (Table 14). While the main focus of concern is violent crime, sexual attitudes and swearing and bad language – unsociable rather than anti-social behaviour – are also sources of concern for the majority of people. However, within the overall tendency for concern, there are noticeable differences between people with differing value orientations. Those with primarily liberal views are much less likely than those holding a neo-Aristotelian position to be very concerned about any of these behaviours. This reflects the earlier finding that the liberal group were the most likely to agree that they didn't care about other people's behaviour. (See Table 10.)

Broadcasting and Other Media

While the preceding section, and earlier chapters, showed that the media are not generally regarded as the major force underlying anti-social and, to a lesser degree, unsociable behaviour, there is also no doubt that people do have distinct concerns about how the media operate, and what safeguards there are over content and timing.

% How concerned, if at all, are you about?	Very concerned	Fairly concerned	Not concerned/ Don't know
Violent crime in this country	64	27	9
Current sexual attitudes and standards of behaviour in this country	36	35	29
Swearing and bad language in this country	36	34	30
% very concerned with:	**Neo-Aristotelian**	**Neutral**	**Liberal**
Violent crime in this country	71	56	48
Current sexual attitudes and standards of behaviour in this country	41	31	23
Swearing and bad language in this country	40	33	25

Table 14. Concerns with anti-social and unsociable behaviour.
Survey 1 n = 1062.

The desire for the existence and maintenance of broad safeguards for media consumers is widespread: clear majorities felt that relaxation of regulation would make standards of television, video and cinema get worse. Virtually no one believed that removal of regulation would improve things, regardless of the actual medium or channel under consideration.

Further analysis of these results shows clearly how individuals' underlying value structures have a direct effect on their opinions about media regulation. Those who fell into the neo-Aristotelian values group were consistently more likely than liberals to believe that the removal of regulation over *any* of the sources asked about would have a negative impact. This finding also suggests that changes in regulation in either direction – lighter or tighter – are likely to elicit unfavourable reactions from one or other values group camp, depending on the direction of change: something that is very likely to be familiar to past and present media regulators.

So far, only broad-based opinions have been reported. While these are useful for indicating broad currents of opinion, there is no doubt that specific questions are also necessary in order to focus upon the different issues which the portmanteau term 'broadcasting standards' means in practice. For example, some people are perfectly happy with 'soft' pornography being available, while being vehemently opposed to graphic violence. Others have no objection to swearing, but do not like the portrayal of 'deviant' behaviour or lifestyles.[5] Both surveys contained questions about specific instances of violent and sexual content that could occur on different types of channel or medium, in order to gauge opinion and reaction on as realistic a basis as possible.

If there was no regulation at all over……would that make it better, worse or the same as it is now?	Worse	No change/ Don't know	Better
Cinema films	65	34	1
Video material	61	38	1
BBC1	58	42	1
ITV	59	40	1
BBC2	57	42	1
Channel 4/S4C	60	39	1
Satellite & Cable channels (total sample)	55	42	2
Satellite & Cable channels (cable/satellite users only)	60	37	3

Survey 1 n=1062 (Note: Channel 5 not on air at time of study). Figures in percentages.

% saying no regulation would make channel worse:	Neo-Aristotelian	Neutral	Liberal
Cinema films	72	65	51
Video material	69	43	46
BBC1	65	45	38
ITV	68	45	38
BBC2	65	45	39
Channel 4/S4C	68	43	41
Satellite & Cable channels (total sample)	63	41	38
Satellite & Cable channels (cable/satellite users only)	69	85 [a]	43

Survey 1 n= 1062 (Note: Channel 5 not on air at time of study)

Table 15. Media regulation.

Violent Content

The question of violent content was approached by asking about five separate scenarios: editing of violent content in television news; news reporting of a murder trial; violent content in a dramatized novel; true-life crime publications and videos; and the showing of unedited violent films.

Most people (72%) feel that television companies should edit the news before it is transmitted, in order to cut out the most graphic or horrifying scenes. However, a more considered view was also sought, offering a range of strategies which could be adopted by broadcasters in covering news items. Starting from the position that a news programme wanted to show exactly what had happened, including details and graphic scenes, most people wanted one or more forms of restriction applied to such an item. A bare majority

If a TV company felt that events in the news should show exactly what has happened, including details and specific scenes, which of the following options should apply?	% choosing this option
Could only be shown after a clear warning to viewers	51
Could only be shown after 9 o'clock	33
Could only be shown late at night	28
Should not be shown at all	8
Could only be shown on BBC2 or Channel 4/S4C	1
Could only be shown on paid-for cable or satellite	1

Table 16. News content.
Survey 2.

opted for an on-air warning to viewers of what would be shown, while just over half opted for timing restrictions on transmission of such a story (after 9pm or late at night). Few, though, felt that such a story should simply not be shown at all, or only restricted to a small audience channel.

When the reporting of a murder trial is considered, together with a range of different media which might report the trial in great detail, a picture emerges of the relative role of the different news media. Fewer people think that television news should be able to give details compared with a television documentary programme. However, newspapers, magazines and radio are slightly less restricted in what they can cover. In none of the options, though, was acceptance chosen by a clear majority, and the level of acceptance is 'fairly' rather than 'very'.

Also, cable and satellite viewers' opinions do not differ greatly from the norm. Nor, in this case, did those with different value systems – while the neo-Aristotelians were marginally more likely to find any of the examples unacceptable, this was a very small-scale effect.

Similar results are found for the dramatization of a violent torture scene; acceptance is limited and conditional.

Of course, material of this type, graphically describing crimes of violence, is already available in magazine and video form. Two in three adults feel that such publications should be available if people want them. However, they also want limited distribution routes: the most popular options were via specialist book shops and mail order, and relatively few wanted such publications available through more accessible routes such as newsagents. In particular, the principle of supermarkets having such material available was not supported by more than a small minority.

Overall, opinions about the suitability of showing violent material late at night on different TV channels show that all channels are regarded as equal, regardless of whether the individual pays for access. (See Table 19.) It should be borne in mind that the key issue here is 'late at night' rather than 'channel identity': the 'rules' about watersheds and late-

During a particularly gruesome murder trial, full details of the killing and the events leading up to it are revealed in the court. How acceptable, if at all, would it be for ……… to report all the trial details?	Very acceptable	Fairly acceptable	Not acceptable/ Don't know
A TV documentary programme	12	45	43
Newspapers	10	41	49
Radio news	9	41	50
Magazines	8	40	52
The news on the 4 main TV channels	8	35	56
Cable or satellite news channels (total sample)	8	35	56
Cable or satellite news channels (cable/satellite viewers only)	8	40	52

Table 17. Murder trial coverage.
Survey 1. Figures in percentages.

A best-selling book includes scenes which describe torture in great detail. How acceptable, if at all, would it be for ……. to include a scene like this?	Very acceptable	Fairly acceptable	Not acceptable/ don't know
A TV drama based on the book on the main TV channels	4	40	56
Drama on cable or satellite channels (total sample)	4	42	54
Drama on cable or satellite news channels (cable/satellite viewers only)	5	51	44
Extracts from the book in a newspaper	5	42	53
Extracts from the book in a magazine	4	43	53
Drama based on the book on radio	5	47	48
A cinema film based on the book	7	49	44

Table 18. Dramatized violence.
Survey 1. Figures in percentages.

night relaxation on some forms of content are very well established among viewers. Cable and satellite viewers' opinions were not different from the overall view.

It is interesting to note that, on these particular issues of principle, the two main values groups did show considerable differences of opinion. On all three options, the neo-Aristotelians are almost twice as likely as the liberals to reject the possibility of late-night

	Agree Strongly	Agree	Neither/ Don't know	Disagree	Disagree Strongly
BBC2 and Channel 4/ S4C should be allowed to show material with a lot of violence in it late at night	6	23	22	28	20
BBC1 and ITV should be allowed to show material with a lot of violence in it late at night	6	23	21	29	21
Satellite and cable channels which you have to pay a subscription to watch should be allowed to show material with a lot of violence in it late at night	9	29	22	21	19

Table 19. Violence on different channels.
Survey 1. Figures in percentages.

violence on terrestrial channels (Table 20). However, they do not show quite such divergent views when paid-for viewing is concerned. This aspect of public opinion – payment for something changing its acceptability – is also addressed in the following section on sexual content.

Sexual Content
As in the case of violent material, the surveys asked about specific aspects of sexual material and its availability under different circumstances. The two questions asked focused entirely upon the specific cases of pornography on television, using the examples of other countries as a starting point. In both the examples given, the majority were not in favour of allowing pornography to be shown.

However, there was a marked difference in the balance of opinions when the question of paying to watch pornography was raised: 38% found this very, or fairly, acceptable compared with 20% for unrestricted late-night showing. This closely reflects the opinions voiced in the focus groups.

As far as sexual material is concerned, the differences between the two main value groups is relatively minor, and large majorities disapproved of unrestricted access to pornographic materials. This contrasts with the findings for violence, shown in the previous section. This may well be due to disapproval, at the official level, of pornography being a very long-established element of British life. The portrayal of violence has never received such blanket and continuing disapproval – indeed, in several forms it has been consistently celebrated in the media: war films, westerns, crime drama, reporting and so on.

% in each values group *disagreeing* with each statement	Neo-Aristotelians	Neutral	Liberals
BBC2 and Channel 4/ S4C should be allowed to show material with a lot of violence in it late at night	60	53	32
BBC1 and ITV should be allowed to show material with a lot of violence in it late at night	60	54	35
Satellite and cable channels which you have to pay a subscription to watch should be allowed to show material with a lot of violence in it late at night	48	42	30

Table 20. Violence on different channels: the role of values. Survey 1.

What is equally clear is that opinions are influenced – among those with neo-Aristotelian views as much as everyone else – by the principle of paying for programming. The current surveys did not address this issue in detail, but the focus groups did devote time to it. In general, the act of paying appears to establish certain rights and privileges for the payee, in that accidental or unsuitable access – by children, for example – is presumed to be prevented.

Causing Harm or Offence

Another area where sometimes contradictory beliefs are exhibited is that of physical or mental harm. There is little doubt that the basic concerns underlying people's views about regulation of violence and sexual content involves the concept of harm.

Harm and offence lie on a spectrum rather than in separate domains, ranging from physical harm – violence which could be engendered by media exposure – through to cognitive harm or offence – core beliefs being challenged. From the focus groups it was clear that one particular model of media effects has generally entered the public consciousness, that of the *'unstable personality'* who can be influenced by violent or sexual content.[6] The surveys followed this up with a number of specific questions.

The questions about harm included reference to expert opinions. This element has a strong and consistent impact on people's opinions about whether or not each item ought to be broadcast; the strength of 'expert' opinion is directly linked to the proportions saying such an item should not be transmitted; 62% said a programme should not be shown if experts thought a programme with disturbing scenes might trigger violent behaviour in a few unbalanced people, down to 17% when experts believed that such harm would not result. This pattern was found across all sub-groups, including the values groups.

Programmes which have the potential to *offend*, rather than harm, do not attract the same levels of censure. In all the cases considered across the two surveys, few (between 8 and

Some of the main TV channels in other countries have hard-core pornography films, which at the moment would not be shown on British television. These are free, and shown very late at night so that children do not get to see them. Would it be acceptable for the main television channels in this country to be allowed to show such films very late at night?	Very acceptable	Fairly acceptable	Not acceptable/ Don't know
	6	14	80
Among neo-Aristotelians	2	13	85
Among liberals	9	14	77
Some cable TV channels in other countries have hard-core pornography films, which at the moment would not be shown on British television. You would have to pay for them if you want to watch them. Would it be acceptable for cable channels in this country to show such films for people who wanted to pay for them?			
	12	26	62
Among neo-Aristotelians	5	26	69
Among liberals	17	23	60

Table 21. Pornography and television.
Survey 2. Figures in percentages.

15%) considered that offence *per se* was a justification for preventing a programme from being shown.

Privacy and Publicity

Both surveys approached the issues of people's rights to privacy and the ethics of intrusion by the media. In the focus groups, discussants made detailed distinctions between different types of individual and their rights to privacy from the media. Accordingly, this aspect of the privacy issue was incorporated into the surveys.

If experts believed that a TV programme with some unpleasant and disturbing scenes *would definitely* trigger violent behaviour in a few unbalanced people, which of these options best applies?	% of sample
Should not be shown at all	62
Could only be shown late at night	11
Could only be shown after a clear warning to viewers	18
Could be shown after 9 o'clock	1
Could only be shown on BBC2 or Channel 4/S4C	★
Could only be shown on paid-for cable or satellite	2
Could be shown on any channel	2
Don't know	4

If experts were *divided* over whether a TV programme with some unpleasant and disturbing scenes might trigger violent behaviour in a few unbalanced people, which of these options best applies?	% of sample
Should not be shown at all	38
Could only be shown late at night	15
Could only be shown after a clear warning to viewers	27
Could be shown after 9 o'clock	6
Could only be shown on BBC2 or Channel 4/S4C	1
Could only be shown on paid-for cable or satellite	2
Could be shown on any channel	2
Don't know	9

If experts believed that a TV programme with some unpleasant and disturbing scenes *would not* trigger violent behaviour in a few unbalanced people, which of these options best applies?	% of sample
Should not be shown at all	17
Could only be shown late at night	23
Could only be shown after a clear warning to viewers	30
Could be shown after 9 o'clock	12
Could only be shown on BBC2 or Channel 4/S4C	1
Could only be shown on paid-for cable or satellite	3
Could be shown on any channel	4
Don't know	10

Table 22. Causing harm.
Survey 2.

Rights to Privacy

In the first survey, the right to privacy – operationalized as the degree of control a specific individual should have over being shown or mentioned in television news or documentaries – was studied in detail. Nineteen different types of person were asked about, covering a range of different roles and formal positions in society. For each, a range of options (A to F)[7] was chosen from, again drawn from the focus groups. These ranged from complete control (prevent any mention) through to complete loss of control (no rights to prevent or comment).

The responses generated by this approach show very large differences in response according to the particular 'character' being evaluated. Broadly speaking, there are very large differences in perceived rights to privacy, which depend upon the social and moral position of the fictitious person involved. Three broad groupings can be seen.

First, there are those who could be termed *innocent victims*; the young, the sick, the injured party or the 'lucky' person, such as a lottery winner. These have very high levels of protection against intrusion onto their privacy.

Television news and documentaries often feature different kinds of people. Which of these best describes your view of how much say they should have in how they might be shown in a TV programme	OPTIONS					
	Full rights		⟷		No rights	
	A	**B**	**C**	**D**	**E**	**F**
A child	54	19	10	6	3	3
A patient with Alzheimer's disease	54	20	12	4	3	2
A parent of a murder victim	54	24	13	4	3	2
A person with a severe disability	49	23	14	6	3	2
A witness to a crime	48	28	11	6	3	2
A victim of crime	47	26	12	5	4	4
A lottery winner	46	31	10	5	4	3
A member of the Royal Family	16	19	22	22	12	6
A schoolteacher	13	24	17	20	17	5
A senior policeman	11	18	15	23	21	9
A senior civil servant	10	15	16	27	21	7
A businessman	9	17	21	28	17	4
A film star	8	13	21	21	10	3
A religious leader	8	12	18	23	21	11
A politician	6	10	14	28	29	11
A shoplifter	4	8	9	24	26	25
A drug dealer	3	3	5	9	20	57
A rapist	3	3	3	8	19	60

Table 23. The right to privacy.
Survey 1 Don't knows not shown. Figures in percentages.

Secondly, there are public figures with formal positions and duties. They have limited rights to privacy, but can exercise some control over how they might be portrayed in the media. Within this overall group, some have more rights than others. Film stars, religious leaders and politicians have the least right to privacy in this group.

The third group – criminals – have no effective rights to prevent TV coverage of themselves. Only the shoplifter, a non-violent criminal, has the semblance of rights to control his or her coverage on television. For the other examples, their actions have put them beyond the pale.

This division of people's rights according to their role and responsibilities was mirrored throughout all the sub-groups within the overall sample. There is a widely shared consensus over what rights different 'players' have in respect of personal privacy.

The Dynamics of Privacy: The Ambulance Scenario

During the in-depth interviews and focus groups it became very clear that there are no simple answers to the questions which can be asked about rights to privacy and justification of intrusion. Rather, each case discussed tended to be analysed and judged on its individual details and merits. However, it was felt that it would also be a benefit of the research if the general principles which people appeared to apply to their decision-making could be tested more widely in the survey element of the research.

Accordingly, a single, complex multi-stage scenario about a serious road accident was designed to explore the different judgements which people would arrive at under highly specific sets of circumstances. This was discussed in the groups held before the second survey wave and, after some amendment, turned into a set of survey questions for use in the survey. Each survey interviewee was asked to imagine himself or herself as an actual participant in the sequence of scenario events.

This approach is very different from conventional survey research. By focusing upon a single event, and stopping along the way within it, key aspects and decision points could be examined and the relevant choices explored from a variety of points of view. Overall, there were seven linked but separate parts to the overall scenario, starting with the accident itself, to which the interviewee had to imagine they were involved as an innocent bystander. Each of these parts required the interviewee to make judgements as to which one out of a range of possible actions involving issues of privacy should be followed by the film crew.

The reason for adopting both the technique and the specific setting was to gauge reactions to a well-established and popular programme genre of real-life, fast-moving documentary series based around everyday life in the various emergency and allied services. An inevitable consequence of such programmes is the showing of members of the public, often distraught in stressful situations or caught off their guard.

This scenario starts with a child being hit by a drunk driver. The ambulance which arrives has, by chance, a documentary film crew on board. The documentary crew want to film various people and situations arising from the accident, including the death of the child in the ambulance on the way to hospital. At each stage in the scenario, the person interviewed was asked to judge specific dilemmas and decisions and courses of action reflecting both the film crew's need to record events and the various rights of the individual members of the public involved.

In this and subsequent parts of the scenario the interviewee was asked about the rights that different individuals had in terms of privacy and in terms of their degree of involvement with the event. The questions also asked about the production side of things, in terms of the programme-makers' desire to make as good a programme as possible from the production values point of view, and to use the programme to highlight issues and consequences arising from drunken-driving.

Here there is a fairly clear consensual starting point for most people: permission should be sought by programme-makers, even under times of stress and confusion. Apart from a slight tendency for older people to say 'Yes' (85% among the over-55s) there are no real deviations from this view. One in five, though, did *not* see the need to ask permission under the circumstances.

At this point, opinions are far less cohesive among the sample as a whole. While almost half opt for the established device of blanking out faces, a sizeable minority (30%) chose the option which would effectively prevent the programme being made. A third possibility, making the person's wishes known, but unfulfilled, was not widely chosen. Again, the only consistent variation from the 'blanking out' option was found among the older members of the sample: 39% opted for this compared with 56% of the under-35s.

Overall, few people are asking for complete control over their appearance in a documentary. Rather, most are saying that that the programme can proceed without their permission. It should be stressed that these conclusions can only be applied to this specific genre, and where the programme has an obviously pro-social intent.

Now faced with a clear dilemma, with personal rights pitted against the victim's mother's wishes (Table 26), most people effectively gave way and surrendered their position. Almost equal-sized proportions chose those options which meant that they did

---

I would like you to imagine that a drunk driver has knocked down a neighbour's child playing in the street. You are the first on the scene to help. You go with the ambulance to comfort the child. The ambulance crew has agreed to be filmed in action for a documentary about everyday life in the ambulance service, and there is a film crew inside the ambulance. You are shown comforting the child, but the child dies on the way to hospital. You are very upset and are crying. You are so concerned about the child that you are not aware that the whole scene is being filmed.

In the confusion and rush, should the film crew have asked your permission before they started to film inside the ambulance?	%
YES	77
NO	19
Don't know	4

Table 24. Accident scenario part 1.
Survey 2.

At the hospital, the camera crew do then ask if they can use the film from inside the ambulance in their programme, and you agree. Later at home, when you are more calm, you call them and say that you don't want anything shown with you in it. The programme-maker argues that to show the full tragedy and how the ambulance service deals with such emergencies, the scenes inside the ambulance have to be shown in full.

What should the programme-maker then do?	%
Show the scenes with your face blanked out, although this would reduce the impact of the programme	47
Agree to your request, which means cancelling the entire programme about the ambulance service	30
Ignore your request and show the scenes in full, but making it clear that you didn't want to be in the programme	11
Point out that you originally agreed to the scenes, and go ahead on that basis and ignore your later change of mind	4
Ignore your request and show the scenes in full	4
Don't know	4

Table 25. Accident scenario part 2. Survey 2.

You have refused permission for the scenes featuring you to be shown, but the mother of the dead child insists that the whole programme be shown to show people the tragic consequences of drinking and driving.

What should the programme-maker then do?	%
Show the scenes with your face blanked out, although this would reduce the impact of the programme	39
Agree to the mother's request and overrule your wishes	34
Ignore your request and show the scenes in full, but making it clear that you didn't want to be in the programme	13
Agree to your request, which means cancelling the entire programme and ignoring the mother's wishes	7
Agree to your request and overrule the mother's wishes	3
Don't know	5

Table 26. Accident scenario part 3. Survey 2.

appear in the programme in one way or another. Further, very few were now willing to exercise a right of veto when faced with another person's valid request. The rights of the involved person – the mother – are judged as being more important than the right to privacy under these circumstances.

As the driver is the guilty party, he loses most rights of privacy in the sample's judgements (Table 27). The most frequently given answer was that the programme-maker should simply ignore the driver's views. This fits closely with the general picture of shifting rights according to status, illustrated by the findings shown in Table 23. Taken together with the proportion who chose the 'blanking out' option, three in four believed that the driver's rights should be overruled.

In scenario part 5 (Table 28), the judgements given previously about the driver are almost entirely reversed in the context of the victim's mother's rights. The mother's request has to be honoured, according to over 80% of people, either by cancelling the programme or by preventing the child being identified and weakening the programme.

Again, this reinforces the differential weight that people's circumstances can give to judgements of their rights to privacy over the public right to know.

The position of the driver's wife, innocent of any direct involvement with the accident, but obviously associated with the guilty driver, falls between two stools. Opinions were almost evenly split over whether she should be contacted or not. Those who said 'yes' were not particularly sympathetic in their views on what should happen next. Half of them felt that the programme should mention her unwillingness to take part, while slightly fewer felt that the attempts to interview her should stop if she was unwilling to take part.

Children also have important rights to privacy, with the majority saying that the programme-maker should not attempt to contact other children present at the accident. One in four, though, felt that this was an acceptable aim for the programme-maker. However, it is equally clear that parental permission should be sought for such interviews. Few people felt that permission from the children themselves would be sufficient grounds for including their interviews in the programme.

The drunk driver involved in the accident does not wish to be shown in the programme.

What should the programme-maker then do?	%
Ignore the driver's request	43
Show the scenes with the driver's face blanked out, although this would reduce the impact of the programme	30
Show the scenes in full, but give the driver the chance to explain himself	21
Agree to the driver's request, which means cancelling the entire programme	4
Don't know	1

Table 27. Accident scenario part 4.
Survey 2.

The mother refuses to let her daughter's death be shown in the programme. You, the ambulance crew and the drunk driver want the full story shown to show the tragedy of drinking and driving.

What should the programme-maker then do?	%
Agree to the mother's request, which means cancelling the entire programme	42
Edit the programme so that the child cannot be identified, although this would reduce the impact of the programme	42
Show the scenes in full, but say that the mother did not agree to the programme being shown	12
Ignore the mother's request	3

Table 28. Accident scenario part 5.
Survey 2.

In Table 30 the rights of children again are highlighted, as well as the important role of authority figures such as the schoolteacher. While a minority of the sample felt that it would be acceptable to try to work around the teacher's objections by going to the relevant parents of the victim's classmates, very few indeed thought it was all right to ignore the teacher.

A further set of questions about the interviewing of these children asked about how people thought programme-makers would *actually* behave when faced with the teacher's refusal to allow interviews (Table 31).

Many people appear to hold somewhat jaundiced views about the ethics of programme-makers. While virtually everyone felt that children should not be interviewed without permission from parents or teachers, far smaller proportions felt that this was what programme-makers would actually do in practice. Broadcasters are believed to be willing to flaunt accepted rules of conduct as far as privacy is concerned in order to make their programmes, and some broadcasters are believed to be less trustworthy than others.

Overall, a clear picture emerges from this scenario whereby the informed and considered participation of most parties to such an event – particularly the innocent parties – should be sought as an *a priori* rule by programme-makers.

Where there is an obvious clash between public interest and private rights, the most preferred resolution is that of anonymizing individuals – through using blanking sections on-screen. Importantly, these protections do not apply in full to the 'guilty'.

Programmes of this general type are undoubtedly popular with many viewers and represent a growing genre of reality-based programming. One in five (19%) of the sample said they watched *'programmes where the emergency services are seen at work'* as often as they could, with a further 40% saying they sometimes watched them. There is a large split between the social grades – only 14 per cent of ABC1s claim to watch as often as they can compared with 25 per cent of C2DEs.

The producer of the programme also wants to interview various people connected with the accident. The aim is to show the interviews in the programme itself, in order to give the background to the tragedy, and to show the full impact of drink-driving on people' lives.

Should the programme-maker attempt to contact the driver's wife?	%
NO	47
Don't know	8
YES	45

IF YES: If the driver's wife is clearly reluctant to talk to the programme-makers, what should they do?

Point out in the programme that she refused to be interviewed	18
Immediately give up the idea of interviewing her	14
Keep contacting her and try to persuade her to change her mind	9
Try to get friends and neighbours to talk about the driver and his family	4
Don't know	1

Should the programme-maker attempt to contact the other children who were playing on the street when the accident happened?

YES	28
NO	64
Don't know	8

Should the programme include interviews with these children?

Yes, if the child agrees	10
Yes, if the parents agree	68
No	12
Don't know	10

Table 29. Accident scenario part 6.
Survey 2.

The basic dimensions of these types of programmes' appeal lies, primarily, in their informative and educational content, according to the sample (Table 32). They also describe the genre as being in the public interest, but they can also be upsetting or frightening. More critically, one in four feels that individual privacy is threatened.

The programme-maker wants to interview the classmates of the victim. The class teacher feels that the children are too upset to be interviewed and refuses permission for any interviews to be held in the school.

What should the programme-maker then do?	%
Accept the teacher's opinion and not try to interview at all	83
Try to get the children's parents to agree to these interviews, and so overrule the teacher	15
Go ahead and interview the children as they leave school	2

Table 30. Accident scenario part 7.
Survey 2.

This broad pattern of opinions – some favourable, some critical – was found across all the sample sub-groups. Among those who said they rarely or never watched such programmes, there were strong indications of how these programmes could antagonize some viewers. A key difference is seen in the proportions of each group of viewers saying that such programmes invaded privacy: those who watch infrequently or not at all were almost twice as likely to say this.

What the surveys show, supported by the findings of the focus groups, is that when it comes to discussing moral issues related to the performance of the media then much depends on the values that people hold. We have shown that the notions of the neo-Aristotelian and the liberal help in explaining the distribution of the findings. These two notions also assist in explaining attitudes towards regulation – with neo-Aristotelians favouring more regulation than liberals. The usefulness of these two notions means that, having identified the distribution of these 'types' of people in contemporary British society,

If the programme-maker was working for ...... what do you think their decision [on interviewing the children] would actually be?	BBC	ITV	Channel 4	Cable/ Satellite
Accept the teacher's opinion and not try to interview at all	45	36	34	30
Try to get the children's parents to agree to these interviews, and so overrule the teacher	40	45	41	39
Go ahead and interview the children as they leave school	15	19	25	31

Table 31. Images of the broadcasters.
Survey 2. Figures in percentages.

What do you think of programmes where the emergency services are shown at work, and ordinary people are often seen in difficulties?	%
Informative	58
In the public's interest	45
Upsetting	40
Educational	30
Frightening	23
Invade people's privacy	23
Over-sensational	15
In bad taste	13
Exciting	7
Entertaining	7
No point to them	6
Play on people's weaknesses	5
Unimaginative	1

Table 32. Attitudes to real-life programming.
Survey 2.

we are in a stronger position to predict the regulatory desires of people in an era of changing values.

What the research also shows is that even though people may have difficulty in expressing themselves in moral terms in relation to moral issues, they have no difficulty whatsoever in doing so when it comes to the morality of the invasion of privacy. In that area of the media's performance people can, and do, make moral judgements based on moral reasoning of what is, and what is not, correct behaviour on the part of both the individual and the media.

Notes

1. In the following tables, all figures shown are percentages of the entire sample unless otherwise stated. Percentages may sum to 99 or 101% due to rounding to whole numbers. Where the % figure found was less than 0.5%, the ★ symbol has been used. Where there were no responses at all, 0 is used.
2. Details of the factor analysis are given in the Appendix.
3. These correspond to: ABC1 – professionals, managers, supervisory and clerical workers
   C2 – skilled workers
   DE – semi-skilled and casual workers, state pensioners
   A more detailed description is given in the Appendix.
4. Only the results from Survey 1 are shown. The same questions were included in Survey 2 and give the same pattern of results.

5. These issues were not covered in the reported surveys. However, previous BSC research investigated attitudes to these issues in depth, and the focus groups which accompanied the surveys reported here did go into these topics in some detail – see previous chapter on qualitative research.

6. For example, the Hungerford shootings, the James Bulger killing and the USA Columbine massacre are widely reported as being due to people being influenced by the media, particularly violent videos, regardless of the actual circumstances involved in each case.

7. A The right to prevent the programme showing or mentioning them at all
   B The right to prevent the programme giving any personal details about them
   C The right to control what is shown or said about them in the programme
   D The right to be told in advance what is to be shown, but not to prevent it
   E No right to prevent the programme showing or mentioning them but a right to comment
   F No right to prevent the programme showing or mentioning them and no right of comment.

PART TWO

PART TWO

The Transgression of Privacy

The Second Phase of Study: The Private and the Public

The second study reported in Part Two of this book takes the linked topics of privacy and intrusion and examines how these relate to the core concept already discussed of 'the public interest' and our suggested replacement term, 'social importance'. The study, as was the case with the earlier one, used multiple methods to address the complex issues involved. The initial phase involved interviews conducted with leading figures in the media industries and from organizations with interests in the issue of privacy and the media (see Chapter 6). This provided a basis by which to frame the issues involved and determine thought in the area. Many of the points raised in the course of these interviews were taken to form points for discussion in the focus groups. The comparative point here is the conceptual language used: do media figures operate with different sets of considerations than those of viewers, listeners and readers?

The study then went on to conduct a series of focus groups (Chapter 8a). These showed how people talked about privacy, about their rights and the media in respecting those rights, and the circumstances under which these claims to rights could be overruled. The focus groups also concentrated upon a small number of detailed scenarios involving invasion of privacy, in order to clarify the principles which underlie people's judgements of media practices and of the balancing of individual rights to privacy against the public right to know.

Chapter 8b then presents findings from a specially conducted national survey. The questionnaire was based, in part, on themes and forms of words that emerged in the interviews and focus groups. The survey also asked about a complex scenario, designed to explore different levels of privacy and rights to intrusion, which had also been explored in the focus groups. This stage was not designed to examine all the issues involved in the overall study. Rather, it aimed to provide reliable and representative measures of the proportions of the general public who hold to specific beliefs and opinions.

5 Privacy and the Construction of Self

This chapter introduces the second research study. It examines the idea of privacy, and does so, to begin with, from a legal discussion of rights and interests. This is added to by a discussion on the idea of citizenship and cultural differences between countries in what citizenship means and confers on members of a state in terms of duties and rights. We discuss the concept of the private as being essential for an individual's identity and formation of the idea of the self. Attention is given to the notion of public interest as a defence for the intrusion of privacy.

One of the key problems in deciding what rights the media have to intrude into privacy, against competing claims of the rights of people not to have their privacy intruded upon, is that insufficient recognition has been given to the complexities posed in balancing these competing rights.

The terms used, 'the public interest' and 'privacy', present distinct difficulties in their own right as to how they are being used and what they mean. Where, also, do questions of taste and decency, and news values, feature in coming to a resolution of when it is right and proper for the media to intrude upon privacy? Indeed, the whole question of the social role of the media is overlooked – what authority do people give to the media to represent their interests, and what are the media expected to offer their audiences?

However, the fact that concepts such as privacy and public interest lack precise definitional formulation does not mean that the concepts have no substance. Truth, justice, freedom and so on are also not given to ease of definitional formulation. Whether easily formulated or not, concepts must 'do some work' if they are to be of any value. In the realm of the social, they must be capable of organizing experience, of assisting us in constructing or regulating our social interactions. Thus, to say, as is so often the case, that something is cultural has little analytical purchase, since it says all and nothing – everything is cultural. The terms 'privacy' and 'the public interest' do not fall entirely comfortably into that realm. However, they do have a certain precision in that, although not readily amenable to precise definition, individuals can and do work with them in giving judgement to happenings. People will say something is an invasion of privacy and they will say something is, or is not, in the public interest, and, in doing so, allow debate to take place as to whether or not something was a breach of privacy, or was in, or against, the public interest.

These terms or concepts have a common currency sufficient for them to act as a judgement on acts. They are, however, performance-driven: in coming to a conclusion as to whether privacy has been breached, or public interest served, people will take into account the medium involved and the treatment and methods used to acquire information, together with the circumstances of the situation and the manner and nature of the acts. Thus, someone might agree that, in a particular set of circumstances, an individual has no right to expect privacy when held against a public right to know, but, when considering the manner in which the privacy was intruded upon, it offers itself as a lesson in the fragility of democratic rights by not following 'due process'. In other words, the methods used go against ideas of appropriate behaviour in the collecting of information, which if rolled out as common practice would undermine cherished notions of correct behaviour; of what is considered just practice. A case, therefore, must not only be made for the intrusion of privacy, why it was right to do so, but why it was right to use the methods by which private behaviour became public property. Appropriateness of actions taken by the media is judged in terms of fair play, which varies according to the specific situation.

Poverty is both a concept and a condition. Both the 'work-shy' and the 'deserving poor' of the Poor Law Acts may have shared the same material circumstances to be classified as in poverty, but response to each differed. Moral judgements came into play, which in a way reclassified the condition. To be forced into the workhouse, or to be given out relief, was a dependent of 'judging the situation'. Although not strictly analogous, the idea of the 'deserving' comes into play in judging whether or not privacy has been breached, but more than that, the question posed is one of whether the privacy deserved to be breached in the manner that it was. Embedded in the ideology of the Poor Law Acts was that of poverty as a crime – fecklessness – wherein the poor could not expect, indeed had no right of, assistance from the community. Some poor, the 'undeserving poor', had, by their acts, broken community rules governing how one should order one's life.

Whether or not privacy can be intruded upon, and by what methods, appears to be governed by widely held norms of 'deserving'. Where some act threatens the people, either their psychological or physical well-being, then the claim to the right of privacy is lessened and the severity of the threat determines the manner in which that privacy can be intruded upon. In certain instances, the intrusion of privacy, through, for example, publishing photographs, can have an element of public retribution: the individual must be put before the community for physical display. This element is seen at work later in the findings from the focus groups, where not all participants considered that a teacher who had been caught cheating, by providing pupils with answers to exam questions, ought to have his or her picture in the paper – for some it was quite sufficient for the teacher to be merely named. It was not simply that the crime did not warrant such intrusion, but that the community would not be served any better by the inclusion, in any report, of a picture of the guilty person. It was considered that the teacher would lose their job and this, as such, was sufficient punishment – the picture, it was felt, was akin to hounding a person for a mistake that, although serious, was not of such proportion as to warrant the biographical intrusion offered by a picture. The community, in other words, was satisfied at the level/manner of disclosure on the grounds of level of threat to, or offence against, the community when set against the consequences of such exposure for the individual. The teacher would lose their job in any case, so what was the point of further damage to the individual by pictorial revelation of the individual? In some cases, though, matters are more complicated than this. It might be agreed that something was serious and privacy could be intruded upon, but whether people at large had a right to the information was in some cases doubtful: it was quite sufficient that the guardians of the public's interest received the 'published' material.

What in effect we begin to see is that, although people did operate with the concepts of public interest and of privacy in judging media performance, it tended to take the form of case-by-case analysis. That is, and not surprisingly, rather than apply the concepts in some philosophical or juridical fashion, the concepts of privacy and public interest were brought into play on an instance-by-instance basis. In other words, each case had to be judged on the unique features of the case, but, as with any judgement of right and wrong, that judgement was informed by an existing moral framework of rights; the right of the individual to unique consideration, and the rights of the collective as representing higher authority than the rights of the individual to consideration. This, of course, takes us into the very heart of jurisprudence and philosophical questions as to ideas of freedom.

Freedom and Individuality, the Community and the State

It was not that Victor Hugo's poor of Paris wanted permission to sleep under the bridges of the Seine, but the right to do so. Within western liberal democracies, where we might assume common assumptions concerning the nature of freedom, this is far from the case when applied to specific rights. Koen Raes (2001), reflecting on the degree of homelessness that he witnessed on a visit to the United States, notes the cultural differences in the manner in which the State treats the homeless and the way in which fellow citizens treat the homeless. Firstly, in most European countries, sleeping on the streets or in parks is simply forbidden, a criminal offence, while for a long time being a vagabond itself was considered a crime. Secondly, it is recognized as a primary duty of the state – and towns – to provide shelter to homeless people. In the United States, people have the right to sleep in public places, while taking care of the homeless is, for the greater part, a task performed by charity organizations. In public opinion, homelessness is mainly considered a choice, or at least a consequence of personal choice. It is a dimension of freedom; the freedom to be left alone, and to live alone. For example:

> ...the 'right to beg' is in American case law widely accepted as a fundamental dimension of freedom, while in many European countries, begging is a conditional right, in the sense that the towns may promulgate decrees to restrict begging (to certain streets, to certain periods of time, only with a licence etc.) (Raes 2001: 25)

According to Raes, the difference in the responses to homelessness is, at root, to be accounted for by different conceptions of the state and what its tasks are, and different conceptions of personal autonomy. This would seem an important point in underscoring the complexities of handling the question of the right of the media to intrude upon privacy. Namely, that one requires understanding of how privacy is viewed, of what personal autonomy is taken to mean. Differences in notions of personal autonomy and privacy, the divergent meanings and values in differing cultures and in differing historical periods, have been well documented, in particular in Barrington Moore Jr's classic study, *Privacy: Studies in social and cultural history* (1984). Not surprisingly, differences in meaning between cultures, in relation to autonomy and privacy, find expressions in law; law being the formal regulation of culture. There is thus a difference between Anglo-American 'common law' and continental European systems. As Raes states:

> In both of these cultures personal autonomy and privacy are highly valued, yet they have rather different cultural meanings and implications in discourses about the relationship between the individual, society and the state, which resurface in differences between legal cultures as well. In sociological terms, American society is defined in terms of the predominance of utilitarian and expressive individualism, while in continental Europe utilitarian individualism is for the greatest part a 'second language' within a framework of thought that is largely collectivistic and egalitarian, although more so in Catholic than in Protestant regions. In Europe, the concept of personal autonomy is therefore integrally related to the concept of egalitarian citizenship, while in the United States a libertarian concept of citizenship seems to be the primary point of reference. (Raes 2001: 26)

Basically, it is a difference between inter-dependence and independence; the former being much more a common feature of European legal culture and the latter of the United States. Personal autonomy in the European model implies protection from abuse of power and abuse of dependency, and this is to be afforded in many cases by the State; for example, by welfare rights protecting citizens from the abuse of economic power and exploitation. In the United States, on the other hand, personal autonomy means independence in the sense of the realization of self-sufficiency – dependency is intrinsically wrong.

Such cultural differences, underpinned at a political philosophical level, shape ideas concerning privacy and the rights of the individual to privacy. The difficulty, no matter what the culture, is in deciding where the individual autonomous-self and the social-self conflict. Indeed, the idea of the self is a philosophical question, but at the sociological level the self does not exist other than as a social being; that is, we become human by being in society. It is, therefore, not so easy to say what the autonomous self is, and what rights one has to be autonomous, since one is always part of society. However, it is quite clear from the findings of the group discussions that the notion of the self as an autonomous individual, free from social gaze or inspection, has a geographic dimension. That is, the individual in his or her home has a right to be left alone. We might call this the freedom of intimate space, and that freedom of intimate space is one unanswerable to shared space; namely, the social world outside of the home. But, clearly this is not so. The physical boundary of geographic space represented by the home is not fully autonomous, in the sense of a private world, from the world outside. We are always, and at all times, social and, hence, interests exist as to what goes on in the walled confines of the home – the neglected or bruised child brings prying eyes. Even if living alone, interest exists in what is brought into the home from the outside world, be that the physical importation of prohibited drugs, or the electronic importation of child pornography via the Internet. It is not surprising, therefore, that Peter Alldridge and Chrisje Brants (2001) consider privacy to be a weak right. According to them, the weakness of privacy is shown at practically every turn where there is a conflict of rights and interests – the right of privacy, they say, 'almost always gives way'.

> It has become trite to announce that the problem with the right to privacy is not so much in locating it (which is not without difficulty), but in its lack of purchase. When it comes into conflict with other widely recognised claims, whether based on individual rights (such as those deriving from freedom of speech), or dealing with a claim on behalf of the collectivity (typically criminal justice enforcement) privacy seldom prevails. (Alldridge and Brants 2001: 20)

Alldridge and Brants distinguish between substantive criminal law – the law of criminal prevention – and procedural criminal law, that is, law dealing with immunity. In terms of substantive criminal law, then the philosopher John Stuart Mill offers the classic liberal position. In succinct form, Mill's position is that, in so far as no one else is affected by an act, then the state has no right of interference. This would cover willing participants to acts conducted in private. However, there is no right to give permission for others to inflict harm on oneself and, hence, consenting adults to sadomasochistic acts have been prosecuted. In other words, autonomy is often qualified, even in spheres where it might be considered that what the individual does is up to him or herself. In terms of procedural criminal law, what is at issue is the asserted right of the accused not to have things done to them, against the claimed rights of representatives of the state to do them. However, as Alldridge and Brants note: 'The immunity is almost always qualified, so that privacy claims during criminal investigations are seldom indefeasible'. (2001: 20)

Clearly, the media are not the state or, in the western world, a voice of the State, but the question of privacy, as it relates to state apparatus, is not removed from many of the issues that arise in the publication of activities that the subject (accused) may wish to keep hidden. One does not have to fully agree with the newspaper baron Lord Northcliffe; that news is what somebody, somewhere, wants to suppress; everything else is advertising, but news does consist of a large element of intrusion into the affairs of others that many who are the subject of scrutiny would wish to keep private or hidden. Alldridge and Brants offer the observation that:

> A question that will legitimately arise is as to the relationship between the two types of invasions of privacy (invasion by prohibition and invasion by enforcement mechanism) and the strength of their respective justifications. With arguments about evidence-gathering techniques, the question is to do with process-values, and the usual approach is to say that the more serious the invasion of the privacy, autonomy or dignity of the defendant, the higher the degree of formal scrutiny which is required before it can be invaded. There are some invasions which can be undertaken by anyone, some only by police officers, some which can be authorised only by senior police officers, and some

invasions which require orders from magistrates, or by more senior judges. There are some invasions that cannot be made under compulsion, but from the defendant's refusal to be invaded can be drawn adverse inferences. Whether or not the additional constraints provide substantial checks or easily surmounted formal obstacles is not here in point: what is of concern is the value expressed by having such a body of rules. (2001: 20–21)

They conclude by offering the observation:

In determining whether or not to authorise, permit or institute a particular violation of privacy, one important consideration is how serious an intrusion is made. Underlying the movement from physical to psychological accounts of privacy is a changing notion of what are to count as breaches of privacy rights, and what are to be their respective seriousness. (2001: 20–21)

Importantly, they further suggest that 'In making this evaluation it might be possible to construct a model of the seriousness of an invasion of privacy'. (2001: 21) Indeed, we will attempt, following the presentation of the findings, to do just that, and do so based on how those in the focus groups perceived privacy and judged the right of journalists to intrude into private spheres as a dependent of the seriousness of the issues at stake.

Many of the points that Alldridge and Brants raise in discussing the laws of intrusion into privacy have direct relevance in discussing the public interest and media intrusion into privacy; even the right to remain silent, where, as they note in court cases, to exercise such a right can have adverse consequences. What we see is the extreme complexity of the notions of rights and the private and the public. It is all well and good for journalistic codes of practice to state that everyone has a right to privacy, but not so easy to grasp in substantive terms what that entails or means when opened to analytical inspection. The conclusion of Alldridge and Brants, that the right to privacy is a weak right, is well founded. Privacy is to do with autonomy. But, as they state:

In some ways autonomy, broadly defined, is not an enforceable right in any useful sense. It is the basis of all fundamental rights – namely to be able to behave and to be treated with the dignity that goes with being human, whatever one is, it is that self that commands respect. This underlies all of the rights of the European Convention. Privacy, freedom of expression etc., are the part-expression of this in positive law, for those situations in which the autonomous individual finds him or herself in the context of society. Then, the autonomy rights of one may clash with those of the other and one will give way. Given that it is the social context that will decide which right has the stronger claim, it must follow that many autonomy claims are unenforceable and privacy rights are weak. (2001: 22)

The introduction here of the idea of the social context in deciding the rights of claim-makers moves us already to considerations that, in discussion, intrusion into privacy can only take place in concrete cases and not in abstraction, as if privacy rights can be delivered by *fiat* in some formalistic manner. The right to privacy, as we shall see in documenting the findings from the focus groups, is one that is worked out in practice. It is, in other words, difficult to say, before some intrusive act has taken place, when the right to privacy is broken, since it is quite clear, in so far as the general public is concerned, that the right to privacy is a conditional one – it is conditional on the act or state that is to be observed and the consequences of not intruding on the privacy of others. That, of course, leaves open the question of the manner of the intrusion. However, as we will see, the rules governing the form of the invasiveness link strongly to the consequences that might follow from not invading someone's privacy. There is also a strong argument to be made for invading privacy in order to prevent public harm. The whole question of privacy and autonomy is ambiguous. Alldridge and Brants, in drawing on examples from the treatment of privacy issues in Holland, provide very good illustration of this, especially in the modern era of new forms of communication.

> ...in those cases of claims to privacy that are rooted in autonomy, the very notion of autonomy is ambiguous, for in considering privacy in terms of autonomy we immediately run up against a preliminary question: what is the nature of the self to which autonomy is granted? Is it to be a socialised or an unsocialised self? The European Court of Human Rights is most definite: protection of autonomy rights is restricted to the socialised self. The debate surrounding the anonymity of Internet use is of particular interest to this issue, precisely because it is partly a debate about autonomy and the freedom to escape from the limits of social normalcy. Those who advocate protection for total anonymity in Internet access argue that only thus is 'uninhibited' self to be given full rein. This is the self for whom the Dutch Supreme Court claims to seek vindication, but at the same time the ultimate freedom to be oneself that the virtual society of Internet could provide, is not what the Supreme Court has in mind for real Dutch society. In frequent references to what the majority of the Dutch population regard as immoral or to 'the changing climate of public opinion', it [Dutch Supreme Court] recognises claims to personal autonomy in pornography, drugs and euthanasia cases for example, only insofar as a majority of the Dutch population accept that these are private spheres where autonomous decisions are legitimate. A law which only recognises the autonomy of the socialised self still asserts control, for reasons of paternalism, authoritarianism or moralism, but makes socialisation the principle mechanism of its instantiation. (Alldridge and Brants 2001: 22–23)

The Nature of Privacy

Privacy is essentially normative and, as such, the idea of the private changes over time, with part of that change being driven by technological change affecting communications. It is not to be expected that an e-society would view privacy in the same way as a society where the delivery of news was accompanied by the blast of a post horn or even by telegraph. Camcorders, along with other electronic image retrieval modes, are now a common feature of contemporary life, which it is reasonable to presume alter the nature of what one might be expected to 'give up' in terms of movement, expressions and so on. Modern society is increasingly a surveillance society, from the installation of CCTV cameras in city centres, shops and car parks, to the collection of personal financial data and other information required of a complex economy. Indeed, information has become a commodity like any other commodity: it has an exchange value. However, in accounting for changes in the ideas of the private, and here we might consider the private to consist of the withholding of information about the self; psychologically, emotionally and physically, too much emphasis ought not to be lain in a straightforward manner on purely technological introductions that affect communications. As stated earlier, modernity is configured upon communications; that is, what makes it modern. It is changes in communications, from co-present interactions to interactions over time and space, which alter social ordering, making possible new structures and patterns of living. The growth of the city itself is part and parcel of this change. It takes little reflection to consider that the idea of privacy is transformed in the long movement from the pastoral village to the town. The development of the metropolis alters living space and possibilities of knowing others' business. This gives an emerging sense of protected space, as activities are not engaged in on a community or communal basis. What is open to inspection, both emotively and physically, becomes reduced with modernity. Indeed, the emergence of the private self is a modern phenomenon.

One must always be careful in handling a historical period to make distinctions between strata, but for some strata, most usually the upper classes, then something as intimate as courtship can be seen to have moved from a public to a private sphere. Yet, it would be wrong to see changes in privacy in some linear terms. Certainly, one can document, in broad epoch terms, distinct shifts in what the private is taken to mean, and it is fairly easy in experiential terms of recent history to see that ideas of the private have changed; something that will be demonstrated in presenting the findings from the focus groups. The modern world gives us the heightened idea of the private as performances become individualized, and the city provides shelter from gaze on the 'full individual' – performance is increasingly split in the execution of a number of roles enacted in a variety of different settings, so that, in a sense, no one can fully claim to know the other. At the most crude level, this can be captured by the simple observation that, despite the much heralded phenomenon of home-working, for the vast majority of us, work and residency remain split by often quite considerable geographic distance, to different parts of the city or even separated by different towns.

Very briefly, modernity, and, more so, heightened modernity, gives rise to special problems for the maintenance of reality. Time-honoured ways of behaving of the pre-modern world, where tradition and custom cement the individual to a world of certainty, even cosmic certainty with little separation of the profane and the sacred, creates a knowing unknown to modern man. To be private is not simply, in the legal sense presented, to be left alone; it is to be alone. This is the source of the ontological insecurity that we all must live with, and in some way grapple. To fail to make sense and order of the world around us is to suffer anxiety of varying degrees of disability in terms of social functioning. There is no mystery here as to how this has come about. The dismantling of certainty is a product of the dynamic released by industrialization so that change is structured into the very structure itself, forcing the individual to constantly keep on 'top of the moment'. Older people have greater difficulty in accommodating to this transience than younger, but then, given that their engagement with the central dynamic of social and economic movement is less than that of younger people, they have less need to. They can, to an extent, refuse entry to the heartland of the modern world; even turn their back on it in a way not possible when they themselves were younger. All such factors impinge on what the private will take to mean.

Because the world is fragmented, and fragments with the modern age, we operate in many different spheres and present ourselves, or position ourselves, in our relationship with others in accordance with how we judge the situation. In a world of dynamic change we rarely, if ever, have full information about that which we face. This is where the media come into play in filling the gaps.

Such situations demand trust. Trust in this sense fills in for missing information, enabling us to make decisions and act. This would be the case in terms of romantic, personal relationships, as it would be in business. One way to establish trust, at the inter-personal level, is openness. Openness is the opposite of privacy, allowing the other into the self. In being open, the impression of familiarity is given, where, in a fast-moving transient world of contact, familiarity could never be achieved organically. The vogue, even a value, of openness is a consequence of the transient nature of contacts.

To allow someone into one's close private domain is saying, 'I trust you', but it is also a device for establishing trust, in that to 'open' in such a way is to convince the other person that they know you – the precursor of trust. And, of course, in one sense, one does know this other person because they have told you intimate details about themselves. Through this technique of openness, time and space is squeezed. What may have taken years, and the unfolding of the self to the other, takes place quickly and is part and parcel of the transformation of intimacy that has taken place in modern society (Giddens 1992). Openness has come to be not just a technique, in the sense of a deliberate operation, but has become a value – a norm transformed into a value – and has done so because of its functional benefit. The reluctance to be open can make one 'odd', as witnessed by descriptions of the non-open person as 'keeps himself to himself', 'is a private person', 'can never get close to him', 'a cold fish', and, worst of all, 'lacks social skills'.

Social skills are no more than a social construction of what it is to be social and what are taken to being social changes over time – the life and soul of the party in one age would, in another age, be the boorish person best kept at a distance. This openness as a norm, and it is not too strong to say a value, has within it the opposite of its function; that is, on the one hand, it leads to ready social intercourse but, on the other, introduces the inauthentic. That is, how, in a world marked by openness and the allowing of the non-significant other into one's private space, does one retain some special value about the self that can then be accorded to the significant other – the person of special importance – when one has retained nothing that could be passed off as signifying a special trust in them. This openness, the means by which trust is quickly established, is thus destabilizing to the authentic self and also carries with it, through the lack of boundary maintenance, a general intimacy of knowing that then has an increased capacity to destabilize existing romantic partnerships. That is, the generation of closeness associated with knowing the other makes the transference of affection that much more likely.

Understanding the Social

The above may seem overly theoretical, or too historical, in discussing the media and privacy. However, unless there is an understanding of some central points of what to be social is, what changes have taken, and are taking, place in contemporary society in terms of associations, the discussion of privacy and media intrusion is left in the abstract. The interviews with media industry figures in Chapter 6, for example, revealed that, as well as being guided by guidelines covering privacy and intrusion, they had an eye, in similar fashion to taste and decency, on public standards of what was acceptable. It was realized that what was an acceptable intrusion of privacy was subject to change. Those changes, as pointed out, can be historically and structurally accounted for. Furthermore, such analysis assists in understanding where privacy rests. Time and again, as will be seen from the findings of the focus groups, the home or place of dwelling is the resting place of the private, and to intrude into that domain requires special reasons. One might say that there is a heightened sense of the private within the home, as inspection of the individual, indeed the voluntary opening of the self to others, outside the home has increased.

A sense of the self as a unique being, almost an anthropological necessity for existence, is predicated upon the private, the separation of the self from others, that which we might call identity, and will differ between historical periods and cultures. This will even differ contemporaneously between various forms of political organization: the totalitarian regime emphasizing the subsuming of the individual to the state, and of a theocratic state to religion. Yet, in the contemporary secular western world, to degrees of variation, self-identity, an appreciation of the individual as a unique constellation of characteristics and attributes, is firmly cemented. It is structured into the political ideology of notions of freedom, as well as the social ideology of what to be human is. Yet, it would seem that at every turn we give up our rights to absolute individual expression of who we are through the inter-connectedness of modern life and social organization. The fate of the individual in modern society has occupied social theorists from the inception of the social sciences; indeed, the social sciences were born out of the necessity to understand the rapid changes taking place in the nineteenth century up to the modern day, *vide* Giddens in particular.

Individuals can rarely escape, or only by the most extreme of performances, the assimilation of the self into the organizational and bureaucratic machinery of modern society, such as credit rating and the electronic payment of earnings direct from employer to bank. Not to have a bank account, not to be part of the complexity of financial institutions, and this is a relatively recent state, is not only to be disadvantaged, but is also not to be modern. Not to be modern is not some badge of pride, but lowers one's operating efficiency. However, by extension, to operate efficiently leaves a trail of private transactions which can then be opened to public gaze, the gaze of authorities empowered in the name of the public, or institutions that have claimed for themselves such legal rights to do so; for example, credit authorities. By scanning one's finances for suitability as a creditee, it is not just liquidity that is being examined, but you as a person or, in line with modernity, you as a 'type' of person. Your privacy has been intruded upon and judgement is then made upon you as a person. This enquiry, of necessity, disembeds you from the totality of your existence. It robs you, in a sense, of the 'essential self'. This point was brought home quite forcibly by every focus group, describing targeted mail and 'selling' phone calls as invasions of privacy.

Importance of the Home

Clearly, no one goes around talking in this manner, but that is not to say that the individual does not feel this intrusion, as we will see from the findings. This intrusion can lead to a sense of powerlessness in the face of removed institutions that enquire into the intimate running of one's life, but in the modern world most people expect such invasion to occur and submit in some way or another with the recognition that this is how things are. It does not mean, however, that the world is not increasingly seen as an impersonal place, exemplified perhaps by the telephone call options given by services, so that in many cases exchange takes place with a computerized system. It may be efficient, but it is not 'human'. It is within such a situation that the home provides a level of emotional intimacy and support that the increased impersonalization of the world denies. The home becomes an island wherein the individual can be, so to speak, himself or herself – a domain over which they have control of how they will perform, rather than responding to the demands of impersonal systems. Indeed, the nature of the family has changed, moving historically away from a prime function as an economic unit, to one that functions for affective or emotional support. The fact that such demands may appear as a strain which the structure cannot carry is by the by. What is important in terms of privacy is a heightened appreciation for the enclosed nature of the home; it is a fortress against the world and a breach of that fortress is a serious threat to personal identity. In a world that increasingly demands information about the self, a heightened appreciation takes place for the private sphere, where information demands must cease. This has much to do with a sense of the authority of the self. There has to be an area, in psychological terms, over which one has control. Yet, the closing of the door does not, as we shall see, keep out electronic intrusion; nor, it must be added, does the state leave what goes on within the supposed privacy of the home to its inhabitants. The control of the State over not just what is permissible, but how one ought to perform, goes deep, and no more so than in child-rearing and the extension of the social services to pronounce upon domestic performance.

The world, in the modern state, can never be kept completely at bay, but it is the performity demanded of modern living that, one might offer, pushes the idea of individual autonomy – captured by the right of privacy – to an area that has shrunk to that of domestic space. Hence, in determining what intrusion by the media can legitimately occur, the home emerges as a fierce point of resistance, as if all other ground has been seceded in a long battle of attrition. But, as stated, the demands of late modernity, or heightened modernity, has produced its own tactics for the handling of new conditions; namely, an opening of the self to the other to transform intimacy and notions of what is to be kept private. By way of illustration, one might point to the habit of many Americans, often disconcerting to the British, of offering intimate information about themselves almost on first meeting.

Public Interest and Privacy

Without understanding what is meant by the private, it is impossible to even begin to move to any resolution of what to intrude into privacy means, and in what circumstances it may be considered legitimate to intrude upon an individual's privacy. In an insightful report, *Privacy and the Law*, produced by the British Section of the International Commission of Jurists under the chairmanship of Mark Littman and Peter Carter-Ruck (1970), they remark, and it is worth quoting at length:

> In the course of our work, we have become increasingly aware of the difficulties which seem to beset any attempt to find a precise or logical formula which could either circumscribe the meaning of the word 'privacy' or define it exhaustively. We think that there are two underlying reasons for this. First and foremost, the notion of privacy has a substantial emotive content in that many of the things which we feel the need to preserve from the curiosity of our fellows are feelings, beliefs or matters of conduct which are themselves irrational. Secondly, the scope of privacy is governed to a considerable extent by the standards, fashions and *mores* of the society of which we form part, and these are subject to constant change, especially at the present time. [...] At any given time, there will be certain things which almost everyone will agree ought to be part of the 'private' area which people should be allowed to preserve from the intrusion of others, subject only to the overriding interest of the community as a whole where this plainly outweighs the private right. Surrounding this central area there will always be a 'grey area' on which opinions will differ, and the extent of this grey area, as also that of the central one, is bound to vary from time to time. (1970: 5)

The authors conclude by saying: 'Accordingly, we shall use the word "privacy" in this Report in the sense of that area of a man's life which, in any given circumstances, a reasonable man with an understanding of the legitimate needs of the community would think it wrong to invade'. (1970: 5) Choice, however, comes into this deliberation. Earlier they say: 'Above all we need to be able to keep to ourselves, if we want to, those thoughts and feelings, beliefs and doubts, hopes, plans, fears and fantasies, which we call "private" precisely because we wish to be able to choose freely with whom, and to what extent, we are willing to share them'. (1970: 4) The freedom to choose, though, is an essential part of privacy in the sense of the individual deciding what he or she will divulge. Nevertheless, the freedom to choose what one will or will not give over to the gaze of others is not absolute, but conditional on the right of others as representing collective interests to intrude. Conflict of interest is recognized:

> The opposing force in the conflict is given by the needs of the community of which we form part. By living in close proximity with others and sharing the burden of the common human experience, we are able to live in far greater material comfort, and to develop our potential far more than we could achieve unaided. The price we pay for these advantages is the abandonment of part of our freedom of choice. The benefits which social organisation can make available for any one of its members must, in the nature of things, flow from those which the others have been willing to surrender. In the special area with which we are concerned, there are innumerable examples where the individual's desire to preserve his privacy has had to yield to the greater needs of the community to regulate its affairs for the benefit of all its members.

> The problem, therefore, is one of balancing the individual's need for privacy against the legitimate needs of the community constituted by his fellows. It is to achieve such a balance between conflicting needs that we have laws. Our task, therefore, is to discover, if we can, what we mean by privacy, what limitations on that privacy the community can legitimately claim to impose, and what are the kinds of legal rules and machinery most apt to strike the balance between the two. (1970: 4)

The concept of the public interest here is cast in terms of a community of interest; that is, the interest is social rather than individual. Also introduced is the notion of balance, in the sense of a conflict of interest between the individual *qua* individual and the community. For example, a collection of individuals formed together in an association that generates interests in the continuation of that association, may be damaged by the actions of one of its members. Thus, the community has the right to override the interests of the individual *qua* individual. In an applied sense, the question becomes here not one of determining the political philosophical rights of the collective over the individual, that appears as a settled matter, but of determining the interests of the community, of that which would constitute a public interest.

In the manner that the idea of the private is subject to change, and, as argued, change has been wrought by changes in the very structure of society so that the notion of the private cannot have the same meaning within modernity that it possessed in pre-modern societies, just so with the idea of the public interest. Public interest is that which the public values. What is valued in one society, as forming part of its essential structure and organization, will not be valued in a society organized along totally different lines. What we are talking about here is the values and norms upon which a society is constituted. Thus, a mercantile society, where value is expressed in monetary terms, is highly likely to consider that it is in its interest to protect its financial institutions from subversion by individual acts that do not accord with the system as instituted. It would consider that it had a right to investigate those it deemed to be performing in a manner detrimental to the health of the system, and the seriousness of the alleged breaking of rules might well determine the lengths the collective might go in determining practices and guilt. This would include the degree of intrusion involved and the methods by which activities were brought into the open. Similarly, a pastoral society, where land was held and husbanded in common, having no interest in financial exchange, could well consider that it was in the public or community interest to enquire into the agricultural practices of its members whom it was held did not conform to accepted practices. Or, a society where it was held that the individual had to practice the profession of arms, in order to provide the community with military protection, may well hold physical fitness as a duty of its citizenry and take an interest in the 'health' of the individual, not as concern for the individual but as part of a collective concern over its ability to defend itself – the idea of privacy and community interest would differ in a modern-day kibbutz to that of contemporary Britain, as indeed does the value structure underpinning the respective societies.

Of course, in the latter cases given, the communal nature of the society would be such that not much could take place in private. As stressed, the private would take on an entirely different meaning than in modern society where much activity takes place in space hidden from public or open gaze. The point to stress is that what is considered to be in the public interest represents a document of the values of any particular society. A highly interdependent society, such as that offered by western modernity, means that much that one does affects the collective in some way. What is at debate is the extent to which the collective can claim that its interests may be damaged by some activity that then leads to the call for intrusion into the private affairs of an individual or, for that matter, an institution. What we will see in presenting the results of the focus groups is that, when it is held that privacy can be intruded upon, a set of values spring into operation, values that are drawn from ideas concerning correct social function. It is not so much balance, the weighing up of individual rights versus community rights, that comes into play in giving permission for the intrusion of privacy; the decisional process appears to be that of accepting a course of action when rules that are held to govern correct behaviour are broken. It is not, in that sense, a legalistic working through of rights at all, of judging the claims of one against the other – although that is involved – but, at times, an emotional response based on sets of values that are held. In some cases, as we will see, invasion of privacy is allowed, not because of any objective threat that an individual's 'secret' doings may pose to the community, but distaste at that which the individual's habits, goings-on and so forth represent. There is, attached to the granting of the invasion of privacy, the idea of moral outrage, which no court, in coming to arbitration over rights, would be likely to uphold as a valid reason for invasion.

One thing that can be said before introducing the findings, and be said with certainty, is that the issue of privacy is one of concern to people. This is not surprising. The objection to invasion of privacy is that such invasion runs against ideas of who we are and the nature of the society that we live in. The notion of privacy is related to ideas of freedom and what it is to be free. Hence, it is not uncommon to hear references of the order, 'we do not live in Russia' or 'what do you think this is, Nazi Germany?' Not surprisingly, the issue of privacy is complex and this is why it is essential, in grappling with what appear to be definitionally loose concepts and the normative nature of privacy, to collect individuals' reasoning of why in some circumstances privacy can be intruded upon, why in some other instances it cannot, and in what circumstances certain procedures can be adopted in invading someone's privacy. The question also arises, even where it is held that there is a public or community interest in intruding into someone's privacy, of who has the authority to do so. The police, it will be seen, have certain rights denied to the media. That notwithstanding, the model of the media held by people involves the media having a 'policing' function, not just of exposing wrongdoing, but of exposing moral turpitude. The public interest, as stated, is constructed from values people hold, and values that they wish upheld; hence, intrusion into privacy is not always authorised on what might be considered technical considerations of mechanistic damage to the community, but on the moral implications of acts. Almost any story, whether deliberately so or not, tells a moral tale – stories that we do not tell, that is, doings, happenings or performances that are not made into stories, also tell a moral tale in that they signify that which we do not consider worth recounting. What appears in the media, be it in the form of entertainment or news, tells us much about the value structure of our society. In some ways, when we examine in what situations privacy can be invaded, we hold in mind a core constituent of what we take to constitute the self, a privileged position independent of others, against some idea of moral behaviour where the moral can only be social.

Interviewing the Industry

6 The Problem of Privacy

This chapter reports the interviews made with industry figures collecting their views on media performance as it relates to the intrusion of privacy. The individuals interviewed were drawn from television, radio, the press – both tabloid and broadsheet – regulators, media pressure groups and trade bodies. The questioning ranged from actual practices of the media to a detailed examination of how they construed the term 'the public interest'. The defence of 'the public interest' is seen to suffer from poor conceptualization, and cases are presented where it is difficult to see where, on the constructions given, public interest could be held to be operable.

In the first stage of this part of the research, a series of fifteen face-to-face interviews was conducted with people within or related to the media industry. These included interviews with: a leading media lawyer, senior figures within television and radio (BBC and ITV), the press (tabloid, broadsheet and ethnic), regulators (press, television and radio), trade bodies and pressure groups involved with the media. All the interviews have been anonymized, apart from an interview conducted with John Beyer from the pressure group Mediawatch,[1] who wished to go on record. The researchers also met with senior staff from the BSC and the other bodies commissioning the study.

  The central purpose of these interviews was to gain an understanding of what they understood, or took to be, the defence of public interest in relation to the intrusion of privacy. In the course of these interviews a whole variety of matters relating to privacy were discussed, but the primary aim was to carry the 'idea' of public interest, as expressed by these figures, over to the focus groups for discussion. We wanted to know if there was disjuncture, or agreement, between media figures and those in our sample, in the understanding of public interest as a defence against intrusion of privacy. It was our hope that we would gain a working definition from these interviews that we might then 'test' for agreement in the focus groups. Nothing of the sort emerged. We were left, following these interviews, with the feeling that, although guidelines existed for determining intrusion on the grounds of public interest, and that the individuals interviewed could say what was in the public interest on a case basis, it was clear that there was no definitional clarity as to 'the public interest'. It was certainly the case that absolute documentation could be provided of areas where it was expected that public interest might be engaged – the reporting of crime, health and safety matters and so on – but that did not resolve the definitional problem. Indeed, the lack of an agreed definition, or any definition at all in the sense of precision, means, not that the whole area remains vague, but that dispute is overly structured into the system, and that the defence can easily be rolled out to argue the case for legitimate intrusion.

One of the difficulties that emerged, or seemed to emerge for us, was that because intrusion can be defended by appeal to something called 'the public interest', then, because public interest has the status of a knowable entity, the term takes on a quasi-legal position, suggesting a ready-made test for whether or not the individual had a right to expect privacy. This, in practice, is far from the case, for the simple reason that the term 'the public interest' cannot do the work allotted to it – it lacks objectivity. There is nothing unusual in this in tests of propriety. The notion of taste and decency suffers similar difficulties associated with subjectivity, the difference being, however, that the term 'the public interest' has the appearance of objectivity. It is for this reason, among others, that later we suggest, and make a case for, replacing the notion of 'the public interest' with that of 'social importance'.

What emerged from the interviews, and was of great help in undertaking the focus groups, was the fact that if those professionals within the media and regulatory bodies had difficulty in coming to a definition of public interest, why should it be expected that the general public would be any better placed to provide a definition. The whole issue is full of confusion. In fact, the more we reflected on the issue, the more complex it appeared than we considered it to be when first undertaking the research. What we have done, therefore, is raise the complexities associated with the defence of 'the public interest' as a justification for the intrusion of privacy at the philosophical, social and political level. We can then hopefully put the issue of 'intrusion of privacy' into manageable portions to suggest how future adjudication might proceed. No research can solve administrative problems. That is for administrators to do. What it can do is assist with enlightenment as an aid to reasoned decision-making. At the moment, the real problem in deciding issues of privacy is the very term, 'the public interest'.

This chapter is structured largely in terms of the individual interviews, rather than by the broad themes emerging from the series as a whole. This allows the differences in thought and judgement operating in each medium to be followed in some detail.

The Public Interest: A Definition?
Prior to the interviews, professional codes of practice and regulatory guidelines from a number of different countries were studied. None contained what could be termed a formal definition of 'the public interest', although the term itself was virtually universal. The Presswise[2] interviewee offered his view on this:

> *Well, I think there is a very good reason for that, isn't there? It's interesting that if you're talking as a journalist then you want it [definition of 'the public interest'] to be as broad as possible a definition. I mean there is this definition in the PCC [Press Complaints Commission] Code*

which... says, 'There is a public interest in the freedom of expression itself'. Well, that just about knocks down every hurdle that you can possibly put in its way.

It is not that he objected to an interest existing in the freedom of expression, far from it, but rather used the example to demonstrate the difficulties faced for defending privacy by appeal to public interest when public interest is not actually defined.

He went further by suggesting that it was in the media's interest not to have a clear definition of public interest, since such a loose definition could be brought into play to justify practices.

We mentioned that there might simply exist confusion about the term:

It's not a question of confusion. This is quite deliberate. I'm not saying that there is a nasty conspiracy, but my job as a newspaper editor would be to make sure that everything I publish is justified. So, if I had the opportunity of defining and redefining public interest in the way that justifies anything that I publish then I am going to do so, because my job is to justify anything that is published which is going to sell newspapers.

An example was given of how he considered the term "the public interest" could be used for publication of material that the subject did not wish published.

He mentioned that, in cases involving children, editors *'must demonstrate an exceptional public interest'* and then went on to question the operation of public interest in practice.

I had a case recently where a woman was being hounded by the press and I was trying to get the press off her back... I was talking to a news desk and saying, 'Look, the story you have is wrong. This woman doesn't want to talk to you. What's the justification for having three reporters sitting outside her door all day so she misses a hospital appointment for instance?' And the justification I was offered was, 'That it was in the public interest' and I said, 'Oh really, why is that?' and they said, 'Because she has spoken to the press before'. This is a classic. Somebody is encouraged to talk to the press, not difficult. The fact that they have spoken to the press then declares them to be, in some sense, a public figure and therefore anything that happens to them thereafter is in the public interest. That is an extraordinary definition but it's one that is often used.

The point made above – that it suited editors to have the idea of public interest as vague as possible on the grounds that it offered a ready defence for stories that intruded upon people's privacy – was put to a senior BBC radio news figure. He agreed and said: *'Yeah, I'm sure it does'*, but then added, *'How else would you have it?'* He was not defending a cavalier 'rolling-out' of the defence, but suggesting that

It will always be a grey area. My view is that there are never simply two sides to a story, there's a multiplicity of sides, which stretches out and stretches back. There's a multiplicity of effects and of what's in the public interest, which will vary from issue to issue, from story to story. I don't see how you can logically, and rationally, impose some sort of blueprint which enables you to know whether it's in the public interest or not.

He also reflected on the separate, but linked, concept of the *national* interest:

> *I'm taking public to mean a collection of individuals, and you would say – in general in the public interest. The problem with national interest is that many things are brought to light, which in the short term are certainly not in the national interest. Anything that involves the Foreign Secretary being corrupt etc.... is it all hugely in the national interest to reveal that, just before they go to a summit meeting? It's very, very complex indeed – you can't get away with that.*

The point he is making here concerning the national interest is one taken up at length later relating to public interest. Namely, that something might ostensibly be in the public interest, that is, the public could reasonably have an expectation to know about something, but the consequences of the release of some information, and of what then followed from such a release, has an adverse effect on the public. Therefore, in a functional sense, it is not in the public interest. In discussing the idea of national interest and public interest, it was mentioned:

> *I suppose the concept of national interest has diminished with the apparent diminishment of the nation state... The whole notion of national interest has waned since 1945. But public interest, which presumably came from the left more; is a more lefty concept, particularly grew up in the 60s and 70s with the exposure of companies and of politicians and was seen as something moving from the bottom up rather from the top down. I think national interest is now a ludicrous concept. National interest these days can mean whatever the government wants it to mean, in a particularly cynical way. Public interest, by the same token, could easily mean whatever the editor of a newspaper wants it to mean. We try to be ethical.*

What he is saying here, although frequent reference was made to the BBC's own guidelines, is that the idea of the public interest is one of judgement, and, from his previous statement, given that the idea of public interest is vague, is open to great variation of interpretation. Hence, his comment, *'we try to be ethical'*. What he means is that his organization has standards of behaviour, a code of performance, that guides practices; an ethic that shapes how a journalist confronts his job. Clearly, formal guidelines embody an ethic, but the suggestion here is that practice is governed by feelings of appropriate conduct distilled from sets of principles. His suggestion is, though, that editors in other organizations, particularly newspapers, do not necessarily operate from sets of principles, but from the opportunities presented by a broad concept – the public interest – that can be exploited. According to him, an *'editor of a newspaper'* can take public interest to mean whatever he or she *'wants it to mean'*. In his case, however, the appeal to the ethics of the BBC appeared to give him a great deal of confidence in executing his role.

He was also asked whether, in reporting the behaviour of an individual, he took into account the local situation; in some localities might the behaviour reported cause greater harm or shame to the individual than would be the case if they lived elsewhere? For him, relative standards did not exist, only a single standard:

I couldn't give a monkey's where you lived. And that's something we carry abroad – we don't swallow this thing of comparative standards. We apply one standard. It may be the wrong standard; it may be arbitrary, it may be patronising of us, but it is the only way you can judge.

Neither, furthermore, did he believe that the consequences of intrusion to the individual concerned had to be considered. The duty of the journalist was to be accurate in his or her reportage.

I remember, virtually the first thing I was told on the first day of my journalist course, by a gnarled old hack, was: 'You're covering a magistrate's court, and a 75-year-old woman is up there for shoplifting, and she comes up to you after she has been convicted and says, "Please don't put my case in the paper, I would kill myself…"' You put that in the paper first – that's another sort of ethic. If you're trying to (act) in the public interest, you can't be motivated by too much hold over you that a person might have as a consequence of what you do. It would be very easy then to destroy the public interest by saying 'report this and I'll top myself'.

This is a point well made and assists in understanding what is meant by the public interest, but not in giving definitional clarity. What he is saying relates to his point concerning the public interest involving the public as a 'collection of individuals': if one considered that the individual, in this case the old woman, had a personal right not to have her offence broadcast, then there could be no public interest defence. Public interest must mean that the collective overtakes the individual. Once a public interest has been established, then one acts on behalf of the public, not on behalf of the individual being reported.

This is pretty much in line with the findings in the focus groups – they were against the 'hounding' of an individual and, although they themselves felt that they would find it difficult to expose something if it had strong consequences for the individual involved, it was felt that the media ought to go ahead and not pay much regard to consequences. What ought to be held in mind is 'style of reporting'. It is one thing to report a story following the intrusion of privacy in a flat descriptive fashion, but it is another matter if it is reported in an exiting dramatic style that might, for example, give luridness to the report. But this is where, and we raise this at several points later, taste and decency interact with the question of privacy – they are not always easily separable.

Public Space and Private Space

At the time of the interview, the newsreader Anna Ford, who had been photographed in a swimsuit on a public beach, had taken her case to court for adjudication. We asked the opinion of a senior radio newsman at the BBC about this in terms of the defence of public interest against the intrusion of privacy. He said:

It's problematic… because the last person I would expect to know what was in the public interest was a High Court judge frankly. I think a newspaper editor, or a news programme editor is probably better equipped to know what is in the public interest. Of course, there's always a tension there, because some papers will push it, but it's very, very difficult to know what the public interest was in Anna Ford sitting on a beach. At the same time, I thought the court case ludicrous. I didn't see that it was a grotesque invasion of privacy – it was a photograph taken on a beach – I think that's pushing it. I think it's difficult. The parameters aren't very clear about what is public interest and what is invasion of privacy. I think both are equally difficult to define.

Anna Ford lost her case. The judgement given was that it was not an infringement of her right to privacy. This was taken up with the representative of the PCC:

I. In the case of Anna Ford, I imagine she would argue that she's a public figure, but there are types of public figures. She is not... someone who has actually courted the media, she has not put herself about like that – she's a public figure by virtue of working on television. What would you say to that type of argument there?

His reply was:

Well, yes, this is a matter of judgement and discretion, but I suppose it could be argued that anyone who is a general newscaster is in some ways open to a much broader constituency of the public, even more than a very well-known pop figure. In a sense the problem for pop figures is keeping themselves in the public eye. Suddenly there's a newscaster, it's willy-nilly by virtue of taking that job. A public figure who is perhaps more instantly recognisable, after all, a public performer, whether they're a pop figure or a classical artist is only going to appeal to the constituency of people who follow that kind of music or that kind of art form, but a newscaster is pre-eminently a public figure. Anyone can recognise Trevor Macdonald in the street.

I. But would they take a picture of him on the beach?
I think they might, yes.

I. It wasn't because Anna Ford happened to be a woman?
It might be, but I don't think there's too much gender bias in the types of complaints we get from public figures.

His response also raises the question of degree of invasion of privacy: in his view the level of invasion in this specific case was not *'grotesque'*, implying that there are degrees of unjustness. The case, as it was put forward, rested on the fact that the celebrity was on a public beach:

Well, it wasn't as difficult, I think, as some of the others that we've had, in the sense that there was a factual basis and a disagreement about fact in that here we were presented with a complaint because [the celebrity] considered that she had been on a private beach and our enquiries established that we did not conclude that she had been on a private beach and, secondly, we took the view that there was nothing in that article or photograph that was in any way demeaning, or derogatory, about her as a person; that in the sense a celebrity does put themselves, by virtue of being a celebrity, in a position where there will be arguments about whether or not they have as much closed space as ordinary people. In fact they're not going to, because anybody who recognised them is going to come up to them and that's going to happen. So it's a little bit like the issue of how private can a member of the Royal

Family be? Our view has always been that there must be a public interest for writing about certain aspects of their private lives, but they are still entitled to as much privacy as anybody else.

One of the distinctions that the members of the focus groups made, in coming to judgement about whether or not the taking of a picture whilst on a holiday beach was justified, related to the degree of concentration given; of how the picture was focused. If directly on an individual then it was held to be an intrusion, but not if it was a picture that included many others on the beach. The same was held for a picture taken of a football crowd. The distinction that we make later in Chapter 8a between closed public space, restricted public space and open public space is relevant here. The expectation of being subject to public gaze is dependent on the nature of the space. One is open to the gaze of others on a beach, but, as we discuss later, consideration ought be given to the context within which the picture is viewed – the gaze of others on a beach is not the same as the gaze of the photograph at home; the picture is transformed at the point of reception so that the subject of the picture might well feel their privacy has been intruded upon.

Public Interest as Collective Interest and Judgement

During the interview with a senior BBC policy-maker, we mentioned that, in examining the various codes of practice as they related to privacy, we could find no satisfactory attempt to define that which was in the public interest as justification for the intrusion of privacy. He began by saying:

The difficult bit, as always, is striking the balance between the individual's right to privacy, I was about to say however you define it, but that in itself raises a whole series of issues, but it is very interested in the privacy an individual would have in their own family life, and in their reputation of course, balanced with the public interest of needing to know, where something seriously in the public interest is taking place which may involve infringing that person's privacy, so the rules are quite clear in terms of their nature. Interpretation, of course, sometimes becomes difficult.

To interpret involves judgement, and judgement involves saliency, but interpretation is difficult when it comes to the right of the individual to privacy judged against public interest, precisely because what constitutes public interest is not defined.
He continued by saying:

Well, the BSC and the ITC Codes both kind of indicate areas, as you say, where it's [the public interest] likely to be a consideration, but I think that is precisely the problem – it is hard to define the public interest with any immense clarity, because the moment you start defining things, it's what you thereby exclude and I think, therefore, one wants to give a general indication of where the areas might be, and I think it's as you say, protection of public health, protection of national security, crime and social behaviour, significant incompetence in public office. It's areas where one is trying to suggest that the interest involved is inevitably bigger than any individual, that it affects a group of people, possibly in a dangerous way, in a threatening way, or it affects a group of people in a way that they might need to know that X or Y, elected by them to a certain job, is not doing that job in a way that they might have come to expect. [...] Your public interest test is going to be one where there is some degree of harm to a significant number of people.

A central theme that emerged from the focus groups is that public interest had to involve the interests of, as the above person mentions, *'a significant number of people'*. We have referred to this as 'social importance', as our preferred alternative term to 'the public interest'. But, we will not enter discussion here, since it is given considerable space later. However, it is difficult to see, on the above reflection on public interest, how pictures of Anna Ford on a beach could be held to affect a significant number of people, if by affect we mean having some consequence to their lives.

Indeed, his test of public interest was whether or not 'there is some degree of harm involved to a significant number of people'. We responded by asking: 'Isn't that moving towards the notion of a community of interests?' His response was:

Well, regulators in different parts of the world have all chosen, I notice with interest, increasingly around the phrase 'contemporary community standards', 'acceptable community standards'. In any event there is some sense there of 'the community'. Now that can actually be applied more in the area of taste and decency, as a means to get away from the idea of taste and decency to a concept that whatever is being adjudicated on is in line with the community-at-large's sense of a standard. And if the community-at-large feels that a certain language is acceptable at, say, ten o'clock at night, that is a better test to apply than whether or not twelve members of the great and the good come to the conclusion that it is or isn't acceptable. In other words, you're trying to root your judgement in a proper understanding of where the audience-at-large is likely to be. So it's tended to be more in that territory, though of course privacy is an interesting area in the sense that you do find that people complain not on their own behalf, but on the behalf of other people's privacy that they feel has been invaded by programme-makers and that might most typically happen where the survivor of some trauma or other is interviewed and is close to tears, if not in tears, or people feel that the broadcaster is intruding too closely into what they think should remain private and unexplored.

Later we discuss the very real difficulty with the term 'community standards', and contrast it with recent ideas in moral philosophy, of a 'moral community'. That is, what is right can only be judged from within a particular community's set of operations, values and moral beliefs, and not from outside in some absolute fashion. Leaving aside whether or not the idea of a moral community is simply a philosophical construction to handle certain problems in philosophy, the question is whether empirically such communities exist. The difficulty within contemporary Britain is discovering 'community' that might give rise to a community of interests. Even if one did exist, and this is discussed at some length, it far from resolves the problem of the intrusion of privacy. 'Community of interest', like 'the public interest', leaves unresolved the question of the precise interests we are referring to. Furthermore, one set of interests that a community might have can clash with the interests of another community to provide confusion in the appeal to standards, or, expressed another way, rights.

Taste and Decency

The introduction of taste and decency by the above interviewee is important. At several points in analysing the comments made by the members of the various focus groups, we see the idea of taste and decency fusing with the idea of privacy. The question of taste and decency is ineluctably bound at times with the question of privacy. The question of dignity as an element of privacy is also a valid point made by the above person. This came particularly to the fore when discussing the 9/11 terrorist attacks on the World Trade Center in New York, and whether or not the publication of the last minute telephone calls by those on the stricken airliners was an invasion of privacy. This question of dignity as privacy is not restricted to 'hard news'. This BBC policy-maker mentioned, as an example, the first series of the reality show *Big Brother*, where the members of the house turn against one of the participants to the point where he is close to tears or *'on the verge of a breakdown'*. The concern is *'about programmes where people feel that the participants are being pursued a bit too much'*. Moving to documentaries, he presented another case:

> *A* Panorama [BBC current affairs programme], *which you may have seen, where a boy in care was being asked: would he like a foster parent? And again, the camera is very tight on his face and he's almost, in a sense, waiting for tears to fall and that's another point where people feel that yes, there might be a public interest involved, in terms of what happens to children in care, how easy it is for them to find foster parents, but they are also capable of being, in the viewers mind, exploited by a programme-maker who's looking for that extra dramatic moment.*

The more one examines the question of privacy and the defence of public interest, the greater the complexity involved than might appear on first reflection. An undermining of someone's dignity can well be considered an intrusion of privacy. He continued by reflecting on *Big Brother*:

> *This is of interest to the public. But again, it's that sense of – at what point does someone's dignity as a human being get transgressed by the programme-maker? And, therefore, is it possible in this day and age to retain that sense of essential human dignity, which means that even though it's not a matter of huge public interest in the aforementioned sense, the public interest lies in the issue of dignity and the particular offence to human dignity, and that's terribly difficult. It's positing, in a sense, an absolute at a time when people have gone for small rather than capital 'a's and where Postmodernism has weaved its magical spell, but I do think that there is still a territory there to be explored.*

This question of allowing the individual to maintain their dignity, as a question of the intrusion of privacy, is not easily resolved. The case given of the young boy and the *Panorama* programme dealing with the important issue of adoption is possibly one that viewers might feel uncomfortable about. There are, however, instances where the audience may feel uncomfortable looking at material, but the individual as the subject of the 'intrusion' may not. The idea of what it is to be dignified is not evenly distributed. That which one person might consider undermines their dignity to another might appear as wonderful self-promotion. The very act of agreeing to appear on a programme such as *Big Brother* would act as a message to many, as noted by the focus groups, that the participants either had no idea of what to be dignified meant, or that they construed dignity differently from most people. But one might say this of adult professional television performers who live by making fools of themselves, especially on children's programmes – it is not something too many people would feel comfortable doing. However, whether dignity is undermined, or, more accurately, whether the audience is concerned, is probably dependent on whether or not the person themselves appears bothered. In the case of the young boy in the *Panorama* programme, he did appear bothered by the questioning, and in the case of *Big Brother*, Nick, the person close to tears, was visibly bothered; whether he had any reasonable right to feelings of consideration is an open question.

The issues here are complex, but it was put to the ITC interviewee whether issues of dignity and intrusion into privacy prompted different regulatory responses depending on where the material originated; in the case presented, that of Britain or America. First, however, this official, as with others, raised the difficulties with defining public interest.

> *I don't know whether there is any objective statement of how you define it, because it's too wide. I know that the law has developed by precedent which would inform how a judge would start to sit and consider how the public interest may, or may not, have been served in a particular case, but certainly we would look to what so often informs content decisions, which is precedent, conventions that have surrounded television journalism which may not apply to radio or the press. As ever, it all boils down in the end to judgements. You don't feed any of the propositions into a computer programme and get a yes/no answer. It's weighing up the balance of factors in any particular case and also it's the context of the programme, the channel, the viewers' expectations as well as the actual journalism.*

The above is interesting for several reasons and is a fine example of the practical sense that a regulator must bring to their work, but it does little to add to definitional resolution. Here is a recognition of precedent as witnessed in the legal process, the building up of case material. The difficulty here, however, is that, unlike the law, or to a greater extent than the law, what in the past operated as sound judgement may no longer operate as such with changes in public values, attitudes and so on. A judgement made by a media regulator in the 1960s may not be good precedent for a judgement to be made in 2005, whereas a legal judgement made in the 1860s might still act as a good precedent in law for 2005. Public interest is not amenable to canonical judgement. Furthermore, there is, in the above, a recognition, in terms of actual performance, of expectations between the various media. This came out in the focus groups also. The press were seen to be less rigorous, when it came to respecting the rights of individuals to privacy, than television. This is not to say that they agreed that this was right, but evidence was collected that visuals of television could often give greater 'penetration' than print. In a sense, therefore, there was a higher onus on care when it came to intrusion placed on television than the press.

We do not wish to extend this consideration, since the concept of the public interest is not dependent upon a medium, but exists as a conceptual category. In fact, the ITC official, in talking of television, recognized the unenviable idea of the public interest and did not consider, unlike the area of taste and decency, that different channels, times of broadcast and so on, really altered the strictures placed on the intrusion of privacy:

Channel perceptions, and what viewers expect, are very important when it comes to the taste and decency arena because it conditions what people's dispositions towards, and expectations of, a certain programme will be. Whereas, when you're talking about news or investigative programmes, or surreptitious recording etc.... you bear a relatively high burden of proof operating across all services. I'm speculating now as to whether there might be examples of public interest in an American context, for example, where you make a different decision much closer to home.

We asked about the Jerry Springer programme:

Well, yes. There are times when we've had a higher degree of sensitivity applying to what's happened in Tricia, *or* Vanessa *versus the* Springer *type or* Ricky Lake. *But even with* Ricky Lake *we've picked up things with Channel 4, where we felt that perhaps the level of public interest served has not been sufficient to merit – I'm trying to think of an example... it often brings into focus that parents alone are not the sole arbiter of whether their child should appear in certain programmes in certain contexts because they can have quite mixed agendas and ambitions for themselves and for their children and parental approval doesn't absolve the licensee of responsibility.*

With a body such as the Press Complaints Commission then it is the person who considers that their privacy has been intruded upon who must bring the complaint; someone else cannot bring it on their behalf. However, with a regulatory authority such as the ITC, they themselves could instigate an enquiry where they consider privacy has been unfairly intruded upon, without a complaint actually being made. It is also the case that, since privacy questions can involve questions of taste and decency, matters can be examined without the necessity of complaint:

In the majority of cases a fairness and privacy investigation would be prompted by a complaint, but where it involves issues where we think somebody's privacy may have been unfairly invaded and the public interest is potentially quite weak, and that might get wrapped up in taste and decency issues because it may arise in part out of a discomfort that viewers feel in watching that scenario, where maybe the participant themselves were less bothered than the viewing public, we can intervene. There wouldn't be a huge number of cases where we would, but we're certainly not constrained from doing so.

In terms of levels of complaint, then privacy is not high compared to other objections that viewers raise against the companies. Out of around four hundred complaints a year, the ITC was receiving *'between 40 and 50 cases per year on average'*.[3] One of the concerns, or at least one of the factors that is taken into account in examining any case involving the issue of privacy, is the method of procedures adopted. The official stated, *'there are ways in which we can obtain the information that we want that falls short of secret filming and making sure that it was the last resort and not the first'*. This regulatory consideration, as we will see later by comments made in the focus groups, was also one shared by the audience in our sample. The use of surreptitious recording was a technique of last resort, and often-imaginative examples were provided by participants of how the information necessary for 'standing a story up' might be obtained without recourse to hidden recorders.

Although the ITC official considered that taste and decency might be affected in the absence of a regulatory authority, it was not considered that intrusion of privacy would be to the same extent.

...if there wasn't an independent regulator [and] the industry themselves made a commitment to published codes of conduct and several things would then kick in. One would be – to what extent they set up their own self-policing mechanisms, or to what extent they set up other interest groups and would take upon themselves a role of scrutiny. I certainly think that if the regulator didn't exist in code areas, then I think this area would probably deteriorate less quickly than perhaps taste and decency. [...] I think for a time there would be a degree, of sort, of professional journalistic pride and expertise that would continue and for the sake of the good name of factual television persist. It depends, I suppose, on what people thought the potential of increased ratings was.

The protection on this latter score was that the ITC official did not consider a massive appetite existed for programmes intruding into people's private lives:

I don't perceive what you would call a really unhealthy appetite for lots more of this sort of stuff. I think there is a degree of restraint on the part of the public... Ok, there is a section of the public that has an appetite for public exposition, clearly in the Jerry Springer-type context, but when it comes to entering into areas where you might be seriously invading people's privacy in times of real grief and distress, or just cavalierly exposing behaviour, that sort of deception is not justified for the end result.

An added difficulty for regulators is the sheer extension of the number of channels and services. As the above official said:

The sheer volume of television services is a challenge because long gone are the days when you could monitor everything that goes out. We monitor a tiny proportion of the total television output. What you've got to rely on is your constant scrutiny and reinforcement of codes, the educative nature of the ITC's work.

If no longer possible to monitor output in the manner of the past, another difficulty identified as a result of expansion and change was the inexperience now existing within television:

One of the challenges, certainly in the whole sector, is the staff turnover. Because there are lots of young inexperienced and cheap people going into the smaller services, and so trying to make them understand what the code means, not least because we now license for many foreign language channels, in which our codes do not apply for much of the time.

Taste, Decency and Intrusion of Privacy
In the course of the interview the ITC official mentioned that they had just returned from America, from New England, and reflected on experiences gained during the visit: '*The majority of Americans' willingness to play out their lives on the screen is pretty staggering*'. We asked where the possible boundary between matters of invasion of privacy and bad taste lay:

Yes, well it's very difficult. I mean I had intended to try and check where we were on a particular issue at the moment. You remember a couple of months ago the wedding in Jerusalem where the floor collapsed?

The reference was to a wedding party in full swing when suddenly the floor gave way and the guests, captured by another guest camera, plunged to their deaths. She continued:

We've been in correspondence with a number of broadcasters who put that out. I'm not sure whether in the end we will conclude the code has been breached, although it's primarily to do with taste and decency. It has privacy overtones.

We asked for expansion:

There were layers of issues as I remember it. I was away when it was first broadcast in the UK, so I came back in with a knowledge of the incident. I'd heard on the radio but not seen the pictures, but one of the things we discussed as a group was whether the pictures that had been shown of the actual collapse were pictures that brought people very close to elements of the code where it says that it is rarely justified to show the point of death and there has to be very strong justification for doing that. So we were looking at that and also whether the pictures of people coming out of it were unpalatably detailed for the timing of the bulletins. But also, one of the things that I suppose we were trying to tussle with, and we'd been in correspondence with Sky and ITN, was the preparedness of people to receive pictures like that. Actually, for a number of my staff the worst offence was that certain pictures were rushed to air, literally as the story was breaking, in an afternoon bulletin and came over in a very much starker, less contextual way than in the later, more produced programmes where there'd been a better chance to set the scene, talk about what was going to be shown and prepare the viewers. That's something that I think we're still in correspondence with the licensees about. It raises questions about the invasion of the privacy of the injured and the respect for those who died – was it sufficient to show the scenes of the run-up to the event, rather than the event itself, and then to have just cut away and show the aftermath? These are very tough decisions to make.

Clearly the issues raised by such coverage are difficult and of some concern to the ITC. Given that we were trying to press ahead with an understanding of what is meant by 'the public interest', we asked: *'If we wanted to mount a defence there on public interest, where would the public interest be?'*

Well, I suppose the public interest there works on a number of levels. One is that the public would have an interest in the scale of the loss of life, and why, at the point at which the story was first carried, because it subsequently was revealed to be the fault of inadequate building. You haven't got that degree of justification to be made, just in terms of the scale and unusualness and tragic juxtaposition of people at the height of the happiest occasion falling prey to who knew what? But that's why I think it is worth testing and asking broadcasters, who showed that material, what thought they gave, the minute those pictures came in, in a very competitive broadcasting world now. The temptation gets even bigger to just put those pictures to air.

Here is the definite idea of the public being interested in something, but it was still unclear whether there was an actual definition of the public interest at work. The point was pressed: *'I still can't really see where the public interest is there, and I'm going to come onto a point now, because I have looked at lots of codes from different countries – public interest was in all of them, but there are no definitions.'* She responded to this by saying:

> *Well, when we brought out our new code, a lot of the broadcasters were opposed to it because we used examples, and yet you'd have thought for guidance's sake that they'd prefer to have a few. But I suppose, for them, the looser and less defined a concept is, the more they feel that they've got scope to argue that their material falls within any reasonable definition.*

It was put to this official that 'Presswise' had been interviewed and a similar point was made: namely, that as far as he was concerned, it's the editors who want it ill-defined. We said: *'Are you suggesting that's the case with television?'* To a point it would seem so:

> *I think you'd find in the majority of broadcasters, they would always want to be less, rather than more, fettered, and you'll always get very strong arguments about freedom of expression and how the constraints should be very carefully weighed on fettering that. But I'm trying to say that we won a major battle in including examples, because those examples are not exhaustive and, as you said, they are only examples, not a watertight definition of what constitutes the public interest. But I think we always face a 'damned if you do, damned if you don't' position with the programme code because, in certain areas, you'll find the broadcasters pressing for specificity because they don't want to run the risk of it not being clear, and then in other areas wanting as broad and as loose a definition as possible so that they are not hampered and constrained. So code-making, in that sense, is always a compromise between a load of inappropriate and over-restrictive detail, and principles that are so broad that they both fail to guide the broadcaster significantly and imperil them by making our powers of discretion too wide.*

It is clear from the above conversation that we had difficulty in understanding how the pictures could be held to be in the public interest. We would not argue that for such pictures to be shown needed to be in the public interest, but used the case as a means of grappling with what is meant by the public interest. As also stated, any definitions of the public interest must, if to be of applied use, take into account the working practices, procedures and news values of the industry. However, the lack of a clear definition of the public interest does mean that it is difficult to say on what ground intrusion of privacy is being defended. There was recognition by this regulator that increased competition pushes towards the use of the dramatic as an attention-seeking device to increase or defend ratings – '...in a very competitive broadcasting world now. The temptation gets ever bigger to just put those pictures to air'.

There was also an awareness on the part of the ITC official of the complex relationship between the different media and the particular immediacy, or impact, of television.

We asked: *'If you look at the press they clearly have different standards of intrusion… once you have different levels of public acceptability of what intrusion can involve, does that make your life more difficult?'*

I think you can't, as a TV regulator, not have some views and regard for how the press behaves, because it sets part of the context in which people judge media standards and journalists work in all these different media, but to some members of the public, a journalist is a journalist is a journalist, regardless of the outlet... we know that the public has a general unease about the way in which people in distress and unfortunate circumstances are exploited in newspapers. The way in which a story is treated in the newspapers is far more extreme and intrusive than it is on television. And there is something still, in the nature of how television is received in the home, even if it isn't now as frequently in a cross-generational family situation, just the way in which the media connects with viewers, that people could be simultaneously sitting in their homes reading The Sun's *coverage of an issue and not feeling unduly uncomfortable, but if that were replicated by ITN or the BBC, it could cause a riot. There is a different level of expectation of behaviour.*

We wished to explore, therefore, how cross-media pressure might come into play; that is, that an item of news may not be considered appropriate for a television or radio station but becomes, through press coverage, an important news item, which other media, because of the circulation and publicity given, are 'forced' to cover. In our interview with the senior person from BBC radio, this was admitted to. It was put to him: *'You take the press – you may be honourable etc....– but does it occur that the press themselves actually behave without the defence of public interest and then you are caught on the hop because you've got to pull this news story?'* He was unequivocal:

Yes, that happens quite often. Now the BBC is quite strong in the defence of privacy, in my view ludicrously strong, and self-defeating and blind sometimes. The BBC thinks itself a public service broadcaster, number one. Number two – it also sees itself as 'civilizing'. It is not something which is driven, theoretically, by circulation or ratings, which of course it is, but that's the defence and, of course, it's got a civil service mentality...

The point here is that, although a public service broadcaster is, to an extent, protected against the pressures of circulation or ratings that press on commercial institutions, no section of the media can be regarded, or viewed, in isolation of the performance of the media in general.

Trivial stories can, if taken up with vigour by other media, be made to become news items in their own right, and must be covered, as we have seen recognized above, or rather greater coverage given than might otherwise be the case.

The idea of the press 'running' broadcasting in this manner was taken up with the official from the ITC. The question of the Hamilton case was raised:[4]

I. It probably happens more in the early morning news, that the press run with a story that is an invasion of privacy by your standards, but that then itself becomes a story.
I had something last week. I haven't pursued it because it's quite a difficult one. It's about the Hamiltons, and they gave an extensive interview to GMTV, and it was clearly one of her worst days and she cried. But they invited the cameras in. They could have gone completely to ground on this issue and they clearly exposed themselves very willingly to the publicity. But the following morning GMTV had a psychologist on analysing her demeanour and attitude and behaviour in

that interview, as a hook to talk about how you identify signs of stress, and a little part of me was saying 'I don't quite like that'. They had consented by virtue of their willing participation to the first interview, but how far does that consent maintain after the event is over. Now they would readily accept that that footage would be sold to other broadcasters and used later in the day on other bulletins, and then you think had they any further rights to expect the interview to be treated at anything other than face value and for it subsequently to form the basis for an item where Christine Hamilton's psychological state was subject to this treatment? On balance, quite frankly they were utterly consenting. They didn't ask at any time in that interview for it to stop, they went on until the broadcaster brought things to a halt. So I suppose I thought that if they were really concerned during that interview that she was not in a state to continue, they were quite at liberty to say so. So the footage used the next morning was something that they had still consented to.

I. They consented, but there's something wrong? Can you have a situation where something is still considered an invasion of privacy, even if someone has consented?
    Yes, again, I think we didn't find a breach of the code, but we explored a case where, in the aftermath of the Omagh bombing or some big incident in Ireland, where an interview was secured with a bereaved relative and we had some really severe doubts as to whether she was capable of making a sound judgement about her own preparedness and suitability to be interviewed. I think it was justified on the basis that she had approached them either wanting to make an appeal or something similar. She had, according to the broadcaster, her own rationale, but her degree of distress was significant and her level of intelligence was not apparently that high. You had cause I think to test the processes the broadcaster had gone through. We never received a complaint from the woman, or on behalf of the woman, that was just prompted by our own viewing of the material.

We said to her: *'But taking a moral position rather than a technical one. Now with people like the Hamiltons, they aren't clinically ill or anything. But would you ever say, "I don't think this should go on", even though they've consented?'*
She replied:

I think even with people who have a high degree of media coverage, both not sought and subsequently sought as in their case. I don't think you can say that there would never arise a position where the broadcaster might not transgress a certain boundary. If we take that example of a live interview with them, where clearly the whole stress of the previous weeks was really getting to her, but although she was looking very weak and exhibiting body language that showed that this was very uncomfortable experience, I don't think in that footage, or in any footage I saw last week, I thought that the broadcaster should have pulled the plug. But you could imagine a situation in which someone in her position, having consented to the interview, broke down in hysterics; started to behave in a very irrational way and I would expect the broadcaster to terminate the interview. I wouldn't expect them just to keep the camera rolling.

We asked: *'Is that a case where taste and decency moves into privacy?'*

Absolutely. I think a lot of the public interest areas dealt with in section 2 of the [ITC] code are not really taste and decency, they're about Roger Cook [investigative journalist] and exposing wrong doing, all that kind of stuff. The Taliban one (undercover journalist showing the treatment of women by the Taliban) in which there were elements of taste and decency in that one because of the extreme behaviour towards women and some of the horrible stories that one heard…

When you're coming to areas when you're talking about public interest versus public curiosity, I do think there are still moments where the broadcasters must be prepared to pull the plug and make a judgement that somebody is unfit and that some real damage or harm could come to them. There are real human dignity questions to be asked.

We then asked about the relationship between public <u>curiosity</u> and the public interest: '*I think some people in the focus groups might say, "well look, we have a need to be entertained, for our natural curiosity to be satisfied". And when society is curious collectively, then you say that's almost in the public interest*'.

Well, quite frankly, a lot of the footage one sees on the softer end of television news – like the Beckhams, that is public curiosity. I think again, these are areas where privacy and public interest meet taste and decency.

We intervened with a cable channel that showed some American footage of a 13-year-old boy doing his first parachute jump to become the youngest person ever to do a solo jump and the chute didn't open. He just plummeted to earth and that was it. And this channel showed the build-up to him having a little one on-the-ground practice and going up in the plane and jumping out of it and then you saw a long shot of him coming down, and you could hear – because the camera was placed where the family was standing – the rising distress levels as it became clear that his chute wasn't opening. And although it was in complete long shot, we said that was unacceptable.

We asked her to clarify: '*Is that the intrusion of privacy, or taste and decency there?*'

Well, I think it's both. I think the death of your son in those circumstances is intensely private. Not least because actually, and you could argue this both ways, it was your fault to some extent. But I suppose that the broadcaster would equally argue the public interest case that demonstrates how extremely dangerous it was for parents to approve for a child to do such a dangerous activity. But it seems to me that that was not acceptable material and it was unjustified as an invasion of privacy. Now, interestingly, the broadcaster told us that the family had approved the use of the footage for educational purposes, as a salutary message to the public. So, I suppose they were saying, 'It wasn't a privacy case at all because the family had approved the use of the footage'. But, as a regulator, we took a view that there wasn't sufficient public interest or curiosity value whatever, and it was unjustifiable to show it.

This example also highlights the differences between television and print:

The press, of course, could only show a still. The only equivalent that I can think of would be to show a heap of mangled bodies on the floor, and the PCC may well have upheld a public complaint that it was not necessary to show that image. Again, I think it's to do with the medium, that a static picture of this boy jumping would not have caused an issue, but the fact that we saw the entire plunge and hear the parents, and then they start running in shot, screaming. To me the whole package was an unnecessary quantity of footage to illustrate a point.

Here is clear evidence of the difficulty of applying the defence of public interest. In addition, it confounds matters more by showing how taste and decency becomes wrapped with privacy. We will see later how those in the focus groups responded to images of anguish as an intrusion of privacy. It is worth pointing out, however, that it is difficult to see how the defence of public interest could be mounted in the case of the 13-year-old who fell to his death. Unless, that is, one had reason to believe that parachute jumping was about to take off as a mass pastime in the fashion of skateboarding. It is also difficult to see what warning was necessary that parachute jumping held risks. One would have thought most people understood that, in the same way that one understands the perils associated with rock climbing. What is also interesting here is whether or not the fact that someone consents to an interview, might even seek an interview, then absolves the broadcaster of any complaint that privacy was intruded upon. Also raised is the question of dignity as an issue of privacy. Does someone under stress, grief or whatever, who breaks down on camera, or shows distress, come under the protection of privacy rulings? Dignity, judging from comments made in the focus groups, does fall under privacy, but so also does taste and decency. Even when consent is given, participants in the groups were well aware that, in particularly distressed states, such consent may not be 'rational'; that is, that individuals suffering grief may not be in a position to act in their own best interests.

The question also arises, but this is really for the judgement of the practised eye of broadcasters and journalists, that visible signs of distress that might produce discomfort in viewers may be little more than a staged performance. In the course of the interview with the BBC radio producer, it was mentioned: *'With the Hamiltons, they're queer – they are not clinically mad, that's for sure, but they are odd. Once she broke down on television, though she volunteered to go on...'* Little sympathy was given here.

> *That's another one where they say invasion of privacy – when people cry on the radio, and we occasionally get a couple of complaints about that, but, and I sometimes have sympathy with the people who complain, we never encourage people to cry and we don't really want them to. Christine Hamilton intended to cry the minute she went on that programme, didn't she? And it's interesting, we had an exclusive interview recently with the lad who was beaten senseless in Genoa by the Italian police. Now we got a 'forced' interview with him and he cried. Possible invasion of privacy, but it was absolutely bang on in the public interest. But, I remember, when I watched him cry seven other times during the day I started to think – hang on a minute.*

Methods of Intrusion

This question of intrusion, and the methods employed, was taken up with the Independent Television News (ITN) interviewee. In general, he said that complaints over the intrusion of privacy were not that common. That, working in television news, *'I would say the main complaint area is the one of balance between the parties, I would have thought. People thinking that they are perhaps unfairly treated, not given the opportunity to give an interview when they felt they should have or that we asked the interview in the wrong way'.* He did admit that this was problematic, however:

> *Privacy is a very interesting one, because for us it's a very difficult one, because we don't know whether somebody wants us to interview them or not... let's take the ghastly, ghastly story of the policeman who killed his family. We don't know whether contacting the grandparents to ask them for an interview is intruding on their privacy at a time of intense personal grief, or whether we are giving them an opportunity to say how much, you know, what a lovely chap their son was, how much they loved him and what a great father he was, and all that kind of thing.*

> *Half the people involved in tragedies just want to go away, close the curtains, not speak to anybody and deal with this terrible event in their lives in private. The other half though, really want to come out and, as almost a way of dealing with the grief, to express their anger, to complain about something that had happened in the process, or just to praise the person. They want their neighbours, they want their friends, and the wider world, to know what a lovely person this was.*

> *Our problem is, we never know which category they are going to be in. So, we don't know whether somebody wants to speak after an event or not. So, the rules that we have are quite simple. We are not intrusive. We will not shove a microphone down through somebody's letterbox, or film through a crack in somebody's curtains. We won't shout through the letterbox, 'Will you give us an interview?' What we do in circumstances like that is, we'll deliver a letter, or we'll approach through a third person like a vicar, or a priest, or a family friend and do it like that.*

He also added that even if pictures had been obtained sticking *'a long lens over a wall'* by someone else, *'we won't use them'.* We asked if the situation, with regard to the intrusion of privacy, had changed in face of increased competition. He admitted that

> *We have never been under more competitive pressure, either in terms of competition, or in terms of the commercial composite competition of the company, but also purely journalistic competition, and yet, I am as resolute on this now as I was when we had less competitive times. [...] There is a whole load of technology now, which would allow us to try and record secretly, and all the rest of it, and we don't do that unless there's an enormous public interest to do so.*

Secret filming, which was claimed to rarely happen, had to be cleared at the highest levels of ITN. There had to be a clear case of public interest and no other viable way of getting the story.

Asked for recent examples, he said:

> *Well, we did 5 years ago, so that's not recent but I'll think of some more recent examples, we did a major investigation of child prostitution in the Philippines and a British travel company actually organising holidays of men to go to the Philippines and then use child prostitutes. So, we sent out an undercover reporter and did secret filming of it, and the company was actually prosecuted and the guy is still in jail as far as I know. So, there are clear, I think there are clear examples. I personally have sanctioned at the moment for us to go and do some secret filming in hospital accident and emergency*

rooms. Because, if we apply to hospitals and say, 'can we come and film in your Accident and Emergency?' they clear everything up, and you go in and everything is absolutely fine. Clearly there are some horrific things going on in our A&E rooms at the moment, people waiting on trolleys for days on end, and I feel that is a massive story of public interest. It involves public funding; it involves public policy decisions. It really involves our viewers and that, the only way to get the story is through secret filming, and that's what we are doing at the moment.

Public interest is clearly used here not simply as the defence for intrusion into privacy, but for the collecting of material by surreptitious means. It is tempting to consider that the need for surreptitious means flows from the nature of the medium. Television news without pictures does not make for good television.

We mentioned to this interviewee that the Broadcasting Standards Commission's Code used the term *'overriding public interest'* and asked if this quantification of public interest was necessary in certain cases involving the intrusion of privacy; for example, where children were involved. He replied:

Yes, it's got to be clear. I know you can play with words, but I haven't really thought about it in those terms. 'Overriding' sounds probably too strong, but it needs to be strong, clear, clearly defined and very apparent public interest.

The Public Interest and News Values

These comments introduce an important element of the practice of journalism – news values. Several of the industry interviews seemed to us to present central questions in reporting; where news values are really at work, or dominate, in the presenting of news, but the defence made is that of public interest.

The ITN official was asked if any debate took place concerning the showing of the deaths at the wedding in Israel when the dance floor collapsed:

Oh yes. In fact, we're in the middle of cases with both the BSC and the ITC I think. But… It was a very difficult one, because what was horrific about that is it's very rare. If it had shown bodies flying all over the place and bits of limbs, then we wouldn't have shown it. But, it was one of the most horrific things that you, you could see.

I. I've never seen anything like it.
Exactly. Now, in the end, we decided to run it, but we had a warning. Even at 10 o'clock, post-watershed, we had a warning saying the video included pictures at the moment of the explosion, which some viewers may not want to watch, or words to that effect. And on the earlier programmes, before the watershed, we edited out the less horrific bits, and we certainly cut out of it very quickly. But you can't, and this isn't a privacy [question] anymore this is…

I. I mean, I was going to say, is this a question of, are we talking taste and decency or privacy?
No, this is taste and decency. But, you can't, well no, ok. If it's happening in Israel, it's taste and decency, because we can't, by showing pictures on British television of something in Israel, you

can't be invading people's privacy. But, say that had happened in this country, then you could argue that that was sort of a private event, and a shocking event, and it's invading people's privacy, the survivors, you know, it's overwhelmingly important to show those pictures, as long as you do it in a sensitive way.

I. What was the basis of the story? I mean, later, it did, but at first the media went out and thought it was a terrorist attack. But, it quickly said it wasn't a terrorist attack. And then it turns out later the story is of jerry building.
It's a human story about, of hitting the moment of sheer joy, you know, the happiest day, the happiest event in many people's lives, turning into, in a split second, turning into a tragedy.

I. So you wouldn't say that was a public interest story that's...
That's a human-interest story... Well, there's a difference here. We we're on ITV, we don't take one moment, you can only do stories which are of the public interest. The public interest only kicks in when we are talking about an invasion of privacy. Night after night we cover stories which are just, they have great pictures in them, or, you know, I think, I can tell you, the BBC, which have the sort of perfect type of approach that even they're changing, that there's got to be an issue to a story.

Without becoming mired in any controversy about the changing nature of television news, that it is no longer so issue-led and has moved to a softer human interest approach, the case above shows the complexity of presenting images that fulfil the news value canon of the dramatic, but one might wish to defend on other grounds, such as public interest. Clearly our own reading of this item is that it does raise issues of privacy, and it does raise issues of taste and decency, but we also fail to see how such a news item can be defended on grounds of public interest. It might be presented, as the above speaker does, that it did not really raise questions of privacy because it was not local to Britain. Yet, all this is open to dispute. A case can be made that coverage of the 9/11 attack did raise issues of privacy. However, this moves into the realm of the philosophical and was raised by the senior policy-maker within the BBC, of consideration for some essential of human dignity which then relates to privacy, or respect for the 'essential self'. For a newsman, such considerations may be too restricting, or even too removed from the trade as recognized. Later, however, we discuss the possibility that human interest stories might be considered to be in the public interest depending on how one sees the constituents of sociality.

The idea of human interest stories being in the public interest comes close to being suggested by this ITN official:

You know, there's clearly public interest, which is crime, corruption, bad transport, bad hospitals; my example area about the hospitals. That is in the public interest because it is very important for us to ... that's our job as the news broadcasters to tell them, 'Look, buildings fall apart and these terrible tragedies happen, and a policeman has killed his family', that has happened and it is still in the public interest for people to know, to be told exactly what is happening in their world, and that's why you have got to protect your children, lock up your house at night and all the rest of it...

This providing of information about the world is in the public interest, but the prime question remains of deciding what is a significant fact or event to record. Of all the rivers Caesar crossed, it is the Rubicon that is recorded, for the significance that it held for the constitution of Rome. Similarly, of all the events that occur in the world, why record some and not others? Some reason is required. But, the ITN representative did not wish for an over-formulization of the term. The vagueness, its lack of precision, suited what he saw as the working imperatives of his profession:

> ...*I think you can over-worry about it being a bit of a nebulous concept, but I think it is a concept that has served us very well. Certainly, in my career, I've been a journalist for 20 years and it's a concept that I now have a feeling for and I think it has served us well and that, basically, there is a distinction between a private individual going about their private business, which we have no right to probe whatsoever, and that private person then going into the public arena and doing things which affect the rest of the community and which we do have the right to report on. So, I would urge you not to be so concerned by the looseness of the definition to get rid of it, because it's a very useful tool and I think its one that we can all adhere to, because its just a useful question. It's a useful caution: 'Hold on, think about it', before you go and film somebody on holiday, before you put that letter through the letter box (asking for an interview) you are doing something which is going to cause concern to the person you are about to contact, are you sure you are justified to do it? Do you have a reason why you are right to invade this person's privacy?*

We talked about the future, and the future explosion of channels that is predicted. Following the comment that the media environment *'is not going to stay the same'*, he responded:

> *Well, that's why I think there should be regulation. I mean it's worked up to now. I see no reason why it can't work in the future. I think it's very dangerous to say, 'lets have no regulations'.*

> *I think the regulators themselves have to be careful and have to be not overly prescriptive and unreasonable. I think some [...] rulings have erred towards over-control, but, as long as they're being reasonable, then I think you should have regulation. The thing you want to do is... keep it out of the courts, and the last thing you want to do is <u>not</u> have a regulator and people suing someone else on the human rights act or something. It's a lot better to have this thing regulated within the industry.*

This may look as if this voice within ITN has joined with the voice of Presswise, but not really. The Presswise position was that newspaper editors wished for the definition of public interest to be as loose as possible so that, and by way of overstatement, editors could publish and intrude into privacy, and justify practically all action on the grounds that it was in the public interest. The ITN interviewee considered that the looseness of definition had served television well, and believed that any tight formulation, or putting matters in the hands of the courts, would lead to restrictions on reporting. Although not having a definition to offer on what public interest was, he knew what it meant, or referred to, and acted accordingly.

This appeal for looseness does not join the press and broadcasting together, for the obvious reason that the nature of the journalism differs. Television news does not engage with the type of stories that the press, most notably the tabloid press, does. It does not have an interest in the private lives of people in the same way, or to the same degree, as sections of the press. Rather, it sees itself as interested in private goings-on where it concludes that there is a *prima facie* case that those goings-on are in the public interest, whereas the tabloid press attempts to interest the public in the private goings-on of individuals. In the former case, therefore, a loose definition is seen to assist in promoting the public interest, or good, by allowing journalists lassitude of movement, whereas, in the latter case, a loose definition allows the journalist the freedom to generate interest in the newspaper through the creation of interesting stories. Here, of course, we are only talking about what might be referred to as news items, and it does not refer to the activities of television as a pure entertainment source, where intrusion into privacy operates in similar fashion to tabloid news reporting; namely, generating interest in the programme in the same way that interest is generated in the paper. However, and it is not something that can be handled here for the reason of objection to speculation, consideration might be given as to whether, under increased competition on existing channels and arrival of new ones, television news itself might not in the future give more consideration to attention-seeking devices than at present and do so by way of intruding upon privacy.

Different Media, Different Situations

Different media, and different channels within the same medium, require different treatment in terms of opportunities, or practices, that might prompt accusations of intrusion of privacy. Most commercial radio stations, for example, are music-based, and, in terms of intrusion of privacy, or how privacy might be intruded upon, light years away from that of, say, the BBC's Radio Four. This is not to say that the possibility does not exist. The Radio Authority interviewee commented:

In commercial radio, one of the more interesting show-bizzy aspects of invasion of privacy has come with the 'wind-up' call, and that is something we are addressing in the revision of the programme code, which is going on at the moment. Because the wind-up call is very easy, it's very easy to cock up. It's very easy to do badly, but it's very easy to do – that is an area that did concern us and we clarified how we felt that fell within the privacy regulatory framework, and it is our opinion, as far as wind-up calls are concerned, that... we always insist that the person who is the victim, and there is quite a lot of victim broadcasting around these days, gives their permission for the broadcast, and also gives their permission in an informed way.

Now the ITC do that with something like Brass Eye *[a spoof current affairs programme], which is almost a half-hour wind-up programme in some respects, how they do that – giving informed consent, when someone has agreed to be interviewed and has agreed to a broadcast. But is it an informed consent they're giving In* Brass Eye's *case probably not, I don't know. I can't speak for the ITC, but, had that happened on radio, it would appear to me that one of the problems that we would have is that the people who gave permission – the celebrities in particular – to be interviewed and to give their views about, in this instance paedophilia, did agree for the item to be broadcast, but they didn't realise it was being broadcast as a spoof documentary. So while they gave consent, it was not actually informed consent and I think there is a little bit of a difference there. But it's very difficult to actually start analysing things like wind-up calls without wishing to appear a complete killjoy about things, but we do feel that, in radio terms, the whole idea of having regulation for radio is because it is a scarce resource; it is a limited spectrum and therefore it is actually quite a weapon that can be wielded and therefore does need to be regulated and I think if you actually allow wind-up calls willy-nilly, then you're actually doing the service of radio no good at all. So probably the greatest amount of privacy complaints are to do with wind-up calls, normally the ones that don't work.*

We asked: *'Does the "phone-in" bring problems of privacy, or is it more the "wind-up"?'*

It's more the wind-up because people who take part in the 'phone-in' know – it gives rise to a lot of offence complaints because people ring up with views that are offensive, or the banter with the presenter means that the presenter comes up with views that are offensive, but there is a feeling that everyone knows what they are doing.

If you're ringing a phone-in, particularly if you're ringing a James Whale's style programme, you know that you're not ringing the local vicar for a confidential chat; you're ringing a robust professional who's going to knock you about on the airwaves because you volunteered for it.

The argument presented here is that the audience recognizes the nature of the programme, and, in a sense, volunteers or consents to that which occurs. A not dissimilar defence, for any intrusion of privacy, was discovered in the focus groups in discussing television's *Big Brother*. We wished to know, therefore, about those areas where people might not give consent because they were unaware of what was happening.

We asked: *'What about surreptitious recording?'*

The Radio Authority interviewee's reply is interesting, especially in light of wind-up programmes being considered at the centre of the intrusion of privacy question.

It does happen, and in some ways the wind-up call is surreptitious recording, because, if people don't know that they are being recorded, they will quite clearly say things that they wouldn't otherwise say, so in many ways it does bring us back to that. Commercial radio doesn't run quite as many documentaries as it used to, but it does have quite a lot of the sort of Esther Rantzen consumer things where you will put people on tape, but if you're getting into the wind-up call and into those programmes where surreptitious recording becomes the norm, then the people involved in the programming know full well what the rules are and tend not to bulldoze through. They'll try and wander around them and hope that they get justification for doing whatever they are doing afterwards, which is obviously where public interest comes in. But, by and large, the people in those sort of programmes know the rules and they play the game more cleverly.

Public Interest Frustrated

It is worth noting that the defence of public interest is not necessarily, or at least in a strict sense, the only justification that we came across for making surreptitious recording. Sheer frustration at the inability to collect information was another; namely, where the person would refuse to give an interview and it was felt that the person, given previous conduct, had no right not to talk. In discussing journalistic practices with the interviewee from BBC radio, it was mentioned that the only time such recording was done was to illustrate points. A few examples were given, but one will suffice.

> Now, the Phillips Report into BSE took years and years to do and, during that time, one of the ministers responsible, John Selwyn Gummer, continually said, when asked about BSE, 'There is a report being drawn up and I will be happy to comment when that report is delivered' – seven years. When that report was finally delivered, Gummer said, 'The report's out, it's in the public domain, I have nothing to say'. And, indeed, one couldn't contact him. We tried and tried. What we eventually did was surreptitiously record his wife telling us where he was, on a mobile phone. Now that is, by press standards, a minuscule invasion of privacy; by the BBC standards, a large one. It's a surreptitious recording, and it's not with Gummer, it's with his wife, who is blameless one might argue, but we thought it was justified to demonstrate to our audience that this man was deliberately avoiding an issue for which he was culpable.[5]

It is interesting that this was done, as he says, for *'our audience'*. For 'audience' here one must read 'public'. What he is saying is that the BSE issue was of public interest, if nothing else because there was, and remains, a possibility that it will affect the health of hundreds, if not thousands, of people. John Selwyn Gummer's unwillingness to talk, to answer questions that one presumes the public would wish put to him, was a frustration of the public interest. In that situation, the intrusion of privacy by surreptitious recording was, if not strictly speaking in the public interest, then something the public would be interested in. Indeed, the two here become inseparable. It is a case, furthermore, where public interest extends to the obligation of public figures to fulfil their public duty to speak at key times.

Therefore, not to speak offers itself as a refusal to be publicly accountable, and, thus, the extension becomes a question of public interest. The argument would be that, in a liberal democracy, it is in the public interest that those responsible for policy open themselves to question about the policies that they have helped shape.

Public Interest and Context

The above intrusion of privacy by surreptitious means is a good example of how, in judging any intrusion of privacy, it is vital to understand the context within which it occurs. This was stressed by the Radio Authority interviewee when asked about the intrusion of privacy as perhaps being governed by different rules depending on the position held by a person:

> There is a difference, and it's the same criteria that we would use when dealing with any sort of complaints, or any sort of behaviour of radio professionals. That is entirely down to the context of it, and that's our mantra in the same way that estate agents would say, 'Location, location, location' we would say, 'Context, context, context', and it's very difficult to answer any sort of generalisations like that without the context.

> The analogy that I tend to use is, I get a lot of calls from people who want the sort of advice they know full well that I can't really give, where they are saying effectively, 'can I get away with this?' and it

really depends on the context. Of course I can offer advice to a certain level, but it's a bit like saying 'if I run out into the road, am I going to get knocked over?' and the answer is that it depends if there's any traffic about — it depends on the context.

Much does depend on the context; hence, the benefit of case law to illustrate the various contexts or situations of past judgements to guide decision-making. All is not context, however. All context does is inform how principles have been applied in practice. When asked: *'Is there any other defence of the intrusion of privacy other than public interest, or is it the only one?'* the reply was:

I think it's the overriding thing, because, without it, it is not worth discussing and, with it, that probably is the justification. Again, it depends on each individual case, but I think if one could define public interest, it's if it is of justifiable benefit to the listener. Ok, what's justifiable? — and off we go again.

We were interested in his construction of public interest in terms of information being of benefit to the public. So we asked: *'What's a benefit?'*

Well, yes, quite. I didn't say it was a good definition. What we are not about is making privacy laws, but part of the problem of trying to define public interest is, whatever it is, it quite clearly changes an awful lot because we know that, and in research we've done — the Radio Authority and the BSC together — we know how offence has changed in quite a bizarre fashion, in that you can tell jokes about paedophiles, but yet you can't tell jokes about Welshmen.

This reference to changes, which he relates to public interest, but then gives the case of what might be considered taste and decency, or political correctness, is very valid and something that we take up later. The idea of what is in the public interest is, in part, a dependent of social values, and these values do change with time, in the same way, but by no means as rapidly, as ideas concerning what is decent or in good taste. It is to say, by way of brief introduction, that a religious society will include more principles as being in the public interest, matters of a religious nature, than a secular society. The value structure of the two societies is different.

Public Interest and Changing Attitudes

It was mentioned that we would, in the course of the research, be talking to lawyers *'to try and pin down what is in the public interest'*, to which the Radio Authority interviewee replied:

Well, we're looking towards whatever wording is likely to be used in Ofcom and in the Communications Act, and there the word 'community' keeps cropping up, which on a personal level I'm not particularly happy with because I think that clouds the issue yet again; in that the way we protect everyone's rights to be whatever they want to be or say whatever they want to say — I can see people sitting down and saying, 'Well this is happily acceptable to a community of paedophiles', which I would say is not what you mean by community, but then you start saying, 'Well what do

you mean by community then?' and so to me it just creates yet another diversion, which might allow a
lot of things through.

What is meant by community, and the problems of using community as a definitional point
in determining justification for the intrusion of privacy, is addressed at length later. Even if
communities empirically exist, at the descriptive level the notion of community has
positive connotations, but that is to overlook the fact that, from some wider perspective,
the values held and practices of a community might very well be held to be negative and
not to be supported. A group or community might well have interests that are not seen, in
some general sense, to be in the public interest.

We asked about the idea of 'overriding public interest' and how useful that was for
determining the justification for intruding into someone's privacy. Definitions again
presented a problem:

That term doesn't mean much. 'Exceptional' is another one, or 'clear public interest'. Given that we
don't know what public interest is anyway, it's very difficult to know whether there is clear or
overriding public interest. I'm not sure. I think again this is all just bandying this odd philosophy
around. I think it's a philosophy well worth holding up, but I don't know how far you can analyse it,
which is a bit dangerous really.

Although it is true that, in talking with regulators, practitioners and others, a clear
definition of the public interest was not forthcoming, it was quite clear that what might be
termed an operating understanding of public interest existed. If this were not the case then
it would be impossible to mount a defence on such grounds for the intrusion of privacy. A
senior figure within CRCA (Commercial Radio Companies Association), the trade body
for UK commercial radio, however, had concerns:

One of the things that we do have at the moment is that there are so many people working in the
media. There are more people working freelance than ever, which means you are as good as your last
story, which means you work particularly hard in prising up the pavement. The pressures are now far
greater and, because of this, barriers are being eroded and things that people used to assume would
never be reported on 20 years ago are now being swept away and I don't think I've got some moral
philosophy that says, 'So far and not further', because I don't know what that is. But it's just a fact
of life. And doesn't one instinctively know when something is wrong? But then you'll say, 'What
you instinctively know is wrong is not what a 25-year-old instinctively knows is wrong'. I certainly
think that the younger generation today are pretty well relaxed and a lot less uptight about a number
of things that were terribly important to us 25 years ago. Because I think the blessing is that the more
nonsensical crap that is in the newspapers and to a certain extent on the radio and television, the less it
matters. And so, although the prospect of grief on the part of the person whose privacy is being invaded
is still there, I think the actual damage caused is nevertheless much lower, because yesterday's news
becomes yesterday's news halfway through the morning that it first appears. So, although no one likes
adverse press, increasingly you say 'move onto the next thing'.

In terms of an occupation, to *'instinctively know when something is wrong'* is really to say that one has been successfully socialized into the values and norms of that institution in the manner in which it determines good practice. The use of freelance journalists is, therefore, of importance in that, competition aside, to have a story accepted, it is not likely that one will be socialized into the norms and values of an organization to the same extent that a 'staffer' is. Of course, the corollary of this is that if the norms and values of an organization are ones that have scant regard for individual privacy then one can be, so to speak, over-socialized in a wrong direction if viewed from a regulatory perspective that is concerned with people's rights to privacy.

The BBC journalist, discussing the use of freelancers, said: *'Well if they are working for the BBC they do have the same strictures. They are bunged a copy of the producer's guidelines as soon as they win the commission. It all comes under the same umbrella, and I would still argue that it's still down to the individual editor to decide what's right and wrong. The individual journalist for that matter as well.'*

We do not wish to go into the question of freelance journalists since, as the above individual says, the responsibility, ultimately, for that which is broadcast or published is the editors, although that is not to deny that the difficulty of surveillance may be increased. The above statement by the person from CRCA raises issues that we discuss later; namely, the changes that have occurred to the idea of privacy and the possibility that the media themselves may have been responsible for some of these changes. His comment that the content of the media has led to a more relaxed younger population is indicative of this, but he also offered the view:

> The point is that you have got people who are content to go on television and do exercises with their testicles in public... The most private thing we do, actually, is have sex. You tend to close the door, and, when you throw the door open on that, it's difficult to see what boils down to privacy. What I am trying to say is that when you throw the door open as a society, then you are saying that privacy doesn't matter, which means that coverage of people doing whatever they happen to do in the press, doesn't matter either because you either find it interesting, or, after a bit, uninteresting. And with something like Big Brother, while ten years ago it would perhaps have been embarrassing, in ten years it will be boring.

The BBC Radio interviewee, who was pushed a little further by the suggestion that changing content has altered attitudes to the private, closely mirrored this statement:

> Yes, I think boundaries have been broken down and the tabloid press is responsible for a lot of that, [but] television is responsible for even more. As you say, Big Brother is a good example, and the moves in recent years where ordinary people, both drama-doc, and those awful fly-on-the-wall documentaries, have in a way made public the private to the degree where we all now think we're celebrities or capable of being celebrities. But I think that's different, [an] unwitting invasion of privacy... it's the notion of consent isn't it?

Indeed, what we consent to is what we agree with, and what we agree with says much about our values, attitudes, dispositions and so on. The suggestion above, and something that occupies us further on, is that the idea of the private has undergone change so that areas once considered out of bounds have now become within the boundaries of the acceptable. Yet, even accepting that what we consent to is a mark of what we agree with, that does not obviate that agreement might be gained in a manner that truly indicates consent; that is, we were misled as to what we were agreeing to, or confused sufficiently not to be in a position to give 'informed consent'. This would include where the person was so grief-stricken or distraught that judgement was clouded by pain.

Public Interest and the Public Good

The *Daily Telegraph* interviewee mentioned that, whilst the paper has an ombudsman that deals with complaints, it was his opinion that

> ...*most of the complaints aren't about privacy at all they're about all sorts of things and the grounds aren't often valid grounds at all. People either say that we have got the facts wrong, which is usually not the case, or they say we have misrepresented somebody's point of view, which again is usually just an excuse for them trying to get their own opinion in the paper... Either they go to the ombudsman, or they go to the Press Complaints Commission, or they go to the law if need be, and we don't encourage them to go to the law, but if they feel that it's necessary then of course its perfectly open for them to do so.*

He then added:

> *There isn't in this country a law on privacy. We've got a code of practice which governs all the national press and invasion of privacy is one thing, along with intruding on people's grief, anything involving children, which is the most difficult matter, but any of these things can be overridden if it's something which is in the public interest.*

Not surprisingly this led us immediately to ask for a definition of the public interest:

> *Well, there's a tri-partite, It almost passes for a definition* [of the public interest], *that we have at the back of our code of practice,* [phrases that mention] *detecting or exposing crime, protecting public health and preventing the public being misled by a statement by an individual or an organisation. That's three things.*

This, however, takes us back to points made to the regulators; namely, that such is not a definition, but rather elucidation of areas where it is considered public interest is to be found. This was put to him, with the additional comment: '*Exposing crime might be in the public interest, but, within that, there are personal rights to uphold. How does one actually balance that?*'

> *Well, there's an old lawyers' saying which says that, 'There's no confidence in iniquity', meaning that if somebody's got a duty to confidentiality that's overridden by a duty to expose iniquity of some kind. So that's an element in the public interest defence. To put it the other way round we've got a duty in a way to publish things which are beneficial to the public. It's a question of publishing things for the common good.*

This is indeed interesting and probably the best clarification of the meaning of public interest that we came across. It is comments such as this, when allied to the statements made in the course of the focus groups, that began to fuse in thinking towards the development of the notion of 'public importance' rather than 'in the public interest' as being a more manageable term for the adjudication of the intrusion of privacy.

His idea of the *'common good'* was taken up and used as a basis for discussing the difference between the national interest, public interest and community interest. Again, his comments are thoughtful:

> *I would have thought that the national interest was more to do with the interests of the national against the rest of the world, whereas public interest is a question of what's in the benefit of the nation internally, and I would have thought that would have depended on the constitution of the country in question, which is Britain.*

In talking of constitution he was not referring to the separation of powers and other such matters, but to the structure of the society in a general sense. This became apparent when talking of a community of interests:

> *Well I think that's the difference of people's individual interests and the interests of the whole society. You are talking about particular group interests, aren't you?*

We responded, *'Yes, community interests, which might actually clash with other groups.'* He continued:

> *Indeed, it might be the duty of a newspaper to publish something in the public interest which is against the interests of a community. I don't see any difficulty with that really, it might annoy some people, but all this, I mean we take advantage of this. To resort to a defence of public interest is a typical scoundrel's defence, so it used to be the case, when every time a newspaper wanted to run a story about someone being homosexual, they would say, 'It's a question of security'. That's all water under the bridge, but one thing it isn't is what people are interested in. It seems absurd to have to state that, but you still do hear on the wireless or on the television people defending things, which they say are in the public interest, but all they mean is that lots of people are interested in it and it's just a weasel defence — it seems incredible that anybody can get the two confused, but they are often knowingly or unknowingly confused. In fact, very often the public interest is of no interest whatsoever to the public. Most people are not really interested in provision of safe roads or detailed public health matters — most people do not spend their life reading epidemiological studies, do they? I mean they just take their chance.*

The idea of public interest here is that it must include something of general standing, in that it has to include principles, and not specific interests. That is, those principles have got to enshrine that which is valued by all, or at least include an overwhelming number of people and not be limited to some specific interest, such as that offered by a community of interests.

The *Daily Telegraph* interviewee offered up a very nice example of this, which illustrates the point well:

> *The* Telegraph *at the moment has got this campaign on possession of freedom, and we find that it does make people think about things. Did you hear about the man who kept hawks and there was a raid on his house by the RSPB[6] and they took a goshawk into care, saying he'd taken it from the wild, and the next thing you know the bloody bird's dead. There's no apologies, no explanation, so this much-loved bird has been killed by the law. We thought that came under the category of freedom, that you shouldn't just have the RSPB kicking down your door and ending up with a dead hawk. He wants to have a post-mortem on the bird to see how it died. It's tragic. There was another one about a blind man who was evicted from his house and his guide dog was locked inside so he couldn't get to it. That's the sort of thing that's in the public interest to report, because you've got a powerful body behaving in a monstrously unjust way to an individual who has an insufficient ability to rectify injustice.*

On their own, the death of a hawk and a trapped guide dog are news items of interest to know, although not necessarily 'in the public interest', but what we see is how principles have entered the story to make it in the public interest. Both stories, although perhaps interesting, are not of great importance to the individual in the sense of, as used before by this journalist, *'the common good'*. Indeed, in asking for the difference between tabloid newspapers and broadsheets, he commented that, insofar as they *'report news, we're not that different'*. He then added:

> *It's when they stop reporting news and start playing games of a different kind that a difference arises; as I said before the almost fictionalised account of some unknown person who's being caught in adultery. There's no public interest defence in naming someone as an adulterer at all as far as that goes. It's not something that impinges on the well-being of the 'public body'.*

It is the notion of the *'well-being of the public body'* that is interesting in relation to the case of the hawk and the guide dog. Left as a story of an event, it has little of public interest in the above sense, but once it is exposed as an example of authority, of institutions riding roughshod over the cares of the individual, it is a story that has importance to all – the misuse of power. Since such misuse could affect everyone in our society, and indeed goes against the notion of justice or fairness as embodied in the spirit of a liberal democracy, it is a story that is in the public interest. It is about the individual that *'has an insufficient ability to rectify injustice'*.

Although it has been stated that the straightforward reportage of the hawk and the guide dog are not stories that are unequivocally in the public interest, they do have certain features that raise them above the trivial, or the merely entertaining, but yet fall short of 'in the public interest', in the strong sense with which the term has been talked about in the course of the interviews. But that is the difficulty with the term – it is not simply that it is difficult to define, but that the associations it carries have a gravity that make it difficult in application to cases that are ostensibly not grave; hence, our preference for the term 'social importance'. Social importance could more readily have been applied to the hawk and the guide dog cases, even if those stories were carried in a descriptive manner rather than involving principles of the rights of the individual in the face of authority. Both stories have social importance in that they deal with the predicaments of individuals, but which do not carry forward, without fundamental reflection on the nature of authority, to involve people in general. Hence, having some social importance, some right to intrude upon the privacy of the agencies carrying out the acts would be legitimate.

The *Daily Telegraph* interviewee further observed that the looseness of a definition did not alter the value and usefulness of a concept:

> *Well, if an injustice has been done, then you're right in saying that you publish that story because an injustice has been done. Just because the definition of justice is vague and the borderline unclear doesn't mean... that you were wrong in saying that you were publishing a story in the defence of justice. And just because somebody says something's in the public interest, doesn't mean to say that it is. Any reasonable person can see very often that the story has not been published in the public interest. I agree that there are difficult cases to judge, but that is true of any reality in the world.*

Public Interest and what interests the Public

For the *Daily Telegraph*, complaints concerning the intrusion of privacy were relatively rare. This was not so with the *News of the World* interviewee.
We asked him: *'When you get into trouble, what area is it normally?'*

> *Normally it's minor points of accuracy. The next is privacy I think.*

We asked for clarification: *'So privacy is actually quite high up?'* The response to this was *'Yeah. It's so difficult to be accurate when so many people give you different versions of the same story'*. The feeling gained was that accuracy was a defence for the intrusion of privacy, or, if one intruded into privacy, one had better be accurate; that is, that whatever misdeed was being investigated had to have taken place.

> *Quite often we go for things when there's no clear public interest, but quite often we find it along the way. Sometimes we don't, in which case it goes unsaid.*

Next, we asked: *'Do some people have a lower right to privacy than others?'*

> *No. I think we all have that right. A lot of us have less to keep private, but we all have that right and I do get complaints from very ordinary people who object to having their lives in the* News of the World. *There has to be a reason for it.*

The question remains, however, does that reason mean it has to be in the public interest? Where it was considered by other interviewees that, in the short term, even if there were no guidelines covering intrusion of privacy, the performance of the broadcast media would not alter radically, this was not the case with the *News of the World*.
We asked: *'Would you behave very differently if there wasn't the Commission?'*

Yes. I mean the whole idea of the PCC was to establish a code of practice that we abide by because of the competitive nature of the business. I think people would be transgressing all the time unless we had clear boundaries.

It looks very much that the existence of the PCC acts as a reminder to behave 'decently'. We then asked: *'Does the press have a looser notion of the public interest than broadcasting?'*

Not looser, but wider. Broadcasters don't have to dig as far as we do, they're not competitive like we are, particularly the popular press. We have to win or we go under. The others are going under and we're winning. Because we've pressed things to the limits and tried not to exceed them. But yes, I think we always look for a public interest defence when it applies in the code of practice.

Two things are worth noting here. First, surviving in the press market is very competitive with the unstated assumption that intruding into privacy gives a competitive edge; something that ought to be held in mind as the world of television becomes increasingly competitive. Is it much easier to hold to 'standards' when there is no downside for not doing so? The second point is that his comment suggests that reporting takes place and then the story is examined to see if the defence of public interest can be grafted on as justification for the story. This comes close to the point made previously, that it is not in the interest of sections of the press to have public interest defined in any precise manner, since to do so would cause it to lose its protective strategic value. Given that he saw the *News of the World* as an investigative paper, we said to him: *'The styles are obviously different between, for example, the* Telegraph *and the* News of the World. *Do you see the* News of the World *intruding on privacy more, or is it a matter of style?'*

I don't think we intrude more. We investigate more, because they are not an investigative newspaper so they don't run the risk... they just report what they see. Very occasionally they might have something that no one else knows, but they don't investigate.

Public Interest and Public Morals

It is this approach to journalism that pushes the *News of the World* as an active intruder on the privacy of others. But, there is nothing wrong, as all the codes make clear, with the intrusion of privacy so long as it is justified; the justification, of course, being if to do so is in the public interest. We therefore asked him directly: *'What is the public interest?'*

It's the most impossible thing to define. In every case it's a matter of judgement. It's certainly there, and it's certainly there to a very high degree in some cases and there are marginal cases where I've argued it and failed in my arguments.

We asked how far one could raise the defence of public interest in reporting the story of the Prime Minister's son Euan, being found drunk after a night out in London: *'I don't think public interest comes into it. It's about an offence on the street, picked up by the police – you don't need to argue public interest'*. It was then added, however: *'If he hadn't been picked up by the police, had just got very drunk and been taken home by a friend, I don't know – I think you'd still be buggered if we weren't sure of our facts'.* It would seem that it would still have been reported, on the grounds that *'the Prime Minister is there to set an example to us all, he talks about family values and if he does that he has to make sure they work.'*

This offers a particular view of the role of the press, which is not easily captured by the idea of 'in the public interest'. What he is suggesting is that the public interest may be served by upholding sets of moral values, acting, if one likes, as the moral conscience of society. This is something that is discussed later and, although such 'moralizing' might sit uneasy within a contemporary society that has difficulty in accepting absolute standards, or in discerning a core set of values by which to conduct social life, it would not seem an odd position in the past. Although it may make for strange bedfellows, the *News of the World*, in exposing 'vice', is close in many ways to the position adopted by the pressure group Mediawatch, with its moralistic stance. That is, that moral contours for living ought to be laid down and that we have a right to know the 'moral' behaviour of public and not-so-public figures.

John Beyer (Mediawatch) argued that

> *We are a community of people who are concerned about broadcasting standards and the influence that has on society as a whole. So one could say that our interest is not being served by the majority of contemporary programming which conveys a very immoral lifestyle, which we suggest is undermining the cohesion and wellbeing of society.*

In terms of privacy then, this moral approach to what are often seen as mere technical questions provides a framework for enquiry that does not easily separate off the private from the public. For example, when asked if it was right for the media to enquire into the BBC Director General's private life:

> *Yes, I think that is a legitimate course of enquiry because he is in a public position, he is paid out of public funds [...] I think in terms of public interest the phrase 'right to know' is an important qualification and I think in that particular case you do have a right to know because you can't separate your private life from your public life.*

This idea of 'non-separation' was raised later when he said, *'there is a great deal of hypocrisy in the media, and you see David Mellor, who was Home Office Minister, responsible for public policy in areas related to that (his affair whilst married), so I think the public interest is served by informing people that ministers in the government are acting in that way'.* When it was put to him: *'To stay with the Mellor case, somebody might say "so, lots of people have had girlfriends that you shouldn't have had. It doesn't affect his job".'* In terms of Mellor's private behaviour not affecting his public performance, he said:

> *I don't agree with that. I think your behaviour in private does affect your judgement on a whole range of things, because if you can cheat on your wife and your children then you can cheat on anybody, because if you can cheat on the people you are supposed to cherish the most, then you can cheat on anybody in your public life. I don't think, and it's the same with Clinton, that you can pigeonhole this or that activity, saying from five o'clock on Friday afternoon to nine on a Monday morning you*

are a different person than you are Monday to Friday. I think your whole character and person is a unit. And so I don't go with this idea that the public and the private can be separated.

Morality for Beyer is the core to society, and it is the core of an individual – the two come together in a non-divisible whole. This did not mean that Beyer wished *'the media hounding people so that they can't sleep at night because of people intruding on their lives'*. There was a difference between that and *'informing the public about what's going on'*. Nevertheless, it is a position that moves to see the media functioning as a moral watchdog. We put to him the hypothetical case: *'A schoolteacher, he's married but he also has a mistress, would a local newspaper be entitled to invade his privacy, and write a story on this?'*

Yes. I think teachers have a particular, I think that generally speaking, the public does have expectations about the behaviour of people, and let's not forget the principles of teacher-pupil relationship, and the trust that implies, and to be a teacher you do have to have, because of the position, I believe that parents have a right to expect high standards of behaviour from those whose care they entrust their children.

It was his firm opinion that society is undermined by the absence of objective moral standards:

The old objective values of the past have been elbowed aside. The whole notion of the new morality in the sixties has sort of swept in and everything swept aside, and I think the evidence of 50 years on not supporting the view of permissiveness. The evidence of the damage that has happened in our society, of all the broken relationships and all the rest of it, the evidence supports our view that there should be objective standards that everybody ought to observe.

The watershed principle, whereby certain content is only deemed suitable for broadcast after a designated time in the evening, although it might be approved as a protective device of the young, nevertheless is symptomatic of the often-technical approach to the moral:

Now obviously you don't want children's programmes 24 hours a day but, equally, I think there are objective standards which apply. For example, I don't think that obscene language is not obscene at ten o'clock and it's obscene at eight o'clock. I think it's obscene whenever it's on.

This moral watchdog element, and absolutely genuine in Mediawatch's case – there is no prurience – folds it, in a sense, in with the *News of the World* to give less protection to the private goings-on of some individuals. Concerned with *'cohesion and well-being of society'* private interests are public matters, since, as he said *'the public and the private cannot be separated'*. Furthermore, there are 'objective standards' which, by extension, must be upheld if moral, and subsequently social, collapse is not to follow. His position is that the standards by which we ought to live must be exposed, and one way of achieving that is exposing acts that depart from those standards.

The idea of social solidarity, or social cohesion, was a central theme of the classical sociologist Emile Durkheim. From this we derive the idea of social importance, or at least give an underpinning as to how social importance might be judged – the degree of threat to social solidarity. Durkheim was much taken up with the idea of morality, by which is really meant the norms, as shared values, that bind a society together. Interestingly, in the course of the interview with the person from the *News of the World*, a kind of Durkheimian position was presented as one of the functions of the press:

> *Well, what passes through my mind all the time is that in society some years ago, before the mass media came on the scene, people knew what their neighbours were doing, they knew what they got up to, and it was probably a more healthy society then than now, because people are in their little cells and they don't know what others are up to. Part of our role is to tell people how people do behave – what the norm is, what is abnormal. To describe how people interact with each other.*

It would be mistaken to see this as overclaiming the position of the *News of the World*, either on our part or on the part of the interviewee. The 'moralizing' also sells newspapers and is also a justification of intrusion, as the interviewee recognized: *'There's a joke at the* News of the World *that we always try and find a higher moral ground from which to tell our stories, so if it's something absolutely appalling going on, which is quite titillating, we condemn it, which is the way we do it'*. This prompted the question: *'Can you actually say there is something called the public interest?'*

> *There are so many definitions floating around, it's probably something the establishment doesn't want you to know but the nation wants to know. It's like the definition of news, which is something someone, somewhere, doesn't want you to know. And it's the whole nature of our work to dig out things that people wouldn't otherwise know, which is of some importance to them. Or could be. And it's the difference between 'of interest to the public'* [and 'the public interest'].

This 'digging out' pushes readily into the use of surreptitious methods. We asked about hidden microphones:

> *Well, we only* [use hidden microphones] *when we are pretty certain that we've got very good reason to do it, like with Delallio. Do you remember that? The case where the rugby player was pushing drugs and taking drugs and talking about the English rugby team taking drugs. We knew he had been talking about it so there's no point in going up to him and saying, 'hello, Mr Delallio, we've been told you've been talking about taking drugs. Can I take a few notes?' It doesn't work. So you get him to come to a meeting, you use subterfuge because you are exposing criminal misdemeanours and you have your hidden camera and your tape recorder, and you make sure you get every single word he says, because if you don't, you don't have a story.*

It is not just that without surreptitious recording there would be no story, but the use of such undercover techniques was considered essential if the *News of the World*, with the type of story that they often cover, did not want to find itself in court for libel. The possession of recordings, no matter how obtained, was evidence against fabrication or the accusations of untruth:

It's absolutely vital. The sort of investigations we do are ones that are likely to be challenged in court. We've had many discussions with the police about this in the past, where they've said, 'We'd like to take this up, but where is the evidence? Where are the tape recordings?' So now, to avoid potential libel action, we have to record everything we do.

This would seem a reasonable defence when operating the type of investigative journalism favoured by the *News of the World*. What is interesting, however, is where deception is used in areas where one might not consider the story to be in the public interest; for example, where it is not obvious that something criminal is taking place. The uninvited presence at the Christmas party of the cast of the soap opera *Emmerdale*, mentioned below, is a case in point. We said: *'So, because you have strong grounds to believe that he's doing something illegal, then invasion of privacy doesn't enter into it because of the defence of public interest?'*

Yes. You have to be pretty sure of what you're gonna write. We had a converse case, where we were told last December that the Emmerdale *Christmas party was going to be a riot with drugs and booze and so on. So a couple of our people went very quietly, basing their enquiry on what happened at the previous years party and nothing happened at all until one member of the cast recognized our reporter and said 'what are you doing here? This is not a media party'. He said that he had just popped in to have a look. But they complained to the PCC and I argued possible public interest because you don't know till you look, but we were adjudicated against.*

The public interest was not obvious to us: *'I can see it's a cracking story, but where is the public interest in that?'* The reply: *'Ok, three to six million people sit down and watch* Emmerdale *every night. Two members of the cast have left and have given interviews about having got stuck into drugs, and if that party had turned out to be a drug party, it would have been a great story wouldn't it?'* We agreed, but then said: *'I can't see that it would be in the public interest though. I can see a good deal of social interest, but...'* Back came the response: *'People fawn on stars. They think they're all wonderful people. If they found out that they spent their spare time snorting cocaine and getting drunk, they ought to know about it'.*

It was pointed out that this might include newspaper editors also, and we mentioned Plato's point of who will guard the guardians, but the point to stress from the above is that public interest was extended to include a moral story about the worship of false heroes. Such stories are as old as drama itself, and do serve the function, in the Durkheimian fashion, of staking out the rules by which the collective ought to abide if solidarity is to be achieved. Those that transgress the moral code of society require exposure in order to reaffirm the code. Indeed, the term 'transgressed' was used in connection with whether or not someone such as the television celebrity Michael Barrymore should be followed if on holiday. The response was unequivocal, and in line with the above arguing: *'He's not only thrust himself in the public eye over and over again, he's transgressed, he committed terrible mistakes... and I'm afraid anything goes with him. He has put himself so much in that area'.* That 'area', and examples were provided, refers to behaviour that we have no way of verifying and therefore no point in naming, other than to say that this journalist did not approve – Barrymore had 'transgressed' and, therefore, 'anything goes'. It is a decidedly moral position to adopt, but could be defended on grounds of public interest once one gives a particular moral role to journalism, but, more than that, to give a particular skew to the idea of public interest. It takes the idea of public interest well beyond the protection of people from crime, or the promoting of the public's health, and into the promotion of the moral wellbeing of people. It may not be, for many people, that the chosen vehicle for such promotion would fall readily on the *News of the World*, but there can be no denying, in the complex makeup of that paper, that there is a righteousness to it that goes beyond mere titillation. Indeed, this is a good example of a neo-Aristotelian position in practice.

This shows the difficulty of operating with the idea of public interest as a defence for the intrusion of privacy, and why, to some extent, the *News of the World* is seen as one of the main perpetrators. It has already been noted that the *News of the World* interviewee saw the notion of the public interest as *'the most impossible thing to define'*. Perhaps so, but, in the course of the conversation, he raised a new and interesting aspect to the idea of public interest; that to pursue a policy of public interest might go against the canons of a free and independent press. This came across in discussing the dance floor collapse in Israel. What was wanted here was a view from the tabloid press of whether to show such images could be defended on grounds of public interest in the manner that the broadcasters interviewed had done so.

He considered the footage to have been *'extraordinary'*, and was asked, *'How would you defend the broadcasters that were showing it? Would you show it?'* To this last question there was no doubt, *'Yes'*. When asked on what grounds, it was replied: *'Well, I'd have to say public interest because it's such a graphic, unforgettable illustration of what happens when architects don't do their job properly'*. The conversation turned into an interrogation, and is worth quoting as it unfolded:

I. Ok, but when it was actually shown, they may have suspected it, but nobody really knew. Because at first people thought it might be a bomb, then the Israelis quickly denied it, because obviously all hell would have broken loose. Two days later it looked like jerry building. So when it actually went out they didn't even know.
You can't fail to put something like that out, whatever the cause was. If it was terrorism, then it was showing what terrorism does to happy people. If it was a malfunction of architects, then similar. It's one of those things that tells the most important story of all.

I. Which is?
Complete failure to make people safe.

I. But I would argue that it was an invasion of privacy, it made people very upset – the dead can have privacy. I think it's hard to justify the defence of public interest in that. If I was a newsman, I could defend it on news values. It's got every angle, but I wouldn't defend that in terms of public interest. Would you?
Certainly. I've always defended it.

I. People are interested in it because it is so dramatic, but I can't see how the public interest benefited in any way from showing that footage.
Because it was what happens. Whichever the cause, be it a terrorist bomb or a faulty building, it was either way in the public interest.

I. Let me put it to you that I actually think the behaviour was much more like your paper, in that 'finding' public interest stories sells the paper. This is Israel. I think it would have been shown if it had been in Nicaragua or wherever, just because of the sheer drama. It wasn't in Scarborough [Britain]. What I am saying about this story, and I'm pushing it as far as I can go, is that the journalists in broadcasting did not claim public interest (could not claim it). I cannot see the public interest in the story. If it had been in Scarborough then I can see it – our buildings falling down. Most people wouldn't care less, quite frankly, how they build their houses in Nicaragua or how they build their houses in Israel... The idea that this is in the public interest defeats me. On journalistic grounds, this is a cracking picture.

If there was a suspicion at the time the film came in, very late at night as it was, that it was terrorism, would you have taken the risk of running it? Because that's what they probably did, and the fact that when they found out it wasn't, they thought thank God we ran it anyway.

I. So if it was terrorism, you might not have run it?

No, I'm asking you, if you'd been there that night and there was a suspicion that it could have been a terrorist attack, would you have waited a few days before you ran it?

I. No, I probably would have run it. Well, look at it this way... I might not have run it, in the public interest.

That's censorship.

I. Well the point I want to make here, is that presumably these are all moral decisions. Presumably you can have stuff that is in the public interest to write, but in the long term is not, because you might cause greater damage. If I was an Israeli editor and there was a peace treaty going through and it was a terrorist act, then showing that on television would scupper the plans for peace and that is a serious moral problem.

There were problems during the war in the Falklands, there was an element of censorship which I got caught in the middle of. I am not thinking of any particular example, but there were cases when we had the public interest in mind and took advice from the Ministry. I think it was reasonable – we didn't have any great quibbles.

What this conversation reveals, especially with his introduction of the term 'censorship', is that the term 'the public interest' is more problematic than it might appear from a straightforward definitional difficulty. It may be in the public interest *not* to publish something. If this is the case then, as a defence for procedures, the term is somewhat denuded. It loses, in other words, its authority. The idea of public interest in terms of journalism is exposure, not closure. It becomes very difficult to say privacy *can* be intruded upon in this case because it is 'in the public interest', but intrusion *cannot* take place in this instance because it is 'in the public interest'. Who says, therefore, what the public interest is? If one believed that the peace treaty involving Israel and the Palestinians was not in the interest of the Israeli people, then to show the pictures of the collapsed dance floor, assuming that it collapsed as a result of a terrorist attack, would be in the public interest, but if one believed the reverse, then to show it would not be in the public interest. Public interest, despite definitional difficulties, has too much of a political loading for it to be woven into a principle of media practice. Or, rather, given all the discussion, it is not surprising that it leads to difficulty in adjudication of practices. It is very much a moveable feast open to special and, indeed, specious, pleading.

For this journalist, and from long experience, privacy and taste and decency were in effect one and the same. This was becoming obvious in the course of the interview, but became very clear towards the end when it was asked if the *News of the World* had pictures of '*Princess Di, in the car in the Paris underpass*'. He said, '*Yeah, we had them in that night, yeah*'. Asked, '*why didn't you publish them?*' he replied:

> *Taste! We do have taste and we apply it an awful lot, with a lot of things. At the time of the sinking of the* Herald of Free Enterprise,[7] *we did a massive news operation which I thought was magnificent. And it was all screwed up by David Montgomery, the editor at the time, who used, on page one, the picture of a dead girl sliding off the side of the ship. I was so angry with him. Everything else we'd done was right. You don't want a corpse on the front page of the paper.*

In response to this we said: '*You mentioned taste and decency, you didn't mention privacy*'. His reply was: '*Well, taste and decency and privacy are all the same in that case because if there was even a remote chance of the mother seeing her dead daughter on the front page of the paper within 24 hours, that's an appalling thing to inflict on anybody*'. And he then added, '*Maybe I'm old-fashioned, but privacy is a new word and it is very much part of taste and decency*'.

The Public Interest and Community Interest

The term 'community interest' as a variant of public interest has been raised at several points in discussing the defence of intrusion of privacy and, indeed, we give particular attention to this at the theoretical level later. We question the existence, in any real empirical sense, of communities, as raised by the *Daily Telegraph* interviewee. Even if communities in any meaningful sense did exist, a community of interest might go against a more general interest. For the moment, however, it is worth noting that the term 'community' did not, as far as responses in the focus groups went, feature as part of language as a lived experience. Only the Asian youths in Leeds used the term 'community' to signify a special belonging to a location or group. The African-Caribbean women in London certainly did not use it to identify a group to which they belonged that had special interests. It was decided, because of the currency being given to community interest as a defence for the intrusion of privacy, to interview a representative of *The Voice*, a long-established African-Caribbean newspaper based in Brixton, London. *The Voice* had a sale of around 35,000 at the time, being read nationally as well as in the Greater London area. We asked if *The Voice* received complaints over the intrusion of privacy:

> *Very, very few complaints. I think when you talk about public interest and what is in the best interest of the public, a lot of members, or readers, question the ability of anyone to decide what is of interest to them and what is not of interest to them, and we've had this come up time and time again. For example, we had one incident with a local authority, a councillor. And he felt that we had overstepped the boundaries by prying too far back into his private life. Not so much private, but he was a member of a black section group and we felt that it was relevant to the story and important to mention what*

black section was, and certainly some years down the line we have a new generation of black readers who wouldn't know what black section meant, and we felt that we had to go back a bit to explain what it was, what his involvement was at that time and where he is today, and we were accused of trying to negate projects that he was involved in, which was very far from the truth. Anyway the PCC ruled that we were correct in what we did. That was the first one we've had in terms of public interest... But it seems that there is a vast difference between what we consider the public interest is and what the government's definition of the public interest [is].

The last observation of *The Voice* is very similar to the earlier statement made by the journalist from BBC radio: *'The last person I would expect to know what was in the public interest was a high court judge frankly'*. What we see here is an antagonism towards an 'official' ruling on public interest. But what was particularly interesting about *The Voice* was the recognition that the constituents of the paper had changed over time so that it was not specifically seen as an African-Caribbean paper any more, although that remained its core identity. He noted:

It's very difficult now to draw a line between a black person, a mixed race person and a white reader. The colour issue is becoming very small and due to cultural mix that's happening – with Asians mating with African-Caribbeans and vice versa, the white community, the Welsh. Really it's a melting pot, and although we are specifically an African-Caribbean newspaper, it's trickier now with varying communities and we are not strictly an African-Caribbean newspaper. We've become more general, but we still focus on the issues.

He saw *The Voice*, as he put it, remaining *'a campaigning newspaper on racial issues, the protection of children, equal opportunities, employment – those issues'*. It was quite clear that the paper was locked into the lives of its readers in an almost participatory sense. Frequent reference was made to the culture of its readers and the response, often very direct, that its readers made towards the paper. For example, he said: *'We try not to intrude into people's privacy and there are certain areas, there are standard guidelines here. For example, if someone was killed in a shooting, we would not send a reporter out to the family's home unless we were asked'*. When we suggested that for some papers that would seem a bit unusual, he stressed the nature of the community to which the paper sold. He said that to send a reporter would be *'an intrusion into grief'*, and then added a rather pragmatic point: *'And if you really know the African-Caribbean culture, you are likely to get battered at the door for being heartless for a start'*. The other reason was an appreciation of the readers' taste:

Secondly, it's not what our readers will want to see – that in a time of grief you are speaking to a broken family, unless you have been asked... So it goes back to social responsibility and feeling for the community that you are supposed to serve and, more importantly, knowing what the needs are in a situation like that, especially in times of grief.

Here we have *'social responsibility'* and *'feeling for the community'*. This all makes for good journalistic sense, in terms of being 'in tune' with one's market. Being 'in tune' with one's market is one thing, in this case the community, but the issue arises of whether the interests of the community, the values of a group of people, may be restrictive when seen in terms of values that either exist outside of that community, or clash with values of groups proximate to, but not necessarily of, that community. The following quote shows this:

> You also know that if you push past your readership and you try to do something that your readership is not happy about, then you pay the price that people will stop reading it. We had one issue – a gay issue, and the traditional African-Caribbean people do not believe in gay relationships. People do it, I'm sure they do, but they keep it to themselves. And we carried an event which was a gay event, and the black community and the Church came down on us like a ton of bricks, saying, 'How dare you let these people, who are an abomination to God in the first place in our culture, bring this nastiness into the paper', and they felt it would encourage gay people. Then on the other hand you had gay people who work within the local authority saying 'let's stop dealing with The Voice, because they're anti-gay'. And it's not that we're anti-gay, but from a cultural perspective, it's not the type of thing that...

Of course, no newspaper can afford to offend the political or social sensibilities of its readers. It would be financial death for *The Guardian* to have a page three pin-up in the manner of *The Sun*, and it may not play well for *The Daily Telegraph* to cover gay issues to the extent that *The Guardian* might. But that is not the point. The point to extract is the value that one places on a community of interests as an appeal for the intrusion of privacy. To the above case, we said: *'That's an interesting dilemma'*, which prompted:

> That's right. So we're bashed from both sides. Bashed by the traditional community, and you can see why, because, if you go to the Caribbean, there are people who dress as women, dress as women and they are treated as celebrities and people think they are a laugh, but gay sex does happen in every country, and it's how it's treated. The church in the Caribbean would not permit two men to be married, and certainly you found that in the Bahamas last April, there was a cruise ship stopped in the Bahamas and these gay couples, about 700 of them were going to come ashore, and the government says, 'no, we don't want you. Get back on and get lost'. The British Government said, 'well this is British law, so in future...' So there you are – you've got the colonial power exerting influence on this small crowd of people who, although British, have their own standards and their own way of life. And you're trying to compete with mother country Britain, who is much more open minded, so you've got a dichotomy.

To emphasize the influence of community values on the policy of the newspaper, it was mentioned what had to be done in handling gay sex stories:

> Very carefully, meticulously, because we don't want to upset the other side as well, but the local authorities have the mandate, because regardless of age, gender, whatever, but it's not something that we would want to promote or encourage by having a feature on gay sex. We know what the response would be, and it's normally swift. We're talking about people coming down to the office; we're not talking about a phone call. A couple of weeks ago we carried a piece about the fashion of young people for very baggy, baggy trousers, and the trousers falling off the backside. That fashion was copied from the States where it began in prisons, and anyone who wore those trousers was making a sign that they wanted to have sex with you. Now we did a feature on the way that these notions are perceived by

people and we had people coming into reception saying – 'Do I look like a gay? Just cause me wear me pants down doesn't mean I want someone to come up me backside with a penis! It's all your fault. I've been approached by this man in the street askin' me if I'm gay because me wear me trousers…' And all we were doing was looking at the perceptions and how this thing started in the States. It's the type of thing where we perhaps need to be more careful than the national papers.

We agreed: *'Yes, no people are going to go to a national newspaper with that sort of complaint'*. He agreed: *'Exactly'*, and added: *'And besides, they'd say "get stuffed" and slam the phone down, or throw you out if you went. With us now, people see the paper as part of them, as their personal paper, and through that they must have a personal say'*. From one perspective, of serving the community, one might see this as commendable, but from the point of the central questions of the research this shows the very real difficulty of appealing to community interests as a defence for the intrusion of privacy. To use the appeal to community means that one would have a 'value drift'; that is, no absolute standard by which to judge the merit of intruding upon privacy. If one transferred his example of the clash between Caribbean notions of appropriate sexual expression, as evidenced by the gay boat cruise, to the context of Britain, which, as he said, *'is much more open minded'* about homosexuality, the problem is brought into stark focus. The intrusion of privacy is based on beliefs that there is a right to intrude into someone's privacy drawn from a set of values that determines what is right. Where one has a community whose values stand in distinction to the rest of society, or to other communities, then the question arises of what is the 'court of appeal' to which one turns for the resolution of a grievance. It might be, in the Caribbean community as described, that to intrude into the privacy of a gay person, to expose his or her gayness, say, for example, in the taking up of a public appointment, might well be supported by an appeal to a community of interests where it was held that it was in its interest to know such matters. Indeed, even the use of surreptitious means to demonstrate a person's homosexuality might be approved.

Yet, in cases given to the focus groups, no one considered it right for a head teacher to enquire into whether someone was gay or not in appointing members of staff. An individual's sexual orientation was seen as a private matter – although exclusion was made most strongly if the sexual predilection was that of paedophilia. Within the community as described, we must ask what right to privacy would a teacher have who was gay and appointed to teach in a school within the community, but who came from outside the community and did not share the communities values? We deal with this issue more thoroughly later in dismissing community of interests as forming a reasonable test for the defence of the intrusion of privacy.

The Public Interest and the New Media: The Internet

The rise of the Internet constitutes a significant change in the nature of 'publication', given its ability to deliver material from anywhere in the world, possibly anonymously authored, and largely unregulated. The possibilities opened up by the Internet might also mean increases in intrusion into privacy arising from the ability of any user to post material onto the Internet in one form or another (e.g. website, bulletin board, e-mail) without any ethical, moral or regulatory hindrance. Not all of the Internet operates in this way. Most service providers (ISPs) and website owners are bound by existing local (national) laws, and most adhere to agreed codes of practice.

The Internet is different from traditional publishing outlets in that it is a re-publisher rather than a creator of material, as a senior figure within BBC Online pointed out:

> We tend to aim at target [interest] groups. We do more technology, which the rest of the BBC doesn't, we do more entertainment news, again, which the rest of the BBC doesn't. We don't do much news gathering, so when it comes to privacy, the practical part of that – going out and getting stuff, maybe invading somebody's privacy, is probably done by radio and television. We then publish that.

The fact is that BBC Online is a very filtered production:

> There is a lot more information [than for most news organisations] but it is filtered, it's all rewritten by BBC journalists, none of it ever goes up uncut, or it shouldn't, because we don't have the contract. There is a lot of information but it is coming from trusted sources. A lot of it comes from the World Service. We then filter that because you just can't put up scripts from radio and television, you've got to make it readable and literate. It's pretty well filtered.

The main BBC television and radio news go out live as webcasts and are then archived until the next day's editions replace them. This could present particular difficulties, in that archives can be seen time and time again until taken off by the bulletin that replaces it. It must also be noted that BBC Online has no watershed. The latter, however, is more relevant to questions of taste and decency than privacy. However, BBC Online also offers links to external websites, which could potentially carry troublesome material:

> I would say that when we're getting links, we tend to link to pretty trustworthy sites anyway and if they're not you look more at them. If you're looking at the Barclays Bank site, you know pretty well that it is not going to transgress our guidelines on taste and decency. You take a look at it, and you've probably done it before because with something like that the chances are that we have linked to them before.

> If there were any worries about a site then you would look deeper into it. The thing, of course, [is] that sites change and could change dramatically after you have linked to it. Now there's not much we can do about that, which is why we have a disclaimer saying that we take no responsibility for any material on this site.

We therefore asked: 'In terms of privacy, how difficult is it to control the net itself?'

> Well, it's very difficult. It's impossible to control anything. We find increasingly, people are doing spoofs on our site. It's not a privacy thing; it just illustrates the fact that there isn't much you can do about it.

> People will take the furniture that we put around our items – they'll take the whole of the code, then they'll republish rubbish or sometimes objectionable rubbish, and purport to be the BBC. Whenever we

find that we try to stop it, and we quite often do because we go to the ISP and say what's going on and that we take grave exception to it. They then warn the person or throw them off the ISP. So that's how we control. There is nothing we can do unless we find it and then it takes all day to take action. On the privacy side of things I don't know. It's an international thing, on the legal side of things no one's quite sure how to treat it, because is it the law of the land where you publish? Or the law where it's published? A lot of people are waiting for some test case to define what you can and cannot do.

We mentioned that: *'At the moment it seems to be the provider that is held responsible, as soon as they know about it.'*

Yes, I'm not sure that that is true anymore. I think there were a couple of cases where they said it was nothing to do with them and they were just literally the carrier.

We replied: *'I think the conclusion was that it was your responsibility once you knew about it.'*

As I said, we don't publish anything unedited at all, even our user-generated material is filtered and edited, but BBC Online do have bulletin boards where people can say what they like and some of those are post-moderated, the rule being that offending material has to be taken off within an hour of being broadcast, but where you stand legally on that, I have no idea. And for the big operators, the people whose livelihood depends on literally being a filter between the user and the viewer of huge bulletin boards, where they stand on libel and slander is anyone's guess.

Even though 24-hour broadcast news services mean that images are repeated throughout the day, the archiving of material that occurs on BBC Online presents, if not a new form of publishing, at least new questions relating to publishing. With readily accessible archives, an intrusion of privacy, or even an issue in the realm of taste and decency could be re-enacted time and time again during the period that it was archived. The collapse of the dance hall floor in Israel was taken as an example, since it offers issues both of taste and decency and of invasion of privacy.

We therefore enquired: *'Did you cover the incident in Israel, the wedding where the floor collapsed?'*

Yes we did. We showed everything the television news showed because we're committed to that, and to stop we would have had to intervene because the Ten O'Clock News *goes out live on the Internet and it's archived on the Internet. So in a sense, whatever decisions they make on the* Ten O'Clock News, *we follow because it goes out live. Then you're faced with a decision about whether you actually take the stuff and highlight it. In a news bulletin it comes and goes. On television you can't see it again, but on the web you can see it as many times as you want and you can take it out and say, 'Look, isn't this great!' and watch it over and over again. You have to think about these things because, as I said, there's no watershed.*

BBC Online could edit if it was known *'that there was something really nasty coming up and the* Ten O'Clock News *came and said... Well, it runs, and very often you don't know what's coming because the stuff is actually coming in while it's being shown'.*

We will return to the difference that technology has made to publishing and to the question of technology exacerbating the 'problem' of privacy. In response, however, to the idea of the archive allowing continual repeats of a news item, such as the Israeli dance floor disaster, he mentioned, *'I watched it once, I didn't watch it twice'*. We then asked him: *'With your journalist's hat on, when you show that, one could argue that's an invasion privacy and in a sense an invasion of the privacy of the dead. What kind of defence would one make in showing that?'*

Well, you could say that it was very dramatic and that isn't an argument for it, so you could say we have the pictures and we're not showing them to you. I think what happened was that there was a warning at the beginning wasn't there.

We replied: *'I still think its pretty tough stuff.'* To which he said:

There is an argument that that makes people watch more. There is obviously a competitive element to this: if ITN are running it, you would have to explain why you weren't doing it when the pictures were available to you, but it's a fine line. I think the BBC's view is that if you warn people what's coming, that was obviously seen as acceptable. It's dramatic, it tells the story, but it's something you have to make your mind up about on a case-by-case basis... You have to make a decision about it. It was hugely dramatic, but it was scary – you were taken aback by it, and you ought to be warned about it too.

We then said: *'But you wouldn't really, or would you, raise the defence of public interest?'*

It's an interesting one, isn't it?

We pursued this by saying: *'What's interesting is that nowhere is the public interest ever defined, all you've got is areas in which it might operate'*. This led to interesting observations on his part about the changing nature of news–gathering, or, more precisely, the increased presence of footage available to newsrooms.

The problem [is] the goalposts move all the time and the reason why we are discussing the collapse of the floor is that, firstly, the chances of anyone filming that fifteen years ago are pretty slight. [...] But the last time I was out on a big story, like the plane that came down on the M1, one of the duties of the reporter when they got there was to find the person with the video camera. Huge numbers of people out there these days are potential journalists and you go and get that before the opposition does. These days there is far more being filmed, so the temptation to use that footage is greater. And you're right. How do you define the public interest? Is it to see Anna Ford cavorting about on a beach in a bikini? I would argue not. So in a sense you've got to take it on a case-by-case basis, because the goalposts are moving the whole time, stuff is becoming available that whole time, as you said. We don't take much stuff off freelancers, because if they came to us with pictures of Anna Ford we wouldn't use them. But the pressures on newspaper journalists are going to be more and more.

The increasing presence of amateur video footage is one aspect worth considering when discussing the intrusion of privacy; namely, that there is an increased likelihood of the capture of events as they happen, so that the sheer drama that is caught makes for the news irrespective of public importance of the event. This can be debated, but looks suspiciously the case in terms of the collapse of the dance floor in Israel. Indeed, this increased capturing of events as they happen is something new. The above interviewee said:

> The technology allows you very often to get stuff that you wouldn't have before, so there are more decisions to make. In the past it would be very, very rare to get dramatic pictures of anything. You'd have to actually have a BBC camera there and occasionally they were. But now virtually every disaster – I saw yesterday the balloon that came down killing six people in France – somebody was filming it. And they would. It's like plane crashes at air shows. There's inevitably half a dozen angles on the disaster and twenty years ago that would not have been the case.

The presence of cameras has important implications for the intrusion of privacy when set within the imperatives of what news is taken to be. This means that one of the central tenets of news values, the dramatic, is now more readily furnished than in the past. Which means that some news organizations, for example, the BBC and ITV, would have difficulty in defending news items, or at least on a regular basis, merely because of drama captured on film. Hence, some defence is required, and one defence, where it involves intrusion of privacy, is that of 'in the public interest'. Because the term lacks clear definitional support, it can be used. Had there been no footage of the dance floor collapse, it is certainly questionable whether it would have made television news, and it may not have warranted much attention by the press either. If this is accepted, then it is difficult to see where the defence of 'in the public interest' rests; either the story was in the public interest to be told or it was not, the presence of cameras does not alter that fact. Of course, television is a visual medium and without pictures then one has, so to speak, a limited story. Yet, it looks suspiciously the case that, in the instance of the dance floor, it was the cameras that made the story.

In taking up the story once more with the interviewee from BBC Online, and returning to questions of both taste and decency and privacy, he commented in very reflective fashion:

> You're absolutely right about the taste and decency. When you look at it you think – what about the survivors who are obviously in shock and are being seen as such. There's a woman who loses it completely and is hysterical, and you think, well, is it right to show this? And I think the view throughout the media was that it was worth showing and I think we would defend ourselves by saying it was in the public interest because there was clearly something wrong with this building and it may well be a much wider spread issue. However, we may be kidding ourselves in that because it was hugely dramatic and it would have been very difficult not to use it.

What is interesting, and points to a very real difference between the press and electronic media, something we had not considered, was that the intrusion of privacy by the latter is often by proxy. In referring to the pictures from Israel, the BBC Online interviewee said:

> …it's sort of invasion of privacy by proxy. You've got the pictures there – we didn't take them, you have to make a decision to do it. The newspapers invade privacy, very often, to get the story, which is

a direct invasion of privacy. But what we were talking about in Israel – we weren't there, we didn't do it deliberately. So, very often for us anyway, it's one step back when you're making that decision. But you're right about this idea that it is the journalist making news decisions as they go along and they have to take into consideration what the current state of play is and it moves all the time.

The above statement really stands for itself. In terms of the news at least, then the electronic media is relaying intrusion of privacy, not instigating that intrusion. For the press, given the nature of how information is captured, *they* must do the intruding. Of course, with intrusion of privacy, either by proxy or directly, the outcome for those whose privacy has been intruded upon is probably the same, or, where death is involved, the principle of intrusion is the same. What he is saying is that, with the spread of technologies of image-capture, the media are increasingly faced with reacting to dramatic images, which in terms of news values presents difficult decision-making processes. Whereas, for the press, intrusion is not so reactive, but active, and, hence, in many ways, a much more considered process, or at least is in the terms discussed here.

The reference to *'the current state of play'* is a reference to changes in the number of potential news gatherers that now exist. But, in discussing changes brought about by advances in technology, it was the opinion of a BBC on-line interviewee that such advances have assisted in changing the notion of the private. He considered, when discussing what people take the private domain to be, *'I'm sure that it's changed'*, and, to reinforce previous points, that

By the very nature and number of cameras you're not going to be able to control what is being filmed.

Yet, it was his view that sensitivity to being filmed was not as high as in the past:

I mean if you're in a public gathering of some sort, like a wedding, it's almost certain someone's filming you. A wedding is perhaps not a good example, because you had stills before, but there are other places where you would be filmed and you wouldn't object anymore.

Finally, and he had long experience as a journalist, we wish to clarify what he saw as the difference between something being 'in the public interest' and something being of 'overriding public interest'. It did not appear that he considered it a useful distinction. He said: *'But if you make a decision to use it in the public interest, it doesn't matter how overriding it is. You've used it or you haven't. So is there a distinction where you believe that it is in the public interest but you don't use it? There must be.'* We put an example to him: *'Yes. I imagine something that might involve children'*. He responded by saying:

Let me think of an example. Just say that there was a minor indiscretion by a public official and you've got the story and you're going to use it. It's not hugely in the public interest, but it's of interest and this junior official should be reported for doing this. Somebody then says to you, 'Hold on for two weeks. If you use this story it will cost the public purse two million pounds. It's only two weeks, but it will save us two million pounds'. You know it's mildly in the public interest, but it's overridingly in the public interest to save two million pounds. What do you do?

One answer to this question posed by the BBC Online interviewee is discussed earlier, where the BBC radio journalist said that he would publish; that the consequences were not his concern – that his job, indeed duty, was to report what he found and report it accurately.

Of course, the BBC Online interviewee was not suggesting that he might have a problem with this, although he might have, but was simply being helpful to the discussion by creating a case where public interest and overriding public interest might clash to illustrate the difficulty of the terms. For our purpose it is indeed a nice illustrative point concerning public interest; namely, that it has an element of guardianship attached. It is doubtful that many journalists would consider it their job to protect the public purse by keeping information hidden, but would consider it their job to protect the public purse by revelations of misdeeds. Yet, as he rightfully points out, by not revealing, or delaying information, public interest was best served. It is this term 'public' that gets in the way of clarification when it comes to intrusion. It suggests some higher order activity than one normally associates with journalism, that somehow the journalist is a public servant whose job it is to act on behalf of the public or protect it. This they might do within a framework that sees journalism as the Fourth Estate, but that is to confuse function with purpose. In acting as a Fourth Estate the public is indeed protected from other estates, but when something is in the public interest it most often entails, though not necessarily requires, that the public is interested in it. It is an occupation that principally sells information as a commodity first and foremost in western liberal democracies. Hence, it must tell stories that the public is interested in. It is the coming together of the two words 'interest' and 'public' that results in such confusion. Hence, the preference for a term that suffers none of the contamination that public interest does; namely, 'social importance'.

In the interview with a representative of the Internet service provider Freeserve, the changed nature of publication was raised. It was suggested to him that a possible point of difference between Internet content and more traditional publishing was that a person was *'very unlikely to inadvertently bump into Internet content'*, in contrast to a newspaper headline, or a broadcast. He replied:

> I think that within the context of the way regulators seem to be viewing it, they're quite clear that Internet service providers are publishers and they're looking to find ways to avoid ISPs picking up the responsibility of the publisher, because they happen to have served as the conduit through which the information has been conveyed. But I think there is also an obligation that if we find ourselves, through the act of being a medium, presenting information which is obscene, which is defamatory, then we have an obligation to remove it as quickly as possible. So not only is there an issue here for me in terms of what is contrary to, or pro, the public interest, but I have to ask myself the questions of 'Well, let's assume that something is contrary to the public interest, what's my judgement in terms of how we should deal with that?' And I can't look to anything under the threat of litigation and damages as being the arbiter of how the company responds. Whereas I think I'd prefer to be directed to something a little more concrete than that, but I am not sure, because what is in the public interest varies.

If regulation is unclear, and little clarification exists concerning the precise definition of public interest, then journalists must fall back on their personal judgement about the areas in which public interest is considered to operate. This does not create a consistent environment and may lead to the same situation creating very different outcomes.

In the area of the Internet, it seems that some decisions are down to the personal judgements of individual operators: *'Freeserve's approach to public interest issues will be dictated pretty much by how I "smell it" on the day and I'll refer it to my boss. He and I take different views; because I am a lawyer by training I'm instinctively more risk-averse than he is, and he's far more liberal than I am'.* Following discussion of pressure on him to remove a site during the general election from *'local Tory candidates who were being "slagged" off by local Labour candidates... we thought this was fantastic, we didn't take any of those down'.* He mentioned that he would only have done so if it was defamatory: *'If it's clearly defamatory we try to get rid of the defamatory content...'*

He was unclear about what the public interest is, or, more accurately, of what the definition of public interest refers to. Therefore, since his medium is faced by confusion as to what its legal responsibility is in carrying information, it is not surprising that to take action on the grounds of 'in the public interest' would not be of utmost consideration. The very fluidity of the Internet means that it does not make particular sense to run it in accordance with regulations that have been developed for established media who know their legal position in terms of publishing much more clearly.

During the interview with a senior lawyer, who advises on regulatory matters relating to the media, it became obvious just how unclear the whole area of what constitutes the public interest is, and how it might be used as a defence for the intrusion of privacy. To begin with, the idea of 'acceptable community standards' raised arguments similar to those which we develop later, when he said: *'Does that mean that, in part of Bradford, that standards are set by three or four self-appointed leaders of the Asian community?'* To press the point of the relativity of using community standards, he added, *'You can't even say "family values", because the family operates differently in different cultural settings'.* The lawyer was not unclear on points of law as they related to reporting, but as to the central usefulness of the term 'in the public interest'. The point was made:

> *I think the law's very good at stating the principle that certain things are overridden by a higher public interest. But our legal system, as you probably appreciate, being a common law system going from precedent, is very good at leaving judges to develop, meeting it on a case-by-case basis... [For example] in litigation, relevant documents have to be exposed to your opponents. But there is a principle of public interest immunity that says that certain documents shouldn't be disclosed because the public interest in them being disclosed to allow a fair trial between individuals is overridden by a greater public interest in keeping certain things secret.*

Applied to the media and the intrusion of privacy then, an individual interest can be overridden by a higher interest. The problem is in deciding what that higher interest is. A difficulty with the media and privacy is that, as the interviews show, there is such a wide range of situations and different media. It is difficult to see how they can be squeezed into a mould that would allow a single judgement of something being in the public interest. The areas to be adjudicated are so different to each other at times that it is not obvious that the same principles of intrusion are being applied – they can go from the trivial to the serious, from entertainment to national security. At other times it looks as if the intrusion of privacy is really one of taste and decency and would have no place in a court of law for a decision to be made concerning whether higher interests were involved. And, yet again, the intrusion of privacy appears necessary simply to inform the public about general happenings in the world, which people may consider they have a right to know, but not a right that is overriding of anything.

It is for these reasons that we consider the term 'social importance' to be a better, and non-legalistic, notion to apply when judging the merits of intruding upon privacy. Indeed, at one point in discussing the legal complexities of the Anna Ford case, with the lawyer pointing out to us where one might draw in law for a case to be made that her privacy had been wrongfully intruded upon, we mentioned that we were working to develop a new term, which, at that point in our thinking, we referred to as social interest (it gave way later to social importance). The lawyer said, *'Yes, I think that's a better label myself'*.

It is the idea of entering the social that makes the whole area more manageable and, we would argue, better capable of testing the merits of any case. Also, by getting rid of the term 'interest', confusion over whether it means 'in the public interest' or 'the public are interested in something', vaporizes. To clarify matters: there might well be social interest in the picture of Anna Ford in a swimming costume, but by using the idea of social importance – that it had impact on social association – the publication of the picture would fail that test. This also does away with debates concerning the nature of the public space from which the picture was obtained. As the lawyer pointed out to us, in discussing some secret filming that took place in a high-street store, there is a presumption *'that people would normally expect to be free from secret filming'*. The interesting word here is 'normally' and, again, the idea of social importance can be applied to provide consideration as to whether appeal can be made to a higher interest. But, that interest must be detached from the notion of the public, as if such interest existed as an established entity. The lawyer said at the very end of our conversation with him, in discussing the concept of public interest, that *'at its simplest, and everyone can see that there is an interest, as I said earlier, in equality of arms for a fair trial, but they can also see that if that results in secrets getting out that will be seriously compromising to national security (say in the Cold War days) then they can see that that is a higher need'*. He then added, *'Well, I suppose it depends on your politics'*.

Everything may depend on one's politics, but it does not seem satisfactory to us that in the realm of media performance one can leave matters as vague as that.

Notes

1. Formerly the NVALA founded by Mrs Mary Whitehouse.
2. Presswise is a media pressure group.
3. In the review period of 04/05, Ofcom Content and Standards Group reached decisions on a total of 4,184 programme complaints, of which 3,994 were complaints about programme standards and only 190 were complaints about fairness or alleged breaches of privacy. (See Ofcom Annual Report 2004–05.)
4. Controversial couple, former Conservative MP Neil Hamilton and his wife, Christine, were arrested in May 2001 by police investigating an alleged, albeit falsely, sexual assault, amid an inevitable blaze of publicity.

5. The BSE [Bovine Spongiform Encephalopathy] crisis (commonly referred to as 'mad cow' disease) severely damaged the farming industry of Britain and led to an independent inquiry, headed by Lord Phillips, about the way it was handled by the Government. John Gummer, former Conservative agriculture minister, was criticized (amongst others) for the way he presented assurances by the Government that beef was safe – most notably, for feeding his 4-year-old daughter with a beef burger in front of press photographers in an alleged publicity stunt.

6. Royal Society for the Protection of Birds.

7. On 6 March 1987, the Townsend Thoresen cross-Channel roll-on roll-off ferry *Herald of Free Enterprise* capsized outside the Belgian port of Zeebrugge with the loss of 193 lives. Its bow door had been improperly closed, allowing the car deck to flood.

The Public and the Private: The Self-Monitoring of Behaviour

7 Clarifying the Conceptual Problems

This chapter begins with a discussion of the self as a self-monitoring being. This involves an exposition of the individual in terms of his or her self-awareness and his or her social awareness, and how the individual moves between states of awareness as a dependent of social location and realization of being observed. The central part of the chapter critically analyses the notion of public interest as representing more than simple self-interest. The notion of public interest is then compared to other referents for judging the performance of the media in terms of intrusion of privacy, such as community interest and national interest. The chapter concludes that the term 'the public interest' is so vague as not to form a viable test for the justification of the intrusion of privacy. The argument is made that the notion of social importance forms a better basis for judging when it is right to intrude into someone's privacy, and that a test for social importance is the degree to which acts, that the media might wish to expose, threaten social solidarity. We propose that the test of social importance, based on an idea of threat to social solidarity, can handle exposure of values in a way that the defence of the public interest cannot.

The phrase 'in the privacy of one's home' is redolent with meaning. Above all, perhaps, it suggests security. To anyone who has woken up to find someone staring at them it is disconcerting, even disturbing, and particularly disturbing if that someone is a stranger or one who they are not over-familiar with. It disturbs because, whilst asleep, one is at one's most physically vulnerable, but it also disturbs because one has been 'studied' without permission having been given. To sleep is to remove oneself from the world of known existence and is, most usually, only voluntarily entered into when it is considered safe to do so. Mostly our waking moments are, to varying degrees, typified by being on guard, knowing that others are watching us to varying degrees of concentration. Hence, the waking world is one of performance and, to be caught unawares, by, for example, someone entering the room without one knowing, can result in a feeling of embarrassed foolishness that private acts were not private at all, but public. Indeed, the feeling of foolishness stems, in some measure, from not knowing what one was doing in the unguarded moment of believing one was alone – it takes a little time to forcibly reflect on what the 'intruder' might have observed. It is not that acts performed alone are unconscious, but that they do not have a lived apparancy to them as those conducted in public have. Quick reflection is needed to remind oneself just what it was that one was doing, or, perhaps more accurately, since one knows, for example, that a cup of coffee was being poured, what the detail of the manner of the acts were – was it that a funny face was being pulled whilst pouring the coffee, was one talking to the coffee cup telling it how lovely it was or scolding it for being chipped?

Not to give others permission to observe the self, and then find that one has been observed, is not surprisingly unsettling to say the least, since it involves the non-monitoring of the self. Therefore, should one not wish to be observed, special precautions are usually taken to guarantee that one will not be observed. All social interaction and exchange involves self-monitoring, although one's ability to self-monitor may in some circumstances be reduced; in sexual passion or extremes of drunkenness. But self-monitoring can also collapse through being overwhelmed by circumstances, faced by a terrifying situation or grief over the loss of a loved one. In such situations, self-control goes. One no longer cares what others see, although one might care what others have seen once the period of pain or fear has passed.

Yet, even in situations where self-monitoring has been set aside, it is often the case that others close to oneself take over the role. In the case of the drunken evening, then advice may be given not to do something that will only be regretted in the morning. Or, in the case of grief, a friend or family member may stay with the individual, not simply to care for the person in a period of functional incapacity but to protect in the sense of monitoring engagement with the outside world, to act as a screen between the individual and the gaze of others – phone calls will be taken and so on. In fact, there are rules or social conventions to protect the grieving person in periods of collapsed self- monitoring, captured, for example, by the phrase, 'not intruding into personal grief'. In other words, the person is in no position to grant, in rational fashion, access to their emotions. To watch, therefore, an interview with someone distraught with grief is not only painful, in the sense of witnessing in sympathetic fashion the pain of another, but can offer the uncomfortable sight of someone who may not have given 'full' permission to be put on such public display. The question arises in such situations of whether one is witnessing the invasion of privacy, even though the stricken has given permission for the interview, because the self-monitoring process has broken down in the face of overwhelming events that have led to a collapse of the individual in a normative sense. One speaks of someone going mad with grief to indicate that they are not themselves, and therefore are not their previous rational self. We will see later that a person in one of the focus groups felt that to even ask for an interview with someone in such a state was to invade their privacy. The wearing, in the not too distant past, of a black armband acted as public signification that the rules of normal intercourse should be adjusted in dealings with those making the statement of sorrow – politeness of exchange would be extended and allowances made for behaviour that at other times might have resulted in challenge. The defence, and we have seen this from the interviews with media personnel, that often the grief-stricken wish to talk, even that it is good for them to do so, as if the media have suddenly become an arm of the social services, is fraught with difficulty when seen in terms of the capacity of the individual for effective self-monitoring. The sobbing individual is not the acting of the professional mourner given to some cultures, but the individual throwing off the 'armour' with which they normally confront the world to display that which they cannot control. The individual is hopeless in despair. The condition, for example, following the tragic events of 9/11 in New York, is so personal that no immediate help can be given to those confronting the loss of a loved one. But, yet, at that most private of moments, there is a total non-concern for the presentation of the self, self becomes public to millions around the world via television.

News Values, Privacy and Taste & Decency

It says much about our culture that such pictures would be transmitted. We make no evaluative judgement here, preferring instead analysis and description. The media presentation of the tragic events of the World Trade Center goes in some way to the centre of the difficulties in discussing the media, privacy and the defence of public interest in justifying the intrusion of privacy. Public interest and news values interact in the most complex manner. It is difficult at times to say where a news value masquerades as public interest, and where public interest has become a news value. In a liberal democracy, then one of the functions of the media is to facilitate the democratic value of the public's right to know – it is part of the democratic theory of the press captured by the idea of the Fourth Estate. No one would deny that the destruction of the World Trade Center, and the subsequent scale of the loss of life, was a story that had to be told; that the public indeed had a right to know what took place. This is supported even further by the fact that in Britain the government acted on behalf of its people, in taking up arms against terrorism, and attacked a foreign state. Detailed coverage was undoubtedly in the public interest, and the event fulfilled many of the criteria of news values laid out by Galtung and Ruge (1965) in their seminal work in the area. It was a big news story. Yet, simply because an event can unequivocally be cast as a news story on almost any definition of news values, does not mean that the manner of its coverage, of how the news values are operationalized, can be defended in terms of news values, or justified in terms of the public interest. In short, the tension point is in the manner that the public interest is served when set against news practices that only tangentially touch core news values. The dramatic and the negative are core news values, of how something becomes defined as newsworthy. However, the playing of the mobile phone messages from those about to die in the hijacked planes does not readily spring into the categorization of news values, but more into narrative procedures for telling a story. One thing is for sure; it was not the intention of those making the heart-rending phone calls to their nearest and dearest that the content of the calls were for public consumption. Indeed, it is almost impossible to think of anything that might be more personal or private than a farewell message before life is extinguished. Nevertheless, the recordings of these messages were relayed via the media to those to whom the messages were not intended. It might be argued that it was in the public interest to broadcast and print the farewells in order to convey the full horror of what took place, but it is a flimsy defence given that the horror was all too apparent and hardly required amplification. What one is looking at is where a story that is in the public interest is underpinned by classic news values. This then cuts with questions of taste and decency that are independent of the rights of an individual to privacy when set against the public's right to know. It is difficult to see how the public had a right to intrude into the private anguish of those making the calls, and no permission of those receiving the calls to broadcast the recordings alters that moral fact. It is not simply, one would have thought, a question of the intrusion of privacy, but also one of taste and decency, and often the question of privacy is, as we shall see, intertwined with questions of taste and decency.

However, privacy, as with taste and decency, is normative. Ideas of what is in poor taste change with time, and so do ideas of what is private. News values, or what is considered newsworthy, rest on the value structure of the society to which the media refer. Communist Russia, to take one example, had a different set of news values to that of the capitalist countries of the West, for the obvious reason that each system was underpinned by different ideologies that then structured what was considered worthy of observation or comment. News is a social construction. What we accept as correct is often a question of performance. That is, what we accept as correct is what we are familiar with and, as with taste and decency, what we become familiar with becomes accepted as a norm in the full sense of that term. Yet, changes in media content relating to matters of taste are a product of social change itself that makes representations acceptable that were not acceptable in the past, but, also, representations themselves have the capacity, over time, of altering how we think about the acceptable. It is, in the strict use of the term, dialectical. In the dialectic of acceptance one also ought to extend the process to that of portrayals of the private; namely, that what we take the private to be is what we are used to seeing portrayed. Only in a culture that was used to the media intruding into the private aspects of individuals' lives could media personnel consider it appropriate to broadcast the last statements of those trapped on the planes that struck the World Trade Center. In other words, to 'accept' those messages, the public had to have been prepared, over a period of time, by the performance of the media itself. There is a further fact here and that is the elevated position given to the news in our society that has an impact on what we consider the private to be, or, perhaps more accurately, on what we can expect to remain private.

News as a Commodity

News is a commodity like any commodity and, indeed, from the days of the establishment of the great wire agencies, such as Reuters and Agence France Press, news followed trade. What we have seen, and relatively recently at that, with the advances in news-gathering techniques, improvement in communications and increased news outlets, is an explosion in the amount of news on offer, perhaps best signified by the development of CNN and other twenty-four-hour news services. One talks of an information society, but one can also talk of a news society and the cultural capital to be had by being informed. In a service society, knowledge itself forms a central part of the productive basis of the creation of wealth, and, hence, there is a high premium, at almost every level of interaction, placed on knowing. It is within this social transformation that the news industry has achieved its present place and status, so much so that it can be expected to be given 'rights of entry' not possible in the past and, in doing so, if not exactly transforming ideas of intimacy, has created the expectation that few secrets will remain. By this is meant that when something newsworthy occurs, we will be there, superbly demonstrated in the continuous and detailed coverage of the dramatic events of the attack on the World Trade Center.

What this means for privacy is difficult to say with certainty, but it can be posited that the news has gained a position in public consciousness where it is expected that the operations of the world are open for close inspection. This does not mean, despite the position of the news, that it is given absolute freedom to roam into the private domains of individuals, unless it can demonstrate good cause for doing so. The suggestion here, however, is that of a winnowing away of what the private is taken to be. This is something that we will see in the course of the focus group findings. But, and here we return to the events of 9/11, it could be expected that the media would not simply 'get the story', but cover it in intricate detail. Without making any criticism, what in essence was a political story, involving massive human drama, was bound to flow in the direction that it did: a focusing upon the individuals caught up in the disaster area that lower Manhattan became. Within this then, the relaying of the last statements of those on the hijacked airliners before their death becomes a feature of the news, and more, played over and over again. To play such voices, and there is no question that to do so is an invasion of their privacy, has a ready logic to it so that it no longer seems strange. One could easily imagine that, only a few years ago, to do so would have resulted in a massive outcry at such a practice. The point to stress is that it is not sufficient to point to what ought to happen in the sense of laws governing conduct, but of what will happen in terms of the acceptable, and what is acceptable has been framed by past performance very much in line with what is considered tasteful and decent.

Privacy as Sanctuary

If we now move away from the performance and position of the media in loosening the idea of the private to the public itself, then, as pointed out, structural changes, in the course of long history, have occurred that have redefined the private and altered the nature of the presentation of the self. As stated, we self-monitor all our public performances, and much of our time is spent in public space, be that the office, shopping and so on. We do not self-monitor when alone, although we may reflect upon what we are doing. The statement 'I'm going home to take my shoes off and put my feet up', represents more than just a desire to relax, it marks the end of performance. The individual, in other words, is moving from the glare of public performance to the non-penetrable world of the private represented by the home. Even if the home is shared with others, the script has been rehearsed so many times that the effort of performance is minimal. The home is a place where one is not on public view. It offers sanctuary, it offers safety and it offers security. In its furthest extreme only self-observation occurs. Not surprising then that something which offers itself as a retreat from the world, where defence against judgement is at its minimum, should be so highly prized and any intrusion vigorously defended.

In a sense, therefore, privacy is taken as a moral or human right, in that it is encrusted with ideas of freedom, of what to be an autonomous human being is taken to mean, and, in another sense, privacy is taken as a necessary condition for functioning of the individual. But how we function is what we are. It is not the case drawn from some biological model that humans require privacy to survive. Soldiers billeted together and performing collective tasks have little access to privacy and, in certain situations, even their letters may be read by others to check the content. Soldiers, at times, must not think of themselves in individual terms, but as part of a functioning whole. Yet, for all the reasons given, the situation of contemporary civil life privacy is valued, and expected to the point where it is seen as a right. It marks in western liberal democracies the boundary between the individual and the state. The idea of an Englishman's home being his castle is a statement of political philosophy based on the idea of autonomy of the individual; that there is an area of life where permission or authority must be gained before entry is made, and that authority must be gained on clearly determined grounds as laid out in law.

If we hold in mind the idea of modern life being one of self-monitoring in a sea of rapidly changing situations, so that one has to present to many publics, then it becomes all the more readily understandable that the home should be a highly prized zone free from self-monitoring, or at least a space where self-monitoring is at a minimum. To get home is a welcome relief, or at least it is for those where home offers tranquillity. Even where tranquillity is not an empirical fact, the idea of the home as a place of tranquillity free from the observation of others is a cherished ideal. Once one understands this then it is that much easier to understand how people in the group discussions came to define and see privacy. It was invariably linked to place of residence, both conceptually and in practice. It did not stretch, in terms of rights, much beyond the home, if for no other reason than that, in the modern world, privacy could not be expected once outside one's door. This has manifest implications for how the media operate and what rights were granted to it in terms of gazing upon, or enquiring into, the activities of people, institutions and so on. The right to privacy did not appear to be a transportable one and in that sense appears as a strange right.

If privacy is linked to the notion of freedom (the idea of the autonomous individual), then one might expect that the notion of autonomy would be carried over to dealings in the world in general and not simply one specific place. What it suggests is that the modern world, from the functional necessity of its interlocked nature, has stripped away at the right of non-observation. Information about the individual is sought and given. Over time there has occurred a gradual erosion of the private sphere in public. Indeed, surprising to us, but perhaps not to others, there was almost universal agreement among the participants that CCTV cameras in inner-city centres, supermarkets, and so on, were a good idea. Some even welcomed the thought that cameras would be placed in their own streets to monitor other people's comings and goings. The reason given was that capturing activity by camera served to make life safer. They [CCTV cameras] were not felt as intrusive of the self. Furthermore, people had no reason to fear 'publication' of captured pictures, provided one was doing nothing wrong. In other words, there was a ready willingness to be under surveillance, since to do so was in the public interest. The idea of public interest here is interesting and will be unpacked in greater detail later, but it has at its core a very individual dimension that takes it in some ways away from more abstract notions of the good of the collective. Public interest appeared as that which was in their interest *qua* individual, but the nature of that individual interest meant that it was also in the interest of others. Now, one might argue that this is what public interest is, that the community's needs are being protected or served but what is interesting, and we will see this in practice later, is how individuals reasoned towards the idea of public interest.

The Individual Nature of Public Interest

One might consider that to posit some idea of the public interest would involve some theoretical consideration of a higher good than one's own, but being a member of the community one would also benefit by the establishment of such a good. Yet, at the theoretical level, the idea of public interest being of some higher good than mere individual ambitions means that it is quite possible, and indeed likely, that, in the enacting of the public interest, the individual might well subsume his or her personal interests to the higher good. In this sense, public interest takes on a collectivist philosophy that holds to principles of association, which cannot be broken merely at the whim of the individual because, in some particular instance, the carrying out of the public interest does not suit or match the interest of the individual. One might argue that the whole ideal of public service broadcasting has behind it the notion of public interest, that only by all paying a licence fee can a certain type of culture be provided. Some individuals will not like or benefit from the entirety of the product, indeed, may not wish for the product at all, but, if operating from a collectivist ideology, could nevertheless agree that such a service was for the common good and gladly support the principle.

To operate some idea of public interest from the perspective of a distinct individual benefit is not like this at all, even though what is of interest to you may be of interest to all. An interest in the self is not the same as having an interest in the community. For example, to believe that the media can gather information on practices in the health service, by covert means, on the grounds that you yourself might someday become victim to such practices, does not show a collectivist spirit, but rather one of self-interest that is reflected by the interests of many. The thought does not move, so to speak, from the top down, but from the bottom up. It is the collectivization of individual interests, but not cemented by a moral commitment to the well-being of others in a disinterested sense.

It is this reason, the way people view the world, and how the world operates, that makes the whole idea of public interest a difficult concept to operationalize. Or, perhaps better expressed, the idea of public interest becomes difficult to define. One did not receive, or hardly so, collectivist expression to give firm support to the idea of something being in the public interest. Having said that, statements were received regarding when privacy could be intruded upon by the media based on ideas of the importance of a story. When one then looks at what makes a story important, it is found to include what we might term stories of public importance, which may be another way of saying public interest. However, we think not, or, if so, we consider that the lexicon of public importance is superior to that of public interest in that what it refers to is less confusing.

Public Importance and Public Interest

Public interest is suggestive of a community of interests and, in the broadest sense, the totality of the community expressed as society, or a community that is nationally bounded. But, as argued previously, it is unclear what the communality of interest would be. Indeed, it is not dissimilar to the idea of national interest. For a Marxist and a free-marketeer, different understandings would be given. For a Marxist, the term 'national interest' would be seen as representing no more than the interests of the ruling class and hence have only ideological power, not analytical power. The whole idea of community interest, in other words, is equally fraught with difficulties, in the empirical sense of deciding upon the existence of a community. Public interest and community interest face, furthermore, the danger of reification; that is, they come to be objectified in the sense of standing outside and above people to take on claims of their own. In short, they become objects with an independent existence so that one can speak of needs, desires and so on. To objectify in this way is to breathe life into that which has no life and imbue it with an inappropriate facticity that can be appealed to in the way that one might appeal to some law.

Furthermore, the term 'public interest' could not, for many in the groups, be separated easily from ideas of that which the public was interested in. Although, it was quite apparent that what the public was interested in was not to be confused with what, in regulatory terms, is referred to as the public interest. People could quite easily grade stories in terms of importance; whether a leading footballer's wife had, or had not, undergone cosmetic surgery was not seen as important when compared with stories, say, of how the National Health Service was run or terrorist activities. Interesting, maybe, but important, no. For something to be important it had to be socially important. That is, it had to have relevance or impact upon how we conduct our lives, either as it affected individuals directly or indirectly. Included here would be things that did not affect us directly or indirectly in a material sense of conducting our lives or associating with others, but events of such a nature that they might be held to have us reflect on the nature of things as enquiring individuals. This would include far-off famines, earthquakes and so on.

The idea of 'publicly important' is really '*socially* important', and we would claim that this has far greater purchase in adjudicating in cases of the intrusion of privacy than the term 'public interest'. The term 'public interest' is redolent with the notion of having a stake in the outcome of something. That is, that one has an interest because one has a vested interest. Or, equally, that one ought to have an interest and, if not, then the media can still act in one's name as if an interest existed. Public interest here takes on a quasi-legalistic tone; that the interests of the public must be upheld. It also follows, given this quasi-legalistic flavour of the term, that any publisher might seek to defend the invasion of privacy by invoking the plea that they were acting in the public interest by in some way protecting the public from harm. This may be material harm, psychological harm, or a revealing of the fact that the public was being deceived as to some true state of affairs. But, as noted at various points, the public had a great deal of difficulty in judging the merits of the invasion of privacy by reference to public interest; they had little difficulty in doing so from a position of that which they considered was socially or publicly important.

Social Importance versus Public Interest

The term 'public interest' has other drawbacks when handling the issue of the intrusion of privacy. It is simply too grand and, in being grand, overlooks the actual performance of the media. Much of that which is relayed by the media is not of earth-shattering importance, but consists of the mundane, even trivial. Yet, what is mundane, trivial, or of no interest to one person may well form the centre of another person's life interests. Not to be interested in cricket may give rise to no interest whatsoever in the professional conduct of the sport, of whether games have been lost through players taking bribes or simply cheating by interference with the ball. For others, as our group of young Asians demonstrated, such events were the very life stuff of their world; they were obsessed with the game. Their passion, and years of following the sport and careers of individual cricketers, meant that they felt they had rights over the game and, out of genuine affection for certain players, felt that if such figures became ill they should know about it, even to the extent of the players' privacy being intruded upon. For example, in discussion, they wished, in the same way that one might wish to know about a family friend, to know the detail of the circumstances should a player be injured or even die. It is hard here to invoke the notion of public interest, with all that implies in terms of a defence of interests in the sense of some social harm or protection of well-being. Using the idea of social importance, a case could be made for the intrusion of privacy in such circumstances. To these young men, the death or serious illness of one of their 'adopted' players was a disruption of their world. The player had been incorporated into their lives and they felt that they had a right to know as much as possible about the condition, or manner of departure, of the player. Such demands were based on absolute affection, not prurience or morbid fascination with death. It is hard to say that what these young men were demanding was in the public interest, it was social interest, by which is meant that it was relevant to their lives in a significant manner. Also, that it affected more than a single individual, but all those who had chosen to construct a life where cricket played an important role. It had public importance or social importance, but not public interest. For nothing would be served by the revelation of this type of information that assisted the continuation of social association, something that is implied by the idea of public interest.

To move towards a defence of intrusion of privacy based on the idea of social or public importance, and away from the idea of public interest, captures the actual performance of the media themselves in what they offer for consumption. The attachment of 'public' to 'interest' has accredited to it ideas of the polis or polity and, hence, at the same time as being vague when coming to understand what the public interest means, gives it an unduly narrow feeling by association with politics; here crime and law would be, and ought to be, subsumed under the political. It is, one would suggest, one of the reasons that, at the popular level, discussants in the groups had difficulty in articulating what was meant by public interest in justifying the intrusion of privacy. It was certainly not a term that they used.

What they did do, in coming to a decision of how far a person's privacy might be intruded upon, and by what means, was decide the level of importance of the story of what was being revealed. The extent of the intrusion and the extremes of methods used to intrude into someone's privacy were determined by considerations of the public importance of knowing. And here we come to values. What was held as important was that which they valued. The idea of public interest suggests some functional disservice to a community or the community at large; that is, society, which really means the nation – it moves it into a political category in the widest sense. That is, 'anti-social' meaning 'against society', rather than how the term is most often and wrongly used in implying unsociable behaviour. But not all acts that one might wish to expose through the invasion of privacy fall into that category. To be hypocritical might offend against values that we hold, and we might wish for the hypocrite to be exposed as such by intruding into his or her privacy to show the nature of the hypocrisy. However, the hypocrisy itself cannot be said to damage the public's interest in the manner that the term was invoked by the regulators interviewed. An example here might be where someone, perhaps a journalist, claimed through his column to uphold the Christian sanctity of marriage, but was found to have, what the press might term, a 'secret love nest', by another newspaper prying into his private life. It is difficult to say how the public interest, in the sense of forestalling some damage or whatever, was served by this story, but it might be of some public or social importance in offering a moral tale that one's sins will find one out. It might be of social importance in that the local golf club would not wish for such a character to be a member, or a church group no longer wished his attendance and so on, but it is hard to cast the interest in terms of public interest. That is, it is difficult to see where non-exposure would have altered the interests of anyone. No harm was being done, but knowledge of the facts serves the function of allowing a public demonstration of moral assertion of what is and is not correct behaviour. For others, it gives satisfaction that a hypocrite has been exposed, providing the feeling of social justice and an opportunity to assert a dislike of hypocrisy. In other words, moving away from the term 'the public interest' and replacing it with 'social' or 'public importance', can make a defence for intrusion into privacy on moral grounds. However, more than that, by moving away from the baggage of the political and legal connotations of public interest, one can take into account the actual feelings of people about what is and what is not important.

The Public Interest: A Disenfranchising Term

What is being said here is that to continue to run with the idea of public interest as a defence of the intrusion of privacy disenfranchises most people from entering the debate in any meaningful sense. It is not a term that they use, although, as stated, the manner in which they make judgements about intrusion into privacy is not unrelated to how it has come to be seen in the various regulatory codes of practice. People make judgements in coming to the appropriateness of intruding into privacy in terms of justice, and in terms of what they feel is important to know. As we will see from the group discussions, although it might be fun for people to follow the private lives of the famous, there is no attempt on their part to justify such interest in terms of a right to know, or that knowing about the antics of the famous is important. It is the equivalent of taking pleasure in gossip. Even so, this aspect of the performance of the media should not be downplayed – gossip, be it social or political, has always been a feature of the press and performs the social function of integration into the fabric of community life. However, given that such information is not essential to the conduct of society at a general or individual level it is seen for what it is – essentially trivial. Therefore, the intrusion of privacy is limited by considerations of the rights of those reported on. Rights are conditional and not absolute. Much depends on the status of the individual reported on, film star, sportsperson, politician and so on, and the manner in which they conduct their lives. (See Tables 37–39 in Chapter 8b for survey results on this issue.) Thus, a footballer that courts publicity cannot be expected to be awarded the same degree of privacy, at times when it suits him to be private, as a footballer whose fame is restricted purely to his performance on the pitch. Nor, by and large, is it seen appropriate to intrude into a politician's life if the area under investigation has nothing to do with his or her performance as a politician. That which is applied in coming to a judgement is the idea of reasonableness.

The idea of reasonableness is really the legal observation relating to that which 'the man on the Clapham omnibus' would consider reasonable, and also the notion in libel of releasing information that would lower the reputation of a person in the eyes of right thinking people. And again, as in law, this is framed by the conduct of the parties in question. Thus, those who appeared on *Big Brother* were considered by those in the focus groups, by and large, to be the type of person who had no reputation to lower, therefore no sympathy was extended to any intrusion into their lives.

Underpinning the idea of reasonable is the notion of fairness, where fairness is determined by consideration of what might be expected to occur in the circumstances balanced by the concept of damage – the damage to the individual by intrusion into his or her privacy, and damage to others by not knowing some information or other. However, even where it is held that the damage to others, of not knowing something, outweighs the damage to the individual through exposure, consideration is given to how the material is collected, the method of intruding into someone's privacy. This is subject to almost arithmetic resolution. The strength and intrusiveness of the methods adopted for gaining information can, in effect, be 'calculated' by gauging the degree of damage to others caused by not offering this information.

Overriding Public Interest and the Idea of Damage

It has already been noted that the term 'the public interest' does not sit easily in the vocabulary of most people. It has also been pointed out that the term suffers from flaws, in terms of that which it appears to refer to – the objectifying of social arrangements. Consequently, the term 'overriding', as found in the vocabulary of regulation, only compounds the problem. That is, it enhances the objectification, and does so by imputing something that is abstract – public interest – with absolute desires, needs, wants and so forth. One might talk of an individual being outraged, and one might talk about the public being outraged, in that the public is a collection of individuals, but it is difficult to talk of an interest being outraged. An interest is not something; indeed, an interest cannot have an interest. It becomes difficult, therefore, to talk of an overriding public interest as if it were a living thing. It is because of this that even the regulators, media personnel and such had great difficulty in handling, in any meaningful way, the idea of overriding public interest. Talking about overriding public interest formed the most unsatisfactory part of the interviews with the media and media-associated figures. The conversations at this point tended to take the form of commentary on the seriousness of that which was being withheld from public gaze. And seriousness here really means damage to people. Damage to people can be damage at the direct individual level, such as pollution of a water supply, or damage in a removed sense of, for example, the undermining of the security of the state, or a master institution, such as a banking system.

The idea of damage, therefore, we would suggest, ought to be the fulcrum around which the discussion of the intrusion of privacy takes place. The insertion of the notion of damage also elides easily with social or public importance. Importance is to be determined by the degree of damage to the public, where public, very much, is the collection of individuals. The notion of the public is not such an abstract concept as that of the state, a term which is the subject of much political philosophical discussion. Yet, when we speak of the public it is as if it is a uniform, even unified, knowable thing. We speak of public opinion, yet when we do so as a firm social fact, of something that is objectively known, we are really speaking of majority opinion on something and then turning it into what we might call the collective will. Of course, public opinion in this sense does not really exist, but for reasons of social management we talk for heuristic purposes as if it did. Furthermore, within a certain type of democratic thinking where numeracy is seen as a defining feature – one is not talking in a political philosophical sense of this is what democracy is, but one of its features in practice that is perhaps valued above most others – it is convenient in a practical sense to do so. There are of course many publics and not something to be simply referred to as 'the public'. And that is why it is difficult to talk in a meaningful way about the public interest, as if there is absolute shared agreement about what this would be. Measures that are taken, in the name of public interest, to present laws governing the vilification of one religious group or another might be agreed upon in a secular state as good and in its interest, but not for religious states, nor even for religious groups within a secular state where a key component of its practice is proselytizing. To hold a belief strongly, be it a political belief, but especially a religious belief, is usually to be intolerant towards counter beliefs, and in many cases not to be tolerant of those who hold such beliefs. It is the organizational structure of advanced capitalist societies, although much also depends historically on the manner in which they have evolved, that makes them relatively tolerant societies to differences: conflict is not functional to the maintenance of the system.

Social Importance

In what has been said, it might be assumed that the idea of social or public importance is not really superior, in moving forward to the clarification of the privacy issue, to that of public interest: that we have merely squared the circle by the substitution of words. There is still the idea of 'the social' or 'the public' as if it is a knowable collective, that it can be said to exist as an identifiable object. In that sense, the term 'social', or 'public importance', does face many of the difficulties presented by the term 'the public interest'. But, and this is important, we are not saying that the term 'the public interest' is valueless, only that it does not work very well as a clarifier in justifying the intrusion of privacy, and does not do so for all the reasons given. It raises nearly as many difficulties as it solves, not least of which is the ever-present charge of 'when we talk of the public interest, whose interest are we talking about?' More so, however, in talking about public interest, we must ask about the nature of that interest. What form does it take and with what intensity?

Because, as we have stressed, the idea of the public interest is infused with the political in the widest sense, it might be expected that elite political groups, or indeed those in the media whose task it is to report the political, will tend to see a greater 'public interest' than the public themselves. That is, those who have built their lives on an appreciation of the political operations of nations, or are concerned with the maintenance of political and social order, will more readily consider something to be in the public interest than other groups if it is defined as having a political aspect to it. There is, if one likes, a biased sensitivity to the political in considering the question of interests. As a case of dramatic proportion, one might here think of the Profumo Affair.[1] Was there a public interest there, or, perhaps better expressed, an over-riding public interest in terms of threat to the state, or the manifestation of the interests, in terms of sensitivity to the political, of particular groups not shared by a wider public?

If we use the terms 'public' or 'social importance' instead of 'the public interest' then certainly not all the problems go away. We are still left with those attached to the idea of the public interest – what is it that one is referring to? The greatest benefit is getting rid of the term 'interest'; again for the reasons given. We are still, however, left with deciding what is important. This, however, is where the social comes in, but for social we can also almost substitute 'public' and, if preferred, can do so. On the whole we much prefer social, in that it removes the problem of saying what the public is. It also allows the handling of issues that are important in terms of social association but may not be recognized as such by the public. Social importance, in the sense of society, suggests that something has wide ramifications at the level of the totality of society – for example, indiscriminate terrorist threats – to ramifications for groups or parties within the society.

What became obvious in the focus groups was that, for the intrusion of privacy to be justified, the outcome of not knowing some information, or exposing some happening, had to impact on more than a single individual. At the most banal and simplistic level, if one individual was to invade another individual's privacy, and the result of doing so was only of benefit to the first individual, then why would such an invasion be justified? Such would be a personal matter, and the claims of one offset by the claims of another. To intrude into someone's privacy, one had to have authority to do so, and that authority can only be drawn by appeal to collective standards of correct performance. The information gained would need to have social relevance, and the wider the social relevance the greater the right to intrusion. At its most naked, it is the individual against the group.

The Collective and Social Solidarity

Time and again, as we will see, when individuals judged whether it was right or not to infringe upon someone's privacy, the judgement taken was based on the importance of knowledge to more than just themselves. They act, in other words, as members of social associations and, in doing so, represented more than just themselves, their interests, when they spoke. They were aware; although this may appear trivial it is nevertheless important, of not being isolated units. Indeed, the whole idea of a society, and the value placed on a particular society, is that it provides greater satisfaction and benefits than not being a member. In extreme cases people do drop out, the hermit being the classical historical example. This would also be the case with religious cults or groups who remove themselves, often for reasons of persecution, to establish self-enclosed communities, refusing contact with other communities and society as a collective expression of the totality of associations. Living in society gives interests that are similar to the interests of others, and also gives an interest in the solidarity of association.

Social interest, therefore, at base, or in its most powerful form, is really an interest in the continuation of social solidarity. Anything that threatens that solidarity is considered of utmost social importance. Therefore, here we might have a model by which to situate the whole question of privacy and the defence of 'the public interest'. That is, the primary claim to the intrusion of privacy is based on the perceived threat to social solidarity. That can be placed at the apex of the model and all other 'interest' placed as variants of social solidarity, as acts that, to varying degrees, threaten social solidarity. In fact, this is how a legal system works in some ways when it apportions punishment to crime. One must not take this last point too far, however, since, although that statement would be true, values of dominant groups enter the legal system. Women, for example, at least historically, can be seen to have less legal rights than men, crimes against property tend to be viewed in a more serious light than crimes against the person and so on. A legal system does reflect the values of a society and the constitution of a society. In the old Soviet Union, fraud involving the state could be punishable by death, since such acts struck at the very foundation of the political and economic system, in a way not seen to be the case in the capitalist West.

The model of social solidarity, of use for examining when and how far one might go in intruding into privacy, must be seen as an heuristic device and not applied in any mechanistic fashion. What it does is serve to show how individual rights give way to social concerns. Clearly, we are uneasy with the term 'the public interest', since it was not a term that many in the focus groups could handle terminologically, even if the principles of public interest were seen in practice operating as a defence for the intrusion of privacy. We have also mentioned that the term 'national interest' suffers from similar problems when brought into use as an appeal mechanism to gain support for action. That is, dispute exists, depending on the values of different groups, as to what is in the national interest. Having said that, most people would consider spying by an accepted enemy or unfriendly foreign nation to be against our national interest and, therefore, spies themselves could legitimately be spied upon. At the apex of the model would therefore be national security, since collapse in that area threatens social solidarity in a very direct sense. It could result in the destruction of solidarity altogether. As ever, the nature and extent of the threat to national security might be open to dispute – the giving away of military secrets through to the activities of anti-nuclear protestors. The primary function of the state, its legitimacy of existence, is the physical protection of its citizens from outside harm. The state is a military construct. It is also the construct of regulation in a whole variety of areas in the conducting of exchange between its peoples – this would include laws to define what constitutes a crime, to business, trade, employment, educations, health and so on. It might even, and most usually does to some extent or another, regulate the provision of culture. How the state actually regulates, and the extent of the regulation, will of course differ between states, even those of similar constructions. For example, the amount of state involvement in steering the economy, or providing healthcare, is lower in the United States than it is in the United Kingdom. If we take, however, the protection of harm from outside forces as the primary function of any state, then one can see why it should, in terms of social solidarity, be considered that its citizens give a high level of permission for the state to intrude, even invade, the privacy of its own citizens, as well as foreigners residing here should suspicion exist that an individual is a threat to state security, which by extension means the physical security of its citizens. Indeed, in the aftermath of the attack on the World Trade Center in New York and the well-grounded fear of terrorist attacks on Britain following that event, the question of the privacy of the individual as a principle of human rights has been seen not to have the same level of protection that it previously possessed. The threat to social solidarity includes not simply a threat to the lives of its citizens but a threat to social solidarity in the sense of the well-being of its citizens, through economic damage, danger of recession and so on. This moves the claim for the intrusion of privacy, the suspension of individual rights, onto the political agenda, and one might propose that this would have a high degree of support among the general public.

Individual Rights versus Collective Rights

The example above is a classic case of where the rights of the individual to privacy give way to the right of the collective to ensure its safety and its way of life, even if part of that way of life must be altered by extending rights of intrusion into the private world of the individual. It is a trade-off. Using the notion of social solidarity to assist in the understanding of when privacy can be intruded upon, and by what means, does not mean the removal or sidelining of moral values. In the case given, that of national security, then the solidarity under threat is that of physical solidarity – physical survival of the collective – and involves little in the way of moral decision-making. The decision is made almost of itself in the will to remain alive: the community is to be protected at almost any cost, in the process of which values, such as the right to privacy, are damaged. Yet, social solidarity, for the most part, is a question of morals; the continuation of support for a set of values that are commonly agreed upon as the preferred way to live. Social solidarity is weakened whenever the moral framework comes under challenge, be this from the breaking of laws, sexual deviance and so forth. From a functionalist perspective, the purpose of punishment is the expression of values. Punishment may be many things; removal of the offender so that they will not offend again, the attempt at inducing reform in the individual, retribution etc., but it is also, through public condemnation, an affirmation of values. It is a demonstration of what will not be tolerated. It is a moral statement as much as a penal act. This functional aspect of publicity ought to be carried over in viewing the social performance of the media. In many ways, it does precisely the same. In the publication of wrongdoings, of giving commentary to behaviour, it is pronouncing moral stories of how one should live, what the values of our society are – the naming and shaming.

The punishment must fit the crime, and the extent of the punishment defines the seriousness of the crime, which in turn is a statement of values. In fact, we will see in the focus groups that, in the area of paedophilia, the right to intrude into privacy is very high, indeed, higher than in any of the other areas that we presented for discussion. Why this should be so can, at one level, be put down to the sheer revulsion towards sex with children, but what is the vehemence of the revulsion? Undoubtedly, complex psychosexual factors are at work. To have sex with children breaks strongly held values governing sexual conduct and values that privilege children in our society. Children are to be protected in the realm of employment, physical punishment, the awarding of lower responsibility towards the rest of society than adults and so on. Given the cherished status that we allot to children, and the emphasis that we put on sex as an intimate democratic exchange, best captured by the high valuation of romantic sex, then sex with children brings forth absolute vilification and severe punishment. The possession of child pornography, never mind the practice of child sex, is a crime, which has caused great concern over the uncontrolled nature of its publication via the Internet. Paedophilia very much threatens social solidarity, not because of the harm that it might do to the children, but because it threatens deeply held sets of values. It promotes distrust of adults by other adults and leads to the social surveillance of children by parents wishing to protect their offspring from harm. For the worrying parent, the world becomes a dangerous place; less stable through its lack of predictability concerning the safety of their children in the course of the routines of everyday existence. Similarly, homosexuality, or aspects of it, most notably the celebration of a homosexual lifestyle, creates confusion. This is best seen in the furore surrounding the decision to include homosexual sex alongside heterosexual sex as a rightful area for discussion in schools. To do so threatens social solidarity because it confuses ways of living. To promote homosexuality in such a way, or rather to normalize homosexuality, runs counter to cherished norms of appropriate sex, which, in turn, underpin ideas of appropriate social structures, the conjugal family.

Of course, the inclusion of homosexual sex within the school curriculum as appropriate behaviour is not that damaging to social solidarity, in that values are not fixed for all time, they only appear fixed at points in time. The late twentieth and early twenty-first century have seen a relaxation of opprobrium towards homosexuals, which makes the inclusion of such material in the school curriculum less threatening to social solidarity than would have been the case decades earlier. Indeed, when we talk of social solidarity we are not talking of some sets of values that lead to solidarity and others that do not, but values that are held in common which bind people together to provide social cohesion. We are not talking here of total harmony, since, if that were the case and tension did not exist between values, it is difficult to account for social change. Within the dynamics of modernity, the compartmentalization of living and the creation of sub-groups within society, it is difficult to see how any person or group can expect their values to hold good for all others in all directions. In fact, a value that has emerged, to provide social solidarity within a disparate world, is the toleration of difference.

System Continuation and Values

Whilst tolerance to difference is a feature of advanced industrial societies, a functional necessity in fact, equally, any society to cohere requires some agreed principles of performance; in short, an agreed moral conduct. What we will see in the course of the discussion, and, hence, why we consider the idea of social solidarity useful is that people showed a uniformity of agreement concerning that which was socially (publicly) important. The degree of that importance framed the deliberations that they made in coming to a conclusion as to whether it was right to intrude upon someone's privacy. Basically, anything that damages systems, and system continuation depends on value support for the system, was considered to warrant protection, and part of that protection might mean the intrusion into someone's privacy. This must be qualified somewhat. A system can continue where there is not value support for it at the general level, so long as those who do value the system are sufficiently powerful to ensure its maintenance. This is why the term 'the public interest' promotes difficulty in a way that 'social importance' does not; namely, what is the public that is being referred to? Power comes in a variety of forms. At its most fundamental, power is the ability to have others do that which one does not wish to do, most usually through the threat of physical harm. In the liberal democracies of the West, system maintenance is by the collection of agreement to the value of a system, and power tends to be exercised through the ability to convince others of that system, hence, the attention to, and regulation of, the means of communication and its ownership. The advent of the Internet, essentially unregulated, as a publisher of information, can give rise to concern in this context.

In talking of systems one must also include systems of beliefs that are held as valuable and given support. A central value of western liberal democracies is that a person's beliefs are his own and not to be enquired into, or restricted, providing they do not harm or limit the freedoms of others. This value was strongly held in the groups. Whether the value will continue to be held with the same intensity should the populace begin to feel threatened by the beliefs of others is an open matter, especially in light of the rise of Islamic Fundamentalism. One can easily hold to a principle when, in doing so, there is little cost to the self – that no other beliefs do threaten one's security. The young Asian men were not quite so firm on this principle compared to their white counterparts; the beliefs of the far right-wing British National Party being a threat to their security. Indeed, the discussion with the Asian young men showed up the fault lines of the term 'the public interest', in that being Asian and sensitive to racial abuse they offered a slightly different 'public interest' than others. They formed a particular public. Whilst sharing the liberal ideal of freedom of beliefs, they were uncertain as to whether they would extend this right to members of the British National Party. They considered, unlike others, that it might be right to intrude into their privacy, by enquiry into their beliefs, before allowing public appointment as a teacher.

At all points in the course of the focus groups what we discover is that, for privacy to be intruded upon, there had to be good reason. Good reason, as we have endeavoured to illustrate, is dependent upon the social importance of the story. What was impressed upon us was the manner in which, when determining what was important to the point where privacy could be intruded upon, the emphasis was away from the individual and towards the collective. Even where, as we will see from one discussant deliberating whether or not a doctor's privacy might be intruded upon to report on the withholding of expensive drugs from patients suffering from cancer who were very old, the reason given for intruding into privacy was prompted by the thought that one day she would be old and it might happen to her, the collective nevertheless was embedded in the personal. It emerged that although she was talking of her own fears she did so in a way that she recognized her fears would be the fear of others, since we all get old. She saw, in other words, the collective through herself. The story was important because it had social relevance, and permission was given to intrude into a doctor's privacy in order for the journalist to get at the truth. If we cast this in social solidarity terms, then the practice of discriminating against people on grounds of age rather than need threatens social solidarity because, by the very act of discrimination, it has divided the world into the worthy and not worthy. Moreover, to withhold treatment for economic reasons, as became obvious from other participants, undermined the ideology of the National Health Service and the right of individuals to health care, something that is deeply woven into the fabric of our society. To withhold through discriminating against the old threatens social solidarity in the sense that it undermines the idea of community support in times of need. It is to make one a non-valued member of the community and, to treat people only as productive units, runs counter to values embedded in our idea of civic culture. In another group, one participant commented that we had a right to know how the Health Service was being run and, therefore, privacy could be intruded upon, because it was *'our Health Service'*. The Health Service was a social amenity. It did not belong to the doctors or managers of the Health Service, therefore, stories such as the withholding of drugs were socially important.

Public Interest and What the Public is Interested in

By substituting 'the public interest' with 'socially important' the whole mess of what is in the public interest and what the public is interested in is tidied up. People could say what was socially important by simple reference to the collective, either in terms of material consequences or value consequences. For example, the groups discussed the case of a schoolteacher who released details of GCSE exam questions so that he would have a high number of successful students to his credit, and also the case where another teacher had behaved similarly, but this time for the reason that his students came from deprived backgrounds with very poor study facilities compared to students in schools in advantaged areas. The response to both cases was the same in terms of the intrusion into the privacy of the teachers in relating the story: It was cheating, whatever the motive, and a limited degree of intrusion into the private domain of the teacher – for example, showing a picture – could be undertaken. Not to cheat, or gain advantage by preferential treatment, is a value that is held to very strongly indeed. This is value support and also system support. It was considered that to gain qualifications in this manner was not the system working at its most effective. The students would be ill-equipped to perform successfully in whatever job the qualification supposedly prepared them for. Therefore, comments were made that, rather than cheating, the teachers should have worked harder and taught more effectively.

This story, which justified some intrusion of privacy, was clearly of social importance, but was not considered of high social importance because it only involved one school and two teachers – it was not a wrong of a systematic nature involving the whole educational system. To use the term 'socially important' here, rather than 'the public interest', as a defence of the invasion of privacy, seems to show the weakness of the term 'the public interest'. 'The public interest' has the connotation of involving the public as a whole; that is, suggesting national importance. In the focus groups, the participants did not think the story to be of that level of interest. 'Social importance' can capture levels of public interest in a way that the term 'the public interest' cannot, and that is why the idea of 'overriding public interest' adds confusion to the defence of intruding into privacy. If it is in the public interest, then the dramatic connotation of the term suggests that no further defence or qualification, such as 'overriding', needs to be added.

The use of the term 'social importance' has an added advantage, which became very clear in the course of the groups. Because at all times it moves away from the individual to the social, it was easy for discussants to say when a story, although interesting perhaps, was trivial and intrusion of privacy could not be justified. Holding in mind the exceptions that we have made concerning the status of individuals involved, and their conduct in courting publicity, comments were frequently made that a story had no consequence other than for the individual in the story – it did not bare upon, or effect, either communities or the community in general. It was not, in other words, a social story, but one that was, in principle, the private doings of individuals. Those doings might be funny, interesting or shocking, and fun or enlivening to consume, but one had no right to know them at the expense of the individual. Not being social, there was no authority by which to appeal for such intrusion. Such 'private' stories did not affect the social order (social solidarity) or have consequences for peoples lives. One can still raise the point here, concerning social solidarity, that to expose someone for being 'a love cheat' offers a moral tale concerning the standards by which we should live. In the long march of history, however, the promulgation of centralized authorities over how we conduct the intimacies of our life, such as sexual behaviour, forms of entertainment and so on, finds little resonance in contemporary life. The State takes little interest. Even divorce laws have been secularized to remove 'at fault' clauses and the whole idea of a guilty party, even where adultery is involved. Instead, the ground for divorce is the non-moralizing and pragmatic one of irretrievable breakdown, of which adultery might be submitted in evidence but, on its own, is not grounds for divorce.

Secularization of Morals

There has been a retreat from public affirmation of morals, and any attempt to do so in a secularized society has a hollow ring to it, even if cast as broadly in appeal as to Victorian values or family values. The dismantling of the moral regulatory structure is an interesting one, but cannot be gone into here. All we need to note for our present purposes is that the conduct of intimate social exchange has moved to be seen as an intensely private matter. This has followed from the retreat of the State, and the Church of England as the established church, to concern itself in such areas. What in fact we have seen is the undermining of all moral authority to leave no institution capable of pronouncing on intimate conduct. As discussed, there is no mystery here, it is a product of the twin processes of industrialization and urbanization, the latter resulting in a technocratic rationality. Such rationality leaves a reduced place for the judgement of individual moral worth – however, vestiges remain in some occupations where judgement of character is entwined with the job, such as judge, lawyer and teacher. Judgement of character in terms of moral worth has no place when compared to technical or managerial competence in, for example, the IT industry. The private can no longer be brought into the public domain, although one might see political correctness as a flaccid attempt to correct for this void – to be known as a wife beater is still not good. The point is that the intimate has now become truly private, and what one does is a matter of personal preference that requires no approval from the collective, however, in institutional terms, the collective is represented.

If we are no longer accountable for our intimate moral conduct in any public way, then stories revealing such conduct to public gaze find it hard to raise social solidarity as a defence – collective interest being served. They are seen for what they are, and were so in the focus groups, as intrusions into privacy for reasons of entertainment. A story of a priest running off with a parishioner's wife may well, of course, be presented as having social importance, by casting them as part of the wider story of the intolerable strains placed on the Catholic clergy as celibates, and that the Church should modernize, but the veil is a thin one. In the past, where religious sentiment may have been deeper and more widely spread, if the story was used as an attack on the Catholic Church in the name of religious struggle then, yes, such a story would be held to have social importance. The intrusion of privacy could then, perhaps, be strongly sanctioned if it served to damage the standing of the Catholic Church. Indeed, the story could still be given social importance in Northern Ireland in a way not so in mainland Britain, since religious sentiment is largely absent in Britain. This is a good example of the claim made earlier that questions of the right to intrude into privacy, and the defences made for doing so, rest on the morals of society at a particular time. Also, that notions of social importance and notions of privacy change with time.

It is this vacating of the intimate aspects of behaviour from the public stage that can be considered to have heightened the home as the resting place of the private. It is nobody's business as to what goes on in the home. If we add to this, comments made earlier concerning the nature of modern life and how the public sphere consists of self-monitoring activity which one is only truly released from within the home, then it becomes that much easier to understand how individuals in the focus groups construed the private. This, by extension, identifies the domain of the public and has important implications as to the rights that the media have to intrude into people's privacy. Invariably, and we shall see this shortly, the idea of privacy was attached to the home, and one had little right to expect respect for privacy outside the home.

Yet, the 'home' is not a fortress. A degree of surveillance does take place even by the state in some matters, for example, childrearing, but the main intrusion which is objected to comes from the penetration of commerce and business through electronic means into the home. To flee indoors is only to be chased by business. In discussing the objection to this intrusion into privacy we will understand much about how privacy is construed; what the private is taken to mean and, as stated, without understanding what is understood by the private one cannot understand what defences can be mounted for intrusion into it, nor understand the methods that might be used when intruding.

Note
1. The Profumo Affair was a political scandal of 1963 in the UK. It is named after the then-Secretary of State for War, John Profumo, who had an affair with showgirl Christine Keeler.

The Idea of Privacy

8a What are the Limits of the Private? Voices from Focus Groups

This chapter draws in great detail on the findings from the focus groups, dealing with a whole range of issues relating to privacy and the performance of the media. The chapter covers some of the ground already laid out, but in doing so allows participants to the groups to comment at length on points made, whilst at the same time extend the discussions to new areas of consideration. The participants detail how they construe the private and give instances of where and how they considered their privacy to have been intruded upon. This ranges from having their privacy invaded by burglars, unwanted junk mail, telephone cold-calling to the media. The notion of space – of where one might expect privacy to be sacrosanct is examined. Views are also presented on who they consider – types of people – have reason to expect their private lives will not be intruded upon, and who can expect little protection. The limits of intrusion, and the methods it is permissible to use in gathering information, are also discussed. The permissible agents of intrusion are similarly documented – from the police to various media. The events of September 11th are used as a case to discuss issues of taste and decency, news values and public interest. A series of scenarios was used, with participants giving their decisions on whether or not the characters in the scenes had a right to privacy, and if so on what grounds – the notion of public interest is here tested.

The Idea of Privacy
All the focus groups started with the straightforward question, *'Have any of you had your privacy intruded upon or invaded?'* This was not so much to gather examples of intrusion, but, rather, by the examples, to determine how respondents viewed or defined privacy. In the first group, the 18 to 25-year-old males in Leeds, the immediate answer given was:

I've been burgled.

We therefore asked: *'In what way is being burgled an invasion of privacy?'*

If they go through your house, go through your stuff; go through your drawers.
There's documents in there and clothing and you don't particularly want somebody else to have their hands on them. Generally you've got your own drawer, you've got your own belongings and you don't want other people to be reading your letters.

We opened this for general discussion:

I. Anybody else?
My mum's been opening my mail?

I. Your mum opening your mail?
Yes, a few years ago that was.

I. Did you have an argument?
Yes, because when I was a kid my dad opened up a letter and he was shocked at what he was to see.

Someone else added his experience of having his mail opened:

Mine was my mum, she deliberately opened it and claimed she mistook it and thought it was for her, but her initials are completely different to mine, but she said it to try and cover her tracks.

I. How old were you?
About 17 or something like that. I was furious when I found out.

I. Any other invasions of privacy you can think of?
Well, I mean I live in a house full of five people, so you know quite often its hard to get time to yourself, you know you're always spending time with other people which is not ideal, because sometimes you just want to be alone, left to your own thoughts?

This last young man jokingly described his living situation as being similar to that of *Big Brother*, and mentioned *'I suppose my bedroom is the quietest place, but you know, sort of, during the daytime my bedroom is walked in and out of. It's not unusual for somebody to walk in.'*
    The manner in which burglary is discussed indicates that, for these young men, it was not so much the invasion of secure space that was bothersome, but rather that letters, documents and so on might be read or examined. In other words, someone has entered their lives without permission. The term 'breaking and entry' is a nice one here. To have someone enter one's life without permission can, straightforwardly, be seen as an affront, but perhaps disturbance follows from the fact that that entry gives the other person power; he or she has seen personal material relating to the self without having established the right to be trusted with the information.
    Other groups (50- to 60-year-old men in Leeds; 50- to 60-year-old African–Caribbean women in London) also spontaneously mentioned burglary as an example of a form of

invasion of privacy. Occasionally, the break-in of a car was mentioned, although that was not seen to be of the same order of intrusion as entry into a person's home. Nevertheless, it does underscore the idea that to possess something is to make it yours, which others do not have a right over.

There is growing recognition that what is private to you, is a commodity to others. Information has become a commodity. After mentioning his privacy being intruded upon *'when you get some circulars through the door'*, one man in the 50- to 60-year-old male Leeds group continued:

'They seem to know a hell of a lot about you and you get phone calls from insurance companies that know that your car is due for insuring and you've never even contacted this company before.

We asked how he felt about this:

I think it is more annoyance... I suppose you feel the [Orwellian] *'Big Brother' thing that people have access to all this information. I mean you know they do it and they can get it a lot easier now than they used to do. It bothers me. I don't like people knowing my business.*

One man simply added: *'I've never really thought about it to be honest'*. Others had thought about it though:

It is just an everyday occurrence that you get into unfortunately. You either tear it up or you know what it is.

I think a lot of it though is quite well targeted if you look at what actually comes through your door. It's obvious that they know more than you would like them to know. They've a good idea what you earn, a pretty good idea what you do with your holidays, they've probably got a good idea what sort of hobbies and pastimes you have, and you find that you're targeted and they're not far from the mark when you see what's coming through the door. Whether you read it or not is irrelevant. All it says to me is that somebody knows a hell of a lot about me, which I haven't told them about.

We enquired if this had increased over recent years:

I think we're finding that more now with the Internet and computers. You can go on, I mean I can go on myself now and find out different things about people, especially where they live and telephone numbers, things like that, it's just a matter of putting names in and I think it's very easy.

What is being voiced here is a general perception of an increased ease with which information about an individual can now be collected, but what seems to bother some people is the 'selling on' of information between agencies. Again, the main complaint was about failure to seek permission in collecting this information, and of agencies knowing things about individuals that they do not wish these agencies to know. If asked to give the information, they would have refused. The attitude, at times, comes close to viewing this collection of information as straightforward theft – such information is theirs, and theirs alone, not to be taken away from them by others. At the heart of privacy is the principle of 'protected space' that nothing or no one should enter without permission. Linked to this is the idea of publication, in the sense of the giving of personal information to unknown others without one knowing.

The above shows the difficulties of protecting privacy within a modern and complex society. The rise of information technology and its applications has undoubtedly made life easier for many, in the sense of convenience. However, it also means that this entry into the information age – which cannot be avoided, by the use of cards, mobile phones, e-mail and online services – locks the individual into a system of exchange over which he has no control or knowledge of its operations. To live in the modern world is to accept its benefits, but also to suffer depersonalization.

The electronic storage of information and the exchange between agencies presents the apparent increase in the phenomenon of the private space of the home being broken into by unwanted telephone calls. It is the electronic storage of data and the ease of transmission of the data which produces this feeling of intrusion, as does receiving an e-mail from some unknown or unwanted source.

There is little advantage in documenting the full range of intrusions mentioned, but one or two more will assist in showing how, although the private is valued, it is not readily found. Or perhaps, because it is so difficult to maintain a barrier between the self and others, that the home is a place of heightened appreciation as somewhere one can be private. But, as a site of the private, it is hard fought. In the 30- to 45-year-old London male group, one man who did not, apparently, object to straightforward selling, objected to the 'false' conversations that often accompanied a sales pitch. He said:

> *It was someone trying to sell... it is not necessarily double-glazing, it is like they then try and slide in before they actually mention double-glazing. They try to engage you with something else you know... invade my privacy at home.*

However, the 'mystery' of obtaining telephone numbers and breaking the barriers deliberately constructed to protect privacy prompted another man to add:

> *I had a letter from the Labour Party thanking me for voting Labour last time. I thought, 'Hang on... is there a list somewhere as to who voted.' I am not a member of the Labour Party and I rang them up and said, 'I didn't like the idea of being on a list somewhere saying which way I voted'.*

It is not clear as to the precise details of how this actually came about. It is almost impossible that there was a list as described by him. What is more likely, in our view, is that he had been canvassed by the Labour Party at his door prior to the election, and had told them that he would be voting for them. This may then have led to him being entered into a database and then, in the presumption that he had voted in accordance with his stated intention, been sent the letter. What he objected to was, as he said, *'I thought it was private which way you voted'*. Therefore, what seems to bother people is being on a list. A man in the same group responded:

I think my privacy is invaded mostly on a Sunday, by Jehovah's Witnesses who are knocking on the door. They've got lists haven't they? I find that quite difficult when you see them walking along... they actually work from a database.

One has here the idea of lists and databases: the technocratization of the invasion of privacy. It represents the permanent systematic possibility of an individual's privacy being invaded. It is not the happenchance of the voice of God telling the Jehovah's Witness to select *that* door as a source of recruitment, but being picked on by technology, as represented by a list generated from a database, that worries. On a different note, one woman in the 30- to 45-year-old Leeds group mentioned that, in order to protect her privacy, she had *'put conifers all around and a six foot fence'*, which prompted someone in the group to say:

I've done similar — I've put conifers round and the man at the back of my house has chopped them down. He's taken the tops off to stop them growing. I mean that was for privacy because he was always leaning over and looking in. So I thought we'd put conifers up and they were growing really well, but he's nipped the tops and he's told me that the starlings have done it.

These examples, and other similar comments made across the groups, show that people are sensitive about protecting their privacy in the home. In fact, the home is the area where people considered privacy to exist. This has important ramifications for the intrusion into privacy by the media. But, briefly, the idea of the home, despite the obvious breaches documented, was seen as 'liberated territory' from the interests of the outside world. Yet, as we shall also see, privacy could be intruded upon, even in the home, in specific circumstances. It was not, however, the home as a place that ought to be hidden from the gaze of others, in the sense of providing a space for being alone, but the sets of relationships within the home. In some ways, although the home is geographic space it is also conceptual space structured by the intimacy of exchange within that space and the emotional attachments to each other of those living within the space. The privacy of the home, therefore, was, in a sense, carried outside the home in terms of the non-dissolving of the ties that constitute the emotional integration of the family. Thus, concern was expressed, even where the defence of the social importance of a news story justified intrusion of privacy. For example, telephone calls between a person's office and his home could not be listened into, even where that person was a 'legitimate' target of attention, in case conversations were overheard that related to family or personal matters and were not relevant to the investigation. In other words, it is not the home alone as an actual place of privacy that has special claims for non–intrusion, but the world that is bounded by the home in terms of the sets of relationships which reside within it.

Rules & Expectations

It became clear, in hearing the groups talk about privacy, that what is often overlooked in discussing the issue of privacy, and due in strong measure to the legalistic framework of rights that brackets the issue, is the question of sensitivities. That is, that an aspect of privacy revolves around how sensitive we are to others 'bumping' into our private worlds by accident and not design. We might all agree, and most of us would be upset, one suspects, if a postman opened our mail and read a letter before forwarding it to us through the letter box. Independent of slowing down the mail service, the upset would stem from someone with no authority, by which we mean right, reading something that was intended for our eyes only. We do not wish for others to know all our business, although we might not object to them knowing some of our business – it depends how personal we consider the communication to be.

How we communicate has certain expectations attached to it of how it will be received in terms of decoding, but also of who will see or hear it. The difficulty with modern communications is that one is not quite sure who will view or hear the communications. The fax, for example, is not as secure as the e-mail, which is not as secure as the letter. One may have sole access to a fax machine, but sensitive material to be sent where the machine is in open space is often preceded by a phone call with the instruction, 'to stand by the machine'. Yet, in any office, there is a presumption that people will not read a fax or message not intended for them. Whether one does read it, or not, can depend on the relationship of an individual to the intended recipient. Distrust of someone on the grounds of their known devious behaviour may result in the feeling that one has every right to read his or her fax to see what they are planning next. The defence for the invasion of privacy here would be very similar, if not the same, as public interest, or, since that seems to ring a little odd, social interest. One would not consider an office, no matter how large, to be a public space, but it can be seen as a social association with common interests, depending on the degree of stratification, with some communication considered to be of social importance, rather than merely of personal importance. In this case, one might consider that the right of the individual to privacy is offset by an overriding collective interest.

Openness and Privacy
All the groups were asked how open they considered themselves to be with other people. They were asked, for example, how open they would be about themselves if they met someone on holiday and they made friends with them. They were quite guarded about what they would tell the other about themselves in terms of personal matters. Asked if there had been a death in the family, was that the type of thing they might mention, the response from an 18 to 25-year-old Leeds man was: *'In some circumstances, yes, if it was part of the conversation, or whatever, but you wouldn't go out of your way just to make sure that they knew that type of thing'*. A woman of the same age in London commented: *'It just depends on what sort of things come up and what you might have in common as well. Cos, I mean, if they had spoken about their parents you might then lead on something, "Oh, yeah, I lost my father".'*

To ask questions or seek clarification could appear an intrusion of privacy, even though the person relating their life history would, as likely as not, not mind. The information given is just raw data. One might suggest here that some of the discomfort in watching television shots, and interviews, with grieving relatives of those killed in some disaster operates at this level. It feels like an invasion of privacy because we are being taken into the intimate moments of someone's life that we do not know and we have little right to know how they are feeling. We will return later to this question when discussing whether or not the messages from the passengers on the stricken aircraft of 9/11 over the skies of New York and Washington should have been broadcast.

Openness is related to privacy. How open one cares to be will influence that which one considers private. This overlooks the question, however, of who we will be open to; we are not very open to strangers, or to those where, although we have established a friendship, it is not a deep or long-standing friendship. A reporter is a stranger, and so are viewers, listeners and readers. Quite clearly, those who entered the *Big Brother* programme were prepared to be extremely open to millions of unknown others, but we can, in the main, see them as casting for fame. For most, taking part in something like *Big Brother* – with the inability to create a private sphere – would be as unthinkable as it would be psychologically impossible.

However, it appears that modernity has produced increased openness of the self to the world as a means of establishing trust. This cannot be quantified, but the focus groups revealed that increased openness does appear to have taken place within the home; that is, what was once considered private between members of a household is no longer so. This has both a gender and an age dimension. It is worth examining briefly since, if we are discussing rights to privacy, we need to know attitudes towards privacy in the most private of spheres, the home, which might give an indication of attitudes towards privacy in general and what intrusion is considered legitimate.

All the women in the groups who were married, or had partners, knew how much their husband or partner earned. As one member of the 50- to 60-year-old London African-Caribbean women's group stated: *'It's our money, but we have separate monies from each other because I don't want to be saying, you know, you've bought that so I want this – we do pool it together, but we have our own private accounts.'* This openness about income had changed and they attributed this to the fact that *'In the past the man was the breadwinner and he was the one who worked, but I mean now in the majority of families the women work as well'*. The 50- to 60-year-old men in Leeds shared these views:

> I think the system has changed in that at one time the man was always the breadwinner, whereas now, often, in most households it's a joint effort and you know the wife is often working… it's a team effort from that point of view, whereas before the financial side of it was the man's domain…

This is a notable contrast to the account given by one woman in the Leeds group, aged 30–40, of the situation when she was a girl: *'I remember my Dad used to come in and put a set amount on top of the telly or the mantelpiece and she* [her mother] *didn't get any more or whatever'*. Evidently she now handled all the family accounts and said, *'So I know exactly how much he's* [her husband] *got'*.

This democratic image of the household that has produced more openness, especially on the financial side, is no doubt why all those with partners knew how much each other earned. Also, technological change had assisted in opening the private to household gaze:

> And in the way we're paid as well, it used to be cash and now it's all shown and is clearer. It goes straight into the account and obviously if anybody wanted to be secretive about what he was earning then he could but… [it would be difficult]. (Leeds men, aged 50–60)

The increased openness between partners concerning financial matters was extended, in many cases, to include their children. Whilst sensitive to the outside world having information about their financial standing, people appeared to have little concern about their own family possessing such information. This was not that the respondents were sensitive about financial matters, but that they objected to others having this information without permission.

It seemed, at times, that part of this openness was motivated by a desire to make children responsible with money, a kind of training for the future. According to one African-Caribbean woman, she had told her child, *'because he needs to know the reality of money, that's why I told him'*. This seems to be the applied lesson of informing children that 'money does not grow on trees'. Here again, this might be a case of the internal world of the family changing in response to outside pressures.

Nothing works in isolation, and this financial complexity that has resulted in the idea of financial management – money pages in newspapers and so on – to produce, or so it would seem drawn on the experiences from the focus groups, an openness to have children know the financial standing of the household, is alloyed with changes in affinity within the family. As one of the African-Caribbean women said, in discussing the organization of her household:

> *I think lots of things have changed. I think I am far more open and relaxed than my mother, than my parents ever were with me. So money isn't a secret anymore. You change – you know there's certain things that you think well my mum and dad did that but I'm not going to do that 'cos I didn't like it, so you don't include that as part of your life, so to me that's why the changes have occurred.*

Publication and Privacy

The question of publication, especially with developments in electronic communications, is a difficult one. As far as most individuals are concerned, whether privacy can be considered to have been intruded upon is largely a measure of the concern generated by publication. Publication here is taken to mean reception of material by others, to whom it was not intended. The offence can be amplified in line with the scale of the publicity. What must also not be overlooked in examining privacy is sensitivity towards the release of material. The point to emphasize, and one which has great importance for media intrusion of privacy, is that it is not just a question of what right to privacy an individual has, but also what right an individual has to be sensitive to the intrusion. The nature of sensitivity to privacy has changed over time. This is demonstrated by reactions to a relatively recent technological advance that impinges on privacy; namely, the mobile phone. The following comes from the 30- to 45-year-old Leeds women:

> *I don't know if it's classed as privacy – but mobile phones. I've got one, but I hate people talking on them on the bus. They're like just having a conversation with the whole bus. I'm like, 'Just say you'll ring them back' – do it when you're off the bus. You know what I mean? I don't want to listen to this at eight o'clock in the morning.*

We asked if she considered that to be an invasion of privacy:

Yes. I get up and move, I'll go sit upstairs out of the way.
I am not very sociable.
It's like when you're stood at the bus stop and someone comes and chats.

The notion here is very much one of the right to privacy in public. However, it is difficult to disentangle whether it is considered that an individual's privacy has been invaded, or that one is annoyed because it disturbs the peace in the same way that, prior to the Walkman and the advent of the MP3 player, the senses were often assaulted by the blaring of transistor radios. One might consider it bad manners, but is it an invasion of privacy?

In law there is the tort of nuisance and a presumption that one has a right to freedom from annoyance through sound. Even so, rulings show that context must be taken into account. For example, in the classic case of *Sturges v. Bridgman* (1879), it was held:

> *Whether anything is a nuisance or not is a question to be determined, not merely by an abstract consideration of the thing itself, but in reference to its circumstances: what would be a nuisance in Belgrave Square would not necessarily be so in Bermondsey...*

Perhaps, therefore, the deluge of junk mail received and the telephone cold selling should be classed as a nuisance and not an invasion of privacy. And perhaps it is reasonable to expect, in high-density urban living, to face the sound of people talking over mobile phones; it is not a nuisance and neither is it an invasion of privacy. But this will not do at the experiential level.

We asked whether overhearing mobile phone calls was an invasion of privacy, or just an annoyance:

I think just annoying.
I think it is the other way round – that you are sort of somehow invading their privacy.
Yes, you're listening in.
Yes, cos you do listen.
They're not quiet.
I was just going to say I think it's natural to listen in.
Yes, especially if you're on a bus and it's all quiet. You can't help but listen.
No you can't.
It's like you're invading them.

The idea of invading *someone else's* privacy by listening into conversations is intriguing and goes some way in helping unpack the detailed aspect of privacy. The intrusion of privacy in the above accounts entails annoyance that one is not left in peace to get on, unmolested by the presence of others, with how one wishes to travel. It might be compared to the intrusion of an advertisement when all one wishes to do is get on with watching the film. However, if one elects to watch the film on commercial television there is little reasonable ground for complaint, in that one knows that advertisements will appear, but that does not safeguard annoyance. It is expected these days that a journey by public transport will be interrupted by mobile phone calls. Yet, the annoyance seems different from that. It seems also that it is the presumption that an individual's private world can be 'forcibly' imposed on the private world of another that annoys. Whether one can say that mobile phone conversations invade the privacy of those not making the phone call, or even vice versa, is not for us the point. What the discussion shows is that the idea of privacy is a contested area.

Whether mobile phones offer an example of the invasion of privacy, or are simply the rude intrusion of a noise that grates in the way that the booming laugh might do, what we see at work are definitions drawn from ideas of appropriate behaviour. Some consider it an invasion of privacy and others do not. This then leads us to a very interesting consideration of privacy and the performance of the media; indeed, how the media themselves might lead to a reconfiguring of what the private is taken to mean. If listening into the mobile phone conversations of others embarrasses a person, then it would, perhaps, be expected that they ought to be embarrassed by watching *Big Brother*, finding it somewhat uncomfortable, even if gripping in the way that the women quoted found themselves listening into the mobile phone conversations. *Big Brother* shows how ideas of privacy have changed, or, more precisely, what private behaviour it is now permissible to see. It is difficult to imagine, even a decade ago, that *Big Brother* would be acceptable fare for mainstream television. Acceptable here is used in two senses; acceptable in terms of taste and decency, and acceptable in the sense that viewers would accept it sufficiently for it to gain a satisfactory audience size. Something has occurred: definitions of appropriate behaviour and acceptance of publication – in the broadest sense – have changed.

The groups' estimations of people who volunteered for *Big Brother* were less than flattering. They certainly did not consider the filming in any way an invasion of the participants' privacy, because *'they volunteered to do it'*. It was considered that *'they wanted the publicity'*, but most of all, *'Everyone who goes on it are full of themselves and showy anyway, so they deserve it'* (Leeds men 18–25), meaning that they had no right to complain even if their privacy was invaded. Enjoyment of the programme was mainly restricted to the younger groups. There are many reasons why older viewers should not enjoy the programme as much as younger viewers, but, primarily, the age of the participants and their concerns were the concerns of a particular age group. It would be hard for older people to identify with any of the members of the 'cast' or probably even recognize them as 'type' in a way that younger people could.

Physical Privacy

At the physical level, the need, if not actual right, to privacy in the home has increased over the generations. Young people's demand for their own space has grown; a space that, with technological change, can form a self-functioning place of residence; namely, the bedroom. The television set in the bedroom, the computer, telephone, either as landline or as a mobile phone, and so on, mean that the bedroom is no longer a place simply to sleep, but a place to live in, and be private in. The feeling given in the groups was that this was not simply because people might be in a state of undress, but due to the recognition of its special significance as belonging to the individual who sleeps there. As one of the older men from Leeds said: *'My son's just been back home in the last twelve months. I wouldn't go in his bedroom. I'd give him a shout, give him a warning that I was coming in, but I wouldn't wait till he* said, "Come in". My younger ones, my daughter definitely, when she was about fourteen. "Nicola, hello, can I come in?"' Clearly gender differences enter, but in terms of embarrassment to his daughter such sensibilities appeared misplaced: 'On the other hand my daughter she walks about in the nude, she sits on the toilet with the door open and I say, "Nicola, close it"'. Even so, he said, 'Yet, I still knock on her door'. The younger London women (aged 18–25) gave the clear impression that their bedroom was theirs, and out of bounds even to their mothers, other than to the most perfunctory entry. Asked what they considered a really private area of the house, all members of the group responded, 'bedroom'.

This concept of the closed space within the home is in sharp contrast to past times: all the older men from Leeds (aged 50–60) said that when they were young no such space existed for them: '[Our homes] weren't that big in some cases, so you had no choice'.

Only in one group, the 18 to 25-year-old Asian men, was there a marked difference on this topic. Their bedrooms sounded more like a continuation of the rest of the living space of the house: the household was closely knit and this closeness precluded the allowance of distinct closed space. This absence of physical privacy appeared not to bother them. When asked the opening question put to all the groups, 'Have you ever had your privacy intruded upon?', this was immediately countered by one participant with a question, 'In terms of like parents or what?' We simply replied, 'Any invasion of privacy', which set the group off talking about their parents entering their bedroom. One man said: 'Well personally, yeah, especially my parents. They can come into my room whenever they want to. My privacy is invaded at times, but I'm not too bothered about that, especially if it's my parents'. Asked as a group if this bothered them, there was general agreement that it did not.

Talking to this group, an image was offered of households that were internally very cohesive, but not particularly open to the outside world; indeed, this may, in part, have assisted in the cohesiveness.

In discussing the idea of privacy, a clear distinction emerged in this group of young Asians between 'home' and 'outside', in terms of which events were public, for out-of-home use, and which were reserved for the immediate family:

Personally there are some things that I would like my parents to know and some things I would like my friends to know, but not my parents. It all depends on what it is really.

I wouldn't like to tell my friend what's happening at home, because I would like to keep that at home.

And then whatever happens outside, if it's not important, I won't want my parents to know about it, because it's not important and it's not affecting them.

It's the same for us, y' know what I mean, you don't want to tell the private things to your mates, about your family and everything and if you get up to anything outside you don't want to tell your parents. Especially if it's bad.

What one witnesses is a very closely shared life, and this shared life extends outside the home in terms of parents wishing to know what their offspring are doing. The outside world is brought into the home in the form of 'intelligence', but family matters are not taken out to the world. On personal observation, this seems the reverse of young white adolescents where the goings-on in the home, the misunderstanding of them by parents, is the subject of detailed and agonizing discussion outside the home with friends.

One of the most obvious changes that has occurred in public spaces is the rise of the CCTV camera. In all the groups, the general principle of CCTV was welcomed, albeit with specific reservations. The older men from Leeds (aged 50–60) all supported the use of CCTV cameras. Having mentioned that he was wary about the type of financial information companies collected on individuals, as discussed earlier, one man commented: *'I think that* [CCTV] *offers security as much as you're being watched kind of thing – visibly watched. I prefer that kind of security that maybe deters crime'*. Someone else added: *'I think they are great personally – if you have got nothing to worry about'*. As a check to see if such a response was age-related, that perhaps older people felt more worried about personal security, the same question was put to the younger Leeds men (aged 18–25). Their response was the same; all agreed that to have cameras in city centres was a good thing: *'They do it on the streets of Leeds and there's people walking around, but it's for the public, isn't it'*. *'It's to catch thieves. To stop violence'*. When it was suggested that they might be captured on tape themselves, the response was that the onus was on the individual not to be doing things that would give cause for them to be bothered: *'If you shouldn't have been doing it, then you shouldn't have been doing it, so it's your own choice'*.

For most, this idea of an individual's movements being captured on camera had a straightforward pragmatic base – it was a good technique for ensuring personal safety.

However, the statements by the young Leeds men show elements of appreciation of the eradication of crime as a general good. As one young man expressed it, in supporting the presence of cameras: *'It's for the public, isn't it'*. It is but a small step here to move from the idea of CCTV cameras operating for the benefit of all – having a social benefit and thus social importance – to the media and the grounds upon which it might be said to be justified in intruding into someone's privacy. Intrusion can be justified where a claim to social benefit is made, or where it is in the public interest.

It is also clear, and again this is important for where and how the media can operate when it comes to privacy, that the group did not consider open public space to be areas where the notion of the private held sway. There was nothing to intrude upon, and those who had a need to be concerned were only those who were behaving in an anti-social manner. The continuous surveillance of open public space was, therefore, not a problem and, indeed, without constant surveillance, the effectiveness of the protection of the public would be reduced.

Yet it was discomforting to consider that one might be under constant surveillance in the immediate home neighbourhood. This was seen as restricted public space and an extension of associations with the home. In the cases where there was support for such 'intrusion', then it was invariably based on protection against crime. One individual in London, although he said his neighbourhood was a safe neighbourhood, nevertheless supported the placement of CCTV cameras in his street in the belief that it might stop bottles and fish and chip paper being thrown into his garden – he was a particular victim of such debris because his house was stationed at the precise distance from the 'chippie' where most people on their way home would finish eating. In short, it depended upon the type of area one lived in and the incidence of crime and anti-social behaviour, or, perhaps, on the simple fear of crime.

The 30- to 45-year-old Leeds women were, like others in different groups, divided about supporting surveillance cameras in their street. One woman did not want CCTV in her street on the grounds that, *'I just don't want people spying on you all the time'*. Another woman was equally certain that she did: *'Well, there's many people go around burgling houses and pinching cars and things nowadays. If my car went missing it'd be caught on camera'.*

There is also here an element of the intrusion of privacy, the idea of being spied upon. But this is not necessarily a negative point. For example, the 50-to 60-year-old London women were in agreement with having CCTV cameras in city centres for the reason: *'Well, for your safety as well as anybody else's'.* Interestingly, however, another woman added her support on the grounds that *'They can't accuse you of stealing or anything or abusing someone's child or anything. If you haven't done it... it's a very good way of checking up on things'.* It is a piquant comment on modern society that this woman should feel the necessity to have a record of her 'non-doings'. To remain private, in other words, for this woman, is not to be protected, whilst to go public and be on record is to be protected. A whole tract of social history could be written here, but it is suffice to say that a complex world requires records. Without records on an individual then the individual becomes invisible and, being invisible, cannot take part in, or take advantage of, a complex world. To live in the modern world is to live in a surveillance society. Evidence of existence is the record. The idea, therefore, of a recording of her non-doings offering protection against accusation of that which she might wish to deny moves the idea of privacy into a different sphere of consideration.

Community

The public, the community and society are all concepts, and concepts do not talk, only individuals, but, in talking, people do so using concepts, which may include, as a way of categorizing or organizing reality, those concepts. It must be said from the outset that the term 'community' does not appear to be an organizing category of thought, or, at least, was not found to act as such in the focus groups. Communities, in the sense of collective identity, tend to exist only where there is no escape from a common condition, so that the interest of one is the interest of all. Geographic mobility, occupational variances and so on make such communities largely a thing of the past only existing in isolated pockets and, where they do, they are likely to be areas of economic depression – by definition, they are not modern.

This notion of community, so that one can then talk about a community of interests, was picked up by the African-Caribbean women in London when they explained why they did *not* see themselves as forming a particular community with special interests. This came about following the opening discussion relating whether or not they had had their own privacy invaded. Here, filling in the then recent census form emerged as a clear example of invasion of privacy: The seeking of certain information about them was considered to intrude into their privacy, especially the ethnic origin question. It must be noted that the last census was the first time a question had been placed on the census enquiring into a person's ethnicity. The group as a whole had definite opinions on this:

Yes, the descriptions I thought... I remember crossing it all out and putting what I wanted to put. I can't remember, there was something like... was it Caribbean or African like that. Black African. Black Caribbean.

West Indian.

I think it was just West Indian. I don't think it had Caribbean. I crossed them all out – sometimes people don't actually... classify themselves as West Indians. I've never classified myself as West Indian. That lady could be a Caribbean or... it means the same thing! Well it doesn't really cos its different...

...I won't say West Indian because of the history of the word – the Caribbean isn't the West of India! So I wouldn't call myself West Indian.

I wouldn't say it was an intrusion, but I didn't like the classification. I thought basically it should have been thought out. I can understand the reasons behind asking a lot of the questions.

The woman who made the last comment above was asked what those reasons were:

Well I suppose they want to know the ethnicity of people within a particular area or so I could go along with that... they need to make up the picture of the area and also they need people's needs which is probably... if the needs in certain communities need to be met they need to know how many is in the country and where they live and so forth, so the census form is fine. I happily fill that in, it's other things that you know... 'cos I feel it's a good purpose if it can be used in another way also.

We said: 'We often talk about community you know, do you feel a part of the community?'

Absolutely.
I've never really given it a thought. I suppose I think that as part of the community where I live... for the first twelve years of my life I was in Enfield, but I feel it's where I live and if it's the community of Enfield then yes I feel part of it 'cos I've lived there.

I. Not an ethnic community?
   There isn't, as such, an ethnic community in Enfield. It's just part of living in England. You can't really pinpoint an ethnic community in Enfield [...]. I think the issues that affect African-Caribbean people, you identify with it and you can identify with it on the prospectus that you are a non-white person, you know in the white community, if any issue that comes up that affects you as a non-white person, as a black person obviously you are identifying with that. In terms of community, in terms of where you live, I think generally speaking you know you can live in London and not really know your neighbour.

All members of the group gave support to that statement.
  She then continued by saying: '*So I wouldn't consider myself part of the community in that sense of the word, where I live, and I know who lives across the road by sight, doesn't mean I know them,*

doesn't mean I am part of their community in the sense of community, no'. It was put to her whether or not she considered, if seeing herself as an African-Caribbean, she had *'special interests that are different from other people?'* to which she responded: *'Em, it depends on the individual. It really does because some African-Caribbean people might have something in common and some don't. I just don't know… it is an individual thing'.*

To tease out feelings of further identity that then might give a community of interests, we mentioned that there had been a similar group of Asian people in Leeds, which offered a different picture than the one being painted by the London African-Caribbean group:

Well, I don't physically want to live in the same area… I would like black communities to integrate.

I agree.

Not really assemble ourselves together in a group, I don't like that.

Well, yes a lot of it is all about religion too, and religion is the disturbing thing that goes on. In Caribbean communities we have different religions, whereas in some Asian communities they will be of the same religion.

Yes.

Here is a recognition of, but not agreement with, what are increasingly referred to as 'faith communities'. At the same time, there were some issues raised which were directly relevant to this group, precisely because of their ethnic origins:

If you live in a local area I think you should have some concern about access to education, about the number of African Caribbean children.

Yes.

At one time the idea was, certainly when I was a child growing up in this country, the adults still have that attitude that they were going back so the stake in the community wasn't the same that I have in the community. I'm not going anywhere so therefore I have concerns about healthcare for the elderly cos I'm going to be one, or my family, so I have those concerns and I have those concerns from a black perspective so I think it is an issue.

The Asian young men in Leeds did have a sense of community beyond that of neighbourhood – using neighbourhood to mean an association with an area of residence rather than, as community, having interests in common that bind a group together which may stretch beyond the immediate neighbourhood. The word 'community' was used, for example, when one Asian male participant said: *'I personally feel safe in, you know, my own community and that. It's my own area and I feel safe in it'.* But one could see that, although he did have a feeling of community in a sense of distinctiveness, it did not extend to exclusive immersion in the community. When asked if they read any Asian newspapers, the *Eastern*

Eye was mentioned. But, when followed by the question *'Is it any good?'*, the reply came: *'No, personally, it just talks about mainly Asian stuff'*. It was generally read for the sports news: *'All the newcomers, good boxers, and good cricketers and everything and all sports kind of people, they'll be in it'*.

The Media and Privacy

In any discussion of the intrusion of privacy by the media we first need to clarify what is understood by 'the private'. The advantage of discussing attitudes towards CCTV cameras is that it has allowed us to arrive at a three-way classification of the private; namely, **open public space**, **restricted public space** and **closed public space**. Strictly speaking, the latter is not public space at all, but is useful to use in creating the idea of a continuum of privacy, where open public space rests at one end and closed public space at the other. In practice, of course, it is not always easy to say, with absolute precision, what actual point of the continuum we are looking at and, therefore, where it might be permissible for the media to enter and publish material gained from that sphere. It must be stressed that the existence of this continuum is not an absolute predictor of the acceptance or non-acceptance of publication, as a dependent of the part of the continuum from which the images or material have been collected. It operates as a guide for saying, in the sense of alerting, when a defence for the intrusion of privacy may be necessary or, more expressly, instruction as to when a defence is necessary because that is where the private rests. It is the breaking down of what is meant by 'private' into its component parts that is so essential in judging the performance of the media.

Every group was asked: *'Think of all the media; television, radio, the newspapers, magazines, which would you say intrudes the most in people's private lives?'* The responses to this question are not very interesting, in that they were fairly predictable. In all the groups it was the newspapers and popular magazines that were singled out as the worst offenders, but it was considered that all media invade people's privacy to some degree. To use just the 30- to 45-year-old Leeds women as an example: *'Newspapers'*; *'Newspapers'*; *'Probably newspapers'*; *'OK magazine'*. Even so, this last was a qualified judgement: celebrity magazine *OK*'s coverage of the Beckhams was an example offered by the group, but the rider was added, *'The Beckhams are maybe not much bothered who knows about them, but definitely what is known.'*

The increase in the intrusion of privacy that people are referring to may be no more than a reference to an increased willingness of people to be famous, or willingness to court attention. In short, there are simply more stories around. Generally, the groups had little sympathy for those people who, by virtue of their position, had deliberately projected themselves into the public gaze: *'Well, I think some people deserve to be.'* *'Yes, some ask for it.'* The difficulty was, as one 30- to 45-year-old London man said, referring to celebrities: *'A lot of them go out asking for publicity and don't like it when they get publicity they don't like.'* He then added: *'I don't know whether that is justifiable or not.'* There is a sense of fairness here. Even though there is not much sympathy for the promotional antics of many celebrities, there is an almost grudging acceptance that even they may have claim to privacy.

Types of People and Privacy

It is one thing to consider that the media have increased their intrusion into people's personal lives as if this were a product of pure media activity, but this misses the social context within which the media operate. They are not responsible for the wider social shifts that have taken place, that have led to a revaluation of self-performance and an altered appreciation for performances. Clearly the willingness of the media to exploit these shifts is there, but that is no more than to say that they have a keen understanding of markets and public appetites – both feed upon each other. In other words, the increase that participants perceived in the intrusion of the media, especially newspapers, can in some ways be accounted for by the changes that have taken place in how people define appropriate behaviour; what characteristics have come to be valued. In terms of privacy here, we are not talking about the unfortunate priest who has strayed from the path of sexual propriety, indeed, the very fact that he would consider himself to have a path to stray from, in the sense of his calling, marks him out from the modern world and its values, but of the increased number of people for whom display is an important part of being considered successful; is, in fact, success itself. We are not talking simply of those who have made a profession of display, but of a changed disposition towards the presentation of the self and a rise in a set of values that sees fame, unattached to any qualities that might be worthy of recognition in a fundamental sense, to be respected.

Rather than look at behaviour, status of the individual and so on, which invariably thrusts one into the realm of value judgements, it is more useful, because one can arrive at analytical and descriptive statements, to focus on the areas within which privacy might be held as operating. Here we go back to our closed, restricted and open public space. Following this, having determined the privacy expected of certain spaces, we can then address the questions of where space itself cannot be entered as a defence against entry into that space. Namely, that the right of the individual, no matter what the space, gives way to rights of others in their claim to enter that space. It is the rights of 'other' here that is essential, since journalists themselves have no right of entry. They draw, in the same way that a politician does, their authority to act by reference to those they claim to represent. It is also the case that, even where the journalist acts with such authority, the behaviour itself has not been authorized.

In all the groups, the role and practices of the media were examined in some detail. Some individuals had direct experience of the consequences for individual privacy through encounters with the mass media. One woman from the 50- to 60-year-old London African-Caribbean group drew upon her own encounter with her local newspaper:

My middle daughter [aged 13 at the time] *got hit on the head by a pole in Enfield, in the market. The stalls have canopies and they were never bolted together... and she was in the market shopping and a gust of wind took the canopy and the pole hit her in the head, so there was a big hoo-ha as you can imagine and the ambulance and the fire engines squealing and what have you and one of the stall holders told the local* Daily Advertiser, *so the next minute the journalist arrived at the hospital to find out what was going on and he wanted to know what happened, where she was born, what... everything. My daughter is in there, she's been hit and she's been hurt, and he's asking me all these sensational ideas... the newspaper. I didn't feel that he was in the least bit interested in my child, he just wanted a story.*

The conversation went as follows:

I. Do you think that this was a story that should not have been printed?

Well, I do think it should have been printed. It was printed, and because of it the environmental health people had to go into the market, and now those things are bolted together so the actual canopy thing can come off, but I think he was just talking to people and he could put words into my mouth – he was talking to an anxious, angry, frightened mother, and I was not pleased.

I. What should he have done?

If he'd at least come in and asked how was she, he came in and he was – was it, your daughter that was hit on the head, was she bleeding, is her head... it was all what are the worse things that could have happened to her, how bad is it, because it was to report how bad it was, not that generally that he cared. He just wanted to report how badly she was hurt and his manner was just so offensive.

I. Do you think that was an invasion of privacy?

Well it was an invasion of privacy because he just came storming through – no one invited him in there and he just thought well I've got the right to come and ask anything I want to.

I. You're saying your privacy was invaded, but at the end of the day it was right that they did it, although you didn't like how it was done – because some public good came of it, yes?

Yes, it was just sensationalizing everything.

I. So he wasn't doing the proper reporting.

No. Because of it some good did come of it but... [the coverage] *did say what should have been done, because they did ask us what do you think should be done, there must be a way that these things can be done so that doesn't happen again and, because of it, it will start to get better.*

It is far from clear-cut what has gone on here. It may be that the reporter simply had an unfortunate approach to people; that he was rude, abrasive and so on. The asking of her age and other details about her, whilst construed as an invasion of privacy on the woman's part, is, after all, the stock-in-trade of any local journalist, be it the reporting of the winner of some home-made jam competition, or the victim of a hit-and-run driver. It is always, 'Mrs so and so, aged X', and, indeed, as any junior reporter on a local paper knows, the age must be correct and the name spelt correctly. That is simply a trade practice and style. Even so, such style does raise issues, to which we will return. She also considered her privacy had been intruded upon *'because he just came storming through, no one invited him in'*. We do not know if he asked hospital staff if he could interview the woman, but, even if he had, the women herself did not give permission, nor was her permission sought.

The other charge is that he did not appear to be concerned at all about the well-being of the woman's daughter, only her fate in the sense of the extent of her injuries. This, again, may only be insensitivity on the part of the journalist. She also raises the issue that she felt that words were being put into people's mouths and that she was in a state of considerable anxiety and upset. In other words, she was not quite in control of herself, or, at least, was not in her normal state of mind. She did strike us as a fairly feisty person, who it was difficult to imagine easily losing control, but then it was her daughter that had been injured; as she says, she was an *'angry frightened mother'*.

The key charge against the journalist is one of sensationalism. He was not interested in the version of the story that the mother was interested in, judging by the account given by her. Who, in other words, owns the experience leading to the story? In this case, it is not as if there is another story to tell – that the subject of the story is hiding something – and, therefore, the journalist has every right to take the story from her and treat it as his own. But, she was pleased with the eventual outcome of the story, in that corrections were made to how the stalls were erected, and this safeguarded the likelihood of similar future happenings to other people. On this ground, accepting the mother's consideration that her privacy had been invaded through the asking of personal details, which she considered irrelevant, and the sensationalist interest in the extent of the injuries, the defence of public interest, or in our terms social importance, can readily be used as justification of any intrusion. Unless the journalist was interested in the public safety aspect, then it is reasonable to say that the mother owned the story, and in owning the story was not prepared to give permission for the use of interviews to sensationalize events. Her privacy had been intruded upon, but in a much more complex fashion than asking the mother to reveal details about herself. The end result was, however, agreed to be for the public good.

Importantly though, while public interest was clearly served in this case, and thus intrusion upon the woman's privacy perhaps justified, at the time of the intrusion the journalist may not have known that the story would turn out to be one of public interest. To raise the defence of public interest in its strongest sense one might consider that the journalist had to have reasonable grounds for considering that the story was likely to turn out to be in the public interest.

The above might seem a somewhat minor example, but it was not a minor incident to this woman who had been subjected to particular newspaper practices. Principles can be discerned from a story like this that allow wider consideration of the issues under examination. One of the crucial principles here is the manner in which individuals are 'used', which, if in accordance with media practices nevertheless give rise to offence and feelings of intrusion, is the question of the state of the individual to consent to their privacy being intruded upon. This appears particularly important when examining grieving people, which will be discussed further later. The other closely related question is the persuading of someone to give consent to their intrusion of privacy, which begrudgingly given, but nevertheless given, results in a feeling of loss of control; that they never truly agreed to what follows by the granting of consent.

The Face in the Crowd

The 30- to 45-year-old London male group spent some time discussing privacy in open public space and some of the issues involved. One man observed:

Everywhere you go now you are faced with cameras on the roads, every building, shop you go in.

He raises the important suggestion that we are, perhaps, used to being captured on video without our permission having been given. It is part and parcel of modern living. It was, nevertheless, recognized by another man that people caught up in a crowd scene that was then shown on television might feel uncomfortable, but that they ought not to. His reason:

> *I mean I know they are individual people in the shot… they are just an illustration… the people might find themselves disturbed by the photo but the rest of the world's looking at the whole event.*

This is a nice point. What he is suggesting is that the egocentricity of the individual makes him or her oversensitive to their appearance in a crowd shot, when, in fact, nobody else is really looking at them. To the unfamiliar eye, they do not exist as individuals, they are, as he says, *'just an illustration'* – it could be anybody making up the scene. But, depending on how a scene is shot, intrusion could follow. One man said:

> *If it was a football match and they took a picture… they saw someone behind the goal… if there was no comment made about the people in the background it is not an issue, but if you are watching* Match of the Day *and they pan on the crowd and they focus in on some individual, that is intrusion.*

> *But being at the football match you must know you are open to being viewed by a camera.*

What he is saying here is that, in buying a ticket for a game, it is almost as if it is a condition of the ticket that one might appear on television – one agrees to being filmed by virtue of entry to the ground.

Thus, even in open space it is possible to intrude into someone's privacy, but it is doubtful that, in the case of a football crowd, even if a close and perhaps lingering shot was taken, it would be considered to be a significant intrusion. Nevertheless, such statements do indicate how intrusion is construed. It is different from CCTV cameras because of the nature of the 'publication'. The CCTV camera recording is essentially private publication, with very few – if anyone – seeing it, whereas publication by television involves being viewed by many.

Following the comment about *Match of the Day*, another member of the group offered the following example:

> *Two or three seasons ago a friend of mine, Arsenal supporter… and I think they had just lost the lead and lost the chance of winning the championship – I laughed, he cried. The cameras panned in on him and the next day* Virgin Radio (Chris Evans) *put out a call, 'Does anybody know his name?' Right, that's my oldest friend and he said, 'I don't want to go', but he ended up on television on* TFI Friday […]. *The cameras, it must have been Sky, was it, he was crying his eyes out. He is 38 years old, crying his eyes out, blubbering. He is a great big bloke, blubbering his eyes out 'cos Arsenal aren't going to win the championship and my brother-in-law was watching TV and he phoned me up and said, 'Howard is on the telly'. He was on about 30 seconds or something, they zoomed in on him. I must admit he said it was really embarrassing, but they actually put a call out on the radio the next day and 'Anyone know this man?' and people were phoning up and saying, 'Yes, it is Howard'… but he got a good reception when he got back to the Arsenal when he sent in for his season ticket.*

We asked if he went on *TFI Friday*.

> *He did actually, he relented and he went and had a really good day, they treated him well and he got drunk and held up the League Championship trophy or something.*

Evidently, the picture of him crying also appeared in the *Sun* newspaper. We asked: '*So your friend, did he consider, when he saw that picture of himself crying, did he consider that an invasion of privacy?*' He responded, '*I didn't ask him, but I know he was embarrassed*'.

To be embarrassed in such a way is clearly an intrusion of privacy. As agreed, no one considered that appearing as a member of a crowd at a football match was an intrusion of privacy; it was to be expected. However, it was not expected, or accepted, that they would be singled out for special attention, especially at a moment of emotional breakdown. True, he then in a sense became an accomplice to his own fate by agreeing to appear on *TFI Friday*, but a hunt was on for him. It takes little, in the circumstances, to imagine the pressure, no matter how friendly, that resulted in this person agreeing to appear on the show.

The idea of being singled out for attention was mentioned on several occasions in relation to privacy. In the same group, another man gave a further example:

> *I mean, a friend who I used to work with, his family were totally shocked because they were watching the television one day after an IRA bomb in London and they zoomed in on a bloke being put on a stretcher in an ambulance and it was his brother and they didn't know anything about it and they had this full-frontal, full-face going on. Luckily he was all right.*

Asked if this was an intrusion of privacy, the response was:

> *It was for the bloke on the stretcher but it was also a big shock for the family isn't it, cos they had been frantically phoning around trying to find out what was going on.*

We asked: '*Did they need to show his face and the pain in his face?*'

> *Probably live was it, live telly?*

> *You should perhaps put yourself in the journalist's position, they want to show the pain, to show how bad the IRA are I presume, so I mean, they are obviously balancing things. I think they tend to get it right overall.*

One cannot accuse this group of being unreasonable, or failing to understand the issues involved in covering a tragic or dramatic event. They are very aware that the story has to be told – it has social importance; a bomb exploding in the capital city with people injured by a group that has used terror as one of its major political weapons. Not showing the devastation would have meant not covering the story. Similarly, to not show the consequences of the act upon those caught up in the blast would also be not to cover the story.

Doubts are, though, clearly cast upon whether or not a close-up picture ought to have been transmitted of one of the injured as he was 'stretchered' away. It was considered an invasion of privacy for *'the bloke on the stretcher'*, but concern was also registered for the shock that such an image had on the parents of the injured, who on seeing the picture *'were frantically phoning around trying to find out what was going on'*. Yet, there is an appreciation that such pictures are necessary and they give the journalists credit, in the sense of attributing to them the desire of trying to show *'how bad the IRA are'*. The conclusion is that television tends to *'get it right overall'*, by which is presumably meant fulfilling the function of relaying events in a manner that captures the horror of what has occurred. Leaving aside the obvious concern relating to the parents, it appears that privacy could be legitimately intruded upon here to the extent that it was necessary to capture what had happened. Also, if the victim had been wounded in the street – open public space – another consideration comes into play, inasmuch as people do require public events to be open to public inspection. It was not simply the bomb exploding as part of a terrorist campaign, but the consequences of the political on people innocently caught up in the struggle.

Right to Privacy versus Expectations of Privacy

The previously discussed idea of distinguishing open public space, restricted public space and closed space offers a means of conceptualizing the type of situations where privacy is felt by people to operate under specific conditions, and can help in indicating what their expectations of rights to privacy would be. Indeed, 'expectations of privacy' may be a more appropriate term to use than 'rights to privacy'. Such expectations are illustrated by another example.

Given that celebrities are often photographed relaxing on holiday, we wished to know whether or not such activity represented an intrusion of privacy. The manner in which this was approached was to ask members of the group if they would consider it an intrusion of their privacy to be filmed or photographed on holiday.

One of the 30- to 45-year-old Leeds women related what had happened to her at the seaside:

We were actually filmed in Whitby years ago. When the kids were really young we'd gone to Whitby and the kids were on the donkeys – we saw them filming on the beach and about six months later this programme called One Summer in Whitby *came on, there we all were. On the beach, on the donkeys. The 'phone never stopped ringing all night – everybody had seen it – it was amazing. They showed it again two years later and we got the same people ringing again. It felt weird.*

Rather than ask if she considered that such filming had been an intrusion of her privacy, we simply asked what her response was:

Oh, I was really embarrassed. It was awful. People even shouted in the supermarket, 'We saw you on TV' and everyone's looking to see who it is. It was awful. I was just so embarrassed.

We enquired, *'what was the nature of the embarrassment?'*

Seeing yourself on TV and thinking, 'Oh God, do I really look like that?'

Pressed to consider, *'Is that an invasion of privacy?'* she replied:

I suppose it is. They didn't ask for our permission.

We again asked: *'Do you consider that an invasion of privacy?'* No direct answer to the question was forthcoming. She simply said: *'They just carried on filming and we walked on'.* Not willing to give up on the opportunity presented by this case, we said: *'You don't think that was an invasion of privacy? – you were just embarrassed?'* Her answer was: *'I was embarrassed. I never thought about it being [an invasion of privacy]'.*

What do we conclude here? Although she knew that she was being filmed, she did not connect that fact to the possibility of her appearing on television in sufficient close-up so as to be immediately recognized. As with the Arsenal supporter, she was not in the background. As innocent as this activity was, it is quite clear that she would prefer this private pleasure not becoming a public spectacle – she was embarrassed. Her privacy was intruded upon, in that she did not wish for such exposure, but at no time does she really define what happened in any intellectual sense as her privacy being intruded upon. She sees the whole situation in terms of embarrassment, which is a response to the invasion of privacy, to publication of the private.

In comparing the two situations, although embarrassment may have been the outcome of both, the beach scene was harmless. There was nothing for the individual to be ashamed about and a good deal of joking took place among the participants about the situation, reference being made as to whether the donkey was embarrassed. Thus, in deciding whether something is an intrusion of a person's privacy, one has also got to consider whether the individual had the right to feel his or her privacy was invaded. 'Right' here is not to be taken in the sense of freedom, or in some legalistic manner, but whether or not one ought to be that sensitive, and whether any harm was done in the sense of hurt feelings. Context is all.

What came across strongly in the groups was that places such as beaches were public places and, therefore, the idea of privacy was not really operable. At worst, pictures or filming were low-grade intrusion. Furthermore, acknowledging space as a public place meant that one regulated one's behaviour.

The African-Caribbean women also recognized the fact that open public space was not theirs to control. For example, one woman said:

...I think from the time you step out the door you have to resign yourself to the fact that you'll be on somebody's camera somewhere, in the same way that once you've put something on the computer it's not private anymore.

In other words, one did not do things that might, if captured on film, be harmful to one's self-esteem, or cause shame in the eyes of others. The young men in Leeds, aged 18–25, perhaps in line with earlier arguing about changed attitudes towards privacy, were very relaxed about being filmed on a beach. We asked: *'What if you were on a beach sunbathing, unaware someone is making a programme on, say,* Corfu, What a Scorcher... *and you appear on the news, would that be an invasion of privacy?'* The answers were unequivocal:

It's the same as the city centre.

There's people milling around all the time.

You're in the public; you chose to be there yourself. You know that everybody can see you, so you're not hiding anything from anybody. Most people like being on camera anyway.

The idea of *'most people like being on camera...'* certainly demonstrates a different attitude to publicity than the previously quoted women. The attitude may well be an attitude of youth. The young men also considered that, although one might be caught in situations that one would not choose to be caught in, any 'downfall' that occurred was your responsibility for having taken the risk of, so to speak, 'going public':

There's a good story about that actually. Someone we knew once was away for a week sick and during that week they were on the front page of the Yorkshire Evening Post *drinking a pint and it was saying how good this pub was and how it had won the best pub in the area this week, and he was there, main man. Yet, he'd been thought to be off work sick that week, so that was quite a good story.*

We asked, *'Is that an intrusion into privacy?'*

That's tricky 'cos... if he's stupid enough to pull a 'sicky' and get himself caught, like on video cameras and stuff, then he's asking for trouble.

In other words, individuals must take responsibility for their actions if in open public space. Someone else said:

You know the risk.

This was added to with: *'It's like on the beach. If you go there with someone you shouldn't be there with there's always the chance that anybody on that beach is going to see you'.* What appears to be being said here is that what is open to the eye of other people is open to the eye of the camera; there is not much difference.

The group was then asked whether it would be different if they had gone for a walk in the countryside on a hot day and found a secluded place by a river to swim – a restricted public space – and they were filmed. Would that be an intrusion of privacy?

I think maybe it would be if you were out in the middle of nowhere expecting that there's nobody about, then you're gonna do different things to if there's a lot of people about.

There was little doubt really that this was an intrusion of privacy:

If it's blatantly obvious that they are taking pictures, say for the news, and they're blatantly taking pictures in front of you when there's another 270 degrees they could take the angle from, then I think that it's an invasion of privacy.

The countryside example was considered an intrusion of privacy, but not the Corfu example. The latter was acceptable for, as one young man put it: *'You're not in the privacy of your own home though; you're out in the middle of a public place'*. The beach is open public space; the countryside, providing efforts are taken for seclusion, is restricted public space.

The London women in the same age group offered similar views about the beach. It was put to them that if they were happy enough to have others view them on a beach, it was difficult to see the objection to a wider audience. This may be a gender difference, but the focus was about how one looked:

If you are going to be sunbathing half-naked anyway you must be quite proud of your body. It's like if you are happy enough for everyone on that crowded beach...

Again, however, there are caveats, in that the public nature of the beach does not give *carte blanche* to the photographer or the film crew:

As long as it's not like a picture of you on your own on the beach, generally they are like pictures of like so many people that...

Yeah, I mean if it was just like one or two people on a beach they can't take a picture of you then.

What is being said is that a story can be illustrated by taking a picture of them on the beach, but the picture cannot be of them alone so that, in a sense, they become the story. They must not be the focus of attention. The isolating of the individual is to intrude into a person's privacy, even though the site of the picture is an open public space. It takes the person out of the context within which they are a member of a collective – a public. Focussing on the individual transforms their own experience – a shared activity – into a photo-shoot, something they have not agreed to by entering a public place, nor, and of equal importance, something they might expect. As with the young men, they considered it an intrusion of privacy if they were photographed in a secluded riverside setting, for the reason: *'They have gone out of their way if it's secluded – they have gone out of their way not to be seen'*.

Privacy and Audience Reception

It appears that to find a quiet spot in the countryside is to find anonymity, and to enter an open public space, such as a crowded beach, is to find anonymity by being lost in a crowd. One of the young women in the London group mentioned that she had a child aged two, so it was put to her whether she would mind if a picture of her daughter splashing around without a bathing costume appeared in a newspaper or was filmed. She was adamant that she would object. Asked why, she replied:

Just because I personally would not like my daughter photographed.
It's like the people reading it — you don't know.

What she is suggesting is that, although a child splashing about in the sea with no swimming costume on might illustrate how hot the day was, in the same way that adults sunbathing would, the way the picture taken was viewed by unknown readers could well be different. The unequivocal suggestion was that a reader might have a questionable sexual interest in viewing the picture. This concern was raised when the same scenario was put to the London group of men aged 30–45.

Although not the point of our question, it was taken at first by one individual in terms of taste and decency. He replied: '*It would offend some people I know. It wouldn't offend me personally*'.

For some, the topic seemed to touch a raw nerve, which one suspects is a relatively recent development from coverage of paedophilia.

I'm always quite wary of taking pictures of children in the paddling pool... something in the paper about going to the chemist and getting the pictures back...

That happened to Jan Leeming.

I thought it was Julia Somerville.[1]

Oh yes.

You've got to be so careful, innocent pictures. It depends what you are using them for, but I wouldn't want one published of my daughter [...]. What reasons are there? I think that has changed. We are much more aware of paedophilia now anyway, possibly veering towards paranoia. If someone was taking a photograph of my child then I would certainly want to know about it.

Confusion enters here. At one point reference is being made to how careful one has to be taking pictures of one's own children, in that the charge of paedophilia is an ever-present threat, and then there is the taking of a picture of one's child by others for publication. In the latter case, there was no way this would be sanctioned. Although not expressed this way, it is seen as a true intrusion of privacy because one, so to speak, never consented to the pictures being viewed in the way that some people might view them. Again we come to context. The 'toddler' splashing about in a rock pool on a hot summer day without clothes is, almost like the donkey ride, or the bucket and spade, part of the English summer beach scene.

The importance of the disquiet concerning the publication of such pictures is that the climate within which their reception takes place has changed, and changed dramatically, from the past. So much so that one of the men was clearly concerned about taking pictures of his own children naked; pictures that in the past were stuck into nearly every family album. Of course, this might be said of the picture of a crowded beach, but not in the same way. The picture featuring a single individual can more easily be read out of context than a crowd scene of a beach, even though individuals might be recognized.

The picture of the crowded beach of sunbathers, or swimmers, still carries the context within which it was taken. The individual was part of a scene, and not the focus of attention, and to be singled out for attention is to change the reception of the picture. In the former, one is asked to look at the totality of the picture within which the individual is submerged, whilst, in the latter, one is asked to look at the individual as the subject. At the time of the picture being taken, the individual on the beach was not the subject of anything, but rather part of, and presumably feeling part of, a collective gathering and collective experience. Although the experience is individual, as all experiences are, what one experiences is structured on and through the surroundings, which, in so far as open public space is concerned, means other people. The individual is not the main object of attention.

If this reasoning is accepted, then, when people complain that their privacy has been intruded upon by a picture of them being published, the anger of the complaint is more than likely to be accounted for on grounds other than the straightforward desire to be left alone. It is likely to include feelings of anguish or embarrassment at how the picture might be read, and it matters little whether the picture is flattering or not.

Changing Times

What is seen in the raising of the spectre of paedophilia is the point made in the opening sections of this book; namely, that to understand the issue of privacy it is essential to understand the nature of the society in which privacy is defined. Changes in society will be reflected in changes in the idea of what it is to be private. As stated, it ought to be handled in the same way that taste and decency is handled: that different periods will generate different levels of acceptability towards images. It might be concluded, as research by media regulators has shown, that acceptance of nudity, and sexual portrayal, has changed, even in the recent past. That change, however, is not even, and does not necessarily entail, what might be termed a 'liberalizing' outlook. We can talk, in other words, of the context of a picture, meaning how it was framed, its location and so on, but we can also talk about the context of the times; that is, the emotional mood with which a picture is viewed.

Intrusion and Permission to Intrude

Fictitious examples based around the police and journalists were used to explore when and why permission might be given for entry into the private world of the home. The purpose of this was to examine tolerance to intrusion depending on the status of those intruding and acceptance of intrusion into the privacy of others. What we were looking for was how people negotiated privacy in concrete settings. It is one thing, for example, to hold to the idea of privacy as a right, but another thing to hold to that right in situations where it seems 'sensible' to give up that right, or make accommodation for the claims of others. From the outset, however, the claims of authorities are judged in terms of the status awarded those authorities, but also in terms of the claims put forward for intruding into privacy; roughly stated, the interests that will be served by intruding into privacy. The scenario below was presented to the group of 18 to 25-year-old Asian young men:

I. The police knock on your door and say they have reason to think you are handling stolen goods and would like to look around the house. Would you let them in without a warrant?

The answers ranged from *'Probably not, no'* to *'No way'*. The reason given for not doing so was: *'They don't have authorization to come in and search it'*. Whether they would cooperate was a matter of mood, not of principle: *'It depends if you're in a bad mood. If you're in a bad mood then if anyone asks you something then you say no. Or you're in a good mood and having a good day then...'* It would, however, appear that they would be more willing to co-operate with the police in a search of their car. The difference in response was that, *'You see your home is where you've got belongings and stuff. In your car you've just got your jacket and tools and your cricket bat'*. Here again is a clear formulation of what makes the home private. It is associated with a distinct personal zone captured by the idea of where *'your personal belongings and stuff'* are kept. This response, of not allowing the police access to one's home without the authority of a search warrant, was practically universal to all the groups.

The session then continued with a variation on the original scenario:

I. The police come to your house and say they have reason to believe that the people living next door are planning a robbery and they would like to eavesdrop, to plant a bug in your house to listen on next door. Would you let them?

They were not quite so unequivocal on this. *'No, I wouldn't.'* *'No, I probably wouldn't.'* *'I'd think about it. I don't see any reason why not.'* The hesitation in allowing such access was given by one participant as: *'Well if the police found out that they were wrong and if your neighbours found out that they used your house and that... they won't feel safe with you around. They'll think that you don't care about their privacy.'*

There are some interesting points here, related not just to media intrusion, but intrusion in general. To begin with, the intrusion into privacy requires that you are right to intrude; that is, one has good grounds for believing that something is wrong and requires investigation. This is captured by the statement *'if the police found out that they were wrong'*. The surveillance of others cannot be a 'fishing expedition'. There is also the element of the duty to protect the privacy of others, captured by the statement *'They'll think that you don't care about their privacy'*.

But when, for these young men, does caring about the privacy of others cease? They were presented with a case where the police asked to use their house to observe the activities *'of crooks across the road'*. The idea of community now featured strongly in their responses: *'If they're trying to help the community you should give them a chance and let them try'*. *'If it's good for the community at the end of the day, they could be planning to rob my house, or they could be robbing a bank and putting the money in my back garden.'* Caution was offered: *'The rest of the community is going to say, he doesn't trust his neighbours'*. Much was made of how well one got on with one's neighbours, but the key point is that here, once more, a sense of community emerges. Despite reservations offered by some of the group, intrusion could occur when to do so was to protect the community's interests. The evidence for the existence of a community is not simply extracted from the fact that the term is actually invoked to defend a practice, but that the community exerts a socializing effect. For example, the statement *'the rest of the community is going to say, he doesn't trust his neighbours'* indicates that he cares about the judgement that members of the 'community' make of him. By extension, the fact that he cares makes him a member of the community. Within his neighbourhood there is a shared set of assumptions about what is and is not the correct mode of behaviour, and to break the rules of performance faces him with the prospect of sanctions – disapproval. Indeed, there is the suggestion that he would no longer be a trusted member of the community. Communities of this nature have a collective conformity. In such a situation, but we did not find it elsewhere, it is possible to speak of a community of interests and use those interests as a defence for the intrusion of privacy. However, the existence of a community of interests such as this does not mean that it is right, in some wider sense, to intrude upon the privacy of another. It may be, as already discussed at the philosophical level, that the values of the community, when subject to reason, are held to be wrong. At the sociological level it might be that the interests of a community, underpinned by a set of shared values and norms, run counter to the interests of other communities and, in the most general sense, the wider society. Thus, the notion of a community of interests as a defence for the intrusion of privacy is, to say the least, problematic.

Although the interests of the community were raised as a defence for allowing the police to use their house to intrude upon the privacy of neighbours believed to be robbers, the support for doing so was not without question. Yet much of this remaining reticence vanished in the third scenario:

I. What if you believe there's a paedophile living next door. What if the police came and said not a robbery, but they have reason to believe there's a paedophile? Would your response be any different?
Yes, that's a bit more serious.
I mean, if you've got kids of your own and then you don't care what the neighbours say, you say, 'Yes, go ahead'.

All agreed: '*I would too*'. '*Yes, I'd let them in.*' We replied: 'So there becomes a threshold, a point...?' '*Yes, there does, yeah.*'

In popular consciousness, paedophilia has come to form an organizing point in grading human conduct, a summary statement of behaviour that is incontestably wrong, of which the person so charged has little, if any, right to claims of consideration that might extend to other wrongdoers. What we see here, therefore, and we witness it in other groups, is a set of values coming into play that deny the paedophile what is generally held to be the human right to privacy, if, in fact, privacy is held as a human right, and it most generally is. All rights, however, are circumscribed by behaviour, and the right to privacy is no different. Our difficulty, and the central question of this part of the study, is in what circumstances can a defence for the intrusion of privacy be mounted. The one most open for consideration is if where to do so is 'in the public interest' – leaving aside for the moment the difficulty that we consider the term raises. For something to be 'in the public interest', to stay with that term, then it presumes that some kind of threat or harm is avoided by intruding into privacy, or, perhaps, by doing so, a general public good has been promoted, in the positive sense of promotion. It is in the public interest to protect children from the attention of paedophiles, but what is unclear is the extent of the threat to children from paedophiles. We might wish to consider that the satisfaction of a psychological state might be in the public interest: hounding and vilifying some group, in this case paedophiles, produces a collective feeling of well-being.

The value of the above discussion is that it again assists in emphasizing that ideas of privacy are socially dependent – they change with time and change with changed circumstances. It also emphasizes that the holding to of sets of ideas might be considered to be in the public interest, and that the intrusion of privacy of those who hold counter ideas to the generally accepted, or dominant, ideas might also be considered to be in the public interest in that it reinforces social solidarity. This is something that perhaps needs to be taken on board in light of the events of September 11th in New York: that it might be held to be in the public interest to intrude into the beliefs of others, not because the holders of those beliefs might be terrorists, but because the beliefs themselves come to be seen as threatening a way of life. That is, that political events push for an interest in what other people believe.

The Agent of Intrusion

The perceived importance of the issue, in this case paedophilia, clearly produced a shift in attitudes towards allowing the police entry to their house to intrude upon the privacy of others. But, also, in allowing the police entry, this gave permission for entry upon their own privacy. Taking this most extreme case only, on the grounds that if it did not apply in this case it would not apply in lesser cases, the Asian men were asked:

I. If a newspaper wished to expose them [paedophiles]... what would your response be to allowing a newspaper in?
I'd be a bit sceptical about that.
They're just looking for a story aren't they?

Given comments made earlier about newspapers, especially the tabloids, indicating that they had a distrust of their readiness to intrude into people's privacy, we asked:

I. What if a television crew came, let's say, from the BBC?
Same sort of thing, isn't it. When the person gets exposed on TV or whatever, he's going to find out where it's come from, d' you get what I mean.

If the police are dealing with it, it's private. They don't let it out to the public do they? They don't let it out to the cameras and that.

We follow this by commenting:

I. So you're saying that you would help the police because it would be kept private, but if you helped the TV it's invading your privacy as well as theirs?

This was agreed, and we asked: *'Because your role would be proven?'*: *'Yeah'*.

The police are looking after you, but television isn't – they are there to make a programme.

We did try to avoid contaminating the discussion by telling them to imagine that no one would know the source from which the information came, but this proved impossible. Participants could not rid themselves of the thought that others would find out that they had allowed their house to be used by the media for observational purposes. No matter. What did emerge is most interesting. There is a great deal of suspicion about the intentions and actual behaviour of the media in general, television included. Although they consider paedophilia to be a serious matter, and for that reason would allow the police to use their house, they did not consider that the media, in an intentional sense, were operating for the public good, but rather *'just looking for a story'*. Of course, good can come from poor intentions, just as bad can come from good intentions, but the fact is that the media were seen to be operating from their own interests and not from the public's interest. This was not the case with the police. The impression is given that the media would not be that bothered to protect their identity, that their concern is simply with the story.

Again, the feeling gained is that they see the media as self-serving and self-interested. From the media's point of view, if this feeling is correct, and is generally held, then it is deeply worrying. It is worrying, particularly in a regulatory sense, in that, for a media organization to raise the defence for the intrusion of privacy on the grounds of public interest, it has a hollow ring. From a propagandist position it becomes difficult for a media organization to take the moral high ground in defending its practices by appeal to acting in the public interest if it is seen to be acting out of self-interest. Of course, the intrusion of privacy might well serve the public interest, and the audience might well agree in very obvious cases, for example, the exposing of practices that threatened the safety of rail passengers, but the problem arises in introducing the defence in cases which are not so clear-cut. In short, the lack of credibility, that the interests of the public are at heart, rather than the desire for a good story, undermines the defence – it looks specious.

Suspicion of the Media

The reaction to paedophiles amongst the 30- to 45-year-old London men, some with young children, was particularly strong. Indeed, there was a rather robust attitude towards policing in general. Even so, they were suspicious about the media intruding into people's lives. They were asked if they would let the police into their house without a search warrant. This, one man explained, would *'depend on the attitude of the copper'*. To support this, one man said, in terms of whether or not he would cooperate: *'Whenever I've been stopped – if one [policeman] gets stroppy, I get stroppy back, I can't help it... actually coming into your house, I don't think I would let them'*.

> *Say they are trying to eliminate white cars from certain garages and they say can I have a look in your garage, possibly. But can I go in your house and go through your drawers no way. If you are talking about the whole house, no way.*

We might term a garage restricted public space, depending on how the garage is used and its relationship to the house. In general, these men would not allow their house – private space – to be used by the police for eavesdropping where there was suspicion that the neighbours might be planning a robbery, although one man said he would if *'it went through the proper channels'*. Interestingly, he would allow his office – restricted public space – to be used by the police for surveillance purposes:

> *At work I did a similar thing. They wanted to film the court next door 'cos some people were up on a charge and they wanted to see some of their [colleagues]... researchers came to the court and they wanted to film them and they set the camera up.*

In judging whether or not to allow intrusion into the privacy of others, the seriousness of the supposed offence enters, and the consequence of the alleged behaviour for them personally:

> *Paedophilia – I find that more threatening to me personally, I would react differently than if you put a listening device on the wall to listen about a robbery. I couldn't give a toss about a robbery, but listening device on the wall to hear about paedophiles and my children...*

His support for such action was underpinned by the fact that, if he suspected such individuals were living next door, he would take direct action himself. *'I would tell the people next door, hey, the police think you are a paedophile, so get away. So I would find that helpful to me and I would alert my neighbours as well, straight away. I wouldn't wait for them to get information. It would be more a vigilante approach to that in answer to your question'*. The existence of a paedophile living next door was considered to alter the way he lived his life, in a way that the existence of a robber would not: *'Would you let your kid go out in the road or play out, you would completely alter your life if the police told you that, whereas if the police said to you its a robbery...'* Others in the group were clearly not in full support of his response to paedophiles and the idea of vigilantism. Someone said, in referring to vigilantism, *'I think that is dangerous'*, to which he replied, in an intellectual rather than threatening manner: *'I know, but we could get into a very big argument'*. Nevertheless, despite the stridency of his position, he would not allow journalists to eavesdrop. We thought he might, but he claimed not.

> *I would still react in the same way... one or two innocent people suffer because there is a vigilante approach to the paedophile scenario. I would react very strongly. I wouldn't let the journalists... I would say you can print anything you like, expose these people, even if they are not guilty. I would fuel the situation for the protection of my family.*

Puzzled by this response, we asked, *'Why not, you said a policeman you would, but not a journalist?'* He replied: *'Because journalists like to sensationalize... police should be informed and involved and if the newspaper has enough suspicions... they should be sharing that with the police'*. At no point did we attach the term 'journalist' to a particular medium; it is thus of some note that he should readily attach the term to a newspaper. This may not necessarily indicate that it is newspapers that are associated with intrusion into privacy; it may simply be that the term 'journalist' is identified with the print medium, rather than radio or television. We can extract a few things here. His sheer aversion to paedophiles assists his willingness to allow the police entry to his property to eavesdrop on next door. Even so, although he was in agreement with newspapers exposing paedophiles – *'print anything they like'* – he would not go so far as to allow his house to be used for the purposes of gathering information. That, for him, was the job of the police.

Journalists & Interests

It is the job of the police, not of the media, to protect against crime. This is not to say that the media ought not to inquire though: *'they* [the media] *should be sharing that with the police'*. This 'sharing' of information suggests a move beyond that of giving information over to the police following the completion of a story. The key, perhaps, for his reluctance to give an investigative or surveillance role to the media, although he appears to have the press in mind when he talks, is that *'journalists like to sensationalize'*. It is difficult to say why he would object to this, since he admits that to get things wrong – *'one or two innocent people suffer'* – is acceptable to him, if to *'fuel the situation for the protection of my family'*. Accuracy is not the point then, and one might argue further that sensational reporting is non-accurate reporting; that is, it is more concerned with impact than what actually occurred, or, if that is too harsh, overemphasizes aspects of a story, playing on the emotions, to the detriment of intellectual understanding. The suspicion is there, as in the case of the Asian men, that the reference to sensationalism is a reference to the media being interested in the story and not concerned with the interests of the public. It operates from self-interest rather than public interest.

In discussing the defence of intrusion 'in the public interest', what emerged from all the groups was a consistent doubt about the media themselves, most notably newspapers; that what they do is largely done out of self-interest, even though it might be in the public interest. In other words, they are not really to be trusted as the carriers of anyone's interest but their own. Hence, the police, who are trusted as acting on behalf of those other than themselves, are empowered with a right to intrude into privacy beyond that associated with their strict technical role of upholding the laws of the land. They are seen as operating in the public interest: something that the media – especially the press – have failed to convince people about. This lack of belief presents a very real problem for the media in mounting a claim for intrusion into privacy by way of the defence of public interest.

At no point are we imputing a lack of idealism, or of an ethic of service. All we are saying is that, from the comments made in the focus groups, the media are confronted by a great deal of scepticism as to their motives in pursuing stories. The danger rests that for a medium, which fails to convince that they are acting in the public interest, in the sense of being for the public rather than themselves, the defence of public interest at best looks thin, and at worst raises questions concerning the actual authority of the press to intrude into privacy at all. It is something that requires address. For example, in following through the above scenarios with the African-Caribbean women, the message of distrust towards the media came through strongly. There was also on their part, and this included policed operations, insistence that material, where possible, must be gathered by means other than those involving intrusion into privacy.

Rights of Entry and Right Methods

The African-Caribbean women did have a sensitivity to formal rights, and a strong sense that privacy was important. They realized that open public space was not theirs to control.

However, the right to intrude still carries with it a further consideration – the methods used to get information, especially where these are surreptitious. For example, among the African-Caribbean women, even when the police are the agents, the surreptitious gathering of information was not generally welcomed – *'there must be other ways of doing it'*. If this right was not extended to the police, then for journalists to gather information in such a manner it was very weak indeed. Attitudes differed a little in some quarters when the case of a paedophile was raised: *'My reaction would be, "Go away".'* *'I wouldn't under any circumstances because I've only got their word for it that they are paedophiles, you must as a neighbour see something strange.'* What this woman would want is corroborating evidence. Another woman, again illustrating the sensitivity towards paedophiles, and how attitudes to privacy can shift depending on the emotionality or seriousness of an issue, commented:

> *My reaction would be different if it's something around child abuse or that, my reaction would be different to a robbery or mugging or something... I won't say I would do it, but I would strongly consider it.*

Her position, unlike the woman who wished for corroborating evidence, was that child abuse was a hidden crime:

> *They abuse these children all the time even within people's houses you know and nobody knows until this child gets to be an adult and then they tell – so you should help.*

This was added to:

> *Yes, but like she said I wouldn't say yes straight away but I would have to see, it would make me stop and think whereas other times it would be no, this time I would take a step back and I would think about it and consider it.*

This equivocation did not extend to journalists: *'Not a journalist, no'*. *'Not a journalist.'* When it was put, *'He's doing a serious investigative piece'*, the answer was still the same. Outright entry was not forbidden: *'If it was about the paedophiles and he was with the law, but I wouldn't just let a journalist in, no. Not on their own.'* When we asked, *'Why not?'*, the answer was:

> *I'd want to know that they were doing things properly. Not that the police always do things properly, but I'd want to know that everything was covered because a journalist would use all kind of underhand methods to get what they want and I would like to know that they are within the law and I'd still have to consider it, and they'd twist the truth.*

In case they had tabloid journalism in mind, rather than broadcasting, we asked: *'So what if it was the BBC though, they came and said we're doing this big documentary exposing child abusers'*. Back came the reply:

> *They're journalists as well. I would still say no to that because, again, I think it's because it's the media, because so many times you hear blah blah blah, and a week later it's all change and you know*

but only a week ago they said this and now they are saying that, most people are very wary of the journalists.

News Values and the Public Interest

We are dealing with perceptions of realities here and not actual reality, though perception and reality may well join. The point to stress is that the image of journalism, from evidence presented so far, is not one that puts them in the position of presenting themselves as operating in the public interest, even though the outcome may be that what is reported is in the public interest. Indeed, from this same group, the story has been relayed of how one of the participants considered the journalist who reported the injury of her daughter to have intruded upon her privacy and been not at all, as far as she was concerned, interested in her daughter, only the drama of the event. Nevertheless, she considered that the outcome was of importance – in the public interest – in that it led to improvements in how market stalls were erected in the future and thus saved injury to other people. Yet, matters are not uniform, and this is to be expected; trust is uneven between the different media and between organizations.

The group of 30- to 45-year-old Leeds women gave a slightly different emphasis to the question of the intrusion of privacy, by both journalists and the police. This group also shows that their considerations of what the media can do are clouded by considerations of how they do it. Also, it should not be supposed that people do not like to know the private goings-on of others, otherwise the popular press would hardly be popular. Much of the news is made up of human interest stories, which, on the surface, do not appear to offer justifiable public interest grounds to intrude into privacy. To explore the area of human interest stories being capable of falling into the category of public interest stories we presented the case where a well-known TV star, who is known to have a terminal illness, is on holiday looking very thin and desperately ill:

I. 's that a story that should be picked up?
No.
No.
They probably would. Well they will. They take photographs and publish them, won't they.
Morally it's not right.
What about John Thaw? He's that age.[2]

I. OK, John Thaw.
I think you'd like to know.
I think you'd like to know they were ok, but not the way they'd do it.
Not the way they would do it.
It makes them look bad – well, not bad, but y' know.
In a nice sort of way, yes.
But they do it badly.

I. Could you take a picture of him and print it?
Not if he's on holiday.

No. That's invading.
But I'd be intrigued to know what they looked like. I would. So I could go, 'Oh, my God'.

We enquired: *'Should they ask this person's permission to take photographs?'*

Yes.
Yes.
I think so, yes.

I. Do you think they do?
Definitely not.
No.
They're spying on them.

The group of Asian men were particularly informative and articulate on this topic.

I wouldn't go out of my way to buy the newspaper to read it, but if I saw it was in there then I might have a look. Actually, it depends on who the superstar is.

Even though it's like getting into their personal life it is of interest to the public, y' know what I mean?

You know what it is if he or she then dies you're like, 'Oh, why didn't you know, why wasn't it in the papers?'

You know when you're following a TV star, you know so much, you know through papers about his life, yeah, you sort of do feel that you know him – y' know what I mean?

It should be in the papers when it gets to that point, when it's really important that people should know, like the fans.

The other groups did not differ in any real respect in their opinions.

Intrusion and Curiosity

Within this discussion there is an 'analytical' position – *'morally it's not right'* – and also an 'empathetic' position that admits to wishing to see a photograph of the ill person – *'So I could go, "Oh my God"'*. The latter was not intended in any venal or hostile sense, the respondent wanted to feel sorry for the victim.

Unravelling responses in an area as multifaceted as privacy is a complex matter. Part of this complexity in practice is that rights to privacy interact with questions of taste and decency. If the story was done *'in a nice sort of way'* the feeling is that, although privacy might have been intruded upon, it was acceptable to do so because the public had a strong interest in that person. The question here is whether this is in the public interest or simply a matter of what the public is interested in. Again, we come to the difficulty of the term 'the public interest' and its conceptual limitations in handling actual cases.

At this level, therefore, it is not true to say that these stories about, or pictures taken of, celebrities and so on have no importance at the social level. They do have genuine social importance for a variety of reasons. They have social importance because people consider them important, which is a better-qualified way of saying that such stories are what the public is interested in. Indeed, adopting a functional perspective then, such celebrity stories can assist, and which is why they can be classed as socially important, with psychological maintenance. The death and funeral of Princess Diana in 1997, for example, showed that the media had a massive role in articulating and choreographing people's emotions and actions, but not necessarily reflecting any clear issue which was 'in the public interest'.

One of the 18 to 25-year-old women from London, in discussing pictures of celebrities that are ill, said:

That wouldn't make me feel so bad because I think they are normal, if things like that happen to normal people, people do die, people do get ill and look desperately ill and thin. And I think to myself, 'Well at least they are only human' and I know you are dying but at least they are human and it's not just, they are sort of like still got their gorgeous looks and massive boobs and stuff, they are looking ill. I would read that and think at least they are normal.

Such stories are reminders of some essential features of life. Her mentioning of *'gorgeous looks and massive boobs'*, is noteworthy for its suggestion, in the context given, that life is also made up of other things. One does not wish to overplay this, since clearly people considered questions of taste and decency at such moments when intruding upon someone's privacy. However, the point must be stressed that what the public is interested in, when reformulated in terms of social importance, as laid out, is not to be dismissed as grounds in mounting a defence of intrusion. That is, the public's interest may well have social importance in the sense of people finding out what other people's life experiences are like, but is unlikely in any adjudication to qualify as 'in the public interest'. Despite this, not everyone rejects a limited degree of intrusion in such matters.

The older men from Leeds, aged 50–60, were asked if they had seen coverage of the Jerusalem wedding disaster that was discussed in the interviews with the media personnel and regulators. They had seen it and could remember the incident:

Oh yes.
Yes.
Forty-two killed.
It was a tragedy, wasn't it?

We then said: *'Some say this was an invasion of people's privacy, showing people screaming, Would you defend showing that? Do you think it was right to show those pictures?'*

You see that to me is a newsworthy item. Not that it's spectacular, y' know, but it's something that's happened that people are concerned about. They're showing concern. You don't necessarily have to show all the gory details... they can just edit certain items out, couldn't they?

Y' know obviously we're interested if a certain number of people have been killed in an accident. It's just human nature that you would show an interest in something like that.

We responded by saying: *'But what is the point in showing this?'*

Well, I suppose it's what's classed as news. It doesn't happen every day does it? It's a one off. If suddenly a wall falls down.

We think could we have avoided it, can we avoid it again? Like these people caught up in fires in the night. That does need publicising. There is no escape route.

It's basically something out of the ordinary.

The above participants grasp news values very well indeed. However, the important point to be taken from this is that not all intrusion into privacy appears to require the defence of being 'in the public interest'.

This brings us squarely to the operationalization of the question of the media's performance and the defence of something being in the public interest to justify the intrusion of privacy. The very term, 'in the public interest', forced us to select, for detailed examination, areas that regulators considered to be in the public interest. What it shows is that the term 'in the public interest' does not allow for a very sensitive scaling of issues in the way that social importance does.

From the focus groups, both in the earlier and the later studies, it became clear that the key to understanding the processes and concepts involved, and the interactions between them, was complex and subtle. Accordingly, we decided to use a more complex method in both the qualitative and quantitative levels of the second study. A detailed fictional, but life-like, scenario was created, involving the National Health Service (NHS) and ethical and professional behaviour linked to the question of the cost of treatment under the NHS.

Public Interest and Social Importance: The NHS Scenario

Each group was taken through one particularly detailed scenario, fictitious but based on similar real-life events. The case selected for this detailed enquiry was the National Health Service and the scenario was introduced as follows.

The NHS has issued a secret instruction telling doctors that they must not use an expensive new drug treatment on older patients suffering from cancer, and can only give it to younger patients. Some doctors are obeying this instruction, but others are disobeying.

Each group was asked a series of questions relating to the scenario, providing a framework and focus for the detailed discussion of the various issues and elements involved. The same scenario was also used in the separate national survey stage (Chapter 8b).

- Level of personal interest in the story
- Level of public interest

- Acceptable methods for obtaining information
- Appropriate media for publication of story
- Acceptability of possible consequences

The first question put to the groups was: *'Is this the sort of story that the media should cover?'* Of that there was no doubt. For example, among the young (18 to 25-year-old) Asian men:

Yes.

Yes, definitely.

Oh yes. Especially for all those families that know this may happen to them. If they know that less expensive drugs are to be used on older people, they have the same right as young people.

This was followed by asking how interested they were personally in the story, on a five-point scale from 'no personal interest' to 'very high personal interest'. This scale was used as a device to focus discussion on the matter in hand. All, apart from one man, had high personal interest, with one participant opting for little personal interest. His low personal interest appeared to be accounted for by his age. He explained his response by saying:

My mum's 45, but I don't really sort of bother with it because there's nothing I can do.

We are not quite sure whether he was referring to his mother's age and, by extension, ageing in general, or his inability to affect the outcome of decisions taken by authority, probably the latter.
We asked, however: *'But you don't think you have a right to know?'*

Oh, you have a right to know, yes, but y' know it's like there's nothing really I could do.

This is an intriguing statement and might also offer further indication of why he was not very interested in the story. It suggests a feeling of powerlessness in the face of power. What is being said here is that a feeling of confidence to change things, or that things can be changed, will automatically allow stories to be read differently, or given importance, in contrast to believing that the world is 'ordained' as it is. The African-Caribbean woman mentioned earlier, whose daughter was injured, quite clearly thought that corrections to procedures ought to, and could, occur; hence, her reasons for objecting to the journalist concentrating on the drama of the event rather than the structural features of the event. As she informed us, in relation to the story of her child's injury: *'It did go in the paper and it went in the way I wanted it to go'*.

They were also asked if this story was in the public interest, on a five-point scale from 'no public interest' to 'very high public interest'. Without going back on the statement concerning the fact that these young Asians did not see themselves, or present themselves, as disenfranchised, they gave the lowest estimation of the NHS story being in the public interest than any of the groups. We then said: *'The next exercise is similar, but this time the emphasis is on public interest. What do you understand by public interest?'* At first they did not focus directly on what they understood by public interest, but rather continued from the previous discussion:

It should be of interest, but some people aren't.

Because you know that only someone who is in power can deal with something like that.

There's a lot of old people out there, a lot of people that don't know what's going on.

It may have been that they were responding by projecting personal interest onto what they imagined others to be interested in, but there are elements that suggest not. *'Something that is available and appeals to everyone,'* is suggestive of what the public is interested in, but, *'there's a lot of old people out there, a lot of people that don't know what's going on',* is suggestive of something being in the public interest. They are not thinking of themselves, since they are young, but of those in our society who are old. In other words, they are thinking of a particular collective that has collective interests. If we now go back to where we asked them if the media should cover such a story, we do see the idea of public interest coming together as a statement of clarification as to what it means. For example, one young man said, *'They* [the elderly] *still have the same rights as young people do'.*

Public Interest as Contradiction
For something to be 'in the public interest' for this group would seem to mean that the story had to have social relevance; that is, it had to relate to people in general and not simply affect one person. Rights were involved; namely, that old people had the same rights to good healthcare as young people. What we see, therefore, is public interest embodying an expression that something is of common importance, which we would prefer to call social importance. As such, a story may not affect you personally, or even engage one's interest, but it has to have features that are seen as important to some group or another.

These features may be material information, or could relate to personal beliefs. Either way, it is hard to imagine that a story involving Victoria Beckham, which intruded upon her privacy, could be defended as being in the public interest. It might be that Victoria Beckham had no right or reasonable grounds to object to the intrusion of her privacy, or again she might, but the defence of 'in the public interest' could not readily be mounted. What she does, in the terms discussed above, has no social importance. Her private life has no intrusion on the lives of others; therefore, the defence of public interest cannot be used to intrude into hers. This would cover, for example, her playing with her son in the grounds of her house. However, it may be possible to mount a defence of public interest if, in some way, what she was doing was affecting her husband as captain of the English football team. For the performance of David Beckham, the footballer, could, on the reasoning given, be stated to be in the public interest.

For England to win the World Cup, of which David Beckham has previously been considered to be an integral part in such ambitions, would be an event of historical significance for many people in England. Many could possibly think of nothing of greater importance. The World Cup consumes the nation's interests, and also gives rise to feelings of national identity, national pride and so on. It is an event of significance not only in terms of entertainment, but also of national significance. Yet, one might pose the case where Beckham's form was so poor that the manager was considering leaving him out of the team. His unexpected dip in form might, for example, be the result of his discovery that his wife was having an affair. Does this then, by the defence of 'in the public interest', warrant intrusion into his wife's privacy?

The Leeds white young men, of the same age as the Asian men, scored the NHS story much higher in terms of public interest. All scored it 'Very High'. Asked why the story should be told, the response of *'it needs to be'* suggested it simply had a self-evident importance. One man said, however, *'We pay for the NHS'*. This response emerged in other groups also, and provides a nice insight into understanding what is meant by 'the public interest'. This story had high public interest because the public were seen, so to speak, to own the NHS. The NHS was public property; therefore, the public had an interest in it. The NHS does not exist, by this account, for the benefit of any one person, but for the collective, and that collective includes the old.

The 50- to 60-year-old African-Caribbean women in London gave a similar account to the young Leeds men in terms of the importance of the story and why it should be covered – like them, the NHS was seen as public property and what went on in the service was in the public interest to know. When asked, *'Even though it's a secret instruction'* should the media reveal it?

Yes, it should, because it affects the nation as a whole because most people are dependent on the NHS and if something is wrong with you, you like to get the best treatment there is – well if they give you the drug that is probably more expensive, but it will help you and probably arrest the cancer or whatever I think it should be known [...]. I mean it is a health service, we contribute and pay in throughout our working lives, therefore, we should be able to have access to whatever is available and their decisions shouldn't be financial, we all contribute to that.

Here is a very clear example of public interest. Perhaps because of their age, a great deal of passion was generated in discussing the story. What the passion suggests to us is that one can have layers of public interest, yet, on reflection, it is not layers of public interest in the sense of 'in the public interest', but layers of publics being interested in the story. That is, it was unequivocally decided that such a story was in the public interest and that it took on the nature of an objective fact since it *'affects the whole nation'*, but it does not affect the whole nation equally, or not equally at any one point in time – only when one is old.

One woman, in fact, said that the story *'sounds awful'*, and another added, *'I hope I never get cancer'*. Here is a case, therefore, of where one has a story that is in the public interest, but, because of the closeness of the story to them in terms of age, it took on added interest; they were interested in it. This is a classic case of how, in practice, the two types of interest come together and should not be separated out.

Acceptable Methods of Information Collection

The next step was to show each group a series of cards listing a range of different methods which might be used by the media to obtain information about the NHS instructions:

1. Hidden newspaper photographer
2. Hidden television camera
3. CCTV footage
4. Hidden microphone
5. Reporter disguised as someone else
6. Intercepting post
7. Recording phone calls where reporter identifies himself
8. Recording phone calls where reporter pretends to be someone else
9. Tapping home telephone lines
10. Intercepting e-mail
11. Interviewing family and friends
12. Interviewing work colleagues
13. Interviewing person's children
14. Doorstepping
15. Going through rubbish for relevant documents
16. 'Leaked' information from anonymous sources

No matter how a story is to be categorized, it is the manner in which it is covered that most usually effects whether or not privacy has been intruded upon. As stated, the higher the degree of social importance, the greater one might expect the intrusiveness that will be agreed to.

It is not possible to go through all the responses given as to what was considered acceptable and what was not acceptable, either for individual groups or for all of the groups; neither is it necessary. The point of providing the groups with such an extensive list was to pull out features that might assist us in determining attitudes towards intrusion and, further, form some general principles from those attitudes. The same items also formed a core part of the survey stage.

Some of the above techniques of information collection are illegal, but the point of including them was to see just how far people agreed that privacy could be intruded upon.

Quite a few of the items on the list were simply considered inappropriate for this story and were, therefore, dismissed. For example, it was not thought that 'going through a rubbish bin' would reveal anything of use for the story.

Asked what methods were acceptable in gaining information for the NHS story, the Asian men's responses were varied:

I don't like the hidden stuff. I think it should always be open. I'd go for 'doorstepping' and 'leaked information from anonymous sources'.

I quite like the idea of 'reporter disguised as someone else' – being inside at all times. I quite like the idea.

To try and focus the discussion, to get at the essence of what was appropriate, we asked what they considered to be *'completely out of order'*.

Tapping home phone lines was rejected on the grounds that, *'you might talk about work, but most of the time at home you don't usually bring work home'*. **Intercepting post** and **intercepting e-mail** were also rejected: *'It's too personal'*, *'They're private things like post is your privacy'*. *'Chances are it would have nothing to do with the story.'* *'It's bordering on theft. If the information is not there you're stealing it from somebody, when you have no right to that sort of thing.'*

None of the groups wished for children or the partners of the 'target' to be interviewed: for most individuals in the groups these methods were completely unacceptable under virtually all conditions: *'Interviewing the person's children or family isn't right'*. It was not considered right because: *'That's not what the story's about, that's not the NHS thing is it? That's like a personal story about the doctor or whoever made the statement themselves. It's not relevant.'*

Attempting to get **interviews with friends and family** was also held to be wrong by the group of African-Caribbean women *'because they might not necessarily know or be involved in that person's decisions'*. This is a very similar position to that adopted by the young men from Leeds; that, whatever method was adopted, it had to focus on that which was germane to the story, which in effect meant those directly involved.

It was put to the African-Caribbean women that children often overhear the conversations of their parents and, thus, might make a good source of information for journalists. In the case of the NHS story, when asked if it was permissible to interview children, one woman commented:

Well yes, but you shouldn't do that because the decision to do this was not the children's. The decision was the board's so whether they've overheard a conversation between adults or not they are not the ones who have made this decision.

The children are not culpable, nor are other family or friends, therefore, they should not be intruded upon, even though the information gained might help to construct what was going on. We might make a principle here: only those directly involved in a story can be intruded upon; others, although related to the participants in the story, have the right to privacy.

We wished to know whether the privacy of children was always sacrosanct and, if not, what it might tell us about the defence of public interest and the intrusion of privacy. When we asked about the attack on the World Trade Center, which had occurred the day previous to a focus group, matters were not quite so clear. It was pointed out to the group that *'terrorism by definition is a very secretive business, that's why it's very hard to catch these people, they are very skilled in hiding who they are, the terrorist, like ordinary people in many ways, have children, families… journalists are good like the intelligence service in actually getting a story, could they follow a suspect's child to see where he is going, eavesdropping, they might give clues away, could they do that in this case?'* It was claimed: *'Well they will do it'*. *'They probably will do it.'* We asked: *'But should they do it?'* The responses were:

Well, yes, this is it, the horror of it, it's very hard, it's something that is so now, so happening now, so emotive, people will probably say they should do anything at all to find these people and bring them to justice, but sometimes you think, oh I don't know.

I don't think so because, I tell you something, if people who are planning these kind of things they are not gonna let kids know about it.

After this last point we clarified the question, '*We are not saying the whole operation, but there might be things that the children have picked up – routines of behaviour, who came to the house and things like that*'.

Yes, [...] It's a different circumstance [from the NHS], *it's almost a war where perhaps we're in a situation like that means that perhaps normally what would not be justified... I think we always have to be careful 'cos once you actually open the door it's very, very hard to close it again.*

I still wouldn't choose the children though for the simple reason that they are innocent.

You wouldn't have to interview the children to know, even if they knew anything because children are naturally chatty and they volunteer, their friends are gonna talk to them so if you can listen to them rather than interviewing them that's ok.

One very certain fact can be drawn from this; namely, that when it comes to children and their privacy (our example was around 10 years old) they have a very privileged position. Even the horrors of the attack on the World Trade Center made them reluctant to intrude into children's private domain. However, it is also clear that for some it was acceptable. There is a hint that what might have been at work was not the question of privacy at all, but worry about interference with the child. That is, people did not wish the child to be bothered, as if in a sense the child ought to be protected from what might be termed 'annoyance'. The privacy of the child could not be directly assaulted, but surreptitious means could be adopted to overhear conversations. In other words, what the child does not know will not harm him or her.

Pretending to be someone else was considered '*all right*' – '*The deception is ok – 'cos you still think he hasn't really invaded privacy. It's just deception*'. Such deception was not automatically considered an intrusion of privacy because to be intrusive it had to involve the gaining of information that the person would not expect others to have access to and, therefore, presumably few precautions would be taken to protect information from the eyes of others. Although if one had known the person was a journalist, information would not be given, it would be given to the type of person represented by the disguise. What this overlooks, however, is the question of publication. If disguised as a fellow doctor or ward orderly one would not, in the normal course of events, expect that person to then publish in open forum that which he had seen or heard. In that sense, it does intrude into privacy because one expects the exchange to be kept private or at least given only restricted circulation.

Intrusion of privacy here involves gaining access to anything that is not considered relevant to the story, and protection is to be given where there is a possibility of collecting information – phone tapping or opening mail – that might include material that has nothing to do with the story – it is private. This idea of privacy coloured their judgement of surreptitious recording. Doubts existed about **hidden microphones**, but this was qualified by adding, '*It depends where it is*'. The consideration was '*If it's in a person's home then its* *not...'*, but that it would be acceptable in his office: *'That's his work place, it's a work place decision'.* He means here that the decision to provide or not to provide treatment is taken at work, not in the home, and, therefore, surreptitious recording could take place as the element of capturing the private, that is, material not related to the story, is reduced. Even so, one person had doubts: *'But you've got other patients coming in with their problems and there's patient confidentiality. They haven't given their permission...'* This only serves to reinforce the point that material must not be gathered that is not in the public interest; that is, material not germane to the story.

Did this 'heightened interest' lead to differences in how far intrusion could proceed in terms of techniques? It did not seem to do so. In fact, the African-Caribbean group of women in London were pretty reluctant to sanction many of the intrusion methods at all, apart from one woman who considered practically all the methods to be appropriate given her passion over the wrong she felt was being committed:

> *If he can stand and say, 'I've decided you're too old, you've had your innings, you've had two years more than you should have anyway', and you've got the front to say that and stand up and say it, don't hide yourself – by whatever means.*

Appropriate Media for the NHS Story

Having selected what methods could be used to investigate the story, participants were asked to select which media sources would be *the most appropriate* to carry the story by the methods agreed to. They were then asked to select which media sources were *most likely* to carry the news story by the non-approved methods. The list of media given was:

1. Television news
2. Television documentary
3. Television chat show
4. Broadsheet newspaper
5. Tabloid newspaper
6. Internet news site
7. Magazine
8. Radio news
9. Radio programme

Because of the importance of the story they considered that most media would cover it – television news and television documentaries, radio, the press and even the Internet. It was also considered that shows such as *Kilroy* and *Esther Rantzen* would handle it. Magazines might not though:

> *It's a totally specialist story.*

> *OK's more bothered about Mr and Mrs Beckham.*

> *Magazines are just gossip really, whereas that is probably news.*

The inclusion of the Internet is interesting, in that recognition was given to different sorts of sites. It was mentioned that on a news site it would be *'a very, very brief story. Just two paragraphs.'* But that *'a site giving information on cancer might run the story saying, "You know. Did you know this drug was available?" sort of thing. It depends what sort of site it was.'*

Although it was considered that the story was important enough for all newspapers to carry, how it was handled was seen to depend on the type of newspaper. Referring to the tabloids, one of the young Leeds men said: *'It'd be on page 23 or something like that. They'd be more interested in which doctors had been doing it and who they have been seeing for the past three years'*. This was added to: *'They'd still cover it, but they'd make a totally different story out of it the tabloids. They wouldn't be saying, "Oh why aren't they administering the drug?" They'd say, "Which doctor's not administering it".'*

When asked about those methods that were considered unacceptable, and what medium they considered most likely to use such techniques of information gathering, newspapers were mentioned. Would this include the *Guardian* or the *Times*? *'No, I don't think so. No.'* However, television documentaries were singled out *'Because they have to have lots of evidence. They have to show first time things'*. Given the strictures of documentary-making, which these young men identified, we asked if it would be right for a television company to adopt such methods; the answer was, *'No'*.

The exercise was not simply to see what methods were appropriate as a way of understanding acceptable degrees of intrusion, however, but to understand what was understood by public interest. We therefore created the situation where a 'good' doctor was breaking the rules by giving the expensive drug to old patients. We asked, given that publication of the 'good' doctor's identity might have occupational repercussions, should publication go ahead:

I think you should because they're not doing anything wrong. They're not, or they might not be obeying the rules, but they're doing it for the people, not for personal interests. They feel that should be right and they're doing the right thing.

I. How could you protect them?
   Well they are in the right though, aren't they.

I. Management tend not to see things like that.
   The public sees it that way.
   We see it that way.

Possible Consequences of Publication of NHS Information

Subsequently, participants were presented with a list of possible consequences of publication for the person or persons to whom the story relates — assuming that the privacy of the individual has been intruded upon:

1. Financial ruin
2. Suicide
3. Divorce or breakdown of relationship

4. Consequences involving children of person
5. Nervous breakdown
6. End of career
7. Acute embarrassment
8. Social ridicule
9. Criminal consequences
10. Suffering or distress
11. Unwanted public notoriety

Participants were asked if any of these consequences might justify the editor or producer changing their treatment of the story.

The eventuality that the Leeds young men had qualms about was if publication led to suicide. In fact, this group had a wider view, considering that the real story was not about the doctors, but about *'explaining the financial restraints and blaming it on the government'*. In summary, it was mentioned: *'Virtually anything has consequences'. 'You've just got to run it how you think right.' 'It depends how you put it across. It's a serious job.'*

Privacy as Taste and Decency: September 11

The terrorist attacks on the World Trade Center (WTC) and the Pentagon could only be discussed with the London groups, since the Leeds groups pre-dated September 11. The insights gained from these groups do, however, help greatly in showing how the issues of privacy and decency can and do come together. This is particularly well illustrated by the African-Caribbean women's group. The group was shown a range of the special newspaper editions which featured the WTC and Pentagon attacks: the pictures of the hijacked planes hitting the Twin Towers, people jumping out of the towers as the fires grew, close-up shots of terrified people running away from the centre of the disaster and of exhausted firemen and rescuers. Those fleeing from the WTC area can clearly be seen and, if one knew them, identified. We asked the group of young women in London about this coverage:

I. Is that [newspaper pictures] an intrusion of privacy?
No, I don't think so, no, I wouldn't think so.

I. Why not?
Well, I think it's only an intrusion for a good reason.

I. What?
It is a tragedy, it is something bad that has happened and I don't think they were sent over there just to take photographs of the people running or anything like that, they set out to show people the horror of what is happening, the people caught in the feature is just a by-product of what they are trying to do. I don't think it's an invasion of privacy. I don't think that at all.
I think it is an invasion of privacy, but I think you can justify it.

I. On what grounds?
On the grounds of the act, as the lady said, you're actually trying to show the horror of the situation and to an extent it's probably justifiable.

I. You are saying, it's not about them it's about the tragedy?
    Yes, I think it is [an intrusion] *but it's justifiable, that's what I mean, yes, it's justifiable for showing, but then it's about where you draw the line – I think that's fine.*

There is, in the above, a slight difference of opinion as to whether the pictures did mount to an intrusion of privacy, but, even where it is agreed that intrusion has taken place, it is in effect discounted as not 'real' intrusion. The reason for this is that the pictures are not about the individuals, but about the enormity of the event, which could only truly be captured by the horror and fear on the faces of the individuals running from the carnage. The defence here is also one of intention – *'I don't think they were sent over there just to take photographs of the people running or anything like that'*. The pictures taken were not so much of individuals, but of people caught up in events. The story was clearly, and is seen to be by these participants, of massive importance, not just for America, but also for the rest of the world.

We are not suggesting for a moment that a defence for any 'intrusion' is necessary with regard to the pictures. The whole point of raising the question with the group was not so much to see if they considered that an intrusion of privacy had occurred, but to use it as an opportunity to explore *in extremis* how they saw privacy and how they saw intrusion.

What they were saying was that the September 11 events were so important, and held such political implications, that it was in the public interest to capture, as best as possible, what actually occurred.

Having said that, there is still the question posed in the group – *'about where you draw the line'*. They were asked whether pictures of (unidentifiable) people jumping from the WTC windows should have been shown.

Yes, it could be shown because it shows the horror of the situation.

We followed this by saying: *'I have never seen anything like it – you saw the bodies jumping out, was that an intrusion of privacy in any way at all, the moment of death, these people leaping out?'*

It is but the people kind of faced with… well, I was going to say nameless… but unlike the other pictures these people are faceless, but it's still an intrusion on that person's privacy, but I don't see it as a problem in that respect.

I think it's painting the horror, isn't it. It's the whole thing it made me think 'My God, these people must have been so terrified of what would be in that building they would rather get out of it' so I didn't look at it at all… it didn't occur to me that it would be an invasion of anyone's privacy. I just think, 'Oh my God, it's a good job you can't see their faces', because can you imagine if their families were watching.

We asked: *'If to get the true horror over they had to show more close-ups, would that have been permissible?'*

I don't think that is necessary.

No, that wouldn't have been right at all, that would have been totally unnecessary because it's bad enough that you see this happening, but to actually have this picture of their faces as these people are dying, there is no need for that.

We asked her to clarify: *'What are we talking here, are we talking here about privacy or a question just of decency?'*

I think looking at the faces close-up then we've already got pictures like that. I think we're coming into decency really.

Privacy and decency interact here. All agreed that any intrusion of privacy that did occur was acceptable on the grounds given; indeed, although the term 'intrusion of privacy' was used, it was not used in any really meaningful sense. What is seen is that the conversation moves from a question of privacy to one of *decency*, and showing close-up pictures of the faces of the dead or dying is simply not decent. It *'would have been totally unnecessary'*, because *'it's bad enough that you see this happening'* from the pictures as shown. Cast in terms of privacy, then it is not decent to intrude upon that person's privacy any further than had been done so. When we asked again whether this was a matter of privacy or taste and decency, the response was

I think both.
Yes, privacy and decency, I think both, yes.

At the same time, these women were unsure about whether it was right or not to interview people who were clearly distressed: whether, because they had consented to give the interviews, this could then be classed as an intrusion of privacy. One woman pointed out that, in a particular instance where the mother of a victim was interviewed, the interviewee must have consented to the interview herself: *'It was her son. Her son rang her* [from the doomed aircraft]*'.* Asked if it was right to get the mother's reactions, the response was

I think for the person concerned, if the person... when you're in a situation like that maybe you might not be thinking straight, but if the person consented to the interview, I think that's fine.

I'm making the assumption she got the phone call, she obviously relayed that to someone and told them what it was about — you know in the public arena — that's the assumption I am making. Yes, she had a choice. I don't know.

This is not an easy question to resolve, clearly shown by the point above that the mother had a choice and so it was correct to broadcast the interview, but then she adds — *'I don't know'.* The difficulty is what, in the context of receiving a phone call from a son who is about to die, does choice mean? Choice, under normal circumstances, suggests a rational decision-making process:

They are sort of getting you at the moment when you're not thinking straight, they're catching you when you're at your very lowest ebb and sometimes you just want to talk and maybe months after this

she might be thinking, 'Oh God, why did I ever do that', but at the moment… this is where I think sometimes the reporters they know, and they jump in when something like that happens and they get you, whereas another time you wouldn't give them the time of day, so maybe she's done it – not instigated it – but she might have done it because you know she might have thought I want to tell the world how awful these people are, but then a few months later when things have calmed down a bit she might…

I mean I personally would like to think that if I were ever, God forbid, in this situation, that I would have someone close to me enough to say, 'No, no thank you very much', but we're talking in an ideal world. I would like to think one would have a certain amount of decency and give people time to grieve.

There can be no resolution to this question of broadcasting interviews with people in shock or trauma at events that have overwhelmed them. Indeed, this has already been shown in the interviews made with broadcasters. Whether a particular example is an intrusion of privacy revolves around *consent* – would the mother have consented if she were not so emotionally upset? The fact is she was upset and she gave the interview, and we were allowed to hear her anguish at a moment of acute vulnerability. Her relationship to her son is unique, therefore, her grief is unique in the way it ferments itself, and, hence, we can talk of this as a deeply private emotional sphere, which is then made public. We talk about not intruding into private grief, and this is, on that score, if not other counts, an intrusion of privacy, but the consent alters that – it is agreed that we can witness her private anguish. Although this situation does involve issues of privacy, it is again overlain with decency; indeed, where decency, of what is decent in the circumstances, takes the upper hand. As one woman in the above group said: '*I would like to think one would have a certain amount of decency*'.

It is not our central task to address the question of taste and decency, and we have only done so at times to make the point that privacy, taste and decency do at times come together and cannot always easily be separated out.

As with showing close-up shots of the dead and dying, one of the participants refused to countenance close-up shots in making such interviews on the grounds that it added nothing of real substance to the story. There was already sufficient material to show what had taken place, the extent of injury and damage and so on, so that close-up shots were superfluous overstatement.

A similar discussion took place with the London male (30- to 40-year-old) group, where one man said: '*If you can identify individuals, then that shouldn't be published, but as an illustration it certainly brings home the horror of the situation*'. The voice left on the answer phone was not an unidentified individual, but had a name attached and was often accompanied by biographical detail. Would, for example, this person on the aircraft have granted permission for his last words to be made public? Would he, if he had known they would be broadcast, have made the call? Although some of the voices appear remarkably calm, even have a touching dignity to them, as with the receiver and publisher, it can hardly be said that, in making the message, they would be in a 'collected state of mind'.

The defence of 'in the public interest' in the context of September 11 can be raised in two ways. First, this was an event that was in the interest of all to know about. It offered repercussions of major importance beyond the United States. Therefore, it was essential to get the story over in the fullest possible manner. But then, as the groups demonstrate, the question arises of how much 'detail' it was necessary to relay in substantively telling the story.

The second argument for it being 'in the public interest' to intrude into the private moment before death is the role of the media in fuelling anger at those who committed the atrocity. Here we move into a situation where the media are not simple conduits of what we might term just 'news', but of news as propaganda – with a definite purpose. It seeks a desired outcome: education for a set of aims or goals, most usually political. Most news has an element of this, but here one is talking of degrees.

It takes little to imagine that those who wished to pursue a military course of action following the events of September the 11th would approve of the relaying of the last messages for the effect that they might have on stiffening resolve to strike back and could legitimately claim any intrusion into privacy was in the public interest. But this is precisely where the idea of 'in the public interest' as a test for the intrusion of privacy shows its weakness. What is in the public interest?

There were undoubtedly significant numbers of people – that might be considered to form 'publics' – who did not give their support for military intervention following September 11. They did so on the grounds that it was not in the public interest; for example, believing that it would mean an increase in terrorist attacks in the future. It is also quite clear that sizeable sections of the Muslim community (a public) in Britain, whilst condemning the attacks on the Trade Center, did not support the consequent military response, most likely from the perception that this could constitute a 'religious' war against co-religionists.

The whole point of raising this question is to show, as reasoned in the opening sections of the book, that it is difficult, when referring to the public interest, to assess just what interest is being referred to.

The Internet and Publication

The London 30- to 45-year-old male group talked about the scenes surrounding the destruction of the Twin Towers. In talking of the bodies falling from the building, one man, in recalling his horror at viewing the pictures, said:

You see it in the movies, don't you? You see a body go out of the window and bangs against the wall, but that [the WTC events] is real, you're actually watching people. To see a body go out of the window, go down a couple of storeys and crash into the side of the wall, and this is real. Horrifying.

As horrifying as these pictures were, they thought more horrifying ones might turn up on the Internet:

I think there will be some pictures... which might then appear on the Internet.

Things do have a habit... I was watching, I think it was NBC on satellite yesterday and the reporter said we've got footage we can't possibly show because it was showing broken bodies at the bottom of the building, basically, and there was lots of amateur cameramen around so that has started appearing now… so some stuff is probably going to start appearing on the Web as it always does. After Diana died it did.

This did not appear to cause him too much concern, or, perhaps more accurately, he saw publication via the Internet as different from other publication:

Well people on the Internet – if they want to see it, they are going to look for it, aren't they? The telly is coming straight in the house and you can't stop your family watching it.

We asked distinctly: '*Talking of the intrusion of privacy, is it the same on the Internet as the newspaper or television?*'

I think it is not because there was a case recently where a young guy had a split up with his girlfriend pretty acrimoniously and she actually used… a photo… his head on somebody else's body wearing lady's underwear and superimposed – and the thing is you wouldn't have known about it except that newspapers picked up on it and published it, and that's when it became much more in the public arena.

I. Properly published?
   On the Internet, if you are in the know – visiting the sites that might pick up on that sort of thing, then you will get to know a bit but… [it's] much more of a two or three stage process. You have to go out and look for the stuff, whereas the national press or television, it is there.

   It depends on the site… a site which is viewed by millions of people everyday then it is exactly the same thing, if it is a website that is widely known.

In some ways this looks as if it is a taste and decency question, of who at what age and so on can be exposed to what material. But it is more than that, and does relate to the issue of publication and privacy in a novel manner. What he is saying is that, with broadcast publication, the consumption of it is public, whereas publication by the Internet is consumed privately. The same might be said of print material as of the Internet, but print material is left lying around. At the very best one does not expect to hide a newspaper – it may be for that reason that some of the more salacious papers are not brought into the house.

It was quite clear that the Internet was seen as a different type of publishing exercise than that of newspapers. But, this was only up to a point. The major difference appears to be that one has to search for material. One also, as he pointed out, has to know what to look for and where to look. What this respondent is saying is that the publication has to be actively sought out, and, therefore, intrusion of privacy is not of the same order as if material was produced in widely available form. The technology, the existence of a multitude of sites, only acts to limit the degree to which 'publication' of the intrusion of privacy occurs, but the intrusion of privacy has nevertheless occurred. By the accounts given, the lack of control means that it is more likely that privacy will be intruded upon.

One participant was well aware of the changes that had occurred in the recent past, and, by implication, the alteration that had occurred in the communications landscape as it relates to the intrusion of privacy:

> *Invasion of privacy is probably a phrase that was generated before the introduction of the Internet so it doesn't allow for that new media.*

It is interesting that this man refers to the Internet as a medium, showing that he sets it alongside, rather than apart from, the more traditional media. In terms of publication, it is not seen as something different, indeed, although it is recognized that one has to search for material, which may mean information is less immediately public than newspapers or broadcast media, Internet-based material can be *'viewed by millions of people every day'*.

There is good evidence from a range of sources that unless a website is well known and established, that is, has some authority to it, images and information offered by such sites that are unlikely to trusted. It was mentioned previously, in the case of the bitter girlfriend, that images could be fabricated. This is not something that one would expect of mainstream media, although quite clearly many participants considered that the tabloid newspapers were not beyond making up quotes. The point to raise is whether trust alters reception and, if so, does that reflect on the intrusion of privacy. For mainstream media to print or broadcast material that might be considered an intrusion of privacy carries with it the unstated assumption that it was right to publish such material.

These media assert claims over the rights of the individual or organization to their privacy. They are saying, by publication, that one did not have a right to privacy. Internet sites are not saying that, if we take out those authoritative sites such as the BBC. It may be that the individual had no right to privacy when held against the claim of something being in the public interest, but the lack of 'authority' means that there is no presumption that it is right to publish such material. In other words, publication does not mean that one has no right to privacy; it merely means that privacy has been intruded upon and one might well in fact have a right to privacy. This means that sympathy might well be with the person 'exposed', or, perhaps of more importance, that the story itself is not taken very seriously. To intrude into someone's privacy by an authoritative medium is to legitimate the act of intrusion. It is doubtful that this would occur with many Internet sites, although, of course, privacy has still been intruded upon. As a final point, it might be worth considering how effective a defence of 'in the public interest' can be taken for justifying the intrusion of privacy if, in fact, a site had hardly any public access to its publication. Without an audience, public interest might well look like private pleasure or personal interest. This is not a strong argument, but it does add for a difference when considering the Internet to that of other forms of publication.

Defining 'In the Public Interest'

The manner in which the groups discussed the issue of privacy and the limits of intrusion not only raised public interest issues, but at times brought the definition of public interest into direct play. The approach was to have participants discuss the question of privacy and media performance in the expectation that we would not only gain insight into how they saw rights to privacy, but also gain an understanding of whether or not some sense of public interest operated in coming to decisions of when it was legitimate to intrude upon privacy. One can clearly see, from the accounts given, that notions of public interest did exist. However, it was decided that we would also ask participants directly what they understood by the term 'the public interest'.

At the end of the session with the London 30- to 45-year-old men, we asked: *'Journalists, they actually say, it is in the public interest... what to you does that phrase mean, if it is "in the public interest"?'*

It is hard to define. What is the public interest?

Something that belongs to the public we should know about. Is it in the public interest for someone to say, 'There is a bomb heading for London right at this moment' and everyone panics?

I don't know, is it in the public interest?

The London young women, aged 18–25, said:

Newspapers treat it as anything basically that we are interested in and we want to read, but if someone said to me 'It's in the public interest', then I would think that it is something that helps the public.

Or the public needs to know, like there is a paedophile living next door.

You need to know so that you can protect your kids from it you know, but the fact that Victoria Beckham bought a new pair of shoes and a matching handbag... Ok – interesting, but it's not very in the public interest to know it, you know. It isn't going to make a difference to their life, it's not important.

Yeah, something that makes a difference to the public's life.

Similar comments were made by the Leeds 50- to 60-year-old men:

My personal view would be, the editor. What his priorities are – is it what's in the public interest or in selling newspapers? That would be my sceptical look at it. My view personally would be that he wants to keep his job and sell papers.

Well, it makes a better standard of awareness.

It's such an individual sort of thing. What I might think is the best for the 'public interest' might be different to what you might think. So whatever the paper might say is going to generate an interest in some people and not others. Which is bound to be the case. So the public interest must be everything. There must be nothing that isn't in the public interest. It's very difficult to try and define it, isn't it? I wouldn't like to try and define it.

It's public benefit or when they say interest, is it a benefit.

I don't think it's possible.

In Leeds, the 30- to 45-year-old women said:

If it's going to affect you personally.

Yes, if it's going to affect everybody.

It's about things that happen to change your life.

It's got to affect a good proportion of the population, hasn't it?

Yet, this idea of what we would term 'social importance' – something that affected people in general – then took a different turn when someone entered the casual comment: *'People wouldn't read papers if they weren't curious'.*

We then gave the example of a male television celebrity under police investigation and asked whether this case was a matter of public interest.

He's a public figure, isn't he, because he's on television?

He's courted the publicity.

But it doesn't affect us though, does it really?

Yes, we're interested in it.

It's not just what affects you, it's curiosity.

We just want to know.

For the scandal.

I wouldn't say I'd buy a newspaper for the trials or anything. I'm interested if I see it happening, but I'm not really bothered what comes next.

The 18 to 25-year-old men from Leeds gave similar definitions of 'the public interest':

Not just affecting a single person, a single life.

It's like printing a story about [a female pop singer]. If you put it in there just because you know that a load of people are going to buy it to see the picture and want to know about it – it's not public interest, it's more smut. It doesn't affect anybody, but there's a load of people out there that just want to see a pair of [the singer's] tits. It's just a load of guys who'd just like to see them, but they won't have any life changes through seeing them or not seeing them.

We put it to them: *'Could it be in a newspaper's defence to say, of a picture of her sunbathing with her kit off taken with a long-range camera, that it was in the public interest on the grounds that it cheers everybody up?'*

Well, they could say that news and entertainment is all in the public interest.

These exchanges demonstrate just how elusive the term 'the public interest' can be, or, perhaps more accurately, the confusion that it causes. At some points the term refers to something that has an impact on large numbers of people, and equally, at other times, it refers to material the public is interested *in*. It is undeniable, however, that amidst the statements concerning the nature of public interest there does rest a sense of public interest referring to matters that cannot simply be of personal interest. Or, where it is of personal interest, it must also be not only of interest to others, but also in their overall interest. Equally, a 'public interest' story could exist that hardly anyone was personally interested in, but, nevertheless, the information given was in their interest. This, however, seems somewhat optimistic when set against news values: it is difficult to imagine a news organization, at least with any frequency or taking pride of place, publishing material that its readers, viewers or listeners were not interested in, even though it was in their interest.

If something can be in the public interest, yet people are not interested in it, a serious problem arises in these cases where the 'public interest' defence is used to excuse intrusions into privacy – especially where intrusion involves the surreptitious collecting of material. It is in examining particular cases in some detail that the question of what people understand by the public interest and the permission given for intrusion becomes clear.

Two final cases put to the groups can help here. The first one involves an airline pilot who is suspected of drinking in the non-permitted time before flying. The second is about a schoolteacher who assists pupils by giving answers to exam questions before the actual exams take place.

At first the 18 to 25-year-old Leeds men were somewhat doubtful about whether or not the story of the pilot was of high public interest, but this may be accounted for by a youthful attitude to drinking in general. They did not appear to consider that the after-effects of alcohol were very debilitating: *'I personally wouldn't have thought if someone had been drinking heavily in the last 24 hours before they fly the plane [he or she] wouldn't necessarily be effective whilst they are driving it'*. It was likened somewhat to *'taxi drivers and traffic accidents'*.

As the conversation progressed, the situation was seen as more serious, and they began to talk about the consequences lending a high degree of public interest.

But then that's different. If a plane crashed that would be high public interest.

It's like you say that you shouldn't be driving and in the car there's you and you may just affect anyone who's in the accident with you, but not on the same kind of scale as if you're flying a jumbo with three or four hundred passengers or whatever... if you make a mistake and you're flying the plane, everybody on the plane has no way out. They can't say, 'Oh, you shouldn't have done that.' You can't swerve round them or anything like that.

The scale of the potential disaster enters here, but there is also the suggestion of the pilot being responsible for others who have placed their safety in his hands. Even so, when asked if this story was of high public interest to the same degree as the NHS story, it was considered not to be so: *'I wouldn't say it's as high an interest'*. Someone else added: *'I would say they're both potential life and death stories.'* The fact that they were life and death stories did not, however, make them equitable in terms of public interest: *'The NHS, we all pay towards that, it's everybody who's involved in that. That* [the pilot's story] *is not the public as in, we pay tax – NHS is there for our health. That is completely different.'*

This demonstrates the possibility of different degrees of public interest – some stories are more important than others, even if they are all about matters of public interest. What we see here is really social importance. The airline story, should the plane crash due to pilot error, may be a tragedy, but as one man said, *'you only fly once or twice a year'* whereas with the NHS, the way described, we are all involved. The NHS impacted directly on the whole of society, the pilot drinking in the proscribed period before flying was only of potential harm to those who boarded that pilot's aircraft or, in the most generous definition, those who fly. Further, when asked once more if it was of high public interest, it was said to be *'middling'*. One of the reasons put forward for this was: *'It depends how you see those rules, as being fair or not, y' know. I personally think that's a bit strict.'*

Consequently, intrusion into the pilot's privacy had to be limited: in this context this would break the 'rules'. CCTV cameras in the bar – a public space – were agreed to, but intrusion into the privacy of the pilot's bedroom by hidden camera was not sanctioned: *'With a hidden microphone if it's in their personal bedroom, no. If you're walking around in the bar with a pint in your hand a couple of hours before you are due to fly a plane then you'd expect to get caught. I wouldn't expect to have cameras in my bedroom watching me.'* It was put to the group that maybe the pilot drank in his room from the minibar and did not enter the public arena of the bar. Other methods, it was felt, could be used for collecting the information: *'Well, the person who stocks the mini bar could tell you – stuff like that'.*

There is a valuable point made here concerning intrusion: the degree of intrusion, such as surreptitious recordings, must not occur if the 'evidence' can be gained by other means. The following comment also shows the concern that material will be collected, the more general the intrusiveness is, that is not germane to the story. In objecting to either hidden microphones or hidden cameras in the pilot's bedroom, one man said:

Because that's purely on what's been drunk [getting the minibar count] *and not on his general life in his bedroom and what he's been doing... it's not his life; it's just how much he drinks before flying the plane. That is all you should be interested in, that's the problem.*

This type of qualification arose time and time again in the way that privacy was handled by the groups; the core concern over the intrusion of privacy is that to collect information by surreptitious means – intercepting mail, listening into telephone conversations and so on – involves going beyond the legitimate parameters of the story and into aspects of a person's life that have no bearing on the story. That is where and how privacy is intruded upon. Only in cases of absolute social importance, such as that which might be said to be in the national interest, the apprehending, for example, of the terrorists responsible for the attacks on the World Trade Center, can such activity be readily justified. The other point to draw from the above is the idea of 'fairness'.

Intrusion into individual privacy forms part of the larger question of fairness or justice. This was raised to a degree earlier in relating the issue of intrusion into privacy to matters of taste and decency: here, the question of fairness is out in the open. For some group members the rules on drinking and flying were seen as too strict, or unfair, and the response to the degree of intrusion was coloured by that. It was not that pilots should totally disregard warnings about alcohol, but if the rules are too strict, people have the right to ignore them.

Justice

Another aspect of 'fairness' is that of justice of treatment. This issue was explored by presenting the case of a teacher who, for self-promotion, provided pupils with exam paper answers prior to the exams themselves. The motive was given as the teacher hoping that as many pupils as possible would pass and so bring credit to the teacher. A variation on this theme was again presented with the teacher giving the answers to the exam questions not for reasons of self-advancement, but because the catchment area of the school was deprived. The intention of the teacher was to compensate for having poor home study facilities compared with pupils in more advantaged parts of the town.

In the event, very few differences existed in group responses to the two cases. We asked if the teacher's name should be published in the first case (self-promotion). The 50- to 60-year-old Leeds men agreed unanimously that the identity of the teacher should be published. They also all agreed that a picture of the teacher should accompany the name. In the second case where the teacher's intentions were to help the pupils with no thought of personal gain, they argued that there should be no difference in treatment:

What good is it going to do the children?

It's an impossible situation, because they could appear to have a greater capability than they actually have. They get the job whatever that matches their capability and in the end they can't do it. So he hasn't done them any favours.

When it was put to the group that in both cases it came to light that the teacher concerned had a lot of personal problems, pressure of work and so on, that had led to suicide attempts in the past and it was believed that such publicity might *'push him over the top'*, uncertainty existed about whether they would still publish.

I would. I'm not sure.

It's like a death sentence.

The problem is still the same… that crime of what he's done is exactly the same for me. He's made the same error of judgement.

I suppose if I was a photographer or whatever, it's my job, so I would do it, but whether or not I would agree with it I don't know myself.

In all the groups, no one wished to go any further than publishing a picture, and some did not even wish for that, being content with naming the teacher. It was not considered necessary to interview family or friends and so on. The fact that publicity might result in the teacher taking their life, although it clearly bothers the group, is not a factor to enter the frame. An offence has been committed, and harm done. Indeed, it is the *harm* that is important – the children will not, in effect, be properly equipped for the world. The good intentions of the teacher in the second version counted for nothing, since whatever the motives, the harm was the same. It was in the public interest that such occurrences ought to be revealed. It was the social consequences that took precedence over the individual consequences to the teacher by publicising the case. What these men demonstrate is a fine appreciation for the social over the individual. When rights clash, the individual rights must give way.

This idea of harm was graphically demonstrated in the London group of 18 to 25-year-old women. Given the 'teacher' examples, one woman recounted a real-life parallel from her local school:

Mrs X at School Y – she cheats. She gave us the answers to my German exam, (GCSE)... I got an A★ for it. I was over the moon, and then I went for my A level and I thought, 'Yeah I am brilliant in German.' I failed it because I weren't that good. So it messes up the rest of your life. In my eyes she has ruined my life because I couldn't sort of go to university or do another A level. She sort of made delusions that you were really good at it and you were not. It's just that she cheated to make herself look better and in the long run...

This young woman had an obvious bitterness about what had happened to her. Others in the group agreed that *'Yeah, she cheated you'.* Nevertheless, although she was very happy indeed for Mrs X to be exposed and her picture put in the newspaper, she drew the line at extending the story to include interviews with her family: *'The whole family, no. But no I would have shown a picture of her.'* Here, even with the bitterness, the idea of fairness comes in. She could not agree to the story being extended beyond the individual responsible for her misfortune. The punishment, in a sense, must fit the crime, and only those who are participants to the crime need to be exposed. Yet the reason for exposing Mrs X is not restricted to the harm inflicted upon her as an individual. She saw the giving away of answers as having a social dimension, in that such activity affected others:
We asked her: *'Is there much reason for publishing the story?'*

I don't dislike the woman but... because to make people aware of what could happen and how things could get so out of proportion because I mean it's not just GCSEs – yeah, I know they are a big thing, but say it's degree level. ' If you give someone a First and they are no way as good as that then they go into whatever because they have got a First.

This is a clear case of the individual considering something to be important because it is in their interest, only to discover on further examination that their interest is joined with others' interests. The individual interest is truly a social interest and the story is important not just because it affects them alone, but because it has immediate social consequences, directly affecting real people. This echoes the earlier example of the African-Caribbean woman who wished the story of her child's injury told in order to protect other people from possible future injury through faulty construction of market stalls. It is the social – the lived-in context – that makes a story important and, the higher the deemed social element, the greater the permission given for intrusion of privacy.

End View

The benefit of the scenario approach in understanding the meaning of public interest as a defence for the intrusion of privacy is that it allowed us to see how people construct the legitimate performance of the media. Throughout, there is a sense that when the media act on behalf of readers, viewers and listeners, they are allowed greater freedom of movement than if they are merely acting as performing institutions, by which we mean acting to attract the audience through attention-seeking devices. This is not to say that the attention seeking devices were not enjoyed, for example, intrusive pictures of the famous or whatever, but that, without a claim of social importance, any defence for intrusion was weak. Deep intrusion, such as hidden cameras or microphones, was never readily granted, even where a story was in the public interest, or, in our terms, of high social importance. The reason for this was that 'collateral information' would be collected that had little or nothing to do with the event or happening in question. Hence, people were more ready to agree to intrusion that took place in the office or work setting than that which occurred in the home. This, however, is not simply related to the collecting of 'collateral information', but had much to do with the way in which people constructed the idea of the private, and they did so by differentiating public space. In our typology, open public space, restricted public space and closed public space. Open public space was not private at all, restricted public space was not really private either, or at least it might be expected that one would be on view, whereas closed public space centred, in essence, on that bounded by the home. Or, as we saw in the case of the airline pilot, space that functioned as the home; namely, the hotel bedroom.

The whole question of public interest and privacy, at the beginning of Part Two, is difficult, yet, as we have seen, it is not that difficult in some senses. The major difficulty stems from the term itself, 'the public interest'. It is conceptually vague and insensitive in practice. For that reason, we have preferred the term 'social importance' as a test of when and to what extent privacy can be intruded upon. To find that something is in the public interest does not indicate how far it is in the public interest, and this is not overcome by using the term 'overriding public interest'. In the discussions, it was quite clear that where it was agreed that privacy could be intruded upon is when to do so provided a social benefit. The term 'social importance' was found to handle a greater degree of situations than that offered by 'in the public interest'.

We are not suggesting that the notion of 'in the public interest' has no value. It is obvious from the evidence of the focus groups that, when they discussed the grounds upon which privacy might be intruded upon, they had in mind something such as the intrusion being in the public interest. What we are saying is simply that the term gives rise to profound difficulties, and some other form of words, or a profound re-definition of the existing term, is required. As it stands, the term creates unnecessary difficulties, in that it clearly can encompass differing meanings and can be given a wide variety of interpretations.

Notes

1. TV news broadcaster Julia Somerville and her partner were interviewed by police after a Boots employee complained about family snaps they'd sent to be developed which showed their 7-year-old child in the bath.
2. British actor best known as *Inspector Morse*.

8b What are the Limits of the Private? Voices from Surveys

This chapter discusses the findings from the specially commissioned UK-wide survey of public opinion on key issues relating to privacy and the media. The content of the survey was largely built around the material used in and arising from the preceding focus group stage. The main findings to emerge show that the UK public have well-established views about individual rights to privacy and media rights to infringe these. In essence, there exists a set of rules of engagement together with a parallel set of rules about behaviour: judgement by people as to the rights and wrongs of any specific case involves weighing these two elements against each other. Moreover, many of these rules are shared across the potential divides arising from people's age, gender and social position. Accordingly, there exist cases where media intrusion into an individual's privacy is almost universally held to be acceptable – as in the case of dereliction of duty or unacceptable behaviour towards others. The survey also asked briefly about reactions to coverage of the September 11th attacks on the New York World Trade Center, in terms of balancing public interest and the right to privacy of victims' families.

The focus group stage of the research offered a good understanding of what 'the public interest' referred to in very broad terms, but gave no indication of whether there are any 'dominant' or widely held definitions of the term. The survey included a number of different routes towards establishing what the term meant to people. The survey also asked the sample to define – in their own words – what the key concept of 'the public interest' meant to them individually. The results of this show that there are indeed some generally-shared elements within the broad 'public interest' term, particularly those linked to issues of public rights and private duties, which are relatively widely shared among the public.

Overview of the survey

The focus groups preceding the survey stage helped to clarify the likely lay-of-the-land relating to media performance, expectations of the type and style of coverage of the different media and also offered a rich variety of opinions about the intrusion of privacy and the boundaries and limits that might be set for such activities. Privacy, public interest and intrusion were all seen as important matters. The groups also provided a detailed basis for an understanding of the dynamics of opinion and belief, as well as a good guide to the actual terms and concepts which people tend to use when discussing these issues. They also highlighted topics which might well be overlooked when designing a survey questionnaire from 'cold'. For example, many of the attitudinal questions asked in the survey were largely based on the topics used and examples raised and discussed in the focus groups.

This survey was not designed to be exhaustive. To do so would have required a much longer – possibly unworkably long – questionnaire. The survey questions were designed to provide a reliable and generalizable account of UK public opinion on key issues arising from the theoretical framework developed and informed by the previous stages of the study. The questions aimed to provide information and answers which could have a direct role in the formulation of regulatory and programme-making policy. Also, the survey did not repeat the Values items used in the first study, partly for reasons of space, but also because the nature of the issues to be asked about, judging from the focus group stage, meant that many aspects of these were likely to be effectively universal regardless of personal value beliefs.

A sample of 1049 adults (aged 16+) was interviewed in the last two weeks of October 2001, following the depth interview and focus group stages.[1] The questionnaire covered a range of topics in varying degrees of depth. In the following sections, four broad themes are covered:

- First, the perceived role and personal uses of the main media, and interest in a range of storylines.
- Second, the survey asked about individuals' perceptions of a range of possible media intrusions into personal privacy, and the primary media sources of such intrusions.
- Third, the issue of defining the term 'the public interest'. The survey included more than one method to examine the public understanding of the term the *public* interest, including asking people to define 'the public interest' in their own words.
- Fourth, the survey focused upon one particular scenario which had featured in the focus groups: the case of a National Heath Service (NHS) ruling about treatment for the elderly.

The Survey Results[2]
The survey data were analysed in a number of ways in order to try to look for alternative 'drivers' of opinion and belief, such as different sets of personal values, or different beliefs about the role of the media. The methods used have included factor analysis and other multivariate techniques. However, these in fact revealed very little and have not been included here. Therefore, the following sections should be read as a summary of the data and associated analysis, and they focus solely upon addressing the main issues and questions underlying the research aims.

Uses and Roles of the Media
The focus groups showed that the media can and do perform a range of different roles in people's lives. While this is not a new phenomenon – it has been researched in many

countries and for many different media since the 1940s – the survey gave the opportunity to obtain more up-to-date and representative data about the UK population. The survey respondents were asked how much a number of different possible uses of the media applied to them personally. The items used in the questions were drawn jointly from a number of existing studies and from the previous stages of the project, and reflected both informational and personal gratifications that can be obtained from the media.

Uses of the Media

From the replies (Table 33), it is clear that majorities believed they use the media for 'important' purposes: getting news and information at local, national and international levels. A majority also clearly value the entertainment content of the media. Other possible uses of the media do not have a clear majority appeal, although large minorities in each case did consider that these applied to their own media use.

Two items in Table 33 are of particular interest – *'Keeps me in touch with local issues'* and *'Helps me feel part of my community'* – since they show a clear difference in media role. Information about the local area (which can be taken to include at least some element of 'community') is markedly more relevant (67% saying applies a lot/quite a lot) to people than the more specific but linked function of *belonging* to a community (35%). In part, of course, this must reflect the fact that the media focus on local community does tend to be limited, either in general scope, or restricted to specifically local media themselves. But it

	Applies a lot	Quite a lot	A little	Does not apply at all
Lets me follow important events & crises	46	41	11	2
Keeps me in touch with what's going on in Britain	42	46	10	2
Keeps me in touch with what's going on in other parts of the world	41	45	12	2
Keeps me in touch with local issues	21	46	26	7
Lets me see how society works	18	40	35	8
Gives me a good laugh	17	34	38	11
Shows what people in authority are really like	15	35	35	15
Helps me relax	15	32	33	20
Keeps me company	14	25	36	24
Cheers me up	12	31	38	20
Helps me feel part of my community	11	24	41	24
Shows me how ordinary people live	10	29	46	16
Tells me about famous people who I am interested in	9	30	43	18
Tells me about people I admire	7	27	46	20
Gives advice on personal problems	5	14	40	41

Table 33. Uses of the Media. Different people use the media for different reasons. How much does each apply? Figures in percentages.

also reflects the focus groups, where 'community' did not seem to be a major factor, other than in the sense of the geographically local area.

A further point to note is the fact that, while the media can and do focus on 'the human condition' – reflecting other people's lives and lifestyles, and offering examples and advice – these media functions are *not* a major feature of most people's replies. However, relatively few said that coverage of people – famous or otherwise – applied to any great degree. For example, around 30 to 40% of adults do have an interest in finding out *'how ordinary people live'*, *'people I admire'*, or *'famous people'*. Equally, though, very few said that their media use was entirely *un*related to these features of the media.

The overall conclusion that can be drawn from these findings is that those areas where issues like privacy and intrusion might arise are part of a relatively minor set of media roles – showing what other people are like or how they behave – which the media can play. The major roles of the media are firmly linked to information about living in the world, rather than to the observation of the lives of others. Again, the points made in the focus groups are reflected in the survey.

Overall, the benefits that people get from the media show a high level of consistency across the different demographic groupings. Within this overall picture, though, there are some genuine differences to be seen in the ways different sections of the population use the media (Table 34). Among those in social grades D and E (those in unskilled work 'D', and the long-term unemployed and state pensioners 'E'), the 'observational' aspects of the media – learning about people – have the strongest role.

There are also some age-related differences, with younger people being most likely to say they use the media for 'a good laugh (Table 34). The over-55s are most likely to value the companionship the media can bring (usually in the form of television[3]) and, since social grade E consists mainly of retired people, these also show a similar trend.

However, demographics alone cannot 'explain' differences fully. When looked at in terms of newspaper reading preferences, further differences of opinion are revealed. Detailed statistical analysis shows that these differences are not simply reflections of the different demographic compositions of each type of newspaper read; rather, people read the papers which come closest to their interests.

	Social grade			Age group		
	ABC1	C2	DE	16–34	35–54	55+
Shows what people in authority are really like	44	52	56	No differences		
Shows me how ordinary people live	33	37	47	No differences		
Gives me a good laugh	No differences			60	47	46
Keeps me company	38	36	44	30	36	53
Tells me about famous people who I am interested in	35	40	53	44	33	39

Table 34. Demographics and Uses of the Media. Percentage in each demographic group saying that statement applies a lot/quite a lot.

	Daily paper read most often			
	Tabloids	**Mail/ Express**	**Broadsheet**	**Local/ regional**
Shows what people in authority are really like	55	54	36	51
Shows me how ordinary people live	42	40	25	46
Keeps me in touch with local issues	70	71	55	78
Gives me a good laugh	55	54	45	49
Gives advice on personal problems	22	30	7	21
Keeps me company	37	46	36	44

Table 35. Daily Newspaper Readership and Uses of the Media. Percentage in each readership group saying that statement applies a lot/quite a lot.

Importantly, many people also believe that the media should have a moral role in society. This can be seen in replies to two attitude statements from the survey asking what people believe the media are 'for' (Table 36). These statements were both supported by very large majorities of the sample, with less than one in twenty actively disagreeing. The underlying sentiment of these two items is unequivocal: the great majority of people believed that the media should be doing specific tasks such as moral guidance and reflecting social life. In particular, over four in ten adults 'strongly agree' that the media should show *'the difference between right and wrong'*. By comparison, opinions are less strongly held over *'reflecting the ways of life of different communities'* – relatively few replies were in the 'agree strongly' category'.

Taken together with the findings on the ways the media are used by people, the firm conclusion can be drawn that the great majority of people expect the media to undertake key roles in imparting information about the physical and social world. Within this overall majority sentiment, there were no real differences between different demographic or readership groups: these views are effectively universal.

	Agree strongly	**Agree**	**Neither**	**Disagree**	**Disagree strongly**
The media should show the difference between right and wrong	42	45	8	4	1
The media should reflect the ways of life of different communities in the country	20	63	13	4	★

Table 36. Media roles. Figures in percentages.

There is, though, always the possibility that other factors are at play when such issues are asked about with questions such as these – for example, replies could have been influenced by survey respondents wanting to appear to be thoughtful and responsible, and so tended to choose 'responsible' alternatives in the interview itself. Accordingly, these issues were approached via a second route, using specific examples in the form of storylines.

The Storylines

The survey asked the sample to rate a range of fifteen 'storylines' in terms of personal interest in each. These basic story outlines included local and national, human interest and

'MAJORITY' INTEREST	Very interested	Fairly	Not very	Not at all	Don't know
Foods sold by a major supermarket have been contaminated with bacteria	76	19	3	1	★
Many electrical appliances sold across the UK may be unsafe	71	24	4	1	★
A High Court judge has large investments in foreign companies linked to the illegal drugs trade	54	31	9	5	1
A sex offender, recently released from prison, is living somewhere in the UK under a new identity	52	29	12	6	1
A local bus driver has a history of drink-driving	48	32	13	6	1
A local person has been charged with supplying drugs	46	38	10	5	1
A schoolteacher has been passing on exam questions to her students to help their GCSE grades	43	35	16	6	1
A company testing medicines is suspected of cruelty towards animals	40	40	13	6	1
A local council has greatly overspent its budget despite warnings from its staff	35	39	18	7	1
A leading footballer is badly injured in a car crash	12	36	29	22	1
'MINORITY' INTEREST					
A well-known TV actor who is known to have a serious illness is seen abroad looking very ill	5	32	38	24	1
A film star is rumoured to be having an affair	3	10	31	54	1
The diaries of a dead politician suggest that he had an affair with a woman who is still alive	2	9	30	58	1
A celebrity's daughter is found drunk in public	1	10	31	56	1
A member of a leading pop group has cosmetic surgery to change her face shape	2	8	23	66	1

Table 37. Personal Interest in Media Storylines. I'm now going to read out a number of media stories. For each, tell me whether you personally would be interested in it. Figures in percentages.

political themes, and were designed to reflect typically occurring and familiar areas of media content.

Depending on the specific storyline, levels of personal interest in the items ranged from 95% interested (very or fairly interested) in contaminated food sold by supermarkets down to 10% interested in a pop star's cosmetic surgery (Table 37). Indeed, there is a clear demarcation between those which attract majority interest and those with minority appeal only.

The minority stories in Table 37 have a common link: they are essentially gossip-based stories of the type usually featured in the more popular newspapers. They serve as a useful contrast, though, with the item about an injured footballer (directly based on comments made in the focus groups). The factor of injury – presumably entailing no blame or self-promotion to the footballer concerned – appears to act to remove this particular item from the general realm of gossip.

However, these results are also evidence of the fact that it cannot be taken for granted that there is such a thing as universal interest in any particular story among the public – different individuals can and will have different interests, just as for some topics there is a high degree of general interest. While there is agreement over the broader issues of privacy – shown in Tables 35 and 36, for example – reactions to these more detailed examples are more idiosyncratic.

Some of these individual differences are, however, also linked firmly to individual circumstances, and examples of these are set out in Table 38.

Attitudes towards Privacy and Intrusion

From the focus groups, it was clear that people's rights to privacy are regarded as important, almost sacrosanct under some circumstances, and as a potential source of friction between the media and the public. The sample was asked how much they agreed or disagreed with a wide range of privacy-related issues in the form of attitude statements (Table 39). The items used were derived primarily from issues raised and statements made in the focus groups and industry interviews.

	Children at home		Sex	
	Yes	No	Male	Female
A well-known TV actor who is known to have a serious illness is seen abroad looking very ill	No differences		28	45
A company testing medicines is suspected of cruelty towards animals	No differences		73	87
A sex offender, recently released from prison, is living somewhere in the UK under a new identity	90	76	77	85

Table 38. Demographics and Interest. Percentage in each demographic group saying that they are very/fairly interested in each storyline.

Among the various statements, the sample's response to one item in particular stands out from the rest: 91% felt that the media should not involve children, while only 5% disagreed. Moreover, most of the responses were '*strongly* agree' rather than the milder 'agree'. The rights of children are held to be effectively inviolable in terms of media attention. This pattern is not seen for any of the other statements dealing with privacy and intrusion, although opinions about relatives' rights and partners' or friends' rights show majority – but markedly milder – support.

	Agree strongly	Agree	Neither	Disagree strongly	Disagree
No matter what someone has done, the media should never involve that person's children	56	35	4	3	2
When the media want to cover the life of someone who has died, the relatives should have the right to prevent it	32	50	12	5	1
No matter what someone has done, the media should never involve that person's partner or friends	24	49	16	10	1
The media should always respect people's privacy, even if this means not being able to cover an issue fully	27	39	17	15	1
If some people want to be celebrities, they have to accept some intrusion into their personal lives	19	61	8	10	2
People in important positions have to accept some intrusion into their personal lives	13	63	10	12	2
It's better for a few people to be upset than to stop important issues being covered fully by the media	12	54	20	12	2
Sometimes, the media have to ignore people's privacy in order to report important issues	10	44	22	21	3
Sometimes, the media have to use underhand means in order to report important issues	6	35	19	32	8

Table 39. Privacy and Intrusion. Figures in percentages.

Rights and Limits to Rights

However, most people also believe that the rights to privacy of adults can be put aside if there is sufficient cause. Celebrities and important people are, in effect, fair game and have to accept this. At the same time, a clear majority support the view that the media should always respect people's privacy. The example below shows that 32% of the sample were fully 'consistent' in their opinions on two of the items, agreeing with one and disagreeing with the other. A slightly larger proportion (totalling 36%), though were seemingly 'inconsistent', either agreeing with (34%) or disagreeing (2%) with both.

Our interpretation of this is that it can be perfectly possible to hold to a principle while admitting exceptions to it – the principle survives but can be softened or amended depending upon circumstances, rules can have exceptions. The wording of the questions – 'should' and 'sometimes...have to' – must be assumed to have a role here. Equally, though, there are also other people who value consistency above flexibility and who do not appear to admit to exceptions or consider weighing the evidence.

Three of the items covered the topic of public surveillance in one or other form (Table 41).[4] Closed-circuit TV (CCTV) surveillance cameras were almost unanimously held to be a good thing. As the groups' comments about these suggested, CCTV can serve as a physical example of the balance between a certain degree of risk of being 'caught on camera' when perhaps you would not want it and the direct benefit of security in *public* places – an important proviso – which these cameras are felt to bring. Nor, in similar vein, was there any evidence of a widespread antipathy towards the principle of introducing a formal system of identity cards for all.

The third item – being photographed in a public place – produced a very mixed reaction, with opinions effectively split. Our suggestion is that the question itself is most likely too general and should have been extended to include the differences between close-ups, long shots and so on featured in the focus groups' thoughts on this issue. Nevertheless, it does offer some support for the general conclusion that a person's rights to privacy – in this case being photographed and then shown in a public place – are by no means simple to define, nor can they be ignored simply by dint of being in a particular place at a particular time. In

% of total sample	The media should always respect people's privacy, even if this means not being able to cover an issue fully		
		AGREE	NEITHER	DISAGREE
Sometimes, the media have to ignore people's privacy in order to report important issues	AGREE	34	8	12
	NEITHER	12	7	2
	DISAGREE	20	2	2

Table 40. Privacy and Intrusion.

	Agree strongly	Agree	Neither	Disagree	Disagree strongly
Security cameras in public places are a good idea	51	39	6	3	1
It is a good idea for everyone in the country to have identity cards	40	38	10	8	4
If people are photographed in a public place, the media should be free to use the pictures	6	28	21	36	9

Table 41. Attitudes towards Surveillance. Figures in percentages.

effect, invasion of privacy requires just cause as well as presence. A conclusion which may well then follow is that the media, when operating in those places which could reasonably be regarded as 'public' or 'open' space are expected to operate under a duty of care not to infringe these implicit rights to personal privacy without due cause.

Media Intrusion

A further question asked about the likelihood of media intrusion into people's privacy. The replies (Table 42) show that, in overall image terms, the popular tabloid daily press and to a slightly lesser degree the Sunday newspapers are firmly entrenched in the public mind as the leaders in intrusion. For both, clear majorities said that these were very likely to intrude. However, television and the other daily newspapers, while clearly not as likely to intrude as the tabloid press, are not seen in a particularly flattering light. Radio and local newspapers, by comparison, are generally believed to be less likely to intrude on privacy than the national press or television. However, the dominant response for nearly all the media asked about was that they were at least 'fairly likely' to intrude. These general opinions about the Internet reflect the fact that many people have no experience and little knowledge of it, hence, the very high level of 'don't know' responses to these two items. If these responses are excluded, the resultant figures of at least one-third saying the medium is 'very likely' to intrude puts it alongside television news and current affairs.

Table 42 represents the image of the various media among the whole adult population. In some ways, this could be an unfair basis for comparison, in that readers/listeners/net users themselves are possibly the best qualified to judge the media they know and use. The data in Table 43 are based only on users[5] (readers, listeners, Internet users) of the various media.

In fact, there are few real changes to the overall patterns seen in the previous results. Readers of the popular press are fully aware of their papers' reputations. The only large-scale changes are seen in opinions about the Internet. Despite some Internet users (around 1 in 4) not having an opinion on intrusion, maybe because they are not users of these services, around 50% believe that Internet news pages or chat rooms are likely to intrude on privacy. This level of opinion puts the Internet in line with many of the more

	Very likely	Fairly likely	Not very likely	Not at all likely	Don't know
Popular daily newspapers (*Sun, Mirror, Star*)	68	22	3	2	4
Sunday newspapers	52	33	7	2	6
Television current affairs or documentaries	35	43	15	4	3
Television news	34	43	17	4	2
Other daily newspapers (*Mail, Express, Telegraph, Guardian, Times* etc.)	31	47	13	2	7
Local newspapers	18	39	33	6	4
Radio current affairs or documentaries	17	41	29	6	7
Radio news programmes	14	42	32	6	6
Radio music or chat programmes	11	26	38	16	9
Internet chat rooms	18	15	11	5	51
Internet news pages	17	20	11	4	48

Table 42. Media Intrusion (All). How likely, if at all, do you think these various media are to intrude into people's privacy? Base: Total sample.

established media. At present, though, among non-users, the Internet remains somewhat of an unknown quantity, whereas the older media have firmly entrenched images among the general public.

Every person who said that broadcasters or national newspapers were very or fairly likely to intrude into people's privacy were also asked whether they had any particular service in mind. In most cases, relatively few could name any specific channel, service or publication (Tables 44 to 47). Rather, they felt that all were equally worthy of blame.

Among the television channels, ITV, BBC1, Channel 4 and Sky News were named more than the other channels, as far as intrusion of the news was concerned, by those respondents who said that television news or current affairs programmes were likely to intrude.

For radio services, again most people could not nominate any one service as being intrusive. Commercial local radio and BBC Radio 1 were the most-nominated in terms of intrusion in the news, but at relatively low levels (Table 45).

However, where the press is concerned, a strikingly different picture emerges (Table 46). In contrast to broadcasting, most people could name specific sources of intrusion. Moreover, there is one clear 'culprit' among the national dailies – *The Sun*. Few people believe any other papers intrude, and the only other dailies attracting more than minimal criticism are the other two tabloids.

Interestingly, *Sun* readers themselves did not greatly differ in their views of their chosen paper: 56% named the *Sun* as the daily paper most likely to be intrusive. Despite acknowledging the *Sun* as the 'guilty man', *Sun* readers' views on what is acceptable media practice over intrusion were not markedly different from the average: for example, identical proportions – 41 per cent – of the entire sample and of *Sun* readers agreed that *'sometimes the media have to use underhand measures in order to report important issues'*. Similarly, 68 per cent of *Sun* readers as against 66 per cent of the sample agreed that *'the media should always respect people's privacy, even if this means not being able to cover an issue fully'*. Indeed, for all the various

	Very likely	Fairly likely	Not very likely	Not at all likely	Don't know
Popular daily newspapers (*Sun, Mirror, Star*)	66	27	4	1	2
Sunday newspapers	56	35	6	1	2
Television current affairs or documentaries	35	43	15	4	3
Television news	34	43	17	4	2
Other daily newspapers (*Mail, Express, Telegraph, Guardian, Times* etc.)	31	54	13	1	1
Local newspapers	22	35	36	5	2
Radio current affairs or documentaries	16	42	31	6	5
Radio news programmes	10	44	37	5	4
Radio music or chat programmes	12	24	42	17	6
Internet chat rooms	25	23	19	6	26
Internet news pages	25	31	17	5	22

Table 43. Media Intrusion (Users). How likely, if at all, do you think these various media are to intrude into people's privacy? Base: Users of each medium/type listed, except TV (entire sample). Figures in percentages.

	TV news %	TV current affairs/ documentaries %
No, no specific TV channel	55	49
ITV/ITN	12	12
Channel 4	8	16
BBC1	8	10
BBC2	1	3
Channel 5	3	3
Sky News	8	4
CNN	5	2
Other TV channel	1	1

Table 44. Sources of Media Intrusion – Television. Is there any one particular TV channel where the news is more likely to be intrusive? Is there any one particular TV channel where current affairs or documentaries are more likely to be intrusive?
Base: All saying TV news/TV current affairs very/fairly likely to intrude.

	Radio news %	Radio current affairs/ documentaries %
No, no specific radio service	64	67
Commercial local radio	11	10
BBC Radio 1	11	6
BBC Radio 4	3	6
BBC Radio 2	2	3
Virgin	2	1
BBC Radio 5	2	1
BBC Radio Wales/Scotland	★	★
Talk Sport	1	1
Classic FM	1	1
BBC Radio 3	0	1
BBC local radio	2	2
Another radio service	2	2

Table 45. Sources of Media Intrusion – Radio. Is there any one particular radio station where the news is more likely to be intrusive? Is there any one particular radio station where current affairs or documentaries are more likely to be intrusive?
Base: All saying radio news/radio Current Affairs very/fairly likely to intrude.

	%
No, no specific daily newspaper	20
The Sun	61
The Star	7
The Mirror/Daily Record	5
The Daily Mail	2
Daily evening paper	2
The Daily Express	1
The Guardian	★
The Daily Telegraph	★
The Times	★
The Independent	★
The Financial Times	0
Daily local/regional paper	0
Another daily paper	1

Table 46. Sources of Media Intrusion – Daily Newspapers. Is there any one particular daily newspaper which is more likely to be intrusive?
Base: All saying daily newspapers very/fairly likely to intrude.

issues relating to intrusion which were used, there were no consistent differences of opinion to be found between tabloid readers (daily or Sunday) and other papers' readers.

Clearly, there is a more complex issue underlying these opinions. It would seem unlikely that *Sun* readers were simply lying when they answered the survey questions. What is far more likely is that there are subtle shades of meaning involved in what constitutes 'intrusion' into privacy. As the focus groups showed, there is an important element of 'deservedness' at play in such judgements. This supports the conclusions drawn from the first study (Chapter 4b), whereby the status of the individual determined the treatment given. The key distinction may need to be drawn between *warranted* and *unwarranted* intrusion – and the current results can be argued to reflect warranted intrusion rather than unwarranted. If this is the case, *Sun* readers are neither lying, nor are they being inconsistent.

Similar results to those obtained for the daily press can be seen for the Sunday papers (Table 47). One title – the *News of the World* – dominates, and the other Sunday tabloids account for almost all other replies. Analysis of *News of the World* readers' views on intrusion (as was the case with *Sun* readers set out in the previous paragraph) did not show their opinions to be any different from the general view.

Defining the Public Interest

The survey approached the issue of defining 'the public interest' using four separate routes. This strategy was designed to avoid reliance on any single measure in order to minimise the possibility of the question wordings themselves unduly influencing the type of response given by interviewees.

	%
No, no specific Sunday newspaper	21
The News of the World	62
The Sunday Mirror/ Record	7
The People	5
The Mail on Sunday	1
The Sunday Express	1
The Observer	★
The Sunday Telegraph	1
The Sunday Times	1
Sunday local/regional paper	★
The Independent on Sunday	0
Another Sunday paper	2

Table 47. Sources of Media Intrusion – Sunday Newspapers. Is there any one particular Sunday newspaper which is more likely to be intrusive? Base: All saying Sunday newspapers very/fairly likely to intrude.

Public Interest: Storylines

In the first approach to establishing what the public interest means to people, the set of storylines discussed previously were used again, but this time asking the sample to decide whether each was in *the public interest*, rather than of *personal interest* to them (Tables 48 and 49).

From these replies, it is very clear that there are some issues which are effectively universally held to be in the public interest. Furthermore, there were no large-scale differences in opinions found between the various demographic sub-groups for these items, suggesting that there is a tendency toward consensus over some key issues – in particular those which have the potential for harm or direct impact on society at some level.

The results do also show similarities with those found for *personal* interest in the items (see Table 37) in terms of those items getting a majority 'vote'. However, apart from the

MAJORITY PUBLIC INTEREST	Definitely in the public interest	Probably	Probably not	Definitely not	Don't know
Foods sold by a major supermarket have been contaminated with bacteria	90	9	★	★	1
Many electrical appliances sold across the UK may be unsafe	85	12	1	1	1
A sex offender, recently released from prison, is living somewhere in the UK under a new identity	67	24	5	2	2
A High Court judge has large investments in foreign companies linked to the illegal drugs trade	62	30	5	2	1
A local person has been charged with supplying drugs	59	32	6	2	1
A schoolteacher has been passing on exam questions to her students to help their GCSE grades	57	35	6	1	1
A local bus driver has a history of drink-driving	55	34	8	2	1
A local council has greatly overspent its budget despite warnings from its staff	49	39	9	2	1
A company testing medicines is suspected of cruelty towards animals	45	44	8	2	1
A leading footballer is badly injured in a car crash	12	40	27	19	2

Table 48. Media Coverage and the Public Interest. Tell me if this is a matter for public interest.

MINORITY PUBLIC INTEREST	Definitely in the public interest	Probably	Probably not	Definitely not	Don't know
A well-known TV actor who is known to have a serious illness is seen abroad looking very ill	6	29	34	29	1
The diaries of a dead politician suggest that he had an affair with a woman who is still alive	4	16	34	44	2
A celebrity's daughter is found drunk in public	4	16	34	45	1
A film star is rumoured to be having an affair	4	15	32	48	1
A member of a leading pop group has cosmetic surgery to change her face shape	3	14	29	54	1

Table 49. Media Coverage and the Public Interest. Figures in percentages.

'footballer' item where the majority/minority split was more even, the proportions saying it was 'definitely' or 'probably in the public interest' is markedly higher than the proportions saying they were 'very' or 'fairly interested' in the same item, and with lowered levels of disagreement.

This suggests that for many people, public interest is understood to mean something beyond purely personal interest. At the same time, there does also appear to be a fairly direct link between the two concepts, since the overall rank order of perceived public interest closely matches that given for personal interest.

Equally, those items where there were low levels of personal interest (the 'gossip' items on stars etc. in Table 37) are marginally elevated when considered from a public interest perspective, but the view of clear majorities (63–83%) is that these are *not* of public interest (Table 49).

The Public Interest: Amount of Coverage

The second approach to understanding 'the public interest' used a different criterion for judgement, this time requiring the interviewees to say *how much* media coverage should be given. The items used were not specific stories, but represented general categories of content. No specific medium was mentioned, merely 'the media' in general. The underlying principle is that the degree of coverage – on a scale from 'maximum coverage' through to 'no coverage at all' – is a reflection of the degree of public interest (or similar) which is implied by each content category given in the question. The results are shown in Table 50.

As with the previous results, it is clear that people can and do discriminate strongly between different types of coverage. Two broad trends can be seen in the results. First, there are several topics which are widely believed to warrant high levels of coverage (maximum or quite a lot). These particular topics involve issues and actions which can impact both at the individual level (e.g. crime, local community) and at the broader societal level (e.g. corruption, incompetence).

There is also evidence of a clear barrier to coverage where privacy is concerned – the contrast between politicians' official activities and their private lives is strong: 88 per cent wanted coverage of the official while only 40 per cent wanted the private revealed (and then only at the lowest possible level). However, there was not such a strong feeling about the private lives of other people in the public eye such as sports personalities and rock and media stars.

Here again there is evidence of a broad consensus on some issues, coupled with split opinions on others. Yet, it is quite clear that the general public do not wish for 'tame'

	Maximum coverage	Quite a lot of coverage	A little coverage	No coverage at all	Don't know
Details of serious crimes	42	43	12	1	2
Exposure of incompetence by officials	42	38	15	3	2
Exposure of corruption and hypocrisy	40	38	15	4	2
Exposure of fraud and cheating	37	42	17	2	1
Information about events in the UK	35	50	12	1	2
The lives of people guilty of serious crimes	29	30	28	12	2
News about your local community	28	52	17	1	2
Showing the effects of crime on the victims	28	39	26	6	1
Information about events outside the UK	21	46	28	4	1
Politicians' official activities	13	42	33	10	2
Showing how people cope with misfortune	11	37	41	8	2
The lives of ordinary people	8	26	49	15	2
The lives of sporting personalities	4	14	54	26	2
Politicians' private lives	3	6	31	58	2
The lives of pop stars	3	9	47	40	1
The lives of TV and film stars	2	10	56	30	2

Table 50. Opinions on Amount of Coverage. The various media – both local and national – can give you many different types of information and coverage. How much coverage do you think the media should give to this type of material? Figures in percentages.

media. People do see the media as having a watchdog function in line with democratic ideas of the media as the fourth estate. Some of the highest overall scores are for the media to 'expose corruption and hypocrisy' with 40 per cent considering the maximum exposure should be given to this type of reporting, followed by 38 per cent considering 'quite a lot of coverage' should be given, similarly 42 per cent and 43 per cent respectively considered that maximum coverage should be given to the 'details of serious crimes' or 'quite a lot of coverage' should be given and that the 'lives of people guilty of serious crimes' should be given great attention, 29 per cent considering maximum coverage be given with a further 30 per cent believing 'quite a lot of coverage' should be given.

The Public's Own Definitions of 'The Public Interest'

As the previous chapters have shown, the term 'the public interest' is both conceptually complex from an *a priori* basis, and may not have a commonly agreed-upon meaning as far as the general public are concerned. The third approach used in the survey to explore 'the public interest' was the most direct and asked people to define the term 'the public interest' in their own words, as a further way of establishing public knowledge.

It should be borne in mind that the definitions given in the survey interview are not directly comparable to conversation and comments arising in the more informal and in-depth setting of a focus group. The survey setting has its own rules, with the interviewer controlling the structure of the session and having to write down the verbatim reply. Thus, the statements tend to be more cursory and formalized.

Equally, the overall structure of the survey questionnaire will have had an impact. This particular question came after a series of questions asking about media intrusion into personal privacy. This placement was deliberately undertaken in order to ensure that the broad context of the question was clear: the relationship – if any – between media intrusion into privacy and 'the public interest'. Thus the question has some potential weaknesses; at the same time, though, it offered the survey interviewees a clear opportunity to offer their own thoughts in their own words on what the term meant to them.

Over 90% of the sample did offer a definition in their own words of what they understood by 'the public interest' in this context, demonstrating that the broad term at least is recognized, even if it is not particularly clearly or consistently articulated.

These verbatim replies were then content-analysed into broad categories. The categorization focused upon the underlying rationale of the definitions given by the sample, and up to two different categories were coded for each person's reply.[6] There was no clear shared majority definition to be found in the sample's definitions. Rather, there were three distinct 'clusters' or groupings of specific themes, shown in Tables 51 and 52, together with examples of each grouping.

The largest proportion of the replies (65% of the sample) fell into a grouping where the overall theme is linked to something best described as a **Public Service Ethos**. Within this overall grouping were three more specific categories of reply. The first we have called **Public Rights**. A defining feature of this category is the use of 'imperative' terms – *needs, rights, should* and so on – used in support of the principle of public, democratic rights to information.

Group 1: PUBLIC SERVICE ETHOS – (65% of sample)

Category:	Examples

Public Rights

34%	It's information that the public has the right to know.

Something going on needs to be brought to the public's notice.

Government officials should be accountable for their mistakes – the public should be aware of this. There are certain issues that the public should be made aware of – this is what 'the public interest' means.

That it's important for people to know about what's going on in the world and for them to make informed decisions and opinions.

The Jeffrey Archer[7] case was in the public interest. The general public was made aware what is happening.

If the matter of the subject transcends or supersedes the individual's right to privacy.

I think we have a right to know what famous people get up to as people i.e. children look up to them. The politician found out doing dodgy deals etc., the public have a right to know.

To make things common knowledge.

Public Effects

28%	Issues that affect ordinary people directly.

Something affecting others rather than just that person.

If it's important to other people and it is likely to affect or harm other people.

If it would affect you as a member of the public like war, disasters or floods.

Where the issue has a direct effect on people's lives.

National Interest

3%	If it's to do with the security of the country – deviousness by politicians – that sort of thing.

Something basically important – in the national interest or the people at large.

General public as a whole, all 60 million of us.

In case of danger to the public or the country and national security.

What it means is security of the country. If [popular singer] is wearing pink knickers that's not important to the country, but if she was a spy, that is in the public interest, national security.

Table 51. Public Interest Definitions Given by Survey. Sometimes the media argue that intrusions into privacy are justified because they are in the public interest. What do you understand by this term – 'the public interest'?

The next largest category of definitions – **Public Effects** – centres around the issue of effects and impacts. Essentially, the argument is that large-scale effects on the public at large are *a priori* a matter of concern. The third category centres around a theme stressing the nation as an entity – **National Interest**. All of these carry echoes of a long-standing cultural and political tradition, – encompassing both actions and expectations – of public service, public duty and so on.

A second grouping of replies – which we have called **Consumer-Oriented** (Table 52) illustrates clear confusion for some people between the more abstract concept of the public interest as a form of public good and the specific interests of members of the public, either *en masse* or as individuals. These replies hinge around public interest being defined by the opinions and interests of the media consumer, rather than taking the more abstract form demonstrated by the replies in Table 52. Within this broad grouping of interest-led definitions are three distinct divisions into the **public**, **personal** and **community** levels.

There is a further set of definitions which again reflect a different style of understanding of the public interest concept. These are basically formulated as observations of media practice under the rubric of 'the public interest', rather than reflections upon what form the ideal might take. Two of the categories are unreservedly critical: the media intrude for the 'wrong' reasons (unwarranted intrusion); and 'the public interest' is simply a convenient cover term used by the media for the media simply doing whatever they want (media excuse).

A third set of replies (warranted intrusion) show that media intrusion can be part of the public interest, though again defining the concept more by actions rather than principles, and in effect proposing that the media act to show how badly other people can behave.

What these verbatim definitions given by the sample show particularly clearly is the lack of a common, shared definitional base for the actual term 'the public interest'. While other aspects of the survey data do clearly point to a strong degree of universality among the public in terms of underlying principles which underpin people's judgements of what is deemed acceptable or unacceptable – such as judging principles expressed as specific actions or scenarios – the core terminology often used by the media industries and regulators cannot be assumed to be equally universally understood. This conclusion is reinforced by bearing in mind the fact that this question was preceded in the survey by others which did raise the general issues of public interest – these replies were not given *in vacuo*.

Taken together with the other various lines of evidence arising from the survey, there are several broad conclusions which can be drawn.

First, people need and value information from the media which tells about events, threats, things of interest and life in general.

Second, the media are supremely important for providing content which is valued and needed, but may not be performing exactly as desired by their public.

Third, the precise nature of what constitutes media coverage which is felt to be firmly 'in the public interest' can vary greatly from person to person, depending upon the issues involved, the medium, and the individual interpreting the medium's content. There is no clear or widely shared definition of 'the public interest'. What there is, though, is a

Group 2: CONSUMER-ORIENTED – (24% of sample)

Category:	Examples

Interests of the Public

15%	Some news like war news and New York towers information is interesting. Good for people to know and we can discuss it with friends. Things that the public would be interested in hearing about, celebrities' and politicians' private lives. Anything the public would be interested in reading about. Kind of what people are interested in reading about, what people want to see or read. Giving the public what they want.

Personal Interests

7%	[Public Interest] is not easy to define, some subjects may be of interest to some members of the public and others may be not. Something that is going to interest you or benefit you. Only way would be a paedophile situation because that would affect me, it would be in my interest to know as I have children. It affects the way I live. If it is interesting to me it must have some effect on me, if not, it doesn't. If it's going to affect you.

Local/Community Interest

2%	Nowadays people often don't know their neighbour, so they need to know what is going on in their neighbourhood to protect themselves. The local papers, news etc. does this, this is 'public interest' Relevant to particular sections of society. If there is a local crime or paedophile in the area, anything like that. What is happening within your local area. The people in the community should know what's going on if it affects them.

Table 52. Public Interest Definitions Given by Survey. Sometimes the media argue that intrusions into privacy are justified because they are in the public interest. What do you understand by this term – 'the public interest'?.

complex interaction between people and the media. In some cases, there is indeed almost unanimous agreement that some media practices are 'good' and some are 'bad' in terms of following the established – and generally accepted and familiar – rules of engagement which should apply.

Group 3: MEDIA PRACTICE-BASED (33% of the sample)

Category:	Examples

Unwarranted Intrusion

16%	Just like to be nosy. Not always in public interest.
	Good reporting shouldn't be intrusive.
	I think they want to be nosy – delve into people's private lives.
	Anything you think of, there is anything in public interest.
	I think due to public interest, newspapers take advantage to expose privacy of the person.
	Public interest means that some of the things that come out will be detrimental to the people involved. Sometimes they don't have the facts right.
	It's just gossip, and telling people what they think they want to hear.

Media Excuse

12%	Statement media use to absolve them of all sin. *Carte blanche* because they say it's public interest.
	They are still just trying to sell their newspapers saying it's public interest.
	Public interest is just a way of broadcasting what media want.
	It's a catch-all term that gives the media carte blanche to do what it likes.
	Public interest is when they get a story and make some money out of it.

Warranted Intrusion

5%	Anything that people are interested in, particularly in other people's lives, particularly celebrities and such like, just human instinct to be nosy, particularly if it is not good.
	You know the full character of the person involved, whether they're entirely honest and reliable.

Table 53. Public Interest Definitions Given by Survey. Sometimes the media argue that intrusions into privacy are justified because they are in the public interest. What do you understand by this term – 'the public interest'?

Serving the Public Interest

The sample were also asked to give their judgements on how well the main media 'serve the public interest'. This was the fourth measure of what 'the public interest' means, and this time was based on people's judgements of media practice rather than upon underlying principles. Despite the previously demonstrated lack of agreement among people as to what exactly constitutes 'the public interest' in terms of formal definitions, it is also clear that people can and do make judgements about media performance using such terms.

The samples were asked about their use of different media – TV, radio and press at national and local levels – and how well each served 'the public interest'. Everyone was asked about all the media listed, regardless of whether they were users of each. For each service or medium asked about, those who could make a judgement other than 'don't know' tended to say that the public interest was well served.

As was the case when considering intrusion, this broad comparison based on the entire population may be unhelpful as far as the less widely used services are concerned. Table 55 shows the opinions of those people who said they used each service asked about. All bar one of the services were regarded as serving the public interest as far as their actual users are concerned. The exception was Channel 5, where opinions were more mixed. The television channel results are based on the entire sample, which could affect Channel 5 to a small degree in that some people could not receive the service (and it also has a relatively low audience share). However, the balance between *very well* and *fairly well* would be unaffected by this, and it is the comparatively low level of 'very well' responses which helps to set Channel 5 apart from the other services listed.

Overall, how well does .... serve the public interest?

	Very well	Fairly well	Not very well	Not at all well	Don't know
BBC Television	53	40	3	1	3
ITV	40	52	5	★	3
BBC national radio	34	37	4	1	24
Daily newspapers	30	51	9	2	8
Sunday newspapers	27	47	12	2	12
Local newspapers	24	55	11	2	8
Channel 4	21	46	17	2	14
BBC local Radio	21	43	6	1	29
Satellite TV	21	22	6	1	50
Internet	14	20	6	2	57
Commercial local radio	12	41	13	3	31
Cable TV	12	18	8	2	61
Channel 5	9	31	23	6	32
Classic FM (radio)	7	20	9	4	60
Talk Sport (radio)	7	17	9	5	62
Virgin (radio)	2	15	9	3	71

Table 54. Media Performance – The General Public's View. Base: Total sample.

Overall, how well does .... serve the public interest?

	Very well	Fairly well	Not very well	Not at all well	Don't know
BBC TV	53	40	3	1	3
BBC local Radio	53	33	2	0	8
BBC national radio	47	41	3	★	9
Satellite TV	45	38	5	2	9
ITV	40	52	5	★	3
Daily newspapers	34	54	8	2	2
Local newspapers	33	55	7	1	4
Sunday newspapers	32	52	11	2	3
Cable TV	29	36	15	3	16
Internet	27	38	10	4	21
Commercial local radio [8]	22	53	10	3	12
Channel 4	21	46	17	2	14
Channel 5	9	31	23	6	32

Table 55. Media Performance – Users' Opinions. Base: Users of each medium (TV users = entire sample). Figures in percentages.

The NHS Scenario

The final element of the survey was a series of questions built around a very specific and detailed fictional scenario, using the approach developed for the first study described in Chapter 4b. The scenario used in the second study was based around doctors being secretly instructed by their senior managers to use cheap and less effective cancer drugs on older patients, rather than more expensive and more effective treatments: some doctors want to disobey this instruction. Various elements in the overall 'plot' were formulated as survey questions and each respondent taken through the various elements in turn.

The focus groups all discussed this specific scenario in considerable detail (see Chapter 8a), and it formed a key element in all of them. The survey also featured the basic scenario, using the concepts and categories employed during the focus groups. Of course, the open-ended nature of focus group discussion, argument and debate cannot be replicated in the survey setting. Nevertheless, the key issues are to all intents and purposes the same.

Virtually the entire sample said that this topic should be covered by the media (96%), and a similarly overwhelming majority (98%) also thought it was in the public interest. Nine in ten also said they would be personally interested in this issue – an example of personal interest matching public interest. There were no major differences in opinion found between the main demographic sub-groups.

The next step was to ask people which of a wide range of possible methods were acceptable means for the media to obtain the information needed to cover this story. The

	Yes, definitely	Yes, probably	No strong view	Probably not	Definitely not
First, is this an issue that should be covered by the media?	84	12	2	1	★
Would you say that this is an issue that is in the public interest?	85	13	1	1	★
Would you *personally* be interested in this issue?	74	16	5	4	1

Table 56. The NHS Scenario. A senior manager in the NHS has issued a secret instruction telling doctors that they must not use an expensive new drug treatment on older patients suffering from cancer and can only give them cheaper and less-effective drugs. Some doctors are obeying this instruction, but others are disobeying it. The media want to report this story. Figures in percentages.

list used was the same as that used in the focus groups, with a few minor wording changes to suit the survey setting.

The results show a clear demarcation between a limited number of tactics thought acceptable for information-gathering and others which were thought unsuitable by majorities of the sample (Table 57).

Those generally thought appropriate include basic journalistic techniques: interviewing or telephoning those concerned at the workplace, and the affected patients and their relatives. The use of 'leaked' information was also deemed acceptable by the majority.

Those techniques thought to be unsuitable by majorities included all of the covert or 'sneaky' methods listed, such as disguised reporters, hidden cameras, searching rubbish – some of which are routinely used in the real world. Other less legal strategies such as phone-tapping and mail and e-mail interception are approved by minorities. It might have been expected that CCTV material might be regarded as beyond the pale, but this is clearly believed by most to be a legitimate source of material.

One important point of principle does emerge from these findings: the home is a protected place. In this particular scenario, it is abundantly clear that for most people, the professional responsibility of the NHS official to answer for his or her decisions does *not* extend outside the workplace. This distinction can be clearly seen in the contrast between identical methods in the work and home contexts, where the levels of approval for the home-focused methods are far lower than for their office-focused equivalents. And, above all, the manager's children are effectively sacrosanct.

These results closely mirror the findings from the focus groups. There are clear 'rules of engagement' operating here. But the precise application of these rules must be assumed to be unique to this particular scenario and the particular circumstances it encompasses. If the scenario changes, the ways in which rules are applied or become capable of variation, even

	Very	Fairly	Not very	Not at all	Don't know
Interviewing relatives of elderly patients affected by the decision	41	35	12	11	2
Interviewing elderly patients affected by the decision	40	31	13	14	2
A reporter telephoning the person's office	36	39	13	10	2
Using security camera pictures from the office	28	37	16	15	3
Reporters waiting outside office	24	47	15	12	2
Interviewing person's work colleagues	18	46	17	16	3
Using 'leaked' information from anonymous sources	17	43	20	17	4
Hidden microphone at the person's office	14	28	28	28	2
Hidden TV camera at the person's office	14	27	30	27	2
A reporter at the office disguised as someone else	13	33	27	25	2
A reporter telephoning the person's home	12	32	24	30	2
Hidden photographer at the person's office	12	29	30	27	2
A reporter telephoning the person's office pretending to be someone else	11	29	29	29	2
Going through office rubbish for relevant documents	10	28	27	32	3
Reporters waiting outside person's home	8	28	27	35	2
Tapping office 'phone line	8	22	25	42	2
Interviewing person's adult friends and family	7	26	28	37	2
Intercepting office e-mail	7	23	25	41	4
Intercepting post at the person's office	7	17	30	42	3
Going through person's home rubbish bins for relevant documents	6	16	31	45	2
Hidden TV camera outside the person's home	6	16	30	47	1
A reporter telephoning the person's home pretending to be someone else	6	12	31	50	1
Hidden photographer outside the person's home	5	19	30	44	2
Intercepting home e-mail	4	8	26	58	5
Tapping home 'phone line	3	8	24	63	2
Interviewing person's children	1	3	16	78	2

Table 57. Acceptable Ways of Getting Information. There are a number of different ways in which journalists and programme-makers might be able to get information. In this particular case, the media would try to get information about the senior manager who is responsible for the order on drugs. For each of the different ways of getting information, how acceptable is it to use it in this particular case? Figures in percentages.

	% saying very/fairly acceptable
A reporter telephoning the person's office	76
A reporter telephoning the person's home	44
Reporters waiting outside office	71
Reporters waiting outside person's home	36
Interviewing person's work colleagues	64
Interviewing person's adult friends and family	33
Interviewing person's children	4

Table 58. Work versus Home

abandoned, will also change. Certainly, had this scenario been about severe medical malpractice, or about drug dealing or child abuse, there is little doubt that the patterns of acceptability found would be strikingly different from those seen in this case.

A similar argument can be applied to the question of the consequences of media coverage of the NHS scenario (Table 59). As with the methods of information-gathering discussed

	Very	**Fairly**	**Not very**	**Not at all**	**Don't know**
Acute embarrassment	42	37	12	6	3
Criminal charges brought	39	31	14	10	6
End of career	27	34	20	16	3
Social ridicule	23	35	26	13	4
Unwanted public notoriety	19	40	22	14	5
Loss of friends' respect	19	40	21	15	5
Moving home to avoid attention	16	42	25	13	4
Financial ruin	16	32	30	17	5
Illness	7	22	40	28	4
Nervous breakdown	5	19	31	41	4
Breakdown of marriage	5	15	34	42	4
Partner harassed in public	4	6	26	61	3
Suicide	3	7	19	67	4
Children picked on at school	2	6	13	78	2

Table 59. Consequences. Sometimes, media coverage can have effects and consequences for the people involved. Still thinking about this NHS manager, here are some possible outcomes of this issue being raised in the media. Again, how acceptable, if at all, is it things like this happen as a result of media coverage in this particular case? Figures in percentages.

above, these results show a marked gradation from being acceptable to large majorities to almost complete rejection of the 'harsher' possibilities.

Again, the demarcation between work and home, role and person, can be seen in the data. Those consequences of media attention which bring severe personal hardship, and family hardship, are disapproved of by large majorities. Few, for example, would countenance the NHS manager's marriage breaking up (20%), or the manager's partner being harassed (10%). At the very end of the scale, even less acceptable than suicide, is the prospect of the children being picked on at school (8%). Whilst the focus groups seemed to be slightly more willing to publish and be damned, there was a clear overall similarity of thinking.

These results show the application of rules which, although unstated, can be deduced readily from the trends seen in the replies. As in the focus groups, and in the previous questions about methods, there is a process of calculation, of weighing up in a semi-judicial manner. This works itself out in people's decisions about the questions of 'guilt', 'deservedness' and appropriateness of means to provide people with the information they require from the media.

9/11: Public Interest and Privacy

The terrorist attack of September 11th 2001 on New York's World Trade Center Twin Towers occurred some five weeks before the survey took place. As noted in the previous chapter, some of the focus groups coincided with the attack and its immediate aftermath: the comments made in those groups led us to ask a small number of questions about the event in the subsequent national survey. The attack was a unique event, and the planned survey content and aims clearly meant that some attention should be paid to 9/11 as an all-too-real example of how the media and individuals – living and dead – might have different conceptions of what was and what was not acceptable. Accordingly, the questionnaire was modified to include a limited number of questions on this event focusing on media coverage and the public interest.

Television was *the* main source of information for nine out of ten adults, far outstripping the other media. This is not surprising, given that the main American television news

	%
Television	89
Radio	4
Other people	3
Daily newspaper	1
Internet	1
Sunday newspaper	★
Nowhere in particular	1

Table 60. The WTC Attack. A few weeks ago, the World Trade Center in New York was destroyed in a terrorist attack. Where did you find out most about what happened?

organizations were on the scene within minutes of the first plane attacking, together with BBC1 and ITV, and some radio stations, abandoning most of their schedules for live coverage across the majority of the afternoon and evening. By late afternoon, the national press had also produced special editions devoted to the WTC attacks.

One in five of the sample said that they had encountered material in the attack coverage which they felt was 'not in the public interest'. Anyone who said they had seen such coverage was then asked what it was, and the interviewer coded replies using a supplied list derived from comments made in the focus groups. A large proportion of these answers were very general – about how terrible the event was, or upsetting. Many, though, homed in on specific aspects of media coverage, particularly the pictures of people jumping from the Twin Towers before their collapse, and, to a lesser degree, the replaying of victims' phone calls to relatives, and interviews with victims' relatives (Table 61).

It is difficult to place the reactions to people jumping from the WTC in a public interest framework – if anything, it is closer to a taste and decency issue, a response to something upsetting. The two other most-mentioned themes are conceptually different, in that they centre around grief and reminders of the dead. Certainly, as far as the focus groups were concerned, these types of coverage do involve issues of privacy, both of the dead and of the living. Essentially private acts – making final calls to loved ones, and giving vent to intense emotions – were on public display courtesy of the media.

Did you see, hear or read anything in the media coverage of this which you thought was not in the public interest?

	%
Yes	20
No	80

IF 'YES': What sort of thing did you have in mind?

	% of all saying 'Yes'	% of total sample
Pictures of people jumping out of the buildings	36	7
'Phone calls from the victims to their families	18	4
Interviews with relatives of the victims	16	3
Pictures of bodies being recovered	11	2
Pictures of injured survivors	8	2
Pictures of people on the ground panicking	8	2
Details of what went on in the hijacked aircraft	6	1
Interviews with survivors	4	1
Other type of coverage	46	10

Table 61. The WTC Attack.

The question asked was coded by the interviewers into a limited number of categories provided to them, in turn largely based on the London focus groups' comments about coverage immediately after the event itself. The survey question, though, was asked a month or more after the event. As can be seen, a large proportion of the replies (46% of those who thought there was media intrusion) could not readily be fitted into the categories given. However, there is some evidence from some interviewers' notes of the verbatim answers given which helps us to see what this 'other' category consists of.

Many centred around the 'distressing' aspects of coverage – *'continual repetition of planes crashing'*, *'aircraft crashing into the building was on day after day, very distressing'*, *'cheering children and adults in Arab countries, starvation of children in Afghanistan'*, *'dwelt too long on gory details'*, *'pictures of families at funerals'*. These are best thought of as further reactions to <u>distasteful</u> material.

Others, interestingly, focused on what can be described as 'the *public interest*' issues: *'Opinion, not facts'*, *'Spreading panic about a Holy War'*, *'blaming Muslim fundamentalism before it's had proof'*, *'attacks on religious groups'*, *'Giving out too much military information over the media'*, *'shouldn't know where Tony Blair is at any given time'*.

A third general category within 'other coverage' was that of *repetitiveness* and weight of coverage: *'repetitive coverage of events'*, *'continuous coverage'*, *'over-exposure'*.

The Survey Research: Conclusions

The survey findings of this second stage of the study show a high degree of similarity between the findings of the focus groups and the population as a whole. This in itself is an important finding, in that it suggests that a great deal of uniformity exists concerning privacy, performance of the media and ideas of intrusion. Within the survey results themselves there was also a general trend towards uniformity of opinion across the ages, sexes and social grades: again this is evidence that the opinions and beliefs studied in most cases reflect something approaching consensus. Certainly there are real statistically viable differences found along demographic lines, and these are highlighted where they occur.
Such differences are relatively few and mainly small-scale, though, and there is no evidence in the survey data of systematic demographic differences governing the ways people think about the media, the public interest and privacy. This general trend is in marked contrast to opinions about another key area of concern about the media – that of taste and decency – where opinions, tastes in content and reactions to portrayals are linked *very strongly* to age and sex.

This tendency to similarity of response regardless of individual people's circumstances can be interpreted as good evidence for a high degree of universalism in the British population about the core issues this study addresses: *the right to know about things which might affect them* is firmly entrenched in the British public's view of the world. Equally, the principle of *the right to privacy* is a non-contested matter and shows a population that agrees with itself in terms of rules by which it ought to conduct social life. In essence, privacy is seen as a basic moral right that goes to the heart of our ideas of social association. Linked to privacy is a widely agreed set of *limits to intrusion by the media*, and also a stress is laid on the *protection from intrusion of the innocent*, such as children. Equally, though, there is general agreement that these rights and protections can be forfeit under specific circumstances.

Further, it is clear that these findings hold a direct implication for policy-making. Unlike the realm of taste and decency, where the key approach tends to be to regulate so as best to cater for disparate 'taste' populations – satisfying some will disappoint others – the evidence here suggests that key principles *can* be established as to what 'the public interest' and 'privacy' (including 'unwarranted' and 'warranted'/justified invasions) can be defined as, and that if these principles link with popular sentiment, they will be agreed with by all. At the same time, reactions to the coverage of 9/11 suggest that, for some, there were aspects of coverage, especially TV coverage, which crossed a line and went too far.

Notes

1. Details of the survey method are in the Appendix.
2. In the following tables, all figures shown are percentages of the entire sample unless otherwise stated. Percentages may sum to 99 or 101% due to rounding to whole numbers. Where the % figure found was less than 0.5%, the ⋆ symbol has been used. Where there were no responses at all, 0 is used.
3. Most detailed studies of people's uses of the media have found that television and radio are the main media as far as companionship is concerned.
4. The survey took place a few weeks after the September 11th attack on the World Trade Center. Therefore, there may well be some impact on these questions, since the UK Government had by then made clear that it wanted a national ID scheme to be set up primarily as an anti-terrorist measure.
5. 'Users' were defined as those who said they ever used each medium nowadays.
6. In fact, most replies were codeable into a single category: on average each member of the sample gave 1.2 categories. Accordingly, the percentages given in Tables 51 to 53 total to more than 100%.
7. Novelist and British politician Jeffrey Archer was found guilty of perjury and perverting justice by a London court in 2001. The charges against him stemmed from a 1987 libel suit he won against the *Daily Star*. The paper printed that he had an affair with a prostitute, paid her hush money and falsified records. Outraged at the alleged slander to his good name, Archer sued and won. The paper's allegations were later proved accurate. He was sentenced to four years in jail and fined.
8. The sub-sample size of listeners to Virgin, Talk Sport and Classic FM was fewer than 25 individuals and was too small for further reliable analysis. Their replies have been amalgamated into the overall commercial local radio category.

Epilogue

In the opening of the book we said that, in calling the work *Media Values: Intimate Transgressions in a Changing Moral and Cultural Landscape*, we hoped to capture the idea of media performance as moral performance. By that we meant we wished to view people as moral actors and accordingly have them evaluate the media and media-related issues. It was noted from the first wave of focus group discussions that in coming to judgement about performance people did so without the benefit of a moral language by which to anchor their judgements in sets of moral principles. What we did detect, however, were two sets of traditions of thought, which could be said to characterize responses, namely, the neo-Aristotelian and the liberal. Hence, Chapter 1 was given over to a full discussion of what these positions entailed and what they meant in terms of demand for the control or regulation of culture. These two positions, whilst having major implications for the regulation of culture, are really expressions of the individuals considerations concerning the appropriate relationship of the individual to the state – the neo-Aristotelian wishing for the state to promote the good life, with the liberal wishing for the state to merely provide conditions within which the individual was left to pursue unhindered his or her idea of the good life.

Hence our questioning ranged, both in the focus groups and in the surveys, over the degree of authority people granted to the State in terms of constructing the conditions of their lives, evidenced by questions relating to the compelling of individuals to seek counselling before obtaining a divorce and compelling alcoholics to seek treatment for their condition and so on. For us this was a way of entering into the complexities of people's views on authority and its nature and purpose. By so doing, it was felt that we would be in a good position to understand what individuals wished for in terms of the management of culture: its extent, point and purpose. But, as demonstrated, people did lack a moral language by which to fully engage with moral questions and, by extension, had difficulty in giving expression to the moral base of performance. Nevertheless, as the study shows, neo-Aristotelian as opposed to liberal sentiments dominated questions of control. That is, although in practice individuals moved position depending on the precise issues involved, and very few could be cast as 'pure' neo-Aristotelians or liberals in any immovable sense, people did consider it necessary for the 'good life' to be promoted and not left at the level of the individual pursuing his or her own well-being in order to form the just society.

We do not intend here to go through the arguing set out in the body of the book, but what is interesting in this desire for the promotion of well-being, which, of course, includes cultural fare, is that the march of history, at least in Britain, has been away from promotional efforts of strong regulatory bodies towards that of deregulation to allow the individual to seek out that which they consider satisfactory to their own ambitions. Indeed, what came across strongly in the research was a sense of the individual facing, so to speak, the world on their own: an individualization that they neither liked nor wished for.

It would be wrong to see this in any strong sense as a world marked by estrangement but, nevertheless, a sense of longing for a past world of engagement was present on the part of many. Of course, to collect the past from the present is fraught with difficulties in terms of assessing the nature of emotional change – the feelings collected may, in ever receding manner, have always been present. No matter, the fact is that people did now view the world in such a manner and it matters little if they always did so. What counts is what they believe, not what was actually the case. It would be nice to have data from the past by which to make, through a time comparison, firm statements about the present in the manner so forcefully argued for by Paul Lazarsfeld in laying out the duties of the 1950s pollster for the historian of 1984 (Lazarsfeld 1950). Even so, working historically and theoretically, we do attempt to give account of why the feelings of a lack of engagement ought to be taken seriously as a statement about contemporary life.

We showed, using ideas drawn from the sociology of religion, that one can talk about the secularization of broadcasting culture within which there has been a vacating of values to be replaced by voices devoid of any organizing set of standards. This 'democratisation of broadcasting' as we have called it, beginning in readily identifiable form in the 1960s and gathering apace thereafter, has meant the undermining of collective assumptions about ways of living, or, perhaps more accurately, an undermining of an official culture as it related to ways of living. As we argue, however, this fragmentation of agreed ways of living was not wrought by broadcasting alone, but by crises in moral authority institutions in general, where it could no longer be expected that appeal to a single moral voice – or an elite moral voice that gave the appearance of a single voice – for adjudication of moral issues could be made. As we point out, changes to laws relating to sexual offences and in divorce reform, meant that, instead of appeal to a moral court, calculations of right came to be based on the empirical facts of life. The appeal to the empirical, and, hence, the fracturing of moral authority, in many ways is a mirroring of the fracturing that had taken place in society at large in terms of social association. Again, we do not wish to reproduce the account of this complex process provided in the body of the book, but it is worth noting, in terms of the loosening of over-arching moral codes, that broadcasting, television in particular, has assisted this process by giving visibility to different ways of life. In other words, it legitimized groups and behaviour that had previously being considered illegitimate at one level and at another level began to cater for tastes that had hitherto not been respectable or, at least, had not been considered worthy of representation. Indeed, we argue that it is not developments in the technology of delivery that fragmented the audience, but that social fragmentation allowed the take-up of new delivery systems to cater for what had previously been an empirical fact but which could readily be ignored.

What we see, especially in the focus groups, was that parents found it difficult to accept portraits of life of individuals and groups, and the values and manners accompanying such portraits, that they themselves did not share. It led, although this is only one part of the story, to a feeling that there had been a coarsening of life in recent years. This feeling was given further support by their everyday, as opposed to mediated, experiences of the world. It was at this point that we discussed the difference between anti-social and unsociable behaviour, but on both counts people were familiar with the two categories, especially the latter most readily manifest by swearing in public.

As stated, it is difficult to judge the degree of estrangement in any historical sense, only to record that the feelings presented offer themselves as a commentary on contemporary life as one marked by uncertainty as to place and purpose, a lack of sense of belonging in either a social or ontological sense. This may seem a little severe, and the danger is of pointing to a time when this was not the case, at least in the recent past, but it is hard to determine meaning in a world primarily organized along lines of efficiency and technocratic competence rather than values. Whilst individuals favoured the present over the past, due to economic wealth, their existence in the modern world was accompanied by a sense of loss. This loss, whether mythical or not, appeared to revolve around the vacating from public life of a set of shared values underpinning the 'correct' way to live. Of course, as we have endeavoured to point out at various points in the book, there was no time in the modern era and even in the early modern era, especially with the growth of towns and cities, where a common set of values pertained. This is not to deny the unifying influence of the church, uneven at best, but it is to say that the formation of collective action by groups, and even whole social strata, was infused by values either in defence of group interests or in opposition to the interests of others. Indeed, a central observational point of the book has been the lack of a moral vocabulary by which to discuss moral issues or cultural performance. Neither, we might point out, did any class-based language emerge by which people organized experience that might then have offered protection against the fragmentation of meaning. What we did see, though, was the continuing importance of the family and the importance of the home, or dwelling space, in providing security, both physically and emotionally, in the face of the 'hostilities' of the outside world.

However, the research clearly shows that the security of the home was felt to be in constant danger of breach by media content that embodied no core values but, rather, contained a disparity of values that tripped and bumped up against each other and by intrusion into privacy through unwanted electronic penetration – cold-calling and so on. The latter we can leave for the moment, but the issue of values, the lack, if one likes, of any organizing principle underpinning cultural production is the outcome of the historical process documented and analysed by Leo Lowenthal as discussed in Chapter 2. Although Lowenthal talks of audience-building devices engaged in by the artist once a separation occurred between the artist and the consumer/patron, we have extended this to consideration of social changes that have produced a whole variety of groups to be catered for. Some of these groups have come to have a visibility fostered by the ideology of tolerance to difference, wherein they have become the subject and object of cultural representation. Clearly, for a moral protest group, such as Mediawatch, the values carried by some of these groups are seen as an assault on Christian values. For them, protesting against such content, as pointed out, is not simply a Christian duty, but a battle to protect the home as a space where, for its members, the meanings that they project onto the world can be held intact. Similarly, but not on Christian grounds, many of those in our samples did not appreciate values and manners of behaviour that they objected to in the outside world being carried by television to the inner world of the home, especially so for those with children. This objection does not rest in any major fashion on fears of the effects of, for example, media violence encouraging real-life violence, but rather represented a contestation over how the social world ought to be ordered. In other words, although people may not have had a moral language by which to conduct moral reasoning, or to discuss the moral implications of cultural production, they did have positions on what was decent and correct and what was not. All was not right with the world, and, by extension, all was not right with a broadcasting system that appeared to give legitimation to that world. In short, broadcasting showed a lack of moral purpose, or, expressed another way, it demonstrated no moral language in coming to judge what was worthy of portrayal and what was not. This position is not surprising given the finding that most people in our sample positioned themselves as neo-Aristotelians rather than liberal.

We cannot pretend that there are any clear answers to the above issues, but merely wish to lay out the terrain of values over which broadcasting operates and how this has meaning for how broadcasting culture is viewed. What we have pointed to is a long process of unfolding social change that has built into it the lack of any possibility of moral purpose in the sense of offering a preferred view of social association, social relationships, conduct and values. Cultural production has always involved political struggle in that it offers a contest of approved ways of viewing the world, but what we now witness, in the main, is a lack of a vocabulary by which to mount the argument of battle. This is not restricted, of course, to culture as artistic expression, but also applies equally to political culture as to the expression of power in terms of enacting values. The lack of fundamental social division or the lack of assumed social and cultural superiority of one group or class over others, leading to the necessity of appeal to all, is part of the same wash that has opened broadcasting to the portrayal of all people and the portrayal of all manners. It is all part and parcel of the decline of moral authority so strongly witnessed in the manner in which people in the focus groups spoke of the world.

Of course, this decline or, if one prefers, loosening of moral authority identified by our studies has the corollary of allowing people to conduct their lives relatively free from the sanctions or disapproval of others. However, as the early classical sociologists pointed out, the rise of the city and the freeing of the individual from custom, while liberating the individual, at the same time threatened a new kind of prison formed by the impersonal regulation of life. Indeed, it was in the discussion of privacy and the freedom of the individual to conduct his or her life without account to others that the relationship of the individual to the state, or some other collective variant of interests, came into full view. What we witnessed in the focus groups and surveys was that, although people agreed, almost as a fundamental human right that the individual had a right to privacy, further exploration revealed that this is very much a conditional right. Enough has been said about who, and in what circumstances, could expect to have their privacy respected not to warrant further comment here. What is worth drawing attention to, however, is the changing nature of what the private is taken to mean, and especially the idea of the public interest as a defence for intruding into some one's privacy.

The idea of the private is strongly circumscribed by the home. This fits very closely to that which we have been saying about the home as the resting place for moral authority. That is, unable to identify a world outside the home that reflects ideas of appropriate living and approved social exchange – the coarsening of social life as we have described it – the home becomes a protected space where it is hoped that the transmission of values under the control of parents can take place, and agreed-to ways of living enacted. Hence, the particular attention paid to the values and social performances carried by television. This privileged place of the home, almost a sanctuary from the outside world, meant that that which took place there was seen as of no concern to anyone else. It was liberated territory from a world increasingly seen to involve moral dangers, in the sense of ill-mannered behaviour that assaulted sensibilities, and physical dangers. Outside the home, and this may well be a recent development historically, there was no great expectation that individual privacy would be respected, or that one had too much right to privacy. Indeed, surveillance, especially by CCTV cameras, was welcomed; a direct result of considerable deterioration in social life. What we see, in other words, is that ideas relating to privacy, of what the private is held to entail, shift in relation to wider social movements.

What, however, is most interesting is the attempt to capture the right to the intrusion of privacy by the defence of public interest. We saw, from the interviews with media personnel, regulators and others involved in the media industry, that no satisfactory definition of 'the public interest' was forthcoming. Nor did the focus groups or the surveys offer a satisfactory account of what was meant by something being 'in the public interest'. This does not mean that the concept was without resonance with the ways people judged when it was appropriate to intrude into people's private affairs: rather, it shows that the concept lacked the analytical precision to do the work allotted to it. Without question, the idea of public interest involved notions of some collective interest taking precedence over personal wishes to have information remain secret.

The whole discussion of the defence of public interest demonstrates a single striking fact about contemporary life; namely, that it is impossible to identify a moral court of appeal based on a set of shared values. Given that historically it would also be difficult to do so, there is now no group to which moral deference is given, or, failing that, as a historical fact, no group that by deft of position is awarded the expectation that it will, or can, morally adjudicate. That is, that a group or social strata by claim to superior standing either socially, politically, ecclesiastically or aesthetically could expect its voice to be listened to in pronouncing what is right by an appeal to knowing what is in the best interest of others. This links directly to earlier comments concerning the fragmentation of social association and a lack of clear agreements over how to live, together with a lack of institutions possessing a moral language of seeming relevance to a society organized around instrumental rationality. The appeal to the public interest, or to community interest, even to national interest, simply looks hollow when it is difficult to identify any communality of experience, or ideological bonds sufficiently strong to socially join people together in a belief of having a common interest. In other words, in raising the defence of public interest it is not all clear whose interests are being invoked as a defence for the intrusion of privacy.

Clearly, as the detail of the research shows, one can point to people and one can point to occasions when intrusion might be held to be justified, but that is not the same as giving certainty to the right of intrusion by the defence of it being in the public interest in some quasi-legalistic fashion. Furthermore, and this is not good news for civic culture, the media, no matter what section and what medium, are not seen to have the interests of the public at the heart of their operations. They may perform a public good in terms of individual stories covered and so on, but do so under the suspicion that their real interests are occupational and not moral. From a consequentialist position that may not matter, but it does matter in terms of trust and in terms of authority to pronounce on moral issues, indeed, to even demarcate what is and what is not a moral issue.

We stated at the outset that the book was an empirical investigation of values and how those values framed the way in which people discussed the media, and how they discussed moral issues relating to the performance of the media. It is quite clear from the findings that a neo-Aristotelian position was more common than a liberal one; that, in general, people looked favourably on the regulation of culture in order to promote well-being. The degree of regulation is an open question, but what the study shows is that a concern exists over the regulation of social life in general, in the sense of a decline in authority of the collective, or, rather, institutions acting in the name of the collective, over the individual. The 'Intimate Transgressions' in the sub-title of the book refers therefore to the legitimate rights of the media to intrude upon the citizens' private lives, but also to expectations of protection from values that are considered to undermine the collective. This latter aspect of 'transgression' is really no more than overriding the values that people hold, but, as we have been at pains to point out, no one in contemporary society can expect their values to be met by universal acceptance. Moreover, no institution or group can expect to enshrine values in some totalizing sense or act as a 'court of appeal' for moral decisions. Although cultural and moral performance has always historically been a point of tension and political struggle, the voices in our study show a sense of despair, if that is not too strong a word, over the very lack of judgemental pronouncement over ways to live. Our samples, however, although having a strong sense of right and wrong, were at a loss to know, not having a moral language by which to reason, what were the appropriate cultural distinctions to draw in determining cultural value. Nor can it be said that those regulators and media personnel interviewed had firm ideas upon what moral grounds content ought to be judged. This was seen, for example, in the attempt to give justification for the intrusion of privacy by the defence of 'in the public interest'. This did not flow from any lack of intellectual capacity on their part, but from an inability to make pronouncements about what was in the general social interest when there was no such general interest to be discerned in the first place. A past class or cultural elite basis for judgement would have made this less problematic, but, as we saw in the course of the research, any attempt to come to a sectional judgement about culture was seen to be likely to bring with it the charge of intolerance to difference. That is, if to argue for a set of values, or to show disapproval for ways of living different to their own, they were sure that they themselves would be made to feel in the wrong.

What we see, or at least we consider to have detected in the study, is a lack of certainty in coming to cultural judgement created probably in part, but we can only argue this theoretically, by the media themselves promoting a variety of lives and values that leave cultural consumption as consumption rather than instruction about what is culturally valuable. We make no judgement on this but, rather, point to the process by which this has come to be and empirically document people's views and positions as they stand at a particular point in time. In doing so we have hopefully assisted, through our analysis of 'intimate transgressions', in increasing our understanding of the moral landscape within which the media perform.

Appendix

Details of Research Methods and Recruitment of Samples

A. 1996/7 Study
1997 Face to face interviews with key media and related figures.
A series of 12 depth interviews were conducted with senior personnel from UK broadcasting organisations, political parties, and the religious and medical spheres.

1997 Focus Groups
Fourteen group discussions were run, lasting around one and a half hours, and were carried out in two waves. The first set of groups took place in October 1996 and the second set were conducted in January 1997. RAS Ltd recruited the groups, with eight people in each who were each paid a £15 incentive. The single sex groups were split by age, social grade[1], the presence and age of children living at home, subscription to cable or satellite channels, and geographical location. There were also two groups held with people classified as 'complainers' – these were people who had formally complained about something they had seen on television, or had objected to something strongly enough to switch the television off, walk out of the room, or deliberately change channels to avoid the offending material. Controls were also set to ensure that working women and unemployed men were not over-represented. All group members had not taken part in any other groups within six months, and did not work in the media, PR or advertising industries, or in the Civil Service.

The locations and recruitment criteria of the samples are set out in the table on the following page.

Focus Groups Recruitment Criteria

Town	Sex	Age	Children	Satellite/Cable	Social Grade
Leeds	Men	25–44	4 with girl aged 8–14 4 with boy aged 8–14	yes	C1/C2
Leeds	Women	45–64	no children at home	no	C1/C2
London	Women	25–44	potential complainers – could have children at home	mixed	C1/C2
London	Men	45–64	no children at home	no	C1/C2
Redditch	Women	25–44	4 with girl aged 8–14 4 with boy aged 8–14	yes	C1/C2
Redditch	Men	35–64	potential complainers – could have children at home	mixed	BC1/C2
Bristol	Men	55+	no children at home	at least 3 with satellite or cable	BC1/C2
Bristol	Women	under 55	children aged 10–16	at least 3 with satellite or cable	BC1/C2
London	Women	18–24	no children at home	at least 3 with satellite or cable	BC1/C2
London	Men	under 55	at least one child under nine at home	at least 3 with satellite or cable	BC1/C2
Walsall	Women	under 55	at least one child under nine at home	at least 3 with satellite or cable	BC1/C2
Walsall	Men	under 55	children aged 10–16	at least 3 with satellite or cable	BC1/C2
Leeds	Women	Over 55	no children at home	at least 3 with satellite or cable	BC1/C2
Leeds	Men	18–24	no children at home	at least 3 with satellite or cable	BC1/C2

1997 Surveys

The overall project included two discrete specially-commissioned survey stages in addition to the interviews with key media and related figures and focus groups. Both surveys were designed to be representative of adults (aged 16 or older) in the UK, and were conducted by RAS Ltd.

The first survey had an achieved sample of 1,062 adults (aged 16+), and took place in December 1996. Survey 2, with a sample of 535 adults took place in February 1997. Both waves used the same set of sampling points drawn randomly from Electoral Registers. Within each sampling point, interlocking quotas were set to ensure that the interviewed samples were representative of the UK adult population in terms of age, sex, social grade and employment status. Both surveys were conducted face-to-face in the home. On average Survey 1 was 45 minutes long, and Survey 2 was 30 minutes long.

The dual-stage survey design was chosen in order to be able to explore key issues in detail, and to allow for the first survey wave results, together with the intermediate focus groups stage, to inform the design of the second survey wave. The use of two surveys reduces the risk of respondent 'contamination' which might occur if a single, hour-long questionnaire homing in on a set of linked topics is used. Further, for some key questions repeated on each wave, the design provides the benefit of an enhanced sample size.

B. 2001 Study
Face to face interviews with key media and related figures.
In all, 15 interviews lasting approximately one hour each were conducted. These included interviews with: a leading media lawyer, senior figures within television and radio (BBC and ITV), the press (tabloid, broadsheet and ethnic), a major internet service provider, regulatory bodies (press, television and radio), trade bodies, and pressure groups involved with the media. All the interviews have been anonymised, apart from interviews conducted with the 'Presswise' organisation, which monitors press performance, and the pressure group 'Mediawatch' (formerly The National Viewers' and Listeners' Association founded by Mrs Mary Whitehouse).

2001 Focus Groups
A total of 8 focus groups were recruited in two locations; Leeds and North London. Freelance professional recruiters were used to recruit for all groups. All were held in private homes, and lasted around 1.5 hours, and a £15 incentive was given. All groups were held in September 2001. All group members had not taken part in any other groups within six months, and did not work in the media, PR or advertising industries, or in the Civil Service.

Location	Sex	Age	Social Grade	Other Criteria
Leeds	Men	18–25	C1/C2	Asian, TV user
Leeds	Men	18–25	C1/C2	Internet users and/or with multichannel/digital TV
Leeds	Women	30–45	C1/C2	Read a Daily Paper, TV user
Leeds	Men	50–60	C1/C2	Read a Daily Paper, TV user
London	Women	18–24	C1/C2	Internet users and/or with multichannel/digital TV
London	Men	30–45	C1/C2	Read a Daily Paper, TV user
London	Women	50–60	C1/C2	Read a Daily Paper, TV user
London	Women	50–60	C1/C2	African/Caribbean

2001 Survey
The national survey stage in the 2001 study was designed to provide statistically representative data on public opinion about key issues in the debate about the media,

public interest and personal privacy. The survey quota sample was designed to be representative of adults (aged 16 or older) in the UK, and the fieldwork was conducted by NOP. A total of 1039 individuals were interviewed in the last 2 weeks of October 2001, following the depth interview and focus group stages. The interview took an average of 29 minutes to complete.

C. Social Grade Definitions

The social grade definitions used were those drawn up by the National Readership Survey and used as standard measures in marketing and opinion research in the UK.

Social grade	Social status	Occupation/Definition
A	upper middle class	higher managerial, administrative or professional
B	middle class	intermediate managerial, administrative or professional
C1	lower middle class	supervisory or clerical, junior managerial, administrative or professional
C2	skilled working class	skilled manual workers
D	working class	semi and unskilled manual workers
E	those at lowest level of subsistence	state pensioners or widows (no other earner), casual or lowest grade workers

D. Data Analysis and Weighting

Data analysis was undertaken using SPSS. All survey results and data shown are based upon weighted data unless otherwise stated. The weights were calculated by the supplying fieldwork companies and were designed to weight the data to the known national demographic characteristics of the populations sampled at the time of each study.

E. Schematic Overview of Privacy

What has been done in the following section is to lay out the public's perceived role of the media in relation to the privacy of the individual. We have, for some of the examples provided, taken them directly from cases discussed in focus groups, and in other cases constructed examples drawn from the principles of privacy that emerged in the course of the focus groups. We have therefore taken the principles of privacy and shown them working in practice when applied to known cases. By doing so, our intention is to show how these principles can be applied to media performance in general.

Public versus Private Rights:

- There is legitimate public interest in certain kinds of event: the extreme, the anti-social, the occasions when social codes are broken. The public feel that they have a right to know when these boundaries are broken.

- The status of the individual to a large measure determines his or her right to privacy and also their right to be consulted in representations of themselves.
- Status here refers to *moral* status, not simple economic or social status: high status, for example, means that right is on the person's side, or that his or her actions are justified. Individuals can have different positional status – doctors high, politicians low; innocent victims high, criminals low; adulterers low(ish), adulterers' partners high(ish).
- The higher the moral status, the greater the claim the individual has to privacy and the greater the right to be consulted about his or her presentation.
- Conversely, the lower the moral status, the more these rights are effectively forfeited – they are beyond the pale.

A high status individual caught up in an event of public importance, while giving up the right to privacy, must be compensated for this breach by detailed consultation.

Determinants of moral status:

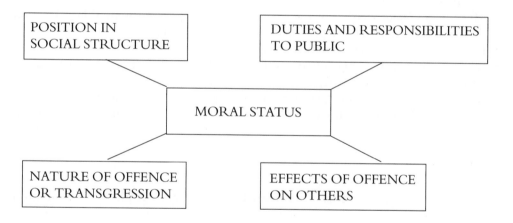

Relative rights to privacy and/or consultation
- Consultation in this sense is used in the strict sense of relevant individuals being informed by broadcasters of their intention to make such a programme, and the amount of attention which should be paid to these individuals' views about the programme.
- The following key cases illustrate how the determining category – status – governs beliefs in the rights to privacy and consultation if the events were to be made into a television programme.

The cases below were selected for discussion because they had received extensive media coverage and the facts of each were well known to the respondents, who could therefore readily discuss the issue of privacy that each case raised. With respect to the Alzheimer's case, this was chosen because the respondents were familiar with the mental impairment it caused and could readily discuss the issue of rights to privacy in a situation where the subject of coverage was in no position to consent to his or her inclusion.

- DAVID MELLOR'S AFFAIR
- HUGH GRANT
- JAMES BULGER MURDER
- A SUFFERER OF ALZHEIMER'S DISEASE
- THE YORKSHIRE RIPPER

David Mellor

	Status	Private Rights	Public Rights	Consultation
David Mellor	Low	Limited	High	None
Antonia de Sancha	Medium	Limited	Low	Limited
David Mellor's wife	High	High	Low	High

- Politicians have low status, but not as low as criminals.
- Mellor was a senior member of a Government which espoused Family Values: he broke the collective moral code – hypocrisy at this level a serious matter.
- His own manner and behaviour increased his low status.
- Mellor's wife was the long-suffering offended party, which increases her status above that of being a politician's wife.
- In this case, where the basic 'plot' is familiar – hypocritical behaviour by a politician – a 'disguised' dramatic treatment with fictionalised characters can be an acceptable substitute.

Hugh Grant

	Status	Private Rights	Public Rights	Consultation
Hugh Grant	Low	None	High	None
Liz Hurley	Low	Low	High	None

- Minor actors and celebrities by definition rarely have high status, especially when they are known to court media attention.
- Hurley's celebrity role, created by being Grant's girlfriend, therefore applies to her.
- Overall, not an important issue – there is a public right to be entertained by the goings-on of figures in the world of entertainment.

James Bulger

	Status	Private Rights	Public Rights	Consultation
Killers of James Bulger	Low	None	High	None
Parents of killers	Low	Low	High	Limited
Parents of James Bulger	High	High	High	Substantial

- Killers were children: but the nature of the crime forfeited the normally high status of childhood.
- Again, very high public interest: how could children do this, what was the role of TV and video and parents?
- Killers' parents have low status – guilt by association – parents are held to be an important formative influence of children. Some consultation, since responsibility questionable.
- High public interest overrules Bulger parents' rights to privacy and/or veto.
- Trade-off for parents is full consultation.

Alzheimer's Disease

	Status	Private Rights	Public Rights	Consultation
The Alzheimer sufferer	High	High	High	Not applicable
The family of the sufferer	High	High	High	High

- Both the sufferer and their family have a high moral status as innocent victims of an indiscriminate disease.
- Unable to think for himself/herself, the sufferer cannot be consulted. Therefore his/her family, who are responsible for his/her interests, have high rights to consultation.
- Public knowledge of this illness, which is not uncommon, is important and therefore generates a high level of public interest. However, this does not overrule the privacy rights of the sufferer and his/her family, who as innocent victims have high rights to privacy.

The Yorkshire Ripper (Peter Sutcliffe)

	Status	Private Rights	Public Rights	Consultation
Peter Sutcliffe	Low	None	High	None
Sutcliffe's victims	High	High	High	Substantial
Sutcliffe's wife	Medium	Low(ish)	High	Medium

- Sutcliffe forfeits all rights due to the nature of his crimes.
- Knowledge is in the public interest - how such crimes can happen, insight into dark corners of human behaviour.
- Sutcliffe's wife's right to privacy is overruled by the high level of public interest, and the insight into the case that she would be able to give – guilt by association.
- Trade-off for victims is full consultation.
- Sutcliffe's wife's rights to consultation are forfeited by the fact that she was his wife.

Intrusion:
- When these rules of engagement are not followed, the result is perceptions of unacceptable intrusion by the media, with the strength of reaction depending upon the degree of rule-breaking.
- Any perceived intrusion on the part of the media results in an assault on viewers' sensibilities.

F. Factor Analysis

In the first survey wave of the 1997 study, a number of attitude statements focussing on personal behaviour, values and moral issues, designed to operationalise the idealised Aristotelian and Liberal positions were included in the interview questionnaire. A five-point agree-disagree scale was used.

The individual scores from these items were entered into the SPSS factor analysis procedures, using principal component analysis with rotation. Three factors achieved eigenvalues of greater than 1, with four out of the six attitude statements most strongly linked with these factors. These four items were then used to create the values scale described in Chapter 4b.

As a further check, a further factor analysis using the same procedure as the first wave was conducted on those items which were repeated in the second survey with a separate sample. Again, three factors were found.

Note

1. See Appendix C for social grade classification definitions.

Bibliography

Ackerman, Bruce (1980), *Social Justice in the Liberal State* New Haven: Yale University Press.

Adorno, Theodor W. (1969), 'Scientific Experiences of a European Scholar in America' in Fleming, D. and Bailyn, B. (eds.) (1969), *The Intellectual Migration: Europe and America, 1930–1960* Mass.: Harvard University Press.

Alldridge, Peter and Brants, Chrisje (eds.) (2001), *Personal Autonomy, the Private Sphere and the Criminal Law: A Comparative Study* Oxford and Portland, Oregon: Hart Publishing.

Appleyard, Bryan (1989), *The Pleasures of Peace: Art and Imagination in Post-War Britain* London: Faber and Faber.

Archard, David (1998), 'Privacy, the Public Interest and a Prurient Public' in Kieran, Matthew (ed.) (1998) *Media Ethics: Public Interest, Privacy and Regulation* London: Routledge.

Aristotle (1965), *Poetics* in *Classical Literary Criticism* trans. Dorsch, T. S., Harmondsworth: Penguin.

Aristotle (1976), *Nicomachean Ethics* trans. Thomson, J. A. K., rev. Tredennick, Hugh, Harmondsworth: Penguin.

Aristotle (1981), *The Politics* trans. Sinclair, T. A., rev. Asunders, Trevor J., Harmondsworth: Penguin.

Asch, S. E. (1955), 'Opinions and Social Pressure' in *Scientific American* 193 (1955), pp. 31–35.

Audi, Robert (1989), 'The Separation of Church and State and the Obligations of Citizenship' in *Philosophy and Public Affairs* vol. 18, no. 3, (1989), pp. 259–296.

Barnett, Steven and Curry, Andrew (1994), *The Battle for the BBC: A British Broadcasting Conspiracy* London: Arum Press.

Bartlett, Robert (1988), *Trial by Fire and Water* Oxford: Blackwell.

Belsey, Andrew (1992), 'Privacy, Publicity and Politics' in Belsey, A. and Chadick, R. (eds.) (1992) *Ethical Issues in Journalism and the Media* London: Routledge.

Berger, Peter L. and Luckmann, Thomas (1966), *The Social Construction of Reality: A Treatise in the Sociology of Knowledge* Garden City, N.Y.: Doubleday.

Berger, Peter L. (1973), *The Social Reality of Religion* London: Penguin.

Berlin, Isaiah (1967), 'Two Concepts of Liberty' in Quinton, Anthony (ed.) *Political Philosophy* (1967) Oxford: Oxford University Press.

Burke, Edmund (1960), *Reflections on the Revolution in France* London:

Burns, Tom (1964), 'Cultural Bureaucracy: A Study of Occupational Milieux in the BBC' University of Edinburgh, Dept. of Sociology.

Church of England Broadcasting Commission (1973), *Broadcasting, Society and the Church: Report of the Broadcasting Commission of the General Synod of the Church of England* London: Church Information Office.

Cox, Harvey (1965), *The Secular City: Secularization and Urbanization in Theological Perspective* N.Y.: Macmillan.

Cumberbatch, Guy and Howitt, Dennis (1989), *A Measure of Uncertainty: The Effects of the Mass Media* Broadcasting Standards Council Research Monograph, London: John Libbey.

Curran, Charles J., Sir (1971), *Broadcasting and Society: A Speech given [at the] Edinburgh Broadcasting Conference, 23 March 1971* London: British Broadcasting Corporation.

Curran, James (1990), 'The New Revisionism in Mass Communication Research: A Reappraisal' in *European Journal of Communication* vol. 5, no. 2–3, (1990), pp. 133–164.

Currie, Robert and Gilbert, Alan D. (1972), 'Religion' in Halsey, A. H. (ed.) *Trends in British Society since 1900: A Guide to the Changing Social Structure of Britain* (1972) London: Macmillan.

Currie, Robert, Gilbert, Alan D. and Horsley, Lee (1977), *Churches and Churchgoers: Patterns of Church Growth in the British Isles since 1700* Oxford: Clarendon Press.

Davies, Christie (1975), *Permissive Britain: Social Change in the Sixties and Seventies* London: Pitman.

Docherty, David, Morrison, David and Tracey, Michael (1987), *The Last Picture Show? Britain's Changing Film Audiences* London: BFI.

Dworkin, Ronald (1977), *Taking Rights Seriously* London: Duckworth.

Dworkin, Ronald (1978), 'Liberalism' in Hampshire, S. (ed.) (1978) *Public and Private Morality* Cambridge: Cambridge University Press.

Dworkin, Ronald (1985), *A Matter of Principle* Cambridge, Mass.: Harvard University Press.

Elliot, Faith Robertson (1986), *The Family: Change or Continuity?* Basingstoke: Macmillan.

Ellis, Anthony (1984), 'Offense and the Liberal Conception of the Law' in *Philosophy and Public Affairs* vol.13, no. 1, (1984), pp. 3–23.

Elster, Jon (1993), *Political Psychology* Cambridge: Cambridge University Press.

Feinberg, Joel (1973), *Social Philosophy* Englewood Cliffs, New Jersey: Prentice-Hall.

Freedman, Jonathan L. (1984), 'Effect of Television Violence on Aggressiveness' in *Psychological Bulletin* vol. 96, no. 2, (1984), pp. 227–246.

Galbraith, John Kenneth (1958), *The Affluent Society* London: Hamish Hamilton.

Galtung, J. and Ruge, M. H. (1965), 'The Structure of Foreign News: the presentation of the Congo, Cuba and Cyprus Crisis in four foreign newspapers' in *Journal of International Peace Research*, vol. 1, (1965).

Gauntlett, David (1995), *Moving Experiences: Understanding Television's Influences and Effects* London: John Libbey.

Gaut, Berys (1995), 'Rawls and the Claims of Liberal Legitimacy' in *Philosophical Papers* vol. XXIV, no. 1, (1995), pp. 1–22.

Giddens, Anthony (1992), *The Transformation of Intimacy: Sexuality, Love and Eroticism in Modern Societies* Cambridge: Polity Press in association with Basil Blackwell.

Greene, Hugh, Sir (1965), 'Conscience of a Programme Director' in Greene, Hugh, Sir (1969), *The Third Floor Front: A View of Broadcasting in the Sixties* London: The Bodley Head Ltd.

Gusfield, Joseph R. (1972), *Symbolic Crusade: Status Politics and the American Temperance Movement* Urbana: University of Illinois Press.

Habermas, J. (1979), *Communication and the Evolution of Society* trans. McCarthy, T., Boston: Beacon.

Habermas, J. (1985), 'Questions and Counterquestions' in Bernstein, R. (ed.) *Habermas and Modernity* (1985) Cambridge, Mass.: MIT Press.

Habermas, J. (1990), *Moral Consciousness and Communicative Action* trans. Lenhardt, C. and Nicholson, S. W., Cambridge, Mass.: MIT Press.

Haley, W. (1948), 'Moral Values in Broadcasting' address to the British Council of Churches.

Hall, Stuart (1980), 'Introduction to Media Studies at the Centre' in Hall, Stuart, et al. (1980), *Culture, Media, Language: Working Papers in Cultural Studies 1972–79* London: Hutchinson.

Hammersley, Martyn (1992), 'On Feminist Methodology' in *Sociology* vol. 26, no. 2, (1992), pp. 187–206.

Hobbes, Thomas (1996), *Leviathan* Gaskin, J. C. A. (ed.) Oxford: University Press.

Hume, David (1975), *Enquiries Concerning Human Understanding and Concerning the Principles of Morals* 3rd ed. Oxford: Oxford University Press.

Hume, David (1978), *A Treatise of Human Nature* 2nd ed. Oxford: Oxford University Press.

Kant, Immanuel (1948), *Groundwork of the Metaphysic of Morals* trans. Paton, H. J. *The Moral Law* London: Hutchinson.

Kant, Immanuel (1970), *Political Writings* Reiss, H. (ed.) Cambridge: Cambridge University Press.

Kieran, Matthew (1996), 'Art, Imagination and the Cultivation of Morals' in *Journal of Aesthetics and Art Criticism* vol. 54, no. 4, (fall 1996), pp. 337–351.

Kieran, M., Morrison, D. E. and Svennevig, M. (1997), *Regulating for Changing Values* Research Working Paper for the Broadcasting Standards Commission, London.

Krippendorff, Klaus (1980), *Content Analysis: An Introduction to its Methodology* Beverly Hills: Sage.

Krueger, Richard A. (1988), *Focus Groups: A Practical Guide for Applied Research* Beverly Hills: Sage.

Lazarsfeld, Paul F. (1941), 'Remarks on Administrative and Critical Communication Research Studies' in *Philosophy and Social Science* vol. IX, no. 2, (1941).

Lazarsfeld, Paul F. (1950), 'The obligations of the 1950 pollster to the 1984 historian' in *Public Opinion Quarterly*, 14, pp. 617–638.

Littman, Mark and Carter-Ruck, Peter (1970), *Privacy and the Law* A Report by Justice, London: Stevens.

Locke, John (1988), *Two Treatises of Government* Laslett, Peter (ed.) Cambridge: Cambridge University Press.

Longford, Lord (1972), *Pornography: The Longford Report* London: Coronet.

Lowenthal, Leo (1961), *Literature, Popular Culture and Society* Palo Alto: Pacific Books.

Luckmann, Thomas (1967), *The Invisible Religion: The Problem of Religion in Modern Society* N. Y.: Macmillan.

MacIntyre, Alasdair (1967), *Secularization and Moral Change* (The Riddell Memorial Lectures) London: Oxford University Press.

MacIntyre, Alasdair (1981), *After Virtue* London: Duckworth.

MacIntyre, Alasdair (1985), *After Virtue* 2nd ed. London: Duckworth.

MacIntyre, Alasdair (1988), *Whose Justice? Which Rationality?* London: Duckworth.

Marshall, W. L. (1989), 'Pornography and Sex Offenders' in Zillman, D. and Bryant, J. (eds.) (1989), *Pornography: Research Advances and Policy Considerations* Hillsdale, New Jersey: Lawrence Erlbaum.

Martin, David (1969), *The Religious and the Secular: Studies in Secularization* London: Routledge and Kegan Paul.

McQuail, Denis (2000), *Mass Communication Theory: An Introduction, 4th ed.* London: Sage.

McQuarrie, Edward F. (1989), 'Review of Krueger, Richard A. 1988' in *Journal of Marketing Research* vol. 26, no. 3 (1989), pp. 371–372.

Meis, Maria (1983), 'Towards a Methodology for Feminist Research' in Bowles, G. and Duelli, Kline R. (1983), *Theories of Women's Studies* London: Routledge and Kegan Paul.

Merton, Robert K. (1968), *Social Theory and Social Structure* Enlarged Edition, New York: The Free Press.

Merton, Robert K. (1987), 'The Focussed Interview and Focus Groups: Continuities and Discontinuities' in *Public Opinion Quarterly* vol. 51, (1987), pp. 550–566.

Mill, John Stuart (1974/1982), *On Liberty* Harmondsworth: Penguin.

Mills, C Wright (1959), *The Sociological Imagination* New York: Oxford University Press.

Montefiore, Alan (1975), *Neutrality and Impartiality* Cambridge: Cambridge University Press.

Moore, Barrington, Jr (1984), *Privacy: Studies in Social and Cultural History* Armonk, N.Y.: M. E. Sharpe.

Morgan, David L. (1988), *Focus Groups and Qualitative Research* Newbury Park: Sage Publications.

Morrison, David E. and Tracey, Michael (1976), *Opposition to the Age: A Study of the National Viewers' and Listeners' Association* A Report to the SSRC.

Morrison, David E. (1978), 'Kultur and Culture, T. W. Adorno and P. F. Lazarsfeld' in *Social Research* vol. 45, no. 2, (1978), pp. 331–355.

Morrison, David E. (1986), *Invisible Citizens: British Public Opinion and the Future of Broadcasting* Broadcasting Research Unit Monograph, London: John Libbey.

Morrison, David E. (1998), *The Search for a Method: Focus Groups and the Development of Mass Communication Research* London: ULP/John Libbey.

Morrison, D. E., Svennevig, M. and Firmstone, J. (1999), 'The Social Consequences of Communications Technologies in the United Kingdom' in Boyce, R. (ed.) (1999), *The Communications Revolution at Work: The Social, Economic and Political Impacts of Technological Change* Published for the School of Policy Studies, Queen's University, Montreal & Kingstone/London/Ithaca: McGill-Queen's University Press.

Morrison, D. E. and Svennevig, M. (2002), *The Public Interest, the Media and Privacy* Research Working Paper for the Broadcasting Standards Commission, London.

Newsome, Elizabeth (1994), *Video Violence and the Protection of Children* March 1994, Child Development Research Unit, University of Nottingham.

Noelle-Neumann, Elizabeth (1991), 'The Theory of Public Opinion: The Concept of the Spiral of Silence' in Anderson, J. A. (ed.) (1991), *Communication Yearbook 14* Newbury Park, CA: Sage, pp. 256–287.

Nozick, Robert (1974), *Anarchy, State and Utopia* Oxford: Blackwell.

Nyamathi, Adeline and Shuler, Pam (1990), 'Focus Group Interview: A Research Technique for Informed Nursing Practice' in *Journal of Advanced Nursing* vol. 15 (11), (1990), pp. 1281–1288.

Parent, W. A. (1992), 'Privacy, Morality and the Law' in Cohen, Elliot D. (ed.) (1992), *Philosophical Issues in Journalism* New York: Oxford University Press.

Parkin, Frank (1968), *Middle Class Radicalism: The Social Bases of the British Campaign for Nuclear Disarmament* Manchester: Manchester University Press.

Philo, Greg (1990), *Seeing and Believing: The influence of Television* London: Routledge.

Plato (1989), *Gorgias* trans. Zeyl, D. J., Indianapolis: Hackett.

Pym, Bridget (1974), *Pressure Groups and the Permissive Society* Newton Abbot: David and Charles.

Rachels, James (1984), 'Why Privacy is Important' in Schoeman, Ferdinand D. (ed.) (1984), *Philosophical Dimensions of Privacy* New York: Cambridge University Press.

Raes, Koen (2001), 'Legal Moralism or Paternalism? Tolerance or Indifference? Egalitarian Justice and the Ethics of Equal Concern' in Alldridge, Peter and Brants, Chrisje (eds.) (2001), *Personal Autonomy, the Private Sphere and the Criminal Law: A Comparative Study* Oxford and Portland, Oregon: Hart Publishing, pp. 25–47.

Rawls, John (1968), 'Outline of a Decision Procedure for Ethics' in Thompson, Judith J. and Dworkin, Gerald (eds.) (1968), *Ethics* New York: Harper and Row.

Rawls, John (1971/1972), *A Theory of Justice* Oxford: Oxford University Press.

Rawls, John (1980), 'Dewey Lectures' in *Journal of Philosophy* vol. 77, (1980), pp. 515–572.

Rawls, John (1993), *Political Liberalism* New York: Columbia University Press.

Reinharz, Shulamit (1983), 'Experiential Analysis: A Contribution to Feminist Research' in Bowles, G. and Duelli, Kline R. (1983), *Theories of Women's Studies* London: Routledge and Kegan Paul.

Reith, John Charles Walsham, Baron (1975), *The Reith Diaries* edited by Stuart, Charles. London: Collins.

Rorty, Richard (1985), 'Postmodernist Bourgeois Liberalism' in Hollinger, R. (ed.) *Hermeneutics and Praxis* (1985), Notre Dame: University of Notre Dame Press.

Rorty, Richard (1989), *Contingency, Irony, and Solidarity* Cambridge: Cambridge University Press.

Rorty, Richard (1999), *Philosophy and Social Hope* London: Penguin.

Ryan, Alan (1993), 'Liberalism' in Goodin, Robert E. and Pettit, Philip (eds.) (1993), *A Companion to Political Philosophy* Oxford: Blackwell.

Sandel, Michael (1982), *Liberalism and the Limits of Justice* Cambridge: Cambridge University Press.

Scanlon, Jr, T. M. (1972), 'A Theory of Freedom and Expression' in *Philosophy and Public Affairs* vol. 1, no. 2, (1972), pp. 204–226.

Scannell, Paddy (1989), 'Public Service broadcasting and modern public life' in *Media, Culture and Society* vol. 11, no. 2, (1989).

Schiller, J. C. Friedrich von (1794), *Letters Upon the Aesthetic Education of Man* in Eliot, Charles W. (ed.) *The Harvard Classics: Literary and Philosophical Essays* vol. 32, (1910), New York: P. F. Collier and Son, pp. 209–303.

Scruton, Roger (1978), *Conservatism* London: Macmillan.

Scruton, Roger (1983), *The Aesthetic Understanding* Manchester: Carcanet.

Scruton, Roger (1996), *Animal Rights and Wrongs* London: Demos.

Scruton, Roger (1998), *On Hunting* London: Yellow Jersey.

Seymore-Ure, Colin (1991), *The British Press and Broadcasting since 1945* Oxford: Blackwell.

Singer, Jerome L. and Dorothy G. (1981), *Television, Imagination and Aggression* Hillsdale: Erlbaum.

Stein, Maurice R. (1964), 'The Eclipse of Community: Some Glances at the Education of a Sociologist' in Vidich, A. J. (1964), *Reflections on Community Studies* New York: Wiley and Sons.

Stewart, David W. and Shamdasani, Prem N. (1990), *Focus Groups: Theory and Practice* Newbury Part: Sage.

Stuart, Charles (ed.) (1975), *The Reith Diaries* London: Collins.

Sturges v. Bridgman (1879), Chancery Division, XI C.D. 852.

Svennevig, Michael (1998), *Television Across the Years: The British Public's View* London: University of Luton Press.

Taylor, Charles (1989), 'Cross-Purposes: The Liberal-Communitarian Debate' in Rosenblum, N. (ed.) (1989), *Liberalism and the Moral Life* Cambridge, Mass.: Harvard University Press.

Tracey, Michael and Morrison, David (1979), *Whitehouse* London: Macmillan.

Tracey, Michael (1983), *A Variety of Lives: A Biography of Sir Hugh Greene* London: Bodley Head.

Vidich, A. J. (1964), *Reflections on Community Studies* New York: Wiley and Sons.

Waldron, Jeremy (1987), 'Theoretical Foundations of Liberalism' in *Philosophical Quarterly* vol. 37, no. 147, (1987), pp. 127–150.

Waldron, Jeremy (1993), *Liberal Rights* Cambridge: Cambridge University Press.

Wallis, R. (1976), 'Moral Indignation and the Media: Analysis of the NVALA' in *Sociology* vol. 10, no. 2, (1976) pp. 271–95.

Walton, Kendall (1990), *Mimesis as Make-Believe* Cambridge, Mass.: Harvard University Press.

Wasserstrom, Richard A. (1984), 'Privacy: Some Arguments and Assumptions' in Schoeman, Ferdinand D. (ed.) (1984), *Philosophical Dimensions of Privacy* New York: Cambridge University Press.

Weber, Max (1948), *The Protestant Ethic and the Spirit of Capitalism* New York: Scribner.

Whiten, Andrew (ed.) (1991), *Natural Theories of Mind* Oxford: Blackwell.

Williams, Bernard (ed.) (1979), *The Williams Report: Report of the Committee on Obscenity and Film Censorship* London: Cmnd. 7772.

Williams, Bernard (1981), *Moral Luck* Cambridge: Cambridge University Press.

Wilson, Bryan R. (1966), *Religion in Secular Society: A Sociological Comment* London: Watts.

Wittgenstein, Ludwig (1969), *On Certainty* London: Blackwell.

Wolfenstein, M. (1958), 'The Emergence of Fun Morality' in Larrabee, E. and Meyersohn, R. (eds.) (1958), *Mass Leisure* Glencoe, Ill: Free Press.

Young, K. (1935), 'Review of the Payne Foundation Studies' in *American Journal of Sociology*, September 1935.

Zurcher, Louis A., Jr, R. George Kirkpatrick, Robert G. Cushing and Charles K. Bowman (1971), 'The Anti-Pornography Campaign: A Symbolic Crusade' in *Social Problems* vol. 19, no. 2, (1971), pp. 217–238.